Trübner's Oriental Series

MISCELLANEOUS PAPERS RELATING TO INDO-CHINA AND THE INDIAN ARCHIPELAGO

Trübner's Oriental Series

SOUTHEAST ASIA
In 7 Volumes

I	English Intercourse with Siam in the Seventeenth Century	
	John Anderson	
II	Ancient Proverbs and Maxims from Burmese Sources	
	James Gray	
III	History of Burma	
	Arthur P Phayre	
IV	Miscellaneous Papers Relating to Indo-China Vol I	
	Reinhold Rost	
V	Miscellaneous Papers Relating to Indo-China Vol II	
	Reinhold Rost	
VI	Miscellaneous Papers Relating to Indo-China and the Indian Archipelago Vol I	
	Reinhold Rost	
VII	Miscellaneous Papers Relating to Indo-China and the Indian Archipelago Vol II	
	Reinhold Rost	

MISCELLANEOUS PAPERS RELATING TO INDO-CHINA AND THE INDIAN ARCHIPELAGO

VOL II

REINHOLD ROST

LONDON AND NEW YORK

First published 1887 by Trübner & Co Ltd

2 Park Square, Milton Park, Abingdon, Oxon OX14 4RN
711 Third Avenue, New York, NY 10017, USA

Routledge is an imprint of the Taylor & Francis Group, an informa business

First issued in paperback 2016

Transferred to Digital Printing 2007

Copyright © 1887 Reinhold Rost

All rights reserved. No part of this book may be reprinted or reproduced or utilised in any form or by any electronic, mechanical, or other means, now known or hereafter invented, including photocopying and recording, or in any information storage or retrieval system, without permission in writing from the publishers.

Notice:
Product or corporate names may be trademarks or registered trademarks, and are used only for identification and explanation without intent to infringe.

British Library Cataloguing in Publication Data
A CIP catalogue record for this book
is available from the British Library

ISBN 978-1-138-98121-8 (pbk)
ISBN 978-0-415-24554-8 (hbk)

MISCELLANEOUS PAPERS

RELATING TO

INDO-CHINA

AND THE INDIAN ARCHIPELAGO.

REPRINTED FOR THE STRAITS BRANCH OF THE
ROYAL ASIATIC SOCIETY

*FROM THE "JOURNALS" OF THE ROYAL ASIATIC, BENGAL ASIATIC,
AND ROYAL GEOGRAPHICAL SOCIETIES; THE "TRANSACTIONS"
AND "JOURNAL" OF THE ASIATIC SOCIETY OF BATAVIA;
AND THE "MALAYAN MISCELLANIES."*

SECOND SERIES.
VOL. II.

LONDON:
TRÜBNER & CO., LUDGATE HILL.
1887.

[*All rights reserved.*]

CONTENTS OF VOL. II.

	PAGE
VIII. Account of the Malay MSS. belonging to the Royal Asiatic Society. By Dr. H. N. van der Tuuk	1–56
IX. Memorandum of a Journey to the Summit of Gunong Benko	57–69
X. Account of the Island of Bali. By Dr. R. Friederich . .	69–200
XI. Notices on Zoological Subjects. By Messrs. Diard and Duvancel	200–209
XII. Descriptions of Malayan Plants. By Dr. W. Jack . .	209–295
Notes to this Article. By Sir J. D. Hooker and the Hon. D. F. A. Hervey	296–302
General and Geographical Index	303–306
Index of Latin Terms	307–309
Index of Malayan and other Oriental Terms	310–313

MISCELLANEOUS ESSAYS.

VIII.

SHORT ACCOUNT OF THE MALAY MANUSCRIPTS BELONGING TO THE ROYAL ASIATIC SOCIETY.

By H. N. VAN DER TUUK.

["Journal of the Royal Asiatic Society," N.S., vol. ii. p. 85-135.[1]]

A.—RAFFLES COLLECTION.

No. 1 (large folio of 460 pages) contains the حكاية غَج توه. About the hero see "Malayan Annals," translated by Leyden, chapters xiv. and xvi. A small extract is found in Crawfurd's "History of the Indian Archipelago," ii. p. 51. Manuscripts of this work, the text of which might be available, are in the possession of Mr. J. Pijnappel, at Leyden; and of Mr. E. Netscher, at Riyow.* The last chapters of this tale are found in No. 2,607 of the manuscripts of the India Office, commencing with that

---

[1] [This article has been revised from the Dutch translation in "Bijdragen," III. vol. i. pp. 409-74. In the references to other collections of Malay MSS. the following abbreviations have been used:—I.O. = India Office Library ("Tijdschrift van Nederlandsch Indië," 1849, vol. i. pp. 385-400); B.M. = British Museum ("Bijdragen," III. vol. vi. pp. 96-101); L. = Leiden (*ib.*, III. vol. v. pp. 142-78); Bat. = Batavia (L. W. C. van den Berg, "Verslag van eene verzameling Maleische etc. Handschriften." Batavia, 1877.]

* I shall make mention of other copies, as it is my opinion that no Malay composition ought to be published without a supply of manuscripts bearing on the same subject. Texts from one manuscript, such as those published by Mr. J. J. de Hollander, in Holland, are not to be depended upon. Even quotations, found somewhere, I shall take notice of, as it may be useful to the editor of a Malay text to consult them.

part where the king of Mălaka intends to make one of his sons king on Mount *Siguntang.**

This composition is very interesting, as it exhibits a faithful picture of Malay life, and is written in genuine Malay.[1]

No. 2 (large folio of 288 pages; the last four pages are filled up with doggrel rhymes by some transcriber). This manuscript appears to be a transcript made by a native of Java, for a great many words belonging to the Malay dialect of Java occur in it; as, for instance, *urĭbang*, flower of the hibiscus rosa Sinensis; *bŏpèng*, pock-marked; *kulòn*, west,† &c. It also abounds with Javanese titles, as *dĕmang*, *ngabéhi*, *kanduruwan*, &c. The manuscript is in many passages too corrupt to be of use in editing the text. The transcriber has often changed words he did not understand into such as resembled them in sound, or nearly so.‡ But what is very strange, it has now and then a form less corrupted than the Javanese; v.g. *nantabóga* (p. 188) instead of the Javanese *antaboga* (a corruption of the Kavi *anantabhoga*). As to the contents, it follows the Javanese poem only to a certain extent, whilst it oftens contains passages which are not explicable otherwise than by supposing that a Javanese original has been translated or imitated, which did not deviate so much from the original Kavi poem, as the one published by Mr. A. B. Cohen Stuart. Although it is evidently taken from the Javanese, its first and last pages contain matter not found either in the Kavi or Javanese work, whilst no trace is found of the introduction, wherein the king, *Jáya Báya*, in whose reign *Mpu Sĕḍah*, the Javanese author,

---

* See No. 66 of my "Kort Verslag der Maleische Handschriften in het East India House, London," where the reader will find a full account of those closing chapters. As the numbers in that account have been since changed, I shall give here the present numbers in the India Office Collection.

[1] [B.M. 9; L. 1762; Bat. 186. Copious extracts are given by G. K. Niemann in his "Bloemlezing uit Maleische Geschriften" (1878), vol. i. p. 1-104; vol. ii. p. 58-120.]

† Even Dutch words, as, for instance, بلاو (*blaauw*, blue), occur in it.

‡ So, for instance, we find passim درهم (Ar.) instead of درما (alms, largesses of a king to priests and religious mendicants).

lived, is spoken of in laudatory terms; moreover, the title *Bărata yuda* (*Bhārata-yuddha*), which is given to the Javanese version, is not known in Malay; and the great war between the *Koravas* and *Pāṇḍavas*, wherever it is alluded to in Malay compositions, is always called *părang Pandāwa Jáya*, "the war of the victorious Pāṇḍavas." Not until we reach p. 134 do the contents of this manuscript resemble the Kavi and Javanese composition. The Malay author says in the opening that his work, although containing the story of the *Pandawa Pancha Kalima*,* gives a great many beautiful tales in the beginning, and afterwards the tale named *Hikayat Pandawa Jaya*. These beautiful tales are, he says, a collection of Javanese dramatic compositions (*lălakon*), to which he gives no particular names. I shall, on another occasion,[1] make an analysis of the whole and divide it into three parts. The first will give a rapid view of the contents from pp. 1–134, being what is not found either in the Kavi or Javanese work. The second will be more circumstantial, as it may illustrate the difficult passages of the Kavi original, and will comprise what is found from pp. 134–208, being the record of the great war. The third will give only a brief account of the contents from p. 208 to the end, as it deviates in this part almost in every respect from the Javanese version,† which closes with a eulogy of king *Jáya Báya*, of which no trace is found in this manuscript. The library of the India Office is possessed of two manuscripts bearing on the same subject, but only containing the description of the war. They are numbered 2,384 (small 4to, 234 pages), and 2,605 (8vo, 176 pages). Both commence with introducing to the reader the chief heroes who figure in it, and then speak of *Kăsna's*‡ mission to demand the half of the kingdom in behalf of

---

* Translation of *pancha*.
[1] ["Tijdschrift voor de T. L. en V.," vol. xxi. p. 1–90.]
† Of the Kavi version only twelve copies (!) have been lithographed by order of the Dutch government. It is not complete, ending with the combat of *Arjuna* and *Aśvatthāmā*.
‡ *Kṛiṣṇa*.

the five sons of *Pandu*.* To enable the reader to form a judgment of the difference of the texts of the three manuscripts, some specimens are here given.

The names of the four holy men (*risi*) that join *Kasna* when setting out for *Hastinapura* as mediator are in No. 2,603: چنتيىك, نراد, رم فراسو , and چکرس ; in No. 2,384, چنتيك, اديكاون, رما فرسو , and جىتركتىر ; and in this manuscript, كوار, كنڤي, بروسي, and رام فرسو.†

The passage where the Javanese version speaks of a human sacrifice being performed by either of the contending parties runs in No. 2,384 as follows:

سىتله هاري سيغ درڤاڬ‌ ٢ هاري مك ماسىغ ٢ ممىلىتىس كوىت كروا ايت برهمان سكىترا نمان دان ممڤالس كوىت ڧىدو ايت انق سغ رجون دان سغ روىن نمان تله سده ممڤالس كوىت ايت مك ڧىدوا ڧون كلورله در دالم كوتان مغادف متىهاري ماىت دان سرىت ممبلاكڠكن سوڠي ڧىچاك ايت &c.

No. 2,603 has:

تله هاري سيغ مك ماسىغ ٢ ممڤلس كوتان ادڤون اكن ممڤلس كوىت كروا ايت برهمان سكىترى نمان دان اكن ممڤلس كوىت ڧىدو ايت سغ ايراوان تله سده مك ڧىدو ڧون كلورله در دالم كوتان مغادف متىهاري ماىت دان ممبلاكڠكن سوڠي ڧىچاك &c.

This manuscript has (p. 147):

سىتله هاري سيغ مك ماسىغ ٢ اكىن مماليس كوتان ادڤون ڤماليس كوىت كوراو برنسكىترا نمان مك ڤماليس كوىت ڧىداو ايىت انق سغ ارجون رڧان ترلال ايلق اروان نمان سىتله سده مماليس مك ايڤون كلورله در دالم كوتا ڠمغادف كمىتهاري ماىت ممبلكاڠي سوڠي ڧىچاك &c.

---

* Leyden ("As. Res." x. 178) mentions the following separate tales about the *Pāndavas*: 1st, *The tale about their gambling*; 2nd, *that about their borrowing a hall*; 3rd, *that about their selling lime*.

† In the Kavi poem they are *Paraśurāma, Kaṇva, Janaka*, and *Nārada* (the Javanese has the same, only differently spelt, according to the Javanese pronunciation).

The Kavi (x. 6) has: *tuwin paḍa tlas makaryya bhisuweng* tgal paprangan | rawan ngaran i kang tawur nṛipati pandava murwwani | kunang tawur i sang nṛipeng kuru ya kārilud brahmaṇa | rikan siru çināpa sang dwija sagotra matiyālaga.* "Then they all performed a sacrifice on the field of battle, *Rawan* was the name of the victim of the Pāndawa king, commencing; as to the victim of the Kuru king, a brahmana was . . . . , thence he was cursed by the twice born, to die with his [whole] family in fighting." This remarkable passage will perhaps attract the attention of some Sanskrit scholar, who may succeed in explaining it. In No. 21 (see below) I have not been able to find it.[1]

No. 3 (large folio of 244 pages, imperfect at the end) contains the حكاية رڠڬ اري كود نستافـ. It is one of the *Panji* tales, containing the adventures of *Inu Kărtapati*, prince of Kurípan. This manuscript commences with the king of Kurípan's getting a son, called at his birth *Asmára ning rat Ondákan Jáya.* Then the birth is

---

* Instead of *bhisuwa* (*bhisuwang* is *bhisuwa+ing*) a manuscript on palm leaves in my possession has *bhisu-eng* (*bhisua + ing*). I should like to read here *bhiṣawa* (*abhiṣawa*). The Malay text gives no explanation, as it is evidently influenced by the Javanese version, where *sagotra* has become the name of a person. Moreover it identifies *Rawan* with a son of Arjuna (of the name of *Irawan*), who is afterwards killed by a demon (xii. 17). The word فماليمس in the Malay version is probably a substantive made from مماليس, which occurs in the *Hikayat Kumala bahrin* with the sense of *to turn off the evil influence of a ghost* from a person who is supposed to have been visited by a ghost, and in consequence of it has got some disease (compare the Ngaju-Dayak *palis*). فماليس must then have the meaning of what is used to turn off the evil influence of ghosts.

[1] In the Malay Panchatandaran (ed. Van der Tuuk, p. 46, l. 17), there is the following allusion to this human sacrifice: ادله فد زمان درماراج
تتكل مريكتمت هندق فركي ميڤرغ سبوه نڬري مك كاتـ
اهل النجومى يغ برنام كسنا چكلو تونك نونه انق تونك اين
بوتكن قربان نسڤاي دافتله نڬري ايت مك سبـ ضرورة
دالم ايت مك دبونهڤله انقى تيادله بردوسر كارن كيت
مملهراكن ڤاو اورڠ بايق. Dharmarâja is the name by which Yu- dhishthira is known in Malay tales [I.O. 87; Bat. 143; J. J. de Hollander, "Handleiding bij de Beoefening der Maleische Taal- en Letterkunde," 5th edition, p. 336, No. 2].

related of *Lăsmining puri Chandra-kirana*, the princess of Daha, also named *Puspaning rat*,* and betrothed to the above-named prince of Kurípan. This princess, when yet a girl, was carried off by *Batára Kála*, and placed with her attendants in a forest, where she changed her name and that of her waiting-women. The prince of Kurípan goes, attended by his followers, in quest of his intended bride, and in his rambles for that purpose takes the name of *Rangga Ariya Kuda Năstapa*, his followers too changing each his name.

No. 4 (folio of 246 pages and ending abruptly) and No. 73 (small 4to. of 420 pages) both contain the حكاية بايين بديمان, an imitation of the Persian طوطي نامه. On comparing the introduction, where the owner of the parrot (خواجه ميمون) is spoken of, I found the readings to be nearly the same. In my possession is a copy (folio of 90 pages) wherein the parrot tells thirteen tales. In the library of the India Office there are two manuscripts of this composition (Nos. 2604 and 2606).[1] The former contains twenty-two tales, but the latter only ten, whilst the introduction about *Khojah Meymún* is wanting in it.† According to Abdu-llah‡ the Moonshee this composition also goes by the name of حكاية خوجه ميمون after the parrot's owner. The two manuscripts of the India Office seem to belong to one and the same version, and only differ in the proper names, which have been changed to Malay ones in No. 2606. The versions in both differ from my manuscript.

No. 5 (folio of 315 pages) contains the حكاية دامر بولي. It is an imitation in prose of the Javanese poem, the commencement of which has been published by Mr. J. J. de Hollander in the Reader, p. 158 sqq., at the end of his "Handleiding bij de Beoefening der Javaansche Taal- en

---

* Compare under No. 14. [1] [Now 285 and 327; L. p. 178; Bat. 173, 174.]
† See further "Kort Verslag der Maleische Handschriften van het E. I. House," p. 394. [For a Makassar version see B. F. Matthes, "Kort Verslag," No. 1, and for one in Bugi, *ib.* No. 90.
‡ See his Journal, p. 95 of the Singapore edition. Of this Journal there is also a reprint in the fourth volume of Meursinge's "Maleisch Leesboek;" and a French translation by Dulaurier.

MALAY MANUSCRIPTS.

Letterkunde" (Breda, 1848). A translation, as it would seem, of the Javanese poem is to be found in Roorda van Eysinga's "Indië" (Breda, 1843), p. 502 (3de boek, eerste deel.). No. 11 (folio of 151 pages, only written half-way down, the open spaces being perhaps intended for a translation) contains the same tale, but considerably abridged.

No. 6. See No. 31.

No. 7 (folio) contains:

I. (71 pages) شعر بيدساري. This poem has been edited with a Dutch translation and annotations by Mr. R. van Hoëvell, in vol. xix. of the "Transactions of the Batavian Society of Arts and Sciences," but may be had separately. A review of this edition is to be found in the "Indisch Magazijn" and the "Gids" (1847), and quotations from another manuscript in Roorda van Eysinga's "Maleisch-Nederduitsch Woordenboek," under دافت, جمم, بوكن, سدير, سندر, راون, دغر, and سنپم. Another copy is contained in No. 36 (folio of 130 pages, and ending abruptly). Both manuscripts may serve to correct the edited text. I subjoin here a specimen of the various readings:

The printed edition, p. 3, line 9 from below, has;

Satălah (baginda sampey)* kapantey | di lihatña părahu (di atas lantey)† ‖ langkap (lah sakaliyan)‡ kajang dan lantey | (báik) § lah putări duduk bărjuntey ‖

Page 5, line 5 from above:

Tidurlah anakku bulang hulu | biyarlah ayahnda bărjalan dăhulu ‖ (anakku pandang) ¶ hatiku pilu | bagey di hiris dăngan sămbílu ‖

Page 6, line 4:

Sămbilan bulan sămbilan hari | (ku kandung)** di dalam (hutan duri) †† ‖

Page 6, line 2 from below:

* No. 7 has *sampey baginda*, and No. 36, *sampey tuwan turun*.
† No. 36, *tărlalu băsey*. ‡ No. 36, *dan*.
§ Nos. 7 and 36, correctly *náik*.
¶ No. 7, *anak kupandang*. ** No. 7, *kukandung*.
†† No. 7, rightly *diri*.

Bărjalan lah baginda (*laju manulih*) * | *rasaña hăndak* (*bărbalik*) † *kămbali* ‖ [1]

II. (69 pages) شعر كن تمبوهن. This poem has been twice edited by J. J. de Hollander, once in the Reader of the first edition of his "Handleiding bij de Beoefening der Maleische Taal- en Letterkunde," and once separately (Leyden, 1856), from an untrustworthy transcript evidently made in Java. The version of this manuscript has hardly anything in common with that of the one edited, but corresponds in many respects with that recension of the poem, from which Marsden has given extracts in the Reader at the end of his Grammar. The king mentioned in the opening is called here *Sări naraindăra di Chămpaka Jajar*, but in the one edited *Ratu Socha windu pura nagara*. As proper names of females, *Kin Tădahan* and *Kin Pangalipur* occur here; whilst the name of the heroine is sometimes shortened into *Kin Tăbuh*, for the sake of rhyme and metre. *Wira Dandani*, *Wira Păndapa* and *Wira Kărta* are found as proper names of males. The hero, the prince who fell in love with the heroine, goes here by the names of *Puspa Kănchana*, *Raden Inu*,‡ *Anak Mantări*, *Inu Bangsawan*, *Raden Inu Kărtapati*,§ and *Anak Inu*. The beauty of the heroine is compared to that of *Januwati*,¶ the goddess of love (*yangyang kăsuma*), and the celestial nymph *Nilautama*. Instead of *taman* (garden), this manuscript makes often use of the Kavi *lălangun*.** *Paduka Mahádewi*, *Paduka Matur* (?), and *Paduka Liku* are mentioned as inferior wives of the old king. The pages of the king employed on errands are called here *pangălasan*, instead

---

* A correction by the editor instead of the words of the manuscript, *sayang tărjalan*. No. 7 has the true reading (*sayang tărjali*).   † No. 7, *balik*.
[1] [L. p. 178; Bat. 256; de Hollander, l. l. p. 309, No. 2. A Makassar prose work of that name is described by Matthes, l. l. No. 9.]
‡ Rhyming on *tărmangu*. See also the extracts in the Reader of Marsden's Malay Grammar.
§ A name of *Panji*.
¶ The name of *Samba's* sweetheart (see under No. 15).
** e.g., *mari-lah ămas ariningsun, kita mandi kalălangun*, and *tăngah hari baginda bangun, părgi mandi kalălangun*. The native tales speak always of delightful gardens, where a bathing-place is one of the first requisites.

of *băduwanda*. This version, moreover, does not end so tragically; Indra bringing the two lovers back to life, accosting the heroine with *anak galuh*.* One of the characters represented is *Si-Tuguk*,† who is described as a kind of Falstaff, big-bellied and fond of fun. There is also a version in prose which goes by the name of حكاية اندكن فنوردت. In this version, the heroine is the daughter of a king of *Wanggar*, and the waiting-maid, who dies with her, is called here, as in the printed edition, *Kin Bayan*. One of her most beloved nurses has the name of *Antarăsmi*, and is addressed by her with *kakak* or the Javanese *ĕmbòk* (elder sister). The principal attendants of the hero are *Panta Wira Jaya* and *Jaran Angsoka*. The place where the heroine is killed is here the wood (Jav. *alas*) *Puchangan*. The lovers are brought to life by *Bătara Kala*, who changes them into lotus flowers, and then veils them in a cloud of incense. The residence is called in the end *Sochawindu*, but elsewhere only *Pura nagara*. The late Mr. H. C. Millies, at Utrecht, had a manuscript of this version. It is not worth publishing, but may be available for a new edition of the poem, of which there is a manuscript also in the library of King's College, if I recollect right. It is beyond all doubt that the poem as well as the tale belong to the widely spread cycle of the tales in which the adventures of *Panji* are related.‡

III. (26 pages) شعر سلندغ دليم. This poem is known on the west coast of Sumatra by the name of شعر سري بنين.§ I possess two manuscripts of it (8vo of 36 pages, and small 4to of 68 pages). A prose version of it is contained in No. 2,715 of the manuscripts of the India

* In the *Panji* tales the princess of Daha, the intended wife of *Chekel*, is commonly called *Raden-galuh*.
† One of the personating characters in the *Panji* tales.
‡ See Raffles' "History of Java," ii. p. 88 sqq., i. 335 and 392; Cohen Stuart's *Djaja Lengkara*, and Roorda's Lotgevallen van *Raden Pandji*, in the "Bijdragen tot de taal- land- en volkenkunde van Nederlandsch Indië," vol. ii. p. 167 sqq., and vol. vii. nieuwe volgreeks, p. 1 sqq. [Bat. 247; L. p. 178; de Hollander, l. l. p. 308, No. 1.]
§ In the end of this manuscript this proper name of the mother of the heroine is spelt سري بانين.

Office, and has been described in my "Kort Verslag der Mal. Handschriften van het E. I. House."[1]

IV. (10 pages) شعر ايكن تمبرا. This is a collection of erotic verses put into the mouths of two fishes (a *tambăra* and a *kakap*) who seem to be desperately in love.[2]

No. 8. See under No. 17.

No. 9 (folio of 160 pages) contains, as do No. 37 (151 pages, and ending abruptly) and No. 55* (small 4to of 262 pages) حكاية اندرا فترا. This tale contains the adventures of *Indăra Putăra*, son of *Bakărma Puspa*,† king of *Samanta-pura*, and is replete with wonderful narratives. The hero is carried off by a golden peacock; is sent by the king *Shahsiyăn* to *Bărma Săqti*; kills a giant or demon on Mount *Indăra Kila*;‡ finds the wonderful sea in the midst of the world (*tasik samu-dăra*); meets with the princess *Kumála Rătna Sări*; contends with the prince *Lela Mangărna* in exhibiting supernatural feats; is carried off by a genie (of the name of تمربوك), whose son (called تمرجلس) he kills; meets consecutively with mountains of gold and other precious metals, the seas of wonder and love; journeys in a cavern during a month; kills a serpent (of the name of مندود), and a demon (called غورقسا); meets with *Dărma Gangga*, who instructs him in supernatural means of conquering his enemies, and with *Bărma Săqti*, &c. At last our hero comes home, and is made king of *Samanta-pura* with the title of Sultan *Indăra Mangindăra*. No. 55 terminates with a great many erotic verses not found in the other copies. Many quotations from this work are to be found in Werndly's "Maleische Spraakkunst" (pp.133, 157, 162, 170 (twice), 171, 174 (three times), 176, 185, 186, 191, 193, 194 and 195), in Roorda van Eysinga's

---

[1] [Now No. 292; Bat. 251, 252; de Hollander, l. l. p. 317, No. 66.]
[2] [Lithographed at Singapore, a. H. 1291.]
* Another copy is in the possession of Dr. Reinhold Rost (small 4to, 148 pages).
† Of course most proper names occurring in this account are transliterated guessingly, such as they would be pronounced by a Malay at first sight.
‡ Where *Arjuna* performed penance to get supernatural arms. Such proper names deserve being taken up in a Dictionary, as they occur very often.

"Maleisch-Nederduitsch Woordenboek" (under *pantas, pandey, puji* and *gărak*), and in the annotations of Mr. van Hoëvell on the Sair Bidasari (pp. 289, 305, 333, 335, 348 352, 375 and 399). Specimens of the reading of the three manuscripts :—

No. 9 :

اد سوڤرڠ راج دنڬري سمنت فوري برنام راج بكرم بسڤ ترلال
بسر كرجاءن براڤ راج ۲ يڠ تعلق كڤد راج دان ممبري افتي
كڤد سڬنڤ تاهن شهدان امڤت فوله راج ۲ يڠ مماكي ماكنت
كاءماسن دباوهن دان براڤ هلبالغ حاضر دڠن سنجتان
ددالم استان دمكينله كبسارن راج ايت حتي ستله براڤ
لمان مهاراج بكرم بسڤ دالم كرجاءن مك استريڽ راج اينڤون
حاملله برنام استري راج ڤتري جمهما رتنا ديوي ادڤون ستله
براڤ لمان مك ترن ڤتوي جمهما رتنا ديوي ايت حامل

No. 37 :

مك اد سوڤرڠ راج دنڬري سمنت فوري برنام مهاراج بكرم
ڤسڤ اكن راج ايت ترلال بسر كرجاءن شهدان ببراڤ راج ۲
يڠ تعلق كڤد بڬند ايت مڠنتر افتي كڤد ستاهن سكال شهدان
امڤت فوله راج ۲ مماكي كله يڠ كاءماسن ننتياس اد حاضر
دڠن سنجتان دباواء مهاراج ڤسڤ دمكينله كبسارن بڬند
دياتس تخت كرجاءن ايت مك اد ببراڤ لمان مك استري
مهاراج بكرم ڤسڤ يڠ برنام ترن ڤتري جمجم رتن ديوي
اينڤون برائق سوڤرڠ لاك ۲

No. 55 :

اد سوڤرڠ راج دنڬري سمنت فور برنام راج بكرم بسڤ دان
اكن راج ايت ترلال بسر كرجاءن شهدان ببراڤ راج ۲ يڠ تعلق
كڤدان ممبري افتي كڤدان ڬنڤ تاهن شهدان امڤت فوله
راج ۲ يڠ مماكي كله كاءماسن دباوهن دمكينله كبسارن مهاراج
بكرم بسڤ سبرمول مك استري مهاراج بكرم بسڤ يڠ برنام
ترن ڤتري جنجم رتن ڤون حاملله [1]

[1] [L. 1690, and p. 178; Bat. 168; B. F. Matthes, "Kort verslag van Makassaarsche en Boeginesche Handschriften," Nos. 13 and 94.]

No. 10 (folio) contains a collection of transcripts of treaties between the Dutch E. I. Company and several native States in the Indian Archipelago. The first treaty is that between Admiral Speelman and the king of *Gowa* (Mangkasar), and the last that between the E. I. Company and the king of Johor and Pahang.

No. 11. See under No. 5.

No. 12 (folio of 444 pages) contains the حكايت برما شهدان. It is very seldom that tales are divided into chapters (فصل), of which there are here sixteen. In the commencement of the tale there is a kind of summary, wherein the hero is said to be a great king, who visited Mount *Qāf*, China, and the land of the inferior gods (*dewa*), subjecting men and ghosts to his sovereignty. On p. 2 a State *Samanda-puri* is mentioned. Its king was called *Săriyawan*, and was sprung from *Indăra Dewa Maharáma Rupa*, whilst his queen was of mere mortal extraction. He had two sons called Raja *Ardān* and Raja *Marsádan*. The two princes went with a large retinue to the forest *Samanta Baranta*, where a dewa of the name *Saráma Dewa* was in the habit of enjoying himself. This god hated the king, their father, who had caused his residence to be destroyed in former times. He changed himself into an old man and visited the princes, saying that he wished to serve them. Contriving to separate them from their followers when engaged in hunting, the god transformed himself into an elephant, whom *Ardān* so hotly pursued, that he got the start of his brother, and at last found himself entirely alone. The god then flew away with the prince to the sky, but was killed by the young hero. *Ardān*, having arrived again on this sublunary orb, made the acquaintance of a *ṛiṣi* called *Báyu Ráma*, who told him that he was not to revisit his country for many years. The prince remained in the dwelling of the holy man, who instructed him in all sorts of supernatural sciences. *Marsádan* goes in quest of his brother, and in his rambles arrives at *Indărapura*, where he marries the king's only daughter, and succeeds his father-in-law.* *Ardān* has a great many adventures of the same kind, delivering a princess with her waiting women, &c. *Bărma Shahdān*, the hero of the tale, is a son of *Marsádan Shāh*, king of *Kalingga dewa*,† and his eldest brother is called here *Rájadirája*. This work is replete with *pantuns*, some of which are worthy of notice. The late Mr. P. P. Roorda van Eysinga possessed a manuscript (two volumes in folio), which he would have published, but for want of a sufficient number of subscribers: what has become of it I cannot say. J. J. de Hollander ("Handleiding bij de Beoefening der Mal. Taal- en Letterkunde," 3rd edition, p. 332) says, I know not on what authority, that the author was *Sheikh Ibn Abu Omar*.[1]

No. 13 is a number I could not find. Dulaurier has also omitted it in the list he gives ("Journal Asiatique," 3rd series, x. 69) of titles of the manuscripts of this collection.

No. 14 (folio of 456 pages: on the back of the cover, *Charang Kurina*) contains the چارغ کلیین حکایة. It is a tale belonging to the *Panji* cyclus. The commencement is about the king of Kuripan having two sons, the eldest being *Kărta Buwána*, and the youngest Raden *Asmára Jaya*, surnamed *Ondakan Rawisărăngga*, who was betrothed to the princess of Daha, called Raden *Puspita-ning Rat*.‡ The name by which this tale goes is the assumed name of the princess when she had fled from her father's residence in order to follow the prince, in the garb of a man.

No. 15 (small folio of 180 pages) contains the حکایة مهاراج بوم. The plot of this tale is nearly the same as that of the *Bhaumakâvya*,§ relating the adventures of *Boma*

---

* Called *Bakărma Dáli raja*. The proper name *Bakărma* is very frequent in Malay tales, and is a corruption of the Sanskrit *vikrama;* it is often confounded with *Pakărma*.

† The manuscript has کالغلت دیو (p. 32).

[1] [According to the same authority (5th edition, p. 353), the printing was actually commenced in 1856, but discontinued in consequence of the editor's death. See also L. p. 178.]

‡ Compare under No. 3. [B.M. 8.]

§ Edited by Friederich in the "Transactions of the Batavian Society."

(the Sanskrit *Bhauma*, son of the earth). He was the son of *Bisnu* (*Viṣṇu*) by the goddess *Părtiwi* (Sans. *prithivī*, earth), and became a powerful king, whom even the gods stood in dread of. As he, demon-fashion, annoyed the penitents, *Kăsna* (*Kriṣṇa*) sends his son *Samba* against him. *Boma* is at last killed by *Hanoman*, after having himself killed *Samba* and *Arjuna*, who were, however, called into life again by *Narâda* (*Nārada*) sent by *Batara Guru* for the purpose. The celebrated episode* of *Dărmadewa* and *Dărmadewi* is here inserted in the same way as in the Kavi poem, *Dărmadewa* following *Bisnu* when incarnating himself into *Kăsna* and becoming *Samba*, whilst *Dărmadewi*, after having burnt herself, becomes *Januwáti*,† and so is reunited to her former love. This tale is also named حكاية سمى سميو. The R.A.S.'s MS. (see also under No. 21) slightly differs from the one in the India Office (No. 2905,[1] 4to, 120 pages). Raffles ("History of Java," i. p. 388, first edition) mentions the Javanese version under the titles *Buma Kalantaka* and *Embatali*. The first name is no doubt *Bhaumakalāntaka* (the death of the demon Bhauma, *kala* being used in Javanese to denote demons and Titans), as may be inferred from the Kavi poem, p. 233, where it is *Bhaumāntaka* (Bhauma's end, the hero dying by the hand of *Viṣṇu*). The Kavi version bears (ap. Raffles, l. l.) the name *Anrakasura*, which is to be corrected into *Narakāsura* (the demon *Naraka*, another name of Bhauma). I shall give on another occasion an analysis of this Malay composition.[2]

No. 16 (folio of 206 pages). A duplicate is No. 62, I. (158 pages). The two manuscripts differ but slightly. They contain the حكاية اسما يتيم. The work has been edited by Mr. P. Roorda van Eysinga (Batavia, 1821), who

---

* This episode is often alluded to in Malay tales and poems (comp. under No. 7, II.).

† *Yajnawatí* is her constant name in the Kavi poem, where she is never called *Dărmadewi*.

[1] [Now 87.]

[2] [This account is to be found in the Batavian "Tijdschrift," vol. xxi. pp. 91-101. Cf. Bat. 142.]

has also given an analysis of it in the tenth volume of the "Transactions of the Batavian Society." The episode of the singing peacocks has been published from another version by Meursinge in the third volume of his "Maleisch Leesboek." In the library of the India Office there are two manuscripts, Nos. 2429 and 2430 (?). Mr. J. Pijnappel has also a manuscript. A new edition of this work is desirable, as that by Roorda van Eysinga has long been out of print. Quotations from it are found in Werndly's "Maleische Spraakkunst," pp. 142, 157, 170, 171, 172, 180, 182, and in the preface xl., xli.[1]

No. 17 contains:

I. The 7th book of the بستان السلاطين (*ărtiña kăbon săgala raja raja*). No. 42 (folio of 440 pages: on the back, *Makota sagala raja raja*) contains but five books of this work, and No. 8 (folio of 367 pages) only four books and a few pages of the fifth; this copy is written with vowel-signs.[2] This excellent work, complete copies of which are very rare, is divided into seven books, each book containing a certain number of chapters. The author calls himself *Nuru-ddīn ibn 'Alī ibn Hasanjī*, son of Muhammad, of the Hamid tribe, and a native of Rānīr (see No. 78, IV.), and he composed it at *Achih* (*Acheen*) in the year of the Muhammadan era 1040, by order of Sultan *Iskander II. Aliyu-ddīn Murayat* Shāh Johan băr dawlat lillu-llahi fi'l'alam*.† The first book (many chapters) treats of the creation of heaven and earth; the second (many chapters) is about prophets and kings; the third (six chapters) on just kings and clever ministers; the fourth (two chapters) on pious kings and holy men;‡ the fifth (two chapters) on unjust kings and foolish ministers; the sixth (two chapters) on honoured liberal

---
[1] [I.O. 89, 90; B.M. 4; L. 1693, 1737, 1747; Bat. 170-72; de Hollander, l. l. p. 352, No. 80. On the Buginese redaction, see Matthes, l. l. p. 32, No. 98, and p. 95, No. 12366.]
[2] [See also No. 70, I.]

* مغاية
† The shadow of God on the world (ظل الله في العالم).
‡ اولياء

men and heroes ; the seventh (five chapters) on intelligence, and on all sorts of sciences, medical, physiognomical, historical, &c. Everywhere a great many tales are given, which might be used for a new Malay Reader. This work gives more than it promises, which in Malay literature may be called a miracle. The twelfth chapter of the second book contains a summary of the history of Malay States ; the thirteenth the history of *Achih* up to the time of the author. In the first chapter of the fourth book there are several tales about the celebrated *Ibrahīm Ibn Adham*, corresponding to some extent with the tale, published by Mr. P. Roorda van Eysinga (Batavia, 1822) and D. Lenting (Breda, 1846) under the title "Geschiedenis van Sultan Ibrahim vorst van Irak."* I have in my possession a manuscript (4to, 194 pages) containing only the first four chapters of the seventh book.[1]

II. An incomplete copy of تاج السلاطين (see under No. 42).

No. 18 (folio of 202 pages) شجرة ملايو. This collection of historical tales has been published for the greater part by Dulaurier in his "Chroniques Malayes," and translated by Leyden ("Malay Annals," edited by Sir Stamford Raffles). This MS., however, contains chapters not found in other copies, and not translated by Leyden. The last chapter but one, for instance, is about *Sang Naya's* conspiracy against the Portuguese at Malaka. There are several versions of these chronicles, as the reader will see from the various readings in Dulaurier's edition. No. 35 (folio of 117 pages), No. 39 (folio 120 pages), and No. 68 (small 4to) end with the death of *Hang Kăsturi*, the last named number having besides an entirely different introduction, and being properly but an abridgment. In No. 76 (small 4to) only a part is found commencing with the chapter on the depredations of a Mangkasar prince (كرايـڠ مـڠـوكو), and ending with the conquest of Malaka by the Portuguese. No. 80 (4to of

---

* The Sundanese version has the title "Hikayat Surtan Oliya Hĕnu Ibrahim waliyullah," a copy of which is in my possession (small 4to, 90 pp.).
[1] [L. 1694 and p. 178.]

MALAY MANUSCRIPTS. 17

312 pages), and No. 5 of the Farquhar collection (small 4to, 259 pages) both end also with the conquest of Malaka by the Portuguese. There are a great many copies of this work* in Holland as well as in the Indian Archipelago, in the Government offices, and in the possession of individuals.[1]

No. 19 (folio of 331 pages) and No. 20 (folio of 365 pages) contain the حكاية دالغ فغود اسمار. This is again one of the *Panji* tales. The title is after a name by which the prince of *Kuripan* was known when he was changed by *Bătara Indăra* into a woman. The beginning of the second volume is not connected with the last words of the first, being—القصه ملك ترسبتله فركتاءن ستله ايت ملك فغيرن كسوم اكّغ فون اغنديك اده كاكغ امفو كدو كاكغ چار بكّمان كدو. No. 43 (small folio of 142 pages; on the back of the cover, *Hikayat Pangeran Kesuma Agung*) contains the same, but only its last part,† the beginning words being—القصه ملك ترسبتله فركتاءن فغيرن كسوم اكّغ ددالم نكري فكمباغن سهاري٢ دغن ممال بون٢ءن دغن سكل كدين, &c. The name of the hero is in this volume دالغ فودق اسمار. No. 51 (small 4to of 149 pages; on the back of the cover, *Hikayat Dalang pudak Asmara*) is the same, but the usual commencement is wanting, its first words being—القصه ملك ترسبتله فركتاءن سري بفات اغ كريفن سلام اي برفنترا اكن انقد بكّند رادن اينو كرتافات, &c.

No. 20. See under No. 19.

No. 21 (small folio of 669 pages) contains the حكاية

---

* That it contains for the greater part but fabulous history is beyond all doubt, as even the history of Malaka is tainted with the *Panji* tales; see, for instance, the chapter about the king of Malaka going to the court of Majapahit, and marrying a princess of the name of *Chandărakirana* (compare under No. 3).

[1] [L. 1703, 4, 16, 36; Bat. 188-90; de Hollander, l. l. p. 356, No. 2. The work was lithographed by Keasberry at Singapore in 1830, and a reprint of this appeared at Leiden in 1884. A French translation, by M. Devic, of part of it (to page 123 of the Leiden edition) was published in Paris in 1878.]

† This part is often found separately, as may be inferred from Bahru-ddīn's list (containing an account of Malay compositions found at *Surabaya*), wherein we find a حكايت فغيرن كسوم اكّغ.

SECOND SERIES.—VOL. II. C

فنداوليم. This is a collection of loosely connected tales, the greater part of which relate to the persons involved in the contest between the *Kaurawas* and *Pāndawas*. To distinguish this composition from that which only relates to the war, I propose to call the last حكاية فرغ فنداو جاي, on account of its being so popular (see under No. 2), and the first حكاية فنداو فنج كليم.* As to the contents of this number, it is evident that it is an entirely different work, and by no means to be identified either with No. 2, or the two MSS. at the India Office (see under No. 2). The commencement narrates the birth of *Parāsu Rama* and *Dewa Bărata*, sons of بسنو روفن by the celestial nymph *Manik*.[1] Then *Santānu* is mentioned, and the birth of his children, who had a peculiar fishy smell about them, as they had been cut out of the belly of a fish, who had swallowed the seed of *Santānu*. On p. 2 *Parasāra* cures the stinking princess *Durgandini*, and calls her afterwards *Sayojana Suganda* (sweet-scented at the distance of a yojana), taking her as his wife. She becomes the mother of *Biyāsa*. Another part of the narrative is about *Băsmaka*, king of *Mandira-săpta*, who had three daughters, called *Amba, Ambi, Ambalika*. *Amba* becomes the wife of *Dewabrata*, who kills her by inadvertence. He therefore vows to surrender his life to a woman, burns his wife's body, and then goes to his brother, *Parasurama*, who consoles him and changes his name into *Bisma*. On p. 34 we find mention made of the birth of *Dăstarāta*,† *Pandu Dewa Nata*,‡ and *Widura Săqma*.§ *Dăstarāta* was born blind, because his mother, when visited by *Biyasa*, from fear closed her eyes; *Pandu's* body was white as crystal because his mother had covered herself with a white veil when she conceived him; *Widura Săqma* was born with one lame leg, as his mother had pulled his leg (?). On p. 38 the birth of *Karna* is related: he was the son of *Sangyang*

---

* This title I derive from the first pages of No. 2, where the author calls the part of his work not bearing directly on the war by this name (see under No. 2).
[1] [Probably Menaka.]
† *Dhṛitarāṣṭra*.   ‡ In Malay the name of *Pāṇḍu*.   § *Vidura*.

Rawi,* by *Dewi Păta*.† After this, the meeting is related of *Bisnu* and the goddess *Părtiwi* (see under No. 15), and then the birth of *Dărmadewa* and *Dărmadewi* (see under No. 15). On p. 91 we have the birth of *Kăsna* (*Krisna*) and *Kakărsana* (a surname of *Baladewa*). The last chapters relate the contest of *Boma* against *Samba* (see under No. 15). Although this composition is but a collection of narratives with no plot whatever to deserve the name of *hikayat*, it is very interesting, as it introduces nearly all the persons acting in the *hikayat părang Pandăwa Jaya*, and the *hikáyat Mahárája Boma*.[1]

No. 22 (folio of 720 pages; the commencement is wanting) contains the حكاية سري رام. It is a very elaborate recension of the Malay Ramayana, from which Marsden has given extracts in the Reader at the end of his Grammar. A far shorter version has been published by Mr. P. P. Roorda van Eysinga (Amsterdam, 1843). A MS. in the Dutch India Office contains also a version of it as elaborate as this; it is in two small 4to volumes (marked Ned. Kolonien. Handschriften C. No. 1), the first volume being of 475, and the second of 654 pages.[2]

No. 23 (folio of 698 pages) and No. 45 (4to. of 278 pages). Two copies of the حكايت چيكل واڽيڠ فاڽت. The first number corresponds in version with a manuscript belonging to the Dutch India Office (folio of 185 pages, and marked Ned. Kolonien. Handschriften C. No. 21; it is not finished), but is more elaborate. No. 45 seems to belong to the same recension as the two copies of the India Office (No. 2,875 small folio, and No. 2,691 large 4to‡). Another version is contained in No. 27 (folio of 347 pages), and No. 28 (folio of 348 pages: on the back of their cover, *Hikayat Dalang Indra Kesuma*). Both these volumes are divided into chapters, each of which contains a tale,

* The god Sun. † Instead of *Părta*, Sansc. *Prithă*, i.e. *Kuntī*.
[1] [See above, No. 2.]
[2] [This MS. is now the property of the Leiden University Library, and is there marked No. 1689; Bat. 141; de Hollander, l. l. p. 336.]
‡ See my "Kort Verslag der Mal. Handschriften van het East India House te London," [p. 385, Nos. 50 and 51; L. 1699, 1709; Bat. 136, 137. On the Buginese recension, see Matthes, l. l. No. 85, and p. 94.]

connected with the chief story; the first volume contains fifty-four tales and the beginning of the fifty-fifth, whilst the second commences with the fifty-sixth tale. The title, چمبل &c., of this *Panji* tale is after a name which the hero takes on his rambles in search of the princess of Daha, disguising himself as a man of the lowest class. This is one of the most interesting Malay compositions, and has influenced almost every literary production of the Malays; on another occasion I shall give an analysis of it. This cycle of stories has received by mistake also the name of حكاية ناي كسوم from its commencement, where a *Bătara Naya Kăsuma*, an inhabitant of *Indra's* heaven, is spoken of as the grandfather of *Kărtapati*.

No. 24 (two folio volumes of 446 and 450 pages) contain the سلسله راج م دتانه جاو. The first volume commences of course with Adam, whose son was *Shīth* (شيت), whose son was *Nūrchaya*, whose son was *Sangyang Wĕnang*, whose son was *Sangyang Tunggal*, whose son was *Guru*, who had four sons and one daughter, being *Sangyang Sambu, Bărahma, Mahádewa, Bisnu*, and *Dewi Sări*. *Bisnu* became king of Java with the title Prabu Seta (? سيبت). Then a chapter treats of the Ratu *Sela Părwata* of *Giling Băsi*. It ends with *Pangeran Dipati* taking the title of *Susunan Mangku Rat Senapati*, &c. The second volume commences with *Susunan Mangku Rat* being at *Bañu Mas*, and ordering the *Dipati* of *Tĕgal* to be fetched, and terminates with *Susunan Pakubuwana's* reign in *Kărtasura*. Two quotations from this work have been given by Dulaurier in the "Journal Asiatique" for 1846.

No. 25 (folio of 304 pages). This *Panji* tale goes by the name of حكاية * الدڠ مالت رسمي from a name the heroine assumes when leading the life of a penitent. The commencement treats of the prince of *Kurĭpan*, called *Kuda Jaya Asmara*, surnamed *Kărtapati*, who was betrothed to the princess of Daha, *Raden Galuh Chandărakirana puspaning rat*. A god falling in love with the

* From the Javanese *eṇḍang* (a female penitent or nun).

said princess asked her of *Batara Guru*, but meeting with a refusal, as she was to be the wife of *Kărtapati*, dropped her with her two waiting-women into a forest, where she led the life of a penitent, and changed her name and that of her companions. She is afterwards married to the prince, here passim called *Raden Inu*, who succeeds his father with the title of *Părabu Anom ing Kurĭpan*, the old king retiring to the woods to do penance.

No. 26 (folio of 239 pages). This *Panji* tale goes by the name حكاية فنج ويل كسوم. The commencement is almost the same as that of No. 23, relating the birth of *Inu Kărtapati*, and that of the *Raden Galuh Puspaning rat*, surnamed *Chandărakirana*. Going in quest of his love, who is carried off by *Batara Kala* into a forest, the hero takes the name *Mesa* Taman Panji Jayeng Kăsuma*. Afterwards in the course of the narrative he is called *Sira Panji Wila Kăsuma* (p. 73 of MS.), but often merely *Sira Panji*. After a great many adventures he becomes king of all Java.† Werndly in his "Maleische Boekzaal" mentions a *Hikayat Mesa Taman Wila Kăsuma*, and van Hoëvell, in his annotations on the Sair Bidasari, has given quotations from a *Hikayat Panji Wila Kăsuma*, pp. 301, 326, 334, 339, 362, 363, and 374.

Nos. 27 and 28. See under No. 23.

No. 29 (folio, 645 pages; ends abruptly). This *Panji* tale has the lettering *Hikayat Naga Bersru* (on the fly-leaf within). I dare not decide whether this is right, as I did not succeed in finding the reason for this title. Leyden, in his "Dissertation on the Indo-Chinese Nations" (As. Res. x.) speaks of a *Hikayat Naga Bisaru*,‡ or story of a princess of *Daha*, who was changed into a serpent, and banished to a lake. It is a pity he gave no explanation of the name. At all events this manuscript belongs to the *Panji* tales. It opens with the king of *Kurĭpan* asking

---

* Jav. *Maèsa* (*Mahişa*, buffalo) is frequent in proper names of Javanese personages, and is sometimes rendered by the equivalent Javanese *kĕbo*.
† *Amutĕr jagad jawa* (Jav.).
‡ This *bisaru* and *bersru* of the lettering, I should like to explain by برسرو in the sense of *to cry invoking the gods*.

for his son, the Raden *Inu Kărtapati*, the hand of the princess of *Daha, Chandărakirana*. The hero is here passim called *Sira Panji* and *Sări Panji*.

No. 30 (small folio of 74 pages; the wrong lettering on the back of the cover, *Salasilah nabi Muhammad*, is owing to the first words, which make *Nuru-ddīn* a descendant of the prophet's) contains the د. فتر شجرة چربون. It is a genealogical account of the kings of Cheribon (properly, *Chi-rĕbon*), commencing with a confused tale about Sheykh *Nūru-ddín*, surnamed the *Suhunan Gunung Jati*, one of the apostles of the Islām in Java. It is probably translated from a peculiar dialect of the Javanese, its language being anything but Malay, and mixed up with Javanese and occasionally with Sundanese words too. Besides the said *Suhunan* ("*Reverend*"), other celebrated apostles, as the Suhunan's *Kali Jaga, Ampel Danta*, and *Bonang* are personated here as people endowed with miraculous gifts, and the conquest of *Majapahit, Bantĕn* (Bantam), and *Pajajáran* (called here too by its ancient name *Pakúwan*) is briefly narrated. The Panĕmbahan *Sura Sohan*, called also *Mowlānā Hasanu-ddīn*, introduces, according to this chronicle, the Islām in *Pajajaran*, the *Lampong* country, *Indărapura, Bangka-ulu* (Bencoolen), and *Balo*. His elder brother, the Panĕmbahan *Pakung Wati* rules the country from Krawang to Cheribon, he himself that from Bantam to Krawang. This manuscript makes use occasionally of the linguals ڊ and ط.* From it some valuable materials might be gleaned for a work on Javanese history, the last pages containing an account of the kings of Cheribon down to Sultan *Anom*.

No. 31 (folio of 411 pages) contains the حكاية شاه قباد. The hero is the son of *Shāh Partsād* † *Indăra Lăqsana*, king of *Thăraf*,‡ situated in the neighbourhood of Mount *Qāf*. This king, although powerful, was forced to pay tribute to the monkey-king *Baliya Indăra*,§ whose residence

* e.g. منوڊڠكن and بطار (*bhatăra*). † فرصاد ‡ طرف
§ According to the Malay history of *Ráma* the same as *Bali*, and brother of *Sugríwa*. Malay compositions borrow from each other proper names; so, for

was *Kurdari* (كوردارى). The king's eldest son, called in the commencement *Qubād Lela Indăra*,* and afterwards *Shāh Qubād Johan 'Arifin*, could not put up with his father's disgrace, and resolved to deliver his parent from the allegiance to the monkey-king. He is in several ways assisted by genii, who prove to be his relatives, and wages war against the powerful enemy. This manuscript ends abruptly, the last words being

ملك بڬند شاه قباد فون ممبري تيىته اكن انق راج ٢ توجه فوله
دان كفد سري فادك كاءندراءن دان كفد راج مڠرن چندرا دان
كفد سڬل راج يڠ سلقسا توجه ريب انم راتس ايت كفد بچار
همب باءتكله سڬل سودار همب

Another copy, in which some of the proper names are different, goes by the name of حكاية شهر القمر (No. 6, large folio of 414 pages). The father of the hero is called here *Shāh Părmat Indăra Lăqsana*, and the residence of the monkey-king *Kărdar* (كردر). An entirely different version is I. (85 pages, and ending abruptly) of No. 58; it goes by the name of حكاية راج شاه جوهن اندرا مڠندرا. The hero is in this recension the son of *Bakărma*† *Chandăra*, king of *Baranta Indăra*. A specimen of the readings of No. 31 and No. 6 deserves being inserted:

No. 6:

اد سبوه نڬري اتوق نمان همفر بوكت قاف نڬرين ايت ترلالـ
بسر كوتاں درفد باءت فوته فنجڠ كوت ايت تيڬ بولں فد
فرجالنن دان نام رجاں شاه فرمت اندرا لقسان ادفون اكن بڬند

instance, we find *Indăra Kīla* (mountain, where Arjuna lived as penitent), *Mintaraga* (name of a cave, where Arjuna did penance, Sanscr. and Kavi *vītarāga*, passionless), and other proper names from the Kavi poem *Vivāha* (in Malay, حكاية داتي بيل كواچ from a Titan conquered by Arjuna) occurring in other compositions. Such proper names ought to be received into the Dictionaries.

* Werndly in his "Maleische Boekzaal" mentions a tale about a person of this very name, and Bahru-ddīn (list of Malay works to be had at Surabaya) has a حكاية راج قباست ليلا.

† See under No. 12.

ايت اصلڽ درفد جن برمول اكن بگند ايت ترلال بسر كرجاءنّ
باڤق منتريڽ توجه راتس دان باڤق هلبالغن تيگ كتي دان
رعيتڽ تياد تركيرٌ لاگ باڤڽ ادفون اكن نگري ايت ترلال
جاؤه درفد نگري يغ لاين ٢ جاڠنكن نگري مانسي يغ اد اكن
همڤر كڤد نگري بگند ايت ادفون بگند ايت سنتياس اي
مڠنتركن افتي كڤد راج كرا درفد ساءت جاؤه درفد نگري يغ
لاءئ شهدان دمكينله ملاڽ ملك سبب راج ايت مڠنتر افتي
كڤد راج كرا كارن اد سواءت راج كرا كردر نام نگريڽ دان رجاڽ
برنام مهاراج بليا ليلا اندرا &c.

No. 31 :

اد راج سبوه نگري طرف نمان همڤر بوكت قاف دان نام بگند
ايت راج شاه فرصاد اندرا لقسان برمول اكن بگند ايت ترلال
امت بسر كرجاءنّ دان كوتاڽ درفد باتو هيتم تيگ بولن
ڤرجالنّ جاؤهڽ برمول اكن بگند ايت اصلڽ درفد جن دان
باڤق منتريڽ توجه راتس دان هلبالغن سڤوله كتي رعيتڽ تياد
تركيرٌ لاگ باڤڽ ادفون اكن نگري ايت ترلال امت مشهور
كڤد سگل مانسي دان جن ڤري ممبغ ديوٌ اندرا چندرا
سكلين ڤون تياد داڤت همڤر كڤد نگري بگند تتاف اكن بگند
ايت سنتياس موسم مڠنتركن افتي كڤد راج كرا دمكينله
اصلڽ يغ جاد بگند ايت مڠنتركن افتي كڤد كرا ايت القصه
اد سبوه نگري كوردراي نمان نگري ايت دان نام رجاڽ
مهاراج بليا اندرا &c.

No. 32* (? folio) contains:

I. (11 pages). An account of various ceremonials, customs, and laws—*e.g.*, of the chief ministers a king should have, the flags they wear, &c.

II. (5 pages). A short story about *Indărapura* being

---

* Dulaurier in his list speaks of two folio volumes, both containing اندغ ٢, but I have only found one, on the back of which the number was obliterated. That number is consequently all but certain.

attacked by *todak*-fishes,* and the stratagem by which they were defeated.

III. (5 pages). The first arrival of the Portuguese, and their stratagem to get possession of Malaka.† A translation of it by Sir Stamford Raffles is to be found in the "Asiatic Researches," xii. p. 115.

IV. Coloured figures representing the flags used by the sovereign and his chief ministers (belonging to I.).

V. (63 pages). A tale the commencing words of which look more like a chapter than like a separate tract. They are:

القصه ترسبتله فركتا°ن اد سبوه نكري برنام طوغان فوري
رجان برنام سلطان اممس ديو ملك راج ايت ترلال امت بسر
كرجا°ئن استريين برنام فتري انتن چهبريم ملك تون فتري
ايتفون ساغت هندق برائق &c.

The last words are:

حتي راج طاهر فري فون ارفلق ارچيم كفد راج ديو بسنو
برتاغس تغيسن لال بگند فون تورن ارجالن حتي بگند راج
سلطان اممس ديو فون دودقله يغ بگمان سلمان

It relates the adventures of *Dewa Bisnu*, son of the king spoken of in the commencement; from which it is probable that the title should be ديو بسنو حكاية .

No. 33 (folio) contains:

I. (11 pages). A collection of laws, commencing with the finding of goods, and what is to be done with them.

II. (44 pages). Laws, some of which are maritime.

III. (8 pages). Fragments of a law book, beginning with the fencing of cultivated fields.

IV. (6 pages). باب فد ميتاكن كتيك رچغ About the ominous qualities of the days of the months, having mystical names, mostly those of animals. The same is found in II. of No. 74.

* The same is told of Singapura (see "Malayan Annals," p. 83) and of *Barus* according to the *Sair Raja Tuktung* (شعر راج تقتنغ).

† The same narrative is found in one of the last chapters of No. 1.

V. (3 pages). باب فد مپتاکن کتیك توجه On the seven ominous times. The same is XVI. and XXXVII. of No. 34, and IV. of No. 74.

VI. (6 pages). فضل فد مپتاکن کتیك لیم On the five ominous times. Compare the "Bataksch Woordenboek," p. 419. The same in No. 34 (X. and XXXV.) and No. 74 (V.).

No. 34 (folio; the number obliterated, and on the back of the cover, *undang undang*) contains:

I. (1 page). A fragment from a law book.

II. (1 page). باب فد مپتاکن ناڬ مغیدر درین On the serpent turning itself round in the sky, the position of which is to be known, especially when going to war.[1]

III. (3 pages). Charms and antidotes.

IV. (15 pages). Malay laws, commencing with the fencing of cultivated fields. The maritime part has been published by Dulaurier in the sixth volume of Pardessus's "Collection de Lois Maritimes."

V. (7 pages). Treaty between the Admiral Speelman and Hasanu-ddīn, king of Gowa, and other Mangkasar chiefs (compare No. 10).

VI. (1 page). Chronicle of Mangkasar, commencing with اینله اصل یڠ فرتام مول ۲ یڠ کرجاءن دتلق ایت برنام کرایڠ لوی د سیرو, &c. (continued in VIII.).

VII. (1 page). Contract of *'Aliyu-ddīn* of Gowa with the Malay merchants.

VIII. (3 pages). Continuation of VI. (continued in XII. and XVIII).

IX. (9 pages). A chapter on the law of inheritance. (فرائض).

X. (2 pages). See VI. of No. 33.

XI. (6 pages). Customs and laws commencing with the duties of the Băndhara, Tumănggung, and other functionaries of the Malays.

XII. (2 pages). Continuation of VI.

XIII. (1 page). A fragment about the discontinuance of praying according to the words of the prophet.

---

[1] [Compare "Bataksch Woordenboek," p. 327.]

XIV. (1 page, 54th page). Formulas used as charms.
XV. (1 page). On ominous days (نحس).
XVI. (3 pages). The same as V. of No. 33.
XVII. (1 page). فصل فد مڤتاكن * رجال الغيب
XVIII. (4 pages). Continuation of VI. (continued in XIX.)
XIX. (3 pages). A fragment of a work on superstitions and continuation of VI. (continued in XXVI.) on charms, commencing with the means of seducing a woman, &c.
XX. (11 pages). Receipts against diseases, commencing with a precept about the regular course of a woman's sperm (ترتيب مني فرمڤون).
XXI. (p. 78). Table of ominous events, which have to be expected on each day of the month.
XXII. (p. 79). Receipts, commencing with a prescription against stomach-ache.
XXIII. (p. 81). The letters of the alphabet with their mystical meaning under each of them.
XXIV. Regulations for the chief of the Malays settled at Mangkásar, his power, &c.
XXV. Prescription to conquer a woman's obduracy.
XXVI. (p. 82). Fragment of a chronicle (VI.) and continued in XXVIII.
XXVII. Continuation of XXIV.
XXVIII. Continuation of VI.
XXIX. Combination of letters attributed to prophets, angels, and holy men.
XXX. (p. 98). A precept of the wise *Loqmān* about the future of a just-born child.
XXXI. (p. 99). On the ominous signification of earthquakes, lightning and eclipses, according to the time of their appearance. A fragment of a similar work is to be found in de Hollander's Reader, p. ٣٢٨.
XXXII. (p. 103). About the choice of the ground to erect a house upon, to make a field of, &c.

* See Herklots' "Customs, &c." p. 395.

XXXIII. (p. 106). Means to know how a man and woman live together.

XXXIV. (p. 110). Means to know whether stolen goods may be recovered.

XXXV. (4 pages). See VI. of No. 33.

XXXVI. Astrological tables of the planets according to the days of the week.

XXXVII. See V. of No. 33. On p. 120, an illustrative table.

XXXVIII. (p. 121). A figure illustrative of the serpent's position (see II.).

No. 35. See under No. 18.

No. 36. See under No. 7.

No. 37. See under No. 9.

No. 38 (small folio of 87 pages), No. 59 (small 4to of 138 pages), and No. 71 (small 4to of 196 pages) contain the حكاية كليلة و دمنة.* In the last-named number the introduction is wanting. Some fables from this book have been published by J. J. de Hollander in his "Malay Reader," p. 18 sqq. I possess a manuscript of it (4to. of 205 pages). A specimen of the various readings of these four manuscripts may not be out of place. The reader may compare with it the fable published on p. 18 of the above-cited work.

No. 38 :

اد سئكر دندغ برمسارغ دياتس سفوهن برقس مها بسر ادفون برقس
ايت برلوبغ ملك د لوبغ فوهن برقس ايت اد سئكر اولر بسر
ددالم كايو ايت ديم دسان ملك افبيل دندغ ايت برائق دماكن
اولر ايت دمكين جو سلمان ملك دندغ ايت فرگي كفد صحابتن
سيكر سريگال ملك كاست سريگال ايت افاته كهندقم دائغ
كفداك ملك كاست دندغ ايت هي توليك ادفون الڬ دائغ اين
تله ببراف كال الڬ برائق دماكنى جو اوله اولر بسر اينله ملك
الڬ اين دائغ كفدام مغدوكن حالك

---

* On the west coast of Sumatra it goes by the name of حكاية ستروبه si-tărubuh) after the name of the bull who became the lion's friend.

No. 59:

اد سڠكر دندڠ برسارڠ دياتس فوهن برقس مهابسر ادفون فوهن
برقس ايت اد برلوبڠ فوهن فرقس ايت اد سڠكر اولر بسر دإم
دسان مك تيف ٢ دندڠ ايت برانق دماكن اولر ايت دمكين
جو سلمان مك دندڠ اينتفون فرڬي كفد سڠكر سريڬال مك
كات سريڬال هي دندڠ اف كهندق اڠكو داتڠ كفدالك مك
كات دندڠ ايت هي توڠك ادفون الك داتڠ اين كارن تله براف
كال الك برانق دماكن جو اوله اولر بسر ابتفون مك الك داتڠ
كڤدام مڠدوكن حالك

No. 71:

مك اداله سڠكر دندڠ برسارڠ دياتس فوهن كايو بسر مك اداله
فوهن ايت برلوبڠ ٢ مك اولر يڠ بسر سڠكر دالم لوبڠ كايو ايت
افبيل برانقله دندڠ ايت داتڠله اولر دماكنن هابس سننتياس
له يڠ دمكين ايت مك دندڠ فون امت حيرانله اكندرين لال
اي مڠادف كفد سريڬال كتان هي هندىك افاله داي افاياك
سننتياس دالم فرچنتا'لك افبيل الك برانق دماكنن اوله اولر
ددالم كايو ايت

My Manuscript:

اد سڠكر دندڠ برسارڠ دياتس كايو برقس مهاتڠڬ مك اد
سڠكر اولر ديم ڤد رڠڬا كايو برقسا ايت تنكل دندڠ ايت
برانق مك دماكنن اوله اولر ايت اكن انق دندڠ ايت دمكينله
سديكال مك دندڠ اينتفون ترلال دكڤت مك دندڠ فون فرڬيله
كڤد سريڬال مڠدوكن حالن دمكين كتان سننتياس همب
برانق دماكنن اوله اولر ايت تولڠله چاراكن اولهم اكنداك
مك اوجر سريڬال هي هندىك

Hence it appears that the manuscript from which de Hollander published some fables must belong to another recension than these four manuscripts. All these versions are from the Persian.*

* The Tamil version has been translated by *Abdu-llah* the Moonshee and published at Malaka [in 1835, 85 lithographed folio pages]. It is divided in the same way as the *Panchatantra*, and bears the title of پنچ تندران . [A

No. 39. See under No. 18.

No. 40 (folio of 320 pages) contains the حكاية ميسس لار كسوم. The hero is the son of a king of كُونَاتُن in West Java. This king had two wives, the younger being *Ămas Ajĕng*, who bore him a son called جِناكر نيبت. She slanders the elder, making the king believe she had tried to poison him. The elder queen is defended by her son, who in consequence falls into disgrace, and is incarcerated. The queen herself is conducted into a forest to be killed, but the executioner, pitying her condition, leaves her in a grotto, where بتار بناو supplies her wants. She is there delivered of a son, who receives the name of رادن ميسس اريا مڠكوستر. The story ends in a strange and abrupt way, as if not finished. I do not think it probable that this composition is the same as that mentioned by *Bahruddīn* under the title حكاية سيير فنج لار كسوم, which is decidedly a *Panji* tale.

No. 41 contains a Malay translation of a Javanese *Wukon*.* It is a miserable composition, not readable without the Javanese original.

No. 42† and No. 64. Two copies of the تاج السلاطين. This work has been published with a Dutch translation by P. P. Roorda van Eysinga ("Der Kroon der Koningen." Batavia. 1827). A great many quotations in Werndly's "Maleische Spraakkunst" are from a better manuscript than that used by Roorda van Eysinga.

No. 43. See under No. 19.

No. 44 (4to of 303 pages) contains the حكاية چابت تڠڬل a *Panji* tale; the title is derived from a banner (*tunggul*), the baneful influence of which occasioned a great mortality in the land,‡ being pulled up (*chabut*) by the hero. It opens with the god *Naya Kăsuma* (see under No. 23)

---

new edition, by the writer of this account, appeared at Leiden in 1866; it has a valuable introduction, and philological and critical notes. A Dutch translation, by Klinkert, came out at Zalt-Bommel in 1871. See also de Hollander, l. l. p. 368; L. 1729, 1757; Bat. 184, 5.]

* See Raffles' "History of Java," i. p. 745 sqq. "Tijdschrift voor Indische Taal- Land- en Volkenkunde" (Batavia, vol. vi. and vii.).

† See also Nos. 17 and 47 II.

‡ Compare Cohen Stuart, l. l. p. 153.

descending into the world, and taking the name of *Mesa Părta Jaya Kălana Banjáran.* He becomes king of *Majapahit,* with the title *Părabu Wira Kărta,* after having married the only daughter of the old king, who retired to do penance. His sons become kings of *Kurĭpan, Daha, Gagălang,* and *Singasári.* In the course of the narrative *Kărtapati* and *Chandărakirána* are again the most conspicuous characters. In his perambulations the said prince calls himself *Ki-ramang Panji Wauhan** (?), and the princess of *Daha,* when leading the life of a penitent, assumes the name of اندغ اسماي دفوري (compare under No. 25). The language of this tale is crowded with Javanese words and expressions. As humble pronoun of the first person, *pun titiyang*† (the man) is here used as in the Balinese.

No. 45. See under No. 23.

No. 46 (large 4to of 306 pages) contains the حكاية د.يو مندو. The hero's father is *Kărma Indăra,* king of *Kangsa Indăra.* This king has heard of a certain white elephant, and orders *Părba Indăra* to catch it. *Părba Indăra,* failing in executing the orders of his master, is discarded from the court, and leaves with his family. He arrives at a hamlet, where a *Sheykh Jădīd* was living in religious solitude, and settles there. He afterwards begot there a daughter called *Siti*‡ *Mangărna Lela Chahya,* with whom the new king, *Pakărma*§ *Raja,* falls in love when coming accidentally to her father's hermitage. *Siti Mangărna* is after due time delivered of a son, who is the hero of this tale. This prince leaves the residence, and rambles about to increase his knowledge of the world. In the course of his rambles he meets with the white elephant, who was a princess of the name of *Lela Rătna Kumála,* and had been transformed by a demon, of the name of *Dewa*

---

* The manuscript: واوهن. A *Hikayat Mesa Kiramang* is mentioned in the "Journal Asiatique," 1833, by Jaquet.

† Compare the use of *ulun* as pronoun of first person, being the same as *ulun* (Lampong) and *ŭlună* (Malagasy spelling *olona*) which signify *man,* and *ngwang* (pronoun first person) and *wwang* (man) in Kavi.

‡ The Arabic ستي. § See under No. 12.

Răqsa Malik, out of spite, as he wanted her for his wife, but met with a refusal at her father's hands. Another copy of this tale is in the library of the India Office (No. 2,871, folio volume),[1] where the introduction is entirely different. According to the last words of that manuscript this tale goes also by the name of حكاية راج كسس اندرا فكرم راج.

No. 47 (4to) contains:

I. The حكاية ميسى اندرا ديو كسوم. The hero is a son of a king of *Kurĭpan* by *Sakărba*,* a daughter of *Indăra*, a king of *Kaling*, who had made himself universal sovereign of the world (چكرا بوان واتس); having subjected the kings of *Gujărat, Mogol, Abyssinia, Machulipatam, Bengal*, &c., he sends a fleet to conquer Java, going himself thither with his sons through the air. *Mesa Indăra Dewa Kăsuma* opposes the conqueror. Amongst the places the Indian king besieged is *Pajajăran*, the king of which had a son called *Ămas Tanduran*, and two daughters, called Raden galuh *Kumŭda Răsmi*, and Raden galuh *Dewi Rina* (?). The opening of this tale is anything but clear. It is besides crowded with Javanese expressions, as for instance, *măngambah jumantăra*† (to tread the air).

II. (64 pages). Fragments of the تاج السلاطين (see No. 42).

III. (18 pages). معجزة رسول الله ممغكل بولن. Another copy in No 62. This short tale about Muhammad's miracle of making the moon pass by halves through his sleeves, has been published by Robinson at the end of his "Principles to Elucidate the Malay Orthography."‡ There are a great many manuscripts of this legend.§

IV. (5 pages). حكاية فرتن اسلام. On the duties of a married woman, about which the heroine of this tale

---

[1] [Now 210; B.M. 1; Bat. 157, 158.]
* Corruption of the Sanskrit *Suprabhā*. [See "Bataksch Leesboek," vol. iv., p. 115.]
† The Sanskrit *dyumāntara*.
‡ P. 222 sqq. of the Dutch translation by E. Netscher [p. 181 of the original work].
§ One in the possession of Mr. H. C. Millies at Utrecht, and another in mine (small 8vo, of 28 pages).

consults the prophet.* A copy is in the possession of Mr. H. C. Millies, where the proper name is spelt فرتنا.

No. 48 (small 4to of 210 pages) contains the شرح يڠ لطيڡ اتس مختصر جوهرة التوحيد.† It is translated from the Arabic of *Ibrāhīm Laqānī*, by the Sheykh *Shihābu-ddīn*, surnamed the Pilgrim, and son of *'Abdu-llah Muhammad*, surnamed the Malay (الجاوي).

No. 49 (4to of 56 pages).‡ A poem, the title of which is uncertain. It contains the celebration of a king of *Bintan*, and the splendour of his palace, garden, &c. The first verses are :—

الحمد لله فوج يڠ سدي
بركة محمد سيد الانبيا
دولة مڠكت تله سجهنترا
عارف بالله تاجم بچار
كامل فرنته سلطان مود

بڬ الله توهن يڠ كاي
برتمبه دولة راج يڠ ملي
د فرنتهكن فادڠ ادند سودار
امڡام شمس منراڠي نڬار
ممرنتهكن كرجاءن فادڠ ككند

The last verses are :

براڠكتله كدو ماكت عالم
دايرڠكن نصب وزير الاعظم
سجهنتراله فكرجاءن دلي ماكت
دڠن انڬرا توهن سمست
سلسيله فترا دلي سمڡاين
برفوله سمبرف برددا ين
تمتله قصه دلي يڠ غنا
دمنتري ددالم قرطاس چين
تمتله رنچان دلي ماكت
جڠ اد § سجق يڠ لت

مغارق فترا ماسق كدالم
مڠنترکن فترا دار السلام
دولة استعادة ددالم كوت
سواست فون جاڠن مار سڠكيت
كلورله هداڠن برلاين
ممبري ايافن هلبالغ سكلين
دكارڠ فقير همب يڠ هين
سجقن § لارت بافق تاء كنا
دكارڠ ضعيف همب كڡست
بربافق امفن دلي ماكت

* It goes also by the name of حكاية بردان سلامة according to de Hollander, l. l. p. 331, No. 14. [On the Makassar recension, see Matthes, l. l. No. 33, III.]

† Another commentary on the same work is called, اتحاف المريد شرح علي جوهرة التوحيد.

‡ The lettering on the back of the cover (*Karangan Bantan*) is wrong. Dulaurier infers from it that it is about the foundation of Bantam.

§ The Arabic سجع.

No. 50 (small 4to of 96 pages) contains the حكاية تميم
الدارى—*i.e.*, the adventures of *Tămīmu-ddāri*, an inhabitant
of *Madīnah*, and originally a Christian. It is taken from
the تاريخ المجرات. He was carried off when bathing
during the night, which the prophet had prohibited, by a
spirit (*jin*) to the country of the genii, that were yet infidels,
and stayed there seven years and four months. He meets
in the course of his rambles with the Antichrist (دجّال),
appearing in the form of a large bitch big with barking
puppies, and becoming large when hearing bad reports
about the Muslims, and small when they are favourable;
with female cannibals on a certain island, with the angels
Jabarāil and *Mikāil*, and the prophet *Hilir* (خضر), who
gives an explanation of the wonderful things *Tămīm* sees
and cannot account for. He meets a bird, too, which
gives him a delicious beverage out of its bill, and is no
other than the bird of *Ishāk*, and leads the erring faithful
upon the right way. He sees a man filling out of a pond
a tub with the bottom off, being a usurer. On his return
to this sublunary orb, he finds his wife re-married, and
squabbles with her husband. '*Umar* (عمر) could not
settle the quarrel, as *Tămīm*, not having shaved and
pared his nails during his absence, looked quite another
man, and was not recognized. '*Ali* (علي) then recollects
a communication from the prophet about a sign by which
Tămīm could be identified, being a whitish spot as large
as a *dărham* behind the knee.[1]

No. 51. See under No. 19.

No. 52 (4to of 140 pages) contains the حكاية راج باتب.
In the opening a king of *Gunung bărapi rantow panjang
tăbing bărukir* is introduced, called طاهير شاه فرى. He
had forty wives, one of whom only, called *Indăra Sori*,
became pregnant. Sending away the other thirty-nine
on account of their sterility, he was cursed by them to have

---

[1] [L. 1719 and p. 178. A lithographed text edition appeared at Singapore, a. H. 1297. On the Makassar recension, see Matthes, l. l. No. 10. Concerning *Tamîm ibn Aûsu-ddâri*, see Slane, "Ibn Khallikân's Bibliographical Dictionary," vol. ii. p. 21.]

a hog as a son. After a pregnancy of seven years the queen was delivered of a boar of a terrifying appearance, with tusks as yellow as a ripe plantain fruit.* The king ordered his minister to throw his son into the woods, where the young hog conquered the king of the hogs, being assisted by a princess who was doing penance on the field of their contest. Having been victorious, he was bathed by that princess, and treated in her residence as her son. After taking leave of her, he is carried away by a *jin*, &c. This composition is replete with *pantuns*, and the text is not much corrupted. The language is genuine Malay as far as I have read it. After a great many adventures, the hero returns in a human shape to his father's residence, and is then called *Indăra Bărma Kala*.¹

No. 53 (small 4to) contains:

I. (98 pages)† the حكاية ‡ سمسكين. It has been published at Singapore (lithographed).² There are a great many manuscripts of this tale. The one in my possession has been vitiated by a Batavian transcriber, who has, for instance, changed سمايم into سممبيڠ !

II. (26 pages) شعر ايكن.³ It commences with exhortations to children, and is a miserable jingling of rhymes about a great many fishes, introduced in it as would-be poets. The composition may be serviceable in correcting the existing Malay Dictionaries in the wrong pronunciation of fish-names. I possess a manuscript of it.

No. 54 (small 4to of 293 pages) contains the حكاية احمد إستو. In the commencement there is a kind of summary, relating that the hero was harmed by a genius called طبر سقتني, that on his rambles he came upon Mount *Langkări Rătna*, where he saw two princes of the genii, that he encountered the princesses *Săkanda Kumála*

باب تفكّل ترلال هيبة رفان تارڠن كونغ سفرت فيسڠ ماسق *

¹ [B.M. 18.]
† The lettering *Angkasa Dewa* is a mistake owing to the tale commencing with these words.   ‡ *Si-miskin* ("the poor one.")
² [In 1857 and 1879; Bat. 175, 176.]
³ [Printed at Batavia in 1865.]

Indăra and *Bumáya Indăra*, fought the king *Makuta Indăra* on account of the first-named princess, and was thrown by order of that prince into the lake *Indăra Sătunang*, where he was swallowed up by a serpent, in whose belly he met the princess *Băranta Maya;* and a great many other adventures of the same kind are told. The hero was the son of *Sahfar Tsaf Indăra*,[*] king of *Burangga Dewa*. In one of the chapters طبر سقتني is said to be king of a State situated in the cavern of Mount *Dewa Rangga Indăra*.

No. 55. See under No. 9.

No. 56 (4to of 412 pages; on the cover *Badiulzaman Anak Hamzah*). In the commencement are contained the adventures of بديع الزمان, said to be the son of *Hamzah;*[†] then follow those of his father, and of *'Umar Maya*, with whose death it closes. Perhaps it is but a part of the حكاية حمزة.[1]

No. 57 (4to of 332 pages) contains the حكاية اندرا كياڠن. *Mangindăra Chuwácha*, king of *Indăra Părchangga*, had two sons called *Raja Sháh Johan Mangindăra Rupa* and *Raja Thahir*[‡] *Johan Shah*. The king having dreamt of a wonderful musical instrument which sounded one hundred and ninety times when but once struck, and longing to have it, the two young princes go in quest of it. They are adopted by a ghost, of the name of راج سلم, who tells them where to find the wonderful instrument. He changes their names, calling the eldest prince *Indăra Mahádewa Săqti*, and the youngest *Bisnu Dewa Kaindăraan*, surnamed *Indăra Lăqsana*. The brothers are separated afterwards, each of them achieving a great many stirring feats by the assistance of the *jin*, their adopted father. Extracts from this composition are to be found in

[*] سڢر صف اندرا .

[†] Of the حكاية حمزة de Hollander in his "Reader" (p. 82 sqq.) has published extracts; and another extract is to be found in Roorda van Eysinga's "Beknopte Maleische Spraakkunst" (Breda, 1839), p. 102 sqq.

[1] [There is a MS. at Leiden, l. l. p. 178.]

[‡] طاهر .

Marsden's "Malay Reader" at the end of his Grammar, according to a manuscript but slightly differing from this one, of which the lettering on the back of its cover, *Indra layangan*, is a mistake for *Indăra Kiyángan*, as the extracts published by Marsden have it.

No. 58 (small 4to) contains:
I. See under No. 31.
II. (34 pages). حكاية فتري جوهر مانكم , which is a more elaborate version of this tale than that published by de Hollander (Breda, 1845), and corresponds more with that of the manuscript from which quotations are found in Roorda van Eysinga's "Maleisch-Nederduitsch Woordenboek" (s. vv. *harām, haji, chiyum, churi, khiyanat, khemah, darah, dapat, dakap, dandam, diri, ridlā, rambut, zadah, salăsey, sălam, sanăschaya, surat, sayid, sisi, shetan, tsahib, pandey,* and *saháya*). In this manuscript the heroine's brother is called منسب شاهد. There was, and perhaps still is, also a MS. copy of this tale in the possession of Mr. Frederick Muller, at Amsterdam. On the west coast of Sumatra the heroine goes by the name of *Johor Malěgan,* which name occurs in Bahruuddīn's list too. Of the Sumatra version* I possess an incomplete copy.

No. 59. See under No. 38.

No. 60 (small 4to of 106 pages) contains the حكاية شاه مردان.† Another copy is No. 66 (small 4to of 223 pages). The hero, assuming in the course of his rambles the name of *Indăra Jaya,* this very popular tale goes also by the name of حكايه اندرا جاي. Part of it has been published by de Hollander in the first edition [and in the fifth from p. ۱۲۷ to p. ۱۵۲] of his "Handleiding bij de beoefening der Maleische Taal- en Letterkunde,"

---

* About a Javanese version, see Raffles' "History of Java," i. p. 394 sqq. [L. 1691, 1727, 1777; Bat. 121-3. See de Hollander, l. l. p. 351. An edition by the same appeared at Breda in 1845.]

† The Persian pronunciation, *shâ-i mărdân* has occasioned the name شيخ مردان cited by van Hoëvell in the annotations to the "Sair Bidasari." On the west of Sumatra شاه عالم is pronounced *sa-i alam;* hence confusion in the title of the dwarf deer between *shā-i 'ālam di rimba* and *shaykh 'ālam di rimba.*

p. ١٧٧-١٩٩. It is also called after the hero's father, حكاية * بكرم دتي راج. It is mentioned by Leyden ("Asiatic Researches," x.) under the title *Hikayet Bikermadi(tya)*. A translated extract about the creation of the world is to be found in No. 60 of the "Indo-Chinese Gleaner." A copy, too, is found in a volume, containing the *Hikayat Pălanduk Jănaka*, belonging to the library of the India Office (No. 2673 ?). I possess a manuscript copy of it of 38 pages folio.[1]

No. 61 (small 4to. of 150 pages) contains the حكاية شمس البر (*shamsu-lbarri*). The hero, called "the sun of the earth,"† is the son of *Dărma Dikăra*, king of *Paruwa Chakăra Nagara* in Hindustan. His name he owes to his being predestined to be a powerful king, ruling over the earth and sea, whence he was surnamed "the moon of the sea."‡ When twelve years old he was carried off by an infidel *jin*, in consequence of which he had a great many adventures before he returned home. On his return he succeeds his father with the title of Sultan *Qamru-lbaḥrin*.

No. 62 (quarto) contains:

I. See under No. 16.

II. See under No. 49, III.

III. (About 60 pages) سريب مسائل. It contains one thousand questions put to Muhammad by a learned Jew of the Khaybar tribe. Having been answered by the prophet satisfactorily, a great many Jews of the said tribe embrace the Islām. It is translated from the Persian. A manuscript of this composition (small 4to of 156 pages) I saw at Barus in the possession of the Tuwanku of *Sigambo-gambo*. A copy is also in the possession of Prof. H. C. Millies at Utrecht. It is a very interesting work, and reproduces the popular belief of the Malays

---

* *Wikramāditya*. No. 60 has بكرم دنت جاي.

[1] [I.O. 373; B.M. 14; L. 1733; Bat. 149, 150, 151. There is a Makassar recension, l. l. No. 11. See de Hollander, l. l. p. 347 f.]

† The manuscript explains the Arabic name by *artiña matahari di darat*.

‡ قمر البحر explained by *bulan yang dităpi lăut*.

about a great many questions of the Muhammadan faith. The orthodox priests condemn it as well as the حكاية مُحمد خنفيه.¹

IV. (8 pages) جرترا نبي الله موسي مناجة د بوكت طور سين. Moses' ascent on Mount Sinai.

V. (5 pages) حكاية فاطمه كاون is a tract about the duties of a married woman, expounded by the prophet to his daughter. A copy of it is in the possession of Prof. H. C. Millies at Utrecht.²

VI. (6 pages) حكاية رسول الله برچوكر. The prophet is shaved by Gabriel, and his hair gathered by the celestial nymphs for the purpose of making amulets of them. Published at Batavia (1853, in 12mo, Lange and Co.).³

No. 63 (4to of 349 pages; on the cover, *Raja 'adil*). It contains the حكاية بختيار.* The wrong lettering is owing to the commencement, where a just king (*Raja 'ādil*) whose name is not mentioned, is forced to flee from his dominions, and is afterwards made captive by an unjust king. This MS. however, contains another version than that from which de Hollander has given extracts in his "Reader" (p. 131 sqq.) and transliterated in his "Handleiding tot de Kennis der Maleische Taal" (Breda, 1845). The name of the person who found the child of which the queen was delivered during her flight with her consort, and which she was forced to leave, is here رسلس. The last tale in this manuscript is the story of Solomon and the Queen of Sabā.† The text is pretty good, but occasionally corrupted. The introduction especially differs widely from that of other versions I know. I possess a copy (folio of 50 pages), wherein the number of tales told by *Bakhtiyār* amounts to nine. Its version

---

¹ [Bat. 82–86; Leiden, l. l. p. 178. Lithographed at Singapore in 1879.]
² [L. 1744; Bat. 94.]
³ [L. 1720; Makassar version, Matthes, l. l. No. 32.]
* The Persian original was translated by Lescalier ("*Bakhtiyar*, ou le Favori de la Fortune." Paris, 1805).
† Of this story there is an elaborate novel on the west coast of Sumatra, where it is called حكاية فتري بلقيس. I possess three manuscripts of it, all written in the Menangkabow dialect. [An edition of it, with translation and notes, by Mr. D. Gerth van Wijk, appeared in the xli. vol. of the "Verhandelingen van het Batav. Genootschap."]

differs from that of de Hollander's text. This tale goes also by the name of حكاية ازباح , حكاية زاده بخت (from the name of the hero's father), and according to de Hollander, also حكاية علام, which last name, found in the Leiden MSS., is by far not so popular, and does not convey an idea about its contents.[1]

No. 64. See under No. 42.

No. 65 (small 4to of 152 pages) contains the شعر اڠريني, a poem the plot of which is taken from the Javanese. It belongs to the *Panji* tales * relating the adventures of *Panji* and *Angăreni*, daughter of the *patih*, with whom he fell in love after having been betrothed to *Sĕkar Taji*, the princess of *Kădiri*. His father ordered *Angăreni* to be killed when *Panji* was absent, having gone in quest of game.† This composition proves to be the story which has suggested the plot of the شعر كن تمبوهن (see under No. 7). This manuscript breaks off abruptly, and is to such an extent replete with Javanese words, that a Malay would not understand it.

No. 66. See under No. 60.

[1] [L. 1718, 1723, 1750; Bat. 132-4, 179. Printed at Batavia in 1880. Makassar translation, ap. Matthes, l. l., No. 89.]

* Other tales belonging to this cyclus, and not existing in this collection, are—I. حكاية فنج جاييڠ كسوم (*jayeng kăsuma* is Javanese, and means "victorious on the battle field," and is often changed in Malay into *Jaya Kăsuma*), from which quotations are to be found in van Hoëvell's annotations (p. 301, 326, 334, 362, 363, and 374). II. حكاية فنج سميرڠ سمرنتاك (after an assumed name of *Chandărakirana*, when dressing as a male, and roving about to subject the States she came upon). III. حكاية ميس تندرامن (No. 2,602, India Office).[2] IV. حكاية فنج چنترا (?) V. حكاية چارڠ ميس كمبر سار يڠ برڬلر رات انوم اڠ ملاي. VI. حكاية سير فنج لار كسوم (see under No. 40). VII. (see II. under No. 7). VIII. حكاية جاي لڠكار (a translation of which into Mangkasar is to be found in Matthes's " Makassaarsche Chrestomathie"). There are more tales belonging to this cyclus, as may be inferred from some manuscripts in the British Museum.

[2] [Now No. 69. See the account of it, l. l. p. 389.]

† The plot does not differ materially from that of the tale of which Mr. Taco Roorda has given an elaborate analysis (see *Lotgevallen van Raden Pandji* in the "Bijdragen tot de Taal- Land- en Volkenkunde van N.I." Vol. vii. Nieuwe Volgreeks). Compare also Raffles' " History of Java," ii. 88.

MALAY MANUSCRIPTS. 41

No. 67. حكاية راجم فاسي. Published by Dulaurier in his "Chroniques Malayes." A list of countries dependent on Majapahit, found in this manuscript, is published by the same in the "Journal Asiatique" for 1846.

No. 68. See under No. 18.

No. 69 (small 4to of 128 pages). According to the lettering on the back of the cover, the title would be باب العقل كفد سگل اورڠ بسرم. It is an ethic work, laying down rules for ministers and great functionaries as to their conduct when officiating. It is illustrated by tales. In the commencement the manuscript says that the tale came from Sultan *Aliyu-ddīn Shāh*, son of *Manṣūr Shāh*, king of *Pătani*. On page 10 there is a story about the sagacity of the dwarf-deer (*pălanduk**) settling a contest between an alligator and a young man about the propriety of the alligator eating the young man, who had delivered it when about to die on the dry land. The last tale is about a Sultan *Al-'ālam Shāh*.

No. 70 (small 4to) contains:

I. (186 pages). The seventh book of the بستان العارفين, an ethic work illustrated by a great many tales. According to the last words of this manuscript, the whole work is divided into seven books. On p. 163 the narrative about *Siti 'Abasah* (see No. 76) is found.

II. (8 pages). A small collection of tales,† belonging most probably to a larger composition (to I.?). The first tale is about Moses and *Qārūn*, who bribed a pregnant woman to say that Moses had committed adultery with her. The second is about a certain بلهم trying to

---

* The حكاية فلندق جناك, two copies of which are in the Library of the India Office (Nos. 3,049 and 2,603 [now Nos. 67, 96, and 373. A text edition was brought out by N. C. Klinkert at Leiden in 1885]), has a great similarity with the European tale about Reynard the fox. (See "Kort Verslag der Maleische Handschriften van het E. I. House te Londen.") The *pălanduk* acts in the Indian Archipelago the part that the fox acts with us.

† Such small collections of tales, the title of which is either arbitrary, or not to be fixed from the contents, are often found in the possession of the poor, who cannot afford to buy manuscripts of the extent of the *Bustānu-ssalāthīn, Taju-ssalāthīn,* and the like. A collection of the same kind is the حكاية ليم فصل in No. 2,603 (Library of the India Office).

outstrip Moses by the force of his penance. The third is about Moses' death. The fourth is about a woman called رابعة العدوية getting ten-fold back what she had given to the poor. The fifth is about a man of the name of دانٍ مسر seeing the mercy of God to the just.

No. 71. See under No. 38.

No. 72 (small 4to of 44 pages; on the back of the cover, *Kitab rasul*). It contains the حكاية مهاراج علي, another version of the " Story of King Skull "* (حكاية راج جمجمة) the plot being the same as that of the حكاية بسف وراج † There are a great many copies of this tale. Prof. H. C. Millies at Utrecht, possesses a copy (small 8vo) bearing the title حكاية علي پادشاه (the Persian *p* is here strange). Of the story of King Skull there is a copy in the India Office, being the third tale in the حكاية ليم فصل (No. 2,603).[1] I myself possess two copies of it (one evidently mutilated by a Batavian transcriber).

No. 73. See No. 4.

No. 74 (small 4to) contains:

I. Laws of Malaka, Johor, and Salangor.

II. (11 pages). See IV. of No. 33.

III. (1 page). Receipts, commencing with that against a kind of leprosy.

IV. (10 pages). See V. of No. 33.

V. (8 pages). See VI. of No. 33.

VI. Fragments of a religious work. On the last pages are found coloured tables representing the *five ominous times* (belonging to V.)

No. 75 (small 4to; on the cover, *undang undang*) contains:

I. (6 pages). A fragment from a law book. The first chapter is about people having plantations and neglecting to fence them.

II. A fragment from some work on Muhammadan

---

* Translated, "Asiatic Journal," 1823.

† Edited by Fraissinet under the title of "Geschiedenis van Vorst Bispoe Radja" (Breda, 1849).

[1] [Now 96; L. 1781; Bat. 106–109.]

law, commencing with the rules about selling and buying (بيع), and ending with the law of inheritance (فرائض).

III. (2 pages). A fragment from an Arabic work on law with Malay interlinear translation.

IV. (15 pages). An Arabic-Malay Dictionary. Under each Arabic word the corresponding Malay is written. The last seven pages are not filled up with the Malay. I possess a complete copy, and a fragment of another work of the same kind.

No. 76 (small 4to) contains:

I. See under No. 18.

II. (9 pages). حكاية سنتي عباسه. It is properly but a tale taken from the بستان العارفين (I. No. 70), but often found separately. Two copies are in my possession (small 4to of 20 pages, and small 8vo of 24 pages).

III. (23 pages). A fragment from a work on religious observances, commencing with the sacrifices (قربان).

IV. (small 8vo of 13 pages). Fragments of a work containing Malay laws, and commencing with goods found on the road.

No. 77 (small 4to) contains:

I. (4 pages). شعر فيفت دان اڠكڠ.

II. (61 pages). Maritime laws.

III. (20 pages). Orders issued by Sultan *Ahmad Tājuddīn Halīm Shāh* of *Kădah* (قدح), some of which refer to the suppression of piracy (Muh. year 1133).

No. 78 (small 4to) contains:

I. (62 pages) شعر فرڠ اڠكرس د بتاوي. A poem, celebrating the conquest of Java by the English forces under Lord Minto. The first words are:

دڠركن تون سواتو القصه   جندرل مسكالق * امفون ماس
تتكل بڬند بربوت جاس   دمستر كورنيليس † ساءت فركسا
بربوت بيڽتڠ د مستير كرنيليس برهمفنله كوني سكلين فرڠچس

It closes with the description of a market, and teems with Batavian Malay words.

* The Dutch *Maarschalk* (Marshal).

† *Meester Cornelis* is the name of a district of Batavia, where there are barracks.

II. (2 pages) شعر چنتس براه. A short love-letter* in verses, of which the following lines may serve as a specimen :

ككند ملاينكن قرطاس سچارق   دترينكن اڭن ريحان العاشق
ڬنت فرتمون يڠ امت باٴٸك   كفد ادند وجه يڠ تحقيق

No. 79 (small 4to) contains :

I. (46 pages) the laudatory terms Malay letters commence with, varying according to the rank of the person addressed. The specimens given here are nearly all in Arabic (continued in III.)

II. (7 pages). Fragments of a Muhammadan law work containing the fines to be paid for wounds inflicted. The انم كوفع امس فوته نكري قده is here explained by مثقال. ياٴنت تيڬ سوك ريل. Each of the Arabic law terms is explained by a Malay phrase written under it, and containing the amount of the fine ; an example will suffice : سمحاق (wound touching the pericranium) is explained by :

لوك فونس داٴع لال سمڤي فد سلافت تولع امفت مثقال
هركاڠ امفت ايكر انت

III. (49 pages) continuation of I. It closes with the model of a letter to the Dutch Governor-General and the Dutch India counsellors (Raden van Indie). I. and III. are consequently fragments from the *kitāb tarāsul*, a book in which precepts are laid down how to write letters.†

IV. (7 pages) رسالة سفاء القلوب (a figurative title, "the physic of hearts"). The author calls himself *Nūru-ddīn Ibn 'Alī Ibn Hasanjī Ibn Muhammad Hamīdi*.‡ This is

* In No. 2,609 (India Office) there is a love-letter, the title of which is yet to be ascertained. Its commencing verses are :

سلام دعا در فد ككند   يڠ دفلهراكن الله تعالي
داٴع كفد تون ادند   بدن يڠ سوچ سدي ترعالي
ايوهي امس مانس شهدا   تمباهن فولق ادند يڠ ملي
تله ترمذكور ددالم داد   اورڠ يڠ عارف مندافتكن دي

It contains 18 pages.

† See Newbold, ii. 338, and Matthes, "Makassaarsch Woordenboek," *s. v.* tarasolo.]

‡ حسنجي حميدي. (See about this author, Note 1 in the Appendix.)

a treatise about the sense to be attached to the word
شهادة. He composed it, he says, in order to combat
those that entertain wrong opinions about the nature of
God.

V. (8 pages). A tract, the title of which I could not
ascertain without reading it through. It begins with
stating the best time for building a house, and contracting
a marriage, and closes with a recommendation of forbear-
ance towards a slave, even when guilty. It is addressed
to 'Ali (علي), each article ending with يا علي.

VI. (2 pages). Questions and answers about the sense
of مقشي (testimony), perhaps belonging to IV.

VII. (9 pages). رسالة فد مپتاکن صفة دو فوله. A tract
on the qualities of God.

VIII. (34 pages). معمدة الاعتقاد.* This treatise is
divided into two introductory chapters (مقدم), four books
(باب), and one concluding chapter (خاتم).

The first introductory chapter : فد مپتاکن اعتقاد اکن
عالم دان الله سبحانه و تعالي.

The second introductory chapter : فد مپتاکن اٺم.

The first book : فد مپتاکن ایمان دان سکلین رکن.

The second book : فد مپتاکن اسلام دان سگل رکن.

The third book : فد مپتاکن توحید.

The fourth book : فد مپتاکن معرفة.

IX. (15 pages). Arabic fragment from a commentary
on the Qur'an, with Malay translation.

No. 80. See under No. 18.

B.—Farquhar Collection.†

No. 1 (small 4to of 51 pages; within, *Cherita Sultan
Iskander*). It contains a pretty good copy of the اندغ م

---

* It is translated by ارتین فوهن اعتقاد. A note by the transcriber calls
the author شیخ نور الدین (the same as the author of IV. ?)

† The manuscripts of this collection were not numbered. I have put numbers
on them in accordance with the list Dulaurier gave of them, with the exception
of two volumes he did not examine.

راج ملاك commencing with what is reserved for the
Sovereign. The seventeenth chapter is about people
going to hunt.[1]

No. 2 (small 4to of 202 pages; imperfect at the end).
It contains the حكاية راج اسكندر ذو القرنين. The last
pages give the history of the defeat by Alexander of a
king who was a worshipper of the sun. A small extract
from this tale is to be found in Roorda van Eysinga's
"Malay Reader" at the end of his "Beknopte Maleische
Spraakkunst" (Breda, 1839), pp. 120–123; and innumer-
able quotations from it are to be found in Werndly's
"Maleische Spraakkunst," and in Roorda van Eysinga's
"Mal. Nederduitsch Woordenboek;" some also in van
Hoëvell's "Aant. op de Sair Bidasari."[2]

No. 3 (small 4to of 175 pages) شعر كمڤني ولند برڤرڠ
دڠن چين, relating the war of the Dutch Company with
the Chinese, and the well-known murder of the Chinamen
of Batavia under Valkenier. It is translated from the
Javanese.

No. 4 (small 4to of 80 pages) عادة سڬل راج ۲ ملايو.
This interesting work was composed at the request of the
Señor Gornador دبرين[3] at Malaka in the Muhammadan
year 1193. It is an account of Malay observances during
the pregnancy of the wives of chiefs, the birth of their
children, &c. After the introduction it continues thus:

القصه فري ميڤتاكن عادة سڬل راج ۲ ملايو يڠ ڤرب كال راج
يڠ بسر ۲ تتكال استري بڬند ايت حامل سمڤي توجه بولن
لمان مك دڤڬڬل بيدن اوله بڬند. On p. 71 there is an
elaborate description of the bier of a king.

No. 5. See No. 18 of the Raffles' Collection.

No. 6 (small 8vo) contains:

I. (17 pages). An erotic poem, the title of which I
could not ascertain. The first verses are:—

[1] [B.M. 20.]
[2] [L. 1696, and at p. 178; Bat. 112, 113; a Makassar translation, ap. Matthes, l. l. No. 87.]
[3] De Bruijn?

MALAY MANUSCRIPTS. 47

دڠركن تون سواتُ رنچان   فتيير مڠارڠ سواتُ بين
اوصل يڠ مانس مود ترون   لاڬ جوهري ببسان

And the last:

دڠ ساجي دودق ممپوج   مڠكت اون نيڬ لافس
افاته داي دڠن بود   قلمن فاته قرطاسن هابس

II. (14 pages). A love-letter in verse. The last verses are literally the same as those on the two last pages of II. of No. 9, commencing with

تون سولت سيا لراڬن   سامله سام ممبله دير
فاته فارڠ لاوت تمو دان   اورڠ مسوكت بتورس باتڠ
سمڤي سكارڠ دراسق دندم   كاسه ترايكت بنچان داتڠ
تتڤ بوله ڤاڬركن دليم   دڠ جوده ددالم ڤون
متنهاري توجه بولن ليم   بهارول سده دڠن مو تون

The last verses are:

اڠڬرس لاوت ملاك   كناله ريبت دتنجڠ تون
تاجمله كرس هلت سنجات   هندق مربت ڤاو تون

III. (11 pages). The same as I. of No. 9.

IV. (27 pages). According to the end the title is شعر فنتن. The beginning verses are literally the same as those of II. of No. 9.

V. (23 pages). A poem without title commencing:

كود داؤن برد نديڬن   باڬيكن ڤوتس راس تلين
مود بڠساون برنتاڠن   باڬيكن ڤوتس راس هتين

The last words are:

انچي علي فرڬي كبڠك   سارت برموت لاد سببج
هاره سكال تيدق كسڠك   ڬاجه دتلن سيولر ليد

No. 6* (small 4to) contains:

I. (14 pages). The same as I. of No. 6.

II. (19 pages). A love-letter in verses. The last verses are:

مرفات برتلر ليم   برتكر دياتس تنجڠ بالي
منجاد بسي افاله كيت   هندق د تمڤا توكڠ يڠ ڤندي

توکڠ برنام خود براهيم فاڤن فنتو لب برکنتڠ
چيت تيدق فد يغ لاأن کڤد تون تمڤت برکنتڠ
بهاڤت کتاءن در فساءن لنتڤکن باتغ تيک دڤا
ڤسن ڤتري در کياءن اين سکارڠ هندق برجمڤا

No. 7 (small 8vo of 55 pages). According to the end the title should be شعر جوهن انق راج ڤيرق. It is a tragic love-story, as the hero dies.*

No. 7* (small 8vo of 55 pages). Another copy of No. 7.

No. 8 (small 4to of 175 pages, imperfect at the end; within: "Presented by Colonel W. M. G. Colebrooke, 6th July, 1832"), contains the بداية الهداية.† The Malay author calls himself *Muhammad sayn*,‡ son of *Jalālu-ddīn*, an Achinese of the Shafi-'i sect. A quotation from this composition is to be found in van Hoëvell's annotations on the "Sair Bidasari," p. 378, where he cites p. 983 of the manuscript. The author of this work says, that he took the subject from the ام البراهين of *Abu 'Abdillah Muhammad ben Yusuf Assanūsī Alhasanī*.

No. 9 (small 4to) contains:

I. (17 pages) شعر بوڠ. A poem where flowers are introduced singing *pantuns*, in this way:

مول برمدح کنتم دليم وجهن سڤرت بولن ڤرنام
لقسان ديوي نيلا اوتام § سکلين عالم تياد اکن سام

* On page 45 we find:

ملک الموت دائغ در حضرة منيڠجڤکن ڤرمان ترلال برت
جوهن سکرا لال له معرت کمبال ڤولڠ کنڬري اخرة

معرت (frequent spelling of the Ar. معراج) *merat*, is in poetry used for "to die," of princely persons whose disease is compared to an ascension to heaven.

† Also mentioned in Bahru-ddīn's list.

‡ He is the author also of a Malay work called کشف الکرام في بيان النية عند تکبيرة الاحرام (a copy of which I saw at Batavia, small 4to, of about 30 pages). [See Van den Berg's "Verslag," p. 7, No. 36.]

§ *Nila-utáma*, name of a celestial nymph ("Tobasche Spraakkunst," § 30, VII. *b*).

MALAY MANUSCRIPTS.

دليم د سورباي   بغان جاته كدالم كولم
تياد كسيهن ممندغ سهيا   دودق برچنت سيغ دان مالم
ممڤهوتي ملح بوغ ڤندن   ممنتغ درجا ترلال حيران

II. (7 pages). A collection of *pantuns*, commencing with:

ݨخود رايم رقنا سولي   بوغ تنجغ دياتس كوىس
راج مأنكم انتن بدوري   د جنجغ بائك جاد مأكت

(See No. 6, II.)

No. 10 (small 4to of 53 pages). اندغ ٢ راج ملاك وقتو اي كرجاءن ددالم نڬري ملاك هڠڬ سمڤي كنڬري جوهر. This work deserves being published; its language is pure, and the text, as far as I have examined it, not corrupted.

NOTE I.

About the Author of IV. *of No.* 79 (*Raffles Collection*).

The author, who calls himself also الرانيري, from *Rānīr*, the place where he lived (مسكنّا), composed, besides the بستان السلاطين (No. 17), also the following works:

I. (No. 39, large 4to, India Office at Batavia) درة الفرائد بشرح العقائد يائت منتيار يغ تركارغ فد ممتاكن سڬل اعتقاد.

II. (No. 3, small 4to, India Office at Batavia) هدية الحبيب في ترغيب والترهيب يائت هلون اكن نبي محمد صلى الله عليه وسلم فد ممتاكن سڬل عمل كبجيكن دان منجاوٴهي درڤد سڬل عمل كجهاتن.

III. (No. 24, Library of the India Office at Batavia) اسرار الانسان في معرفة الروح والرحمن, commenced under Iskandar II. 'Alā uddīn, and finished under the queen Tāju-l'ālam Tsafiyatu-ddīn.[1]

IV. (No. 14, Library of the India Office at Batavia) [2] جواهر العلوم في كشف المعلوم

[1] [Van den Berg, l. l. p. 8, No. 40.]   [2] [*Ib.*, p. 3, No. 10.]

V. فتح المبين علي الملحدين ارتيں كمفاءڽ يغ امت ڤاٿ اتس سگل ملحد, composed by order of Sultan *Muqul Marāyat Shāh*.* against the tenets of the Pantheistical sect, the followers of which were put to death by the said king of Achih, their books being burnt before the mosque *Beyturrahman*. I saw a copy of this work at Barus (small 4to of 40 pages), from which I took this notice.

VI. نبذة في دعوي الظل مع صاحبه ارتيں رسالة فد مڤتاكں دعوي باينغ ۲ دعں يغ امڤون دي, a refutation of *Shamsu-ddīn's* heretical tenets (cf. VII.).

VII. تبيان في معرفة الاديان فكانه ماءالزلال علي قلب الضمان الي الطريق الرحمن ارتيں مڤتاكں سگل اڬم مك ادله سؤله ۲ اير يغ امت سجق مموسكں هاٿ يغ دهاڬ كفد جالں توهں يغ برنام رحمں, composed under queen *Tāju-l-'ālam Tsafiyatu-ddīn Shāh*,† daughter of Sultan *Iskandar Muda Johan bărdowlat*, son of Sultan *'Alā u-ddīn 'Alī Ri-'āyat Shāh*, son of Sultan *Farmān Shāh*, son of Sultan *Mutlafar*‡ *Shāh*, son of Sultan *'Ināyat Shāh*. It is divided into two books, the first giving an account of the religions from Adam till Muhammad, and the second summing up the heterodox tenets of several Muhammadan sects. The purpose of the author was to combat the opinions of *Shamsuddīn* of *Pasey* § and his followers. A copy in small 4to (of 72 pages) is in my possession.

VIII. ماء الحياة لاهل الممات. A fragment of this work is found in a manuscript belonging to the Batavian Society (No. 55 ?).

IX. حجّة الصديق لدفع الزنديق. A copy of this work exists in the Library of the Batavian Society (No.   ?).¶

* مقل مغاية شاه.
‡ مظفر.   † تاج العالم صفية الدين شاه.
§ الشمطرائي as the Arabic introduction has. *Shamaṭarā* is an Arabic corruption of *Samudăra*, the ancient name of *Pasey*, which occasioned the whole island to be called by the Portuguese, who sailed with Arabic pilots, *Sumatra*, a name with which natives, not used to mix with Europeans, are not acquainted.

¶ X. صراط المستقيم. See Roorda van Eysinga's "Indië," III. 1, [pp. 413-435 [and Van den Berg, l. l. p. 1, No. 3.]

Most of these works are directed against the popular writings of *Hamzah* of *Barus*,* and the above-named *Shamsu-ddīn* of *Pasey*. The works of *Hamzah* are, as far as I know:

I. اسرار العارفين. I saw a copy of this at Barus (small 8vo of 24 pages). I read only the preface, which says, that it is an abridgement of a greater work of the same name and by the same author; and that there are three works of this name, the two already mentioned, the large and the abridged one, and one treating on عشق, عاشق and معشوق. This is all I could read, as the owner would not lend it me even for a day.

II. شعر سبورغ فيڠي, an allegorical poem,† wherein the soul of man is spoken of as that of a bird (*kalow tărbagn siburung pingey, 'alāmat badan di makan ulat*, if the pingey flies away, it is a sign that the body will be eaten by the worms).

III. شعر فراة. An allegorical poem, wherein mankind is spoken of as a vessel tossing about on the waves. A small fragment is in my possession.

IV. شعر سيدڠ فقير. A copy is in my possession (small 4to of 14 pages). It is also an allegorical poem, speaking of mankind as forlorn and indigent.

V. كشف السر التجلي السبعاني, a short exposition of God's nature, qualities, and works. Werndly knew it (see his "Boekzaal," p. 354). It is quoted in the second book of the *Tabyān* (see above, in the specification of Ranir's writings, No. VII.) as a book deserving to be burnt.‡

---

* الفنصوري *Fantsur* being the ancient name of Barus [see above, vol. i. p. 164]; hence the Barus camphor (كافر بارس) is called in Arabic كافور الفنصوري.

† The poems of Hamzah were yet much read in Valentyn's time, but that he was a native of Barus that author did not know (see "Beschrijving van Sumatra," p. 21).

‡ The other books, the author of the *Tabyān* speaks of in this way are the دائرة الوجود, the حق اليقين, the حرقة, the مرأة الحقيق, the سر الربوبيه and the تحفة المرسلة.

VI. كتاب منتهي فد مراجناکن سبد نبي. It is mentioned in the *Tabyān*, and seems to be an exposition of the sayings of the prophet.

VII. شعر داڭغ. A fragment is in my possession. It has the same tendency as No. III.

The works of *Shamsu-ddīn** of *Pasey* are :

I. مرأة المحققين كتاب فري نسبة ارتين بڬس مخلوق دغن حق تعالي. It is cited in the second book of the *Tabyān*. A badly mutilated copy is in the Leyden University Library (No. 1,332). The Sultan in whose reign it was composed is there only called مرحوم ماكت.

II. شرح رباعي حمزة الفنصوري. I saw at Padang a copy (8vo of 16 pages), but the owner would not part with it. It is a commentary on the anything but transparent poems of *Hamzah* of *Barus*.

III. مرأة المومن. Werndly ("Maleische Boekzaal") knew it, and says of it, that it is divided into 211 questions and answers, explaining the principal religious terms. In the preface to his "Grammar" a small quotation from this work is given.

NOTE 2.

The Manuscripts of the India Office not mentioned in my "Kort Verslag der Maleische Handschriften van het E. I. House te Londen."

1. حكاية مهاراج بوم. (See No. 15 of the Raffles Collection.)

2. Another copy of the حكاية فرڠ فنداو جاي. (See No. 2 of the Raffles' Collection.)

* He calls himself sometimes ابن عبدالله. He seems to have lived at *Achih* (Ar. اشية). A namesake of his is محمد شمس الدين الحاذق ابن فضل الله, and is cited as the author of the above-mentioned تحفة المرسلة.

3. سمرقندي (17 pages in No. 2,906,* 4to). Arabic with an interlinear Malay translation. It contains the first precepts of the Islām in questions and answers. The commencement is: "If people enquire of you: 'What is the *imān?*' the answer is: 'I believe in God,'" &c. The author is ابو الليث محمد ابن ابي نصر ابن ابراهيم, surnamed of *Samarqand* (السمرقندي). This little book goes universally by the name of *Samarqandī*. Copies with an interlinear Javanese translation† are numerous in the west of Java. A commentary on it (شرح علي السمرقندي) is in the Library of the Batavian Society (No. 29); it has an interlinear Javanese translation. Two copies in Sundanese are in my possession, one of which is in the Arabic character.

4. (No. 2,672, folio) contains:

I. (133 pages). Another copy of the شعر جارن تماس It is of the same version as the other manuscript (No. 2,610).

II. (127 pages). Another copy of the حكاية بودق مسكين (or حكاية فارغ فونغ, so called after a miraculous chopping-knife the hero was possessed of). It seems to belong to the same recension as No. 2,877.‡

AMSTERDAM, *November* 25, 1865.

---

* The other 51 pages of this volume contain: (1) the several positions of the body when praying; (2) the application of the five letters of الحمد to the five obligatory prayers; (3) the formulas of prayers for the dead; and (4) on marriage (حكم نكاح).

† A copy is in the Library of the Batavian Society (No. 26).

‡ There may be other Malay manuscripts in the Library of the India Office which I have overlooked, the Persian, Arabic, and Malay manuscripts being mingled together. I am in hopes the deficiencies in this notice may be filled up by other scholars, who will also call attention to the many valuable Malay manuscripts in the Libraries of London. A New Malay Chrestomathy is urgently needed at the present time, as those published by Marsden, Meursinge, and de Hollander, are anything but trustworthy, each of the texts they contain having been taken from a single manuscript only. It is only by a careful comparison of many that a text can be furnished which may be depended upon by persons desirous of obtaining an adequate idea of the grammatical structure of the Malay language, and reluctant to trust the assertions of those who pretend that Malay is devoid of grammar.

Note 3.[1]

The proper name *si-lindung dalima* (Raffles Coll., No. 7, III.) had better be taken to mean "she who excels the granate-apple in beauty." Thus we have in Menangkabau tales the name of a princess *si-lindung bulan*, "who surpasses the moon in radiance" (compare the Batak name *nan-chilok mata ni ari*, "Miss Sun-stealer," see "Bataksch Leesboek," IV. p. 157). In the prose edition of the poem, the heroine of which goes by the name of سلندغ دليم, the proper name سيدغ دليم also occurs (p. 15 of the I.O. MS.); the heroine's father is there called *Dewa Laqsana*, who had transformed himself into a granate-apple which, being eaten up by *Sari Buniyan*, became the cause of her pregnancy.

Note 4.

To Raffles Collection, No. 62, V.

Mr. Engelmann informs me that there is also a Sundanese recension of this work, a copy of which (small 4to, 36 leaves) is in his possession. In it the prophet's advice is not only given to his daughter *Fâṭimah*, but also to another female whom he calls *Murtasiyah*. I suspect that this proper name is nothing but the feminine of مرتضٰي (a cognomen of Fâṭimah's husband *'Alî*), so that the second female recurring in the Sundanese recension has got in through misunderstanding. It is worth noting that ض has become *s*, since this consonant is pronounced *l* both in Sundanese and Javanese (e.g., *malarat* i.q. Arabic مضرة). But as ض is pronounced as a sibilant by the Persians and Indian Muhammedans, it is not improbable that the Sundanese redaction was subject to Kling or Bengali influence. The forming of female proper names by means of the termination *ah* is a

---

[1] [The following additional Notes (3–10) are found in the Dutch translation of this "Account." See the note at the beginning of this article.]

well-known fact.* May not the Malay word *rubiyah* be explained as formed from ربّي (my lord), as the Malays generally know so little of Arabic that it could not well occur to them that ربّي is properly used only in reference to God? On the west coast of Sumatra they call *rubiyah* a female who keeps the five prescribed prayers (سمبهيڠ فرض), reads the Koran, and, in short, lives in the fear of the Lord, while—strangely enough!—*mande* (mother) *rubiyah*, is a nickname for a procuress, or the keeper of a house of ill-fame. The name ربيعه (Raffles Coll., No. 70, II.) appears to convey an illusion to *rubiyah*. The usual cognomen of *Fâṭimah* in Malay is الزّهرا; hence they say of an unchaste woman: فرمفون بديح چلاك يڠ تيباد براوله ناؤڠ ديباوه فنجم فاطمه الزهرا.

NOTE 5.

Ad No. 79, II., *and No.* 77, III.

On قده for كده see the "Annotation to Panjatandaran" (Leiden, 1866), p. xxii.

NOTE 6.

Ad Raffles Coll., No. 2.

Mr. Cohen Stuart informs me that from an interpretation given him by a Balinese, he has also been led to correct *bisuwa* into *bhishawa*—a reading which I had already suggested in my pamphlet, "Taco Roorda's beoefening van't Javaansch bekeken" (p. 22, note 2).

NOTE 7.

Ad Raffles Coll., No. 7, II.

Concerning *inu* compare vol. iv. of the "Bataksch Leesboek," p. 213.

---

* The Javanese from *Bulkiyah* (for *Bulqis*) is probably due to a Menangkabau form *Bulkih* (cf. "Tobasche Spraakkunst," p. 50).

Note 8.

Ad Raffles Coll., No. 14.

Rawi sarangga, as one of the names of *Panji*, must mean "ray of the sun," and have been chosen as a pendant to *chandrakirana*, "ray of the moon," the cognomen of his betrothed. Compare in Batak the use of *bulan* or *mata ni bulan* for a daughter, and of *mata ni ari* for a son. *Sarangga* must be a corruption of *sàrangga*, "light," so that *rawisarangga* literally means "sunlight."

Note 9.

Ad Raffles Coll., No. 30.

Chi-rĕbon is Sundanese, and originally the name of a river. The Javanese, not understanding its meaning, have changed the word into *Cherbon, Chrebon*.

Note 10.

Ad Raffles Coll., No. 65, note.

Jayeng kasuma has been rendered according to native ideas (*jayeng kusuma* being, i.q., *jayeng sĕkar*). On this subject I owe to Mr. Cohen Stuart the following interesting note: "I would rather think of a real field or meadow, than of a battle-field, and take *kusuma* in the sense of a woman (see 'Bataksch Leesboek,' vol. iv. p. 127, note 2). Such terms of honour, taken from love conquests, are not unknown in Java; I have known at Solo a certain *Jayeng Resmi** ('conqueror in love'), *Jayeng Rana* (the last word in the sense of *pudendum muliebre*†), &c."

---

* *Resmi*, however, must mean "beauty," and not "love;" see "Tobasche Spraakkunst," p. 52, note 2.

† In Malay *rana* (رانى) means "a princess," and is a corruption of *ratna* (*ib.*, p. 51).

IX.*

MEMORANDUM OF A JOURNEY TO THE SUMMIT OF GUNONG BENKO,[1]

OR THE SUGAR LOAF MOUNTAIN IN THE INTERIOR OF BENCOOLEN.[2]

["Malayan Miscellanies," vol. ii. (Bencoolen), 1822, pp. 1-11.]

THIS mountain, which stands detached from the regular range of hills, forms, by its peculiar and remarkable shape, an excellent landmark on this part of the coast. It lies about 18 miles N.E. of Bencoolen, but its exact position and distance had never been correctly ascertained. Two attempts had been made by Europeans to ascend the mountain, but without success, and a general impression prevailed that it was utterly impracticable to gain the summit. Remarkable mountains of this description are generally believed by the natives to be the residence of spirits, and their summits are considered as Kramats or places of peculiar sanctity.[3] A Kramat of this nature was said to exist on the top of the Sugar Loaf, and it was reported that the natives sometimes adventured to visit it from motives of superstition. It was therefore resolved to make another trial, in the expectation that it might afford the means of correcting and extending the observations already commenced on the coast, with a view to a more accurate survey of this part of the country.

* [For the foot-notes the editor is indebted to the Hon. D. F. A. Hervey.]
[1] We should spell it Bengkok. This, which means "winding" or "crooked," hardly tallies with the English name; but the Malays doubtless refer to different characteristics, possibly indicating the tortuous path which leads to it.
[2] The Malay name to which this is the English approximation is *Bengkahŭlu*. *Hŭlu* is source, of a river, and might imply that the Bencoolen river had its source in the Bengkok mountain. But while the mountain is here called Benko', it figures in Baron Melvill's map as Boengka (Bungka) [and in Favre's "Dictionary," as well as in the account of the Dutch expedition ("Midden-Sumatra," Reisverhaal, 1881) as Bukit Bungkuk, or Dwarf Mountain. Veth, in his "Geographical Dictionary," calls it Bukit Bongso.]
[3] For accounts of similar legends regarding Mount Ophir near Malacca and Gunong Dato in Rembau, see "Journal S.B.R.A.S.," No. 13, p. 257; and "N. and Q.," No. 2, p. 41, and Note; [on haunted mountains generally, "Journal Ind. Arch." i. 319; G. A. Wilken, "Het Animisme," p. 139; J. B. Neumann, "Het Pana- en Bila-stroomgebied in Sumatra" (1886), p. 294, and "Midden-Sumatra," Reisverhaal, vol. i. pp. 150 and 405.] Besides these Kramats, there are those formed at the tombs of holy or great men, where Chinese, Hindus, &c., all come and pay their vows, whatever may have been the religion of deceased, so long as he has established his reputation.

A party of gentlemen accordingly proceeded from Bencoolen on the 10th of June, 1821, for the purpose of effecting this object. They crossed the Bencoolen river a little above Tanjung Agung, and proceeding through the Lumba Selapan district, halted the first night at Lubu Pooar, a small Rejang village on the banks of a stream which falls into the Sungey Lamow.[1] Thus far the journey was accomplished on horseback, but it was found impracticable to carry the horses any farther, and the party proceeded on foot to Punjong, a respectable village situated on the banks of the Simpang-ayer, and the residence of the Pasirah of the tribe of Marigi, the chief of the four into which the Rejangs are divided. The others are called Bermani, Saloopu, and Joru Kallang. On the third day they reached Rejak Bessi, the last village in the direction of the mountain, where they rested for the night. It is situated on the Ayer Kiti, a stream which falls into the Simpang-ayer below Punjong. The journey from Lubu Pooar to this might with ease have been accomplished in one day instead of two had the weather permitted.

The mountain was now to be attempted, and in order to ensure success, it was arranged to pitch a tent in the forest in case the ascent could not be accomplished in one day. From Rejak Bessi they proceeded over hilly ground gradually rising for about five miles, when they found their progress impeded by the increasing steepness of the ascent, and then halted under an overhanging rock, where the tent was pitched, as it was impossible to carry it any further, even if space could have been found to erect it on. The course from Rejak Bessi was through deep forests which precluded them from seeing the mountain. The last view they had of it was at Rejak Bessi, which it appeared to overhang, and whence they were able to form some idea of the difficulties they were likely to encounter from the steepness of the ascent and the precipitousness of the declivities. Soon after quitting Rejak Bessi they crossed a small river on a temporary bamboo bridge thrown across a deep chasm between two rocks, which confined the stream within a narrow channel after being precipitated over a fall of considerable height. A fine view of this fall was commanded from the bridge, which was itself suspended about one hundred feet above the stream, and the whole formed, with the surrounding forests, a beautiful and romantic scene. About ten o'clock they commenced the ascent of the cone along the rocky bed of a mountain torrent, until they arrived in front of a perpendicular face of bare rock stretching completely across the ravine which had hitherto afforded a passage, and seeming to bar all further progress. This difficulty was surmounted by placing two of the longest bamboos against the rock underneath where the bare root of a tree projected from above; by the aid of these

---

[1] More correctly Límau or Lémau.

THE SUMMIT OF GUNONG BENKO.

held fast at the bottom, and afterwards secured by a rattan at the top, they succeeded in clambering up to the tree which overhung the precipice. The next acclivity terminated at the head of another ravine, where their progress was again checked by a jutting rock rendered moist by the trickling of a small spring of water from among its crevices. Here the guides declared that further ascent was impracticable, and that from thence the party might return as soon as they pleased. The fact is, they were extremely averse to their proceeding, fearing the vengeance of the evil spirits if they conducted strangers to the summit; they were, therefore, advising to return at every difficulty, and the ascent was ultimately accomplished without their aid, or rather in spite of them. The appearances around were calculated to confirm this assertion, but before determining to return they examined the extent of the precipice, and crossing the ravine, perceived that the opposite side, though almost perpendicular, had a thin coating of soil and moss, with numerous roots of trees half laid bare, by laying hold of which with the hands and placing the toes in the niches, they at length reached the ridge which formed the right-hand shoulder of the hill. Along this a path was found, sometimes along the base, sometimes over the face, of a succession of bare masses of rock, which it was necessary to clamber over by the aid of such twigs and roots as occasionally fastened themselves in their fissures. The last of these precipices was perhaps the most dizzy and dangerous, as it was necessary to make a step or two on a narrow ledge on the face of a cliff of such height that the eye could not discern the bottom, and thence catch at a dry stump barely within reach, by swinging from which it was possible with a considerable effort to clear the rock. The denseness of the moss and the stunted appearance of the trees now indicated their approach towards the top, and at length about two o'clock they found themselves on the summit. This was a bare spot of not more than four or five yards in breadth with a precipice on each side partly concealed by brushwood. Of those who set out together from the foot of the hill a few only reached this point, by far the majority giving up in despair at different parts of the ascent, but the labour of those who persevered was amply recompensed by the view which opened from the summit. The line of the coast from Laye[1] on the north to a considerable distance beyond Buffalo Point on the south was distinctly marked; the vessels in the basin of Rat Island were distinguishable with the aid of a glass, and the white ramparts of Fort Marlbro' were easily discerned. To the south, they looked down on the hills of Bukit Kandees,[2] or the Lion's Rump, and Bukit Kabut (the hill of mist), which formed a straight

---

[1] This appears as Laïs in the Dutch maps.
[2] Kandis is the name of a tree (*Garcinia merguensis*) bearing an edible fruit.

line with the Sugar Loaf. Inland the view was obscured by a cloud, which was evidently directing its course towards the hill, and it was necessary, therefore, to take the desired observations and bearings with all possible dispatch. This was done with a small compass, none of the larger instruments having been got up. The character of the vegetation was decidedly Alpine, the rocks and trunks of the trees being covered with dense moss,[1] and many of the shrubs belonging to genera of higher latitudes, such as vaccinium, rhododendron, &c. There is also found here a shrub which the natives consider a substitute for tea,[2] remarkable by its thick glossy leaves; it will form a new genus in the family of the Myrtaceæ. Having finished their observations, they made haste to descend, as the cloud was now rapidly approaching the hill and threatened a deluge of rain. They found the descent fully as difficult as the ascent had been, but it was occasionally facilitated by fastening a long rattan to a tree above, and then sliding along it down the steepest places. It was necessary, however, to be cautious not to slide with too much velocity in order to be able to keep a footing when the rattan slipped from the hand. When they had got about half-way down, the cloud, which had now enveloped the hill, burst in a flood of rain, and rendered the footing still more insecure. The steepest parts, however, were then past, and the trees for a short while afforded some protection, but by the time they reached the lower ravines, the waters began to swell, and the latter part of the descent was in the very bed of the torrent. They arrived at the tent about an hour before sunset, and found the spot completely flooded; the rain had in no degree abated, and it was impossible to find shelter for the whole party of natives, &c., which was very numerous; it was, therefore, determined to make a push forward to Rejak Bessi, rather than pass the night in so uncomfortable a situation. A sharp walk brought them to the village soon after dark, and a good night's rest repaired the fatigues of the day. The next day was spent at the same place, both for the purpose of resting the people, and of bringing up the tent which had been left in the forest. On the 16th they travelled to Punjong, and the following day they commenced their return by another route, striking across the country in the direction of Bukit Kandees to the Bencoolen river. Sampans had been previously ordered to be in readiness at Tanjong

---

[1] On Gunong Belúmut in Johor, at from 2,000 feet onwards, the trees and saplings are thickly clothed with dripping moss, making stems only wrist-thick appear thigh-thick; hence the name "the be-mossed mountain," from *lúmut*, moss.

[2] There is a similar shrub on the summit of Mount Ophir at a height of about 4,200 feet, a spray of which stirred in boiling water gives it a very pleasant aromatic fragrance. This quality was discovered at the suggestion of Governor Sir F. Weld, who discerned in the plant a likeness to others he had seen possessing this quality on a mountain in one of the Australian colonies.

THE SUMMIT OF GUNONG BENKO.

Sanei, and they arrived there about eleven o'clock, having in the latter part of the journey forded the main stream of the Bencoolen river no less than eleven times. About twelve they embarked on the sampans, and placed the baggage and some of the followers on bamboo rafts; the first part of the course was a constant succession of rapids, in shooting down which some management was necessary to avoid being upset upon the trunks of trees and other obstacles that lay in the way. Twice, by being driven against these, the boat was filled with water and with difficulty saved from being swamped. Below the junction of the Rindowati,[1] the depth of the river increased and the current became more regular; and at length they landed near Bencoolen about nine at night, having thus accomplished, aided by the rapidity of the stream, in one day what would have occupied several in ascending.

Gunong Benko' is not estimated to exceed 3,000 feet in height,* but its shape, and its standing boldly out from the general range of hills, render it the most remarkable visible from Bencoolen. It is almost entirely composed of masses of basalt or trap, which is the most prevalent rock along this part of Sumatra. The whole of the country traversed on this occasion is exceedingly broken and irregular and but thinly inhabited. In the neighbourhood of the hill it is a complete forest and very wild, presenting an infinite number of romantic and beautiful views. The soil near the rivers is remarkably rich, and that of the forest tracts is little inferior, particularly in the bamboo groves, which indeed are generally found to prevail on the finest lands. The greater part of the rice is cultivated in ladangs,[2] but there are a few sawahs. At Tello Anou is a small nutmeg plantation where the trees have never been manured, yet seem as thriving as any about town. The forests abound with noble timber trees; few animals were seen; of monkeys the Kra (*S. fascicularis*), and Chingkau (*S. cristata*), were the most common, and the loud cry of the Siamang (*S. syndactyla*) was frequently heard, though they did not come in sight. It is very singular to observe the young of the Chingkau and Simpai (*S. melalophos*) embracing their mothers, that of the former being fawn-coloured, while the adult is nearly black, and the latter having the young black while the mother is fawn-coloured, appearing exactly as if they had exchanged young ones.

At about half the height of the mountain the temperature of a small shallow spring was tried where it oozed from a cleft in a

---

[1] Perhaps for *rindu háti*, desire of the heart—*i.e.* an enchanting stream.

* [In the new atlas of the Dutch East Indies, by Stemfoort and ten Siethoff, the height of the "Suikerbrood" or Sugar Loaf Mountain, is given as 1,029 metres; in Veth's "Geographical Dictionary" as 3,287 Rhenish feet. In the latter it is also mentioned that on the 11th of August 1857, Lieut. F. G. Steck made a successful ascent.]

[2] *Ladang*, plantation on high ground, dry cultivation; *sawah*, padi or ricefield in swampy ground, wet cultivation.

rock and found to be 68° Fahrenheit. The temperature might, however, have been lowered by evaporation; therefore it can scarcely be assumed as a true mean temperature, or employed in calculating the height. It may, however, be remarked that the mean temperatures given by Mr. Leslie for the level of the sea in the different latitudes will certainly not apply to the low latitudes in the eastern islands: 83°, which is given as the mean temperature in latitude 3, is far too high for Bencoolen, where the range of the thermometer throughout the year is usually from 74° to 85°, rarely falling below 70° or rising above 87° or 88°.[1]

The people who inhabit the interior are Rejangs, and speak a different language from the Malays; they extend northward as far as Laye. From the Sillebar[2] river southward, the Serawi tribe prevails, and the space between that river and the Bencoolen is occupied by the tribe of Dua-blas. Similar customs, with slight shades of difference in each, prevail among all these tribes. At every village where the party stayed for the night, the gadises, or virgins, paid a visit of ceremony in the evening, making a present of betel or siri, and receiving some trifling articles in return. This custom is general, and it is necessary to be provided with a sufficiency of fans, looking-glasses, or such like articles in consequence, as the number of the young ladies is often very considerable. Sometimes an entertainment is given in honour of the visitors, and then all the beauty of the surrounding villages is also called in.

These entertainments, which take place also on occasions of marriages, &c., are not unamusing, and to a European have the additional interest of novelty and originality. They are given in the Balei, or public hall, a large building generally in the middle of the village, appropriated to such purposes and to the accommodation of strangers, &c. When European visitors are present, the ceremonial is generally as follows:—The gentlemen being seated near the upper end of the room, the gadises, dressed out in their best attire, make their appearance about nine o'clock, and seat themselves on the floor, previously spread with mats, in a semicircle, with their attendant matrons behind them; each brings her siri box of various material and elegance according to the rank or wealth of the parties. The chief of the village or one of the elders then makes an harangue in the name of the ladies, welcoming the strangers to their village, and concluding with the presentation of the betel. An appropriate answer is then to be made, and, after taking out the siri leaves, a small present is put into each box, proportioned in some degree to the rank of the parties; this, however, may be put off at pleasure till the conclusion. The amusements of the evening then commence, which

---

[1] This is almost identical with the Singapore temperature.
[2] That is Salébar or Selébar, from *lébar*, broad.

consist, on the part of the young people, of dancing and singing; and of the old, in smoking opium in a circle apart to themselves. The musical instruments are commonly kalingtangs, which are a species of harmonicon formed of a series of small gongs arranged on a frame.[1] A space is cleared on one side for the dance, which is performed by five or six of the young gadises; the step is slow and sailing; the salindang,[2] or scarf, is adjusted in a particular manner over the shoulders so that the ends may be taken in the hand, and the motions of the arms and management of the flowing scarf are not the least graceful part of the performance.

The singing of pantuns in alternate contest is an amusement which seems to be peculiar to the Sumatrans, and of which they are very fond. It may either be formally commenced by two parties, who seat themselves opposite to each other after having danced together, or it may be begun by one of the ladies from the place where she happens to sit. She begins a series of pantuns in a kind of recitative or irregular song; a bujang, or young man, answers her in the same manner, and the contest is kept up indefinitely, or until one of the parties is unable to give the proper answer. The girls and young men relieve each other occasionally as one or other happens to get tired.

The Malay pantuns, strictly so called, are quatrains, of which the first two lines contain a figure or image, and the latter give its point or moral. Sometimes the figure or comparison is accurately suited to the subject, and then the application may be omitted in recitation, the more to try the ingenuity of the respondent; sometimes the whole is couched under one or more figures; while in many the beginning seems only intended as a rhyme, or, at least, has not obvious connection with the subject.[3] Among the Rejang and Serawi people a greater latitude is allowed to the seramba* or pantun, the figure is pursued to greater length, and a kind of measured prose is often employed in place of confining themselves to the trammels of verse. The pantun is frequently framed into a kind of riddle, whose meaning it requires some ingenuity to discover, and a blundering answer to which excites much mirth. These pantuns frequently contain words derived from the lan-

[1] On the same principle as the Javanese *gambang*, in which pieces of wood take the place of the glass in the harmonicon, ranged over a hollow case or trough.

[2] In the Straits *selendang*.

[3] In the majority of Peninsula pantuns no meaning is to be attached to the first two lines as far as any connection with the remaining two is concerned. [See H. N. van der Tuuk's "Bataksch Leesboek," vol. iv. p. 107, ff.; and J. Pijnappel in "Bijdragen" for 1883, pp. 161-75.]

* [The scope of the *serambahs* is somewhat wider than that of the *pantuns*. They are called *berdīwi*, when young people sitting in rows sing them in the daytime; *begandai*, when sung standing; and *nyambri*, when they are sung in the evening, sitting. Specimens are given in "Midden-Sumatra," iii. 2 (1881), pp. 15-35.]

guage of Sunda, which has been partially introduced into the poetry of all the tribes to the southward of Kataun, while to the northward the Menangkabau dialect prevails. The origin of this distinction is referred to the period of the wars between Imbang Jaya, a Javanese prince, and Tuanko orang Muda of Menangkabau, the traces of the Sunda dialect marking the limit of the possessions of the former.

In these contests the pantuns are supposed to be extemporaneous effusions, and perhaps sometimes are so in reality, but in general their memories are so stored with established verses, that they are not often put to the task of invention. Of their force and meaning it is extremely difficult to convey a just idea by any translation: whoever has attempted to transfuse the spirit of an Oriental composition into a European language must have felt the difficulty of doing so satisfactorily, where the whole structure of the language is so different, and the whole current of ideas seems to flow in another channel. This is particularly the case with the pantun, whose chief merit consists in conciseness and point, and in conveying a deeper meaning than is contained in the literal words and expressions. The figures and allusions are often quaint, but occasionally evince a considerable degree of poetic feeling and force of imagination.

It is not only on these set occasions that pantuns are employed, they enter largely into their more common intercourse, and are essential accomplishments to all who aspire to a character of gallantry, or who hope to woo and win their lady's love. Skill and readiness in this kind of poetry is with them a passport to female favour, much in the same way that a readiness at compliment and flattery in conversation and the art of saying soft nothings serves the European candidate for the smiles of the fair; much of this kind of flirtation goes on independently of the open and public display of skill, and is often accompanied with the interchange of flowers and other mute symbols, which have all a mystic meaning intelligible to those who have been initiated into this secret mode of communication. Making due allowance for difference of customs, of wealth, and of progress in civilization, there seems to be much in the conduct of these entertainments and in the general deportment of the Sumatrans towards women to indicate that they possess somewhat of that character of romantic gallantry which marked our own earlier ancestors, and there might be found as much delicacy of feeling and perhaps more of the poetry of the passion in their courtships, than in the over-refinement of modern English society. It must also be remembered that no people can be more jealous of female honour than the Sumatrans, and that all this is conducted with a strictness of decorum far greater than is observed in the free intercourse permitted by European custom.

THE SUMMIT OF GUNONG BENKO.

A few examples of the different kinds of pantuns may not be unamusing, though it would be as difficult to convey an idea of the effect with which they are applied at the moment and on particular occasions, as to record the sallies and evanescent sparkles of wit that sometimes enliven our own tables, and which like the champagne that inspires them, would seem flat and dull if repeated next morning. Of the Malay pantun of four lines, several examples have been already given by Mr. Marsden, the strictness of their form and limits perhaps render them better suited to translation, but they are considered by the people of the interior as too stiff and prosaic and as deficient in that boldness of allegory and recondite allusion which they consider the perfection of their own longer ones. The following are specimens of the Malay pantun, applicable to different occasions, such as the opening of a courtship, complaints of inconstancy, coyness, &c., expressions of compliment, of affection, of doubt, of ridicule or displeasure, and others which the reader may much better imagine to himself than they can be explained by words. In some the connection of the figure and the sentiment will readily be perceived, in others it is obscure, particularly where the allusions are idiomatic or have reference to popular fables or belief, and in others there is none at all.

> Memuti[1] umbak di rantau Kataun
> Patang dan pagi tida berkala
> Memuti bunga de dalam kabun
> Sa tangkei saja iang menggila.

"The waves are white on the shore of Kataun, night and day they do not cease to roll; many are the white flowers of the garden, but one alone hath made me distracted with love."

> Guruh berbuni[2] sayup sayup
> Orang di bumi samoa bembang;
> Jika ada angin bertiup
> Ada kah bunga mau kambang.

"The thunder rolls loud and deep, and the inhabitants of the earth are dismayed; if the zephyrs should now breathe upon it, will the flower expand its blossoms?"

> Ayer dalam bertambah dalam,
> Ujan di ulu bulum lagi tedoh;
> Hati dendam bertambah dendam,
> Dendam daulu bulum lagi sumboh.[3]

---

[1] In the following notes the common (Straits) Malay forms are referred to:—mĕmutih, from *putih*, white; *pĕtang*.

[2] *Bûnyi*; *Sâyup* means primarily as far as the eye can see, or the ear can hear.

[3] *Sĕmboh*, cured.

"The deep waters have increased in depth, and the rain hath not ceased on the hills; the longing desire of my heart hath increased, and its former hopes have not yet been accomplished."

Parang bumban¹ di sabrang.
Pohon di hela tiada karuan;²
Bulan pernama niatalah bindrang,
Sayangnia lagi di saput awan.

"The reed is cut down on the other bank, it is now at the mercy of the stream, draw it towards you; the moon is at the full and shining, a cloud as yet intercepts her light (literally affection)."

Ulak berulak batu mandi.
Kian berulak tenang jua;³
Hindak bertunah tunah ati,
Dewa membawa bembang jua.

"The stream becomes still behind the sunken rocks, and the waters are smooth and calm amid the eddies; I try to quiet the uneasiness of my heart, but there is a fairy that still disturbs its peace."

Permata jatu di rumput,⁴
Jatu di rumput bergelang gelang;
Kasih umpama ambun di ujong rumput,
Datang matahari nischaya⁵ ilang.

"The jewel fallen on the ground, though fallen among the grass, is glittering still, but thy love is like the dew on the flower,⁶ quickly disappearing when the sun comes forth."

Telah lama tiada ka rimbo,
Bumban berbua garangan kini;
Telah lama tiada bersuo,
Dendam berubah⁷ garangan kini.

"It is long since we have been to the forest, perhaps the bumban (a species of flowering reed) is now gone to fruit; it is long since we have met, perhaps thy affections are now estranged."

¹ *Běmban;* this plant, except for its more branching character, somewhat resembles the bamboo. The stem is hollow, but contains a pith; it is split up to make sieves and mats, and the leaves are plaited into baskets. There are two kinds, mangifera thalpa and maranta disticha.
² The tree is being drawn (by the stream) uncertainly—*i.e.*, hither and thither, *běnděrang.*
³ The eddies whirl over the bathing rock; often though they whirl (the surface) is calm.
⁴ *Rumput,* the grass; but many plants are called rumput.
⁵ Lit., surely.   ⁶ Lit., on the point of the grass.
⁷ Lit., changed.

THE SUMMIT OF GUNONG BENKO.

> Jeka sungguh bulan pernama,
>   Mengapa tiada di pagar bintang ;[1]
> Jeka sungguh tuan bijaksana,[2]
>   Mengapa tiada dapat di tintang.[3]

"If indeed the moon is at the full, why does she not appear in the midst of her stars? If indeed thou art true and faithful, why is it denied me to behold thee?"

> Unggas bukan, chintayu bukan,
>   Kira-nia daun selara tubbu;
> Aches bukan, Malayu bukan,
>   Pandei nia amat bermain semu.

"'Twas not a bird, neither was it the *Chintayu*,* 'twas only a withered leaf of the sugar cane; she is not of Achinese, neither of Malayan race, yet is she deeply skilled in the arts of deceit."

> Bagimana menangkap landak,
>   Di hasop pinto-nia dengan api;
> Bagimana mula berkahindak,
>   Deri mata turun ka hati.

"How is the porcupine to be caught? smoke his hole with fire. How is desire first kindled? from the eyes it descends to the heart."

A few specimens of the longer and more irregular Seramba of the people of the interior will be sufficient, and the Serawi dialect is selected as differing least from the Malay. The following may be supposed the opening of the contest.

> Pandak panjang rantau di Musi,
>   Maso meniamo rantau Tenang,
> Rantau Aman pandak sakali;
>   Hendak anggan wong ku puji[4]
> Mimpin bulan sanak bintang
>   Anak penakan mata hari.

"Long and short are the reaches of the Musi (river), think you they are the same with the reaches of the Tenang, the shortest of all the reaches of the Aman; willing or unwilling I will address my opponent, I will take the moon by the hand, though she is of the family of the stars and a daughter of the sun."

It may be answered as follows:—

> Burong terbang mengulindang
> Sangkan terbang pagi pagi,

---

[1] Lit., why is she not fenced in by the stars?
[2] Usually in the sense of wise, prudent.   [3] *Ditĕntang*, lit., meet face to face.
  * The chintayu is a fabulous bird, said to delight particularly in rain.
      [4] Praise or compliment.

Hindakkan bunga jeruju;
Amun wong sintano bulan,
Rinchang sintano matahari
Timbang betating berteraju.[1]

"The bird flies swift and straight, it flies early in the morning in search of the Jeruju flower; if a person resembles the moon, and is also compared to the sun, take them up and try them in scales.

Titiran pikat nibang hari, Ingunan si Jiwo Jiwo, Jadi kampong burong tiong, jadi koum punei siulan, Bringin di mana garangan masak, merangei meruntuh daun, sanalah dio maridawan, Amun sakali kali lagi, Taulah aku di idar' o, Hindak niabong ayam tangkap, Hindak berjudi kandong pitis, Hindak siri rai peliman, Hindak bunga, karang ko tuboh, kundang wong di rindu jangan, amun asso rindu kan dio, tangisi kian dalam hati.

"The turtle dove kept by Si Jiwo Jiwo calls day by day, the minas are collected together and the tribe of pigeons; where the warringin tree is with ripe fruit, bare and stript of leaves, there they are all chattering; Since once more it has come to my turn, if you wish to fight cocks, take up your bird, if you wish to game, bring money in your purse, if you wish to eat siri, draw the siri box towards you, if you wish for flowers, string thyself (*i.e.*, thou art thyself a flower), if you desire a lover, do not pine for him, if you do feel a longing towards him, conceal your feelings within your breast."

As an example of the puzzling questions or figures with which they sometimes try each other's ingenuity, the following may be taken:—

Ada kayu indan sabatang, Tumbuh di padang maha leber, Beringin bukan Beringin, Kruya bukan Kruya, Bodahan ganio[2] ampat dahan, bedaun ganio ampat daun, sadahan chondong ka langit, niat ka mana bulan bintang, sa dahan chondong ka laut, niat ka mana raja ikan, sa dahan chondong ka gunong, niat ka mana gaja indan, sa dahan chondong ka bumi, niat ka mana anak Adam, Amun teritti[3] sili warang, wong ku angkan dio guru, Amun de teritti sili-warang, wong ku angkan anak murid.

"There is a great tree, growing on an extensive plain; it is not a beringin, neither is it a kruya; of branches it has only four, of leaves, too, it has only four; one branch points to heaven, what will become of the moon and stars? one branch points to the sea,

---

[1] Lit., weigh by taking in the hand and scaling.
[2] Bĕrdáhan hánya.
[3] Form of *arti*. *Rĕti* is found in Straits Malay; thus *terĕti* is = *terarti*.

what will become of the king of the fishes? one branch points to the mountains, what will become of the great elephant? and one branch points to the ground, what will become of the children of Adam? If you understand my riddle, I will take you for my instructor; if you do not understand my riddle, I will take you for my disciple."

In these examples several words occur which are foreign to the Malay language; some of these, as wong (orang), indan, sili, &c., belong to the Sunda dialect; and others, as amun (if), peliman, asso, angkan, &c., are Serawi.

To conclude this paper, the following are the results of a series of trigonometrical observations made by the late Captain H. Auber, for determining the distances and height of some of the more remarkable hills in the neighbourhood of Bencoolen.

Distance of the Sugar Loaf from Mount Felix, 17·84 miles.
Perpendicular height of the Sugar Loaf, 2601 feet.
Distance of the Laye or Sungey Lamau Hills, 28·37 miles.
Perpendicular height of their highest points, 7,797 feet.

X.

AN ACCOUNT OF THE ISLAND OF BALI.

By R. FRIEDERICH.

["Journal of the Royal Asiatic Society," N.S., vol. viii. pp. 157-218; vol. ix. pp. 59-120; vol. x. pp. 49-97.]

Dr. Friederich's valuable paper was originally published in vols. xxii. and xxiii. of the "Verhandelingen van het Bataviaasch Genootschap' (1849-50), under the title "Voorloopig Verslag van het Eiland Bali." Part of it (pp. 1-39 of the present volume) was translated for Dr. Logan, and published in the "Journal of the Indian Archipelago," vol. iii. pp. 119-137, 235-250, whence it is here reproduced in a thoroughly revised form. The remaining and by far larger portion appears now for the first time in English; the translation having been made by Mr. A. H. May, at the suggestion and expense of Major-General Sir George le Grand Jacob, C.B., K.C.S.I., who is greatly interested in Balinese literature, and has long been desirous of obtaining a copy of the Kavi Brahmânda-Purâna, according to Dr. Friederich the only Purâna known to the Balinese.

INTRODUCTION.

I MUST request the indulgence of friendly readers for the following paper on Bali. Not having prepared myself for this labour on Bali itself, I had not the means of collecting and properly arranging all my materials. I could only use for this purpose a small portion of the valuable manuscripts of the priests which were placed at my disposal. I could not avail myself of the information of the natives as to many points, and I was deprived of a great part of my manuscripts. These circumstances will, perhaps, in some degree excuse the many deficiencies, best known to the writer, of this preliminary account. I have divided this work into three sections—1st, language and literature; 2nd, religion, worship and cremation; 3rd, castes and royal races. With this is given a short description of the Balinese calendar.

In the "Tijdschrift voor Neêrland's Indië," IX. vol. iii. p. 340, an explanation from the Sanskrit is given of the name Bali in the paper *Usana Bali:* subsequently the title of a work, *Bali Sangraha,* became known to the writer. This work, which however appears no longer to exist, was presented by a pandita to one of the princes of Bali. The name is explained thus—*Bali* = *wiśesha, sangraha* = *kumpulan*. Following the Indian manner of composition, where the word, which must be taken to be in the oblique case, is placed before that in the nominative, it is to be explained thus—*The gathering of the excellent* (the heroes). With this the Sanskrit *sangraha* entirely agrees. Bali is then not to be considered as "offering," but as the nominative of the theme *balin,* a strong person, powerful, a hero. The name *Bali* signifies, thus, a hero, and the name of the country given in Usana-Bali, *Bali angka,* "the lap (birthplace) of heroes," is a very beautiful denomination of the holy land, and one which expresses the bold spirit of the nation.

Crawfurd and Raffles first drew attention to the great importance of Bali in a religious and scientific respect. After their time little progress was made towards a knowledge of the island, and thus the Balinese (from their wanting that courtesy which the Javanese exhibit, which however only shows their submissive character) have been considered as a rude uncivilized people, from whose knowledge not much was to be expected. It cannot, indeed, be said, that the *whole population of Bali*, in arts (wherein they clearly are behind) or in science, stand above the Javanese, but the priests bring before our eye the stage at which the Javanese stood before the introduction of Muhammedanism. They are, also, the only remaining preserves of the old literature and religion. To them must every one repair who desires the elucidation of the Kavi. They are the expounders of all laws and institutions; and of the knowledge of antiquity they have scarcely lost or forgotten anything from their faithful adherence to traditions.

Should circumstances permit, I hope, after some time, to follow up this preliminary account by an extended work on this remarkable island.

Language and Literature.

The language of Bali,[1] like that of Java, is divided into a High and a Low, the first being spoken by the lower to the higher orders, and the last by the higher to the lower. The *High Language* is nearly pure Javanese, but it does not entirely agree with the present high Javanese. It possesses many words which now belong to the low tongue of Java, while other high Javanese words cannot be used in it without giving offence. It is thus easy for a Javanese to understand the high language of Bali, but he is not able to speak it with purity. The *Low Tongue*, on the other hand, has very little in common with the Javanese, and it agrees more with the Malayan and Sundanese, so that it is easily learned by men from Western Java. This language is that of the original inhabitants of Bali before the arrival of the Javanese. It has naturally undergone some changes, but, in general, we find in it a rude Polynesian[2] dialect, which, in the recognized relationship of all these languages, agrees most with the least polished dialects, the Sundanese and original Malay; while it is far behind, and greatly differs from, the polished language of Java, which, in the course of more than a thousand years, has been brought to its refinement. On Bali, four hundred years ago, there were yet savages or half savages without a finely elaborated language. The same we may suppose to have been the case with the Malays before the reception of Muhammedanism, and with the Sundanese before the kingdom of Pajajaran came into existence. From this alone, that is, from the original relationship between all the languages from Sumatra to Bali and further to the east, which has been only distinctly preserved where the people have remained in a lower stage of civilization, we may explain the agreement between the low Balinese tongue and the Sundanese and Malay; an immigration of Sundanese or Malay into Bali is not at all to be thought of. The Javanese conquerors found this language the prevailing one on Bali, and could not expel it, and, for this reason in particular, that the population of Bali was very numerous, and was brought under subjection more by the greater civilization of the Javanese than by the force of arms. The Javanese conquerors preserved as a high language the Javanese which they brought with them; for their intercourse with the people of the land they had to learn the original Polynesian tongue, which alone was spoken by the former, and which, to this day, has a wider prevalence on Bali than the low language on Java. It is still

---

[1] [R. van Eck, "Beknopte Handleiding bij de beoefening van de Balineesche taal," p. 1-8; H. N. v. d. Tuuk in "Tijdschrift v. de taalkunde," vol. xxv. p. 245; Dr. Brandes, "Vergelijkende Klankleer," p. 108-11.]

[2] [Here and in the sequel we should prefer the term "Malayan."]

exceedingly difficult for a common man to express himself intelligibly in the high language; and to speak to each rank of a higher or lower degree with full conformity to the laws of politeness, is an accomplishment which many even of the young princes have not attained. The agreement between the Balinese and the Sundanese does not confine itself to words alone. Both have also only 18 letters, while the Javanese possesses 20; these 18 were as much as the Polynesian organs originally required; the second $ḍ$ and $ṭ$ are properly foreign to these languages, and the distinct pronunciation which the Javanese give to them is not easily discriminated by the ear. Notwithstanding, these characters, as well as the capital letters, exist in the writing of the Balinese, but are only used to express the corresponding Sanskrit characters $ṭ$ and $ḍ$ or $ḍh$ (cerebral), in the same manner as the *aksara murda* or *g'de*, the capital letters of Cornets de Groot.[1] Further, the Sundanese and Balinese agree in preserving the pure pronunciation of the vowel *a* in all cases where the Javanese corrupt it to *o* (â). The *a* is also in these languages, as in the Sanskrit, of far greater range and predominance than the other vowels. The only degeneration is to *pepet è*, and this may also be considered less as a short *è* than a short ejaculated *ă*, which is commonly used with a nasal sound following it (*m* or *n* and *ng*).

The language of Java must originally have possessed a closer relationship to the Balinese. This we conclude principally from the appearance of Malay, and also (according to Humboldt, vol. i. p. 198) of Tagala words, in the Kavi. At the period when the Kavi formed itself, the Javanese language could not yet have been so refined as it might have been if it had been formed in the course of ages in civilized Hindu States.[2] The Malay words of the Kavi, which do not exhibit themselves in the present Javanese, are original Polynesian, and reveal to us the union which once existed between the languages of Sumatra, Western and Eastern Java, Bali, and probably all the Eastern islands, and which, chiefly, in the Eastern or proper Java alone, has been obscured by a higher civilization. The influence of the polished Javanese has also, it is true, made itself felt in the Sunda territories, but the high language of those parts is far less developed than that of Java; it probably first began with the establishment of the kingdom of Pajajaran; as on Bali with the arrival of the Javanese. On Bali the division into castes operated most, which rendered necessary a subordination in the manner of speaking also. By

---

[1] [And of the subsequent authors of Javanese grammars, T. Roorda, J. J. de Hollander, Jansz, Halkema. The ten letters in question are called capital because they are substituted, except when final, for their equivalents in writing names of objects to which honour is due, such as deities, princes, &c.]

[2] [The results of the labours of V. der Tuuk, Kern, Brandes, and other *savants* tend to modify these conclusions; see the following notes.]

the Javanese, however, the language must have been rendered so complicated, since it was developed by them during more than a thousand years. A further knowledge of the languages east of Bali will probably still more confirm this position: *the languages of all these islands are dialects differing from each other, which have departed the less from the original parent the less and the later the people have received Hindu civilization.* Besides the spoken languages, we have on Bali the written language; this is in poems, with the exception of the more recent, the *Kavi*, and in the sacred writings of the priests, the Sanskrit.

Humboldt (vol. i. pp. 188–203) has written best on the origin of the Kavi language.[1] Some modifications, however, in the conclusions of Humboldt must be introduced by the fact that pure Sanskrit writings are still found with the priests on Bali.

Kavi is explained by Humboldt to be "poetical language" (*Kavi* "a poet," *kâvya* "a poem"). With this explanation that of the Balinese agrees; they say that *Kavin* or *Kakavin* signifies "to make comparisons," "to speak in comparisons." This is the mode in which poetry is formed; comparisons are the ornaments and marks of poetry. The explanation of the Javanese by *Khavi* (strong) scarcely needs to be mentioned. Khavi is an Arabic word; first known in Java in the Muhammedan era, and in Bali not at all. How could the Arabs have given the name to a language which they neither produced nor cultivated, but, on the contrary, have nearly destroyed, because it was the prop of Hinduism and of all the institutions on Java which the Arabs sought to overthrow and cast into oblivion? It is due to the Arabs and their followers that the Kavi is no longer understood on Java, and that Kavi works have nearly disappeared there, while an abundance of them has been carefully preserved on Bali. The verb *kavin* or *kakavin* has caused the works to which that name is applied by the Balinese to be regarded as marriage poems, because it reminds us of the Malay *kavin* (to marry). Both words, the Balinese and the Malayan, appear to be referable to the same Sanskrit word. From *kavya* by the suffixing of the Polynesian *an*, *kavyan* is formed; this, by the contraction of *ya* to *e* commonly (however improperly) used in Java, gives *kaven;* and from this, by a careless pronunciation with the common permutation of *e* and *i*, are formed *kavin* and *kakavin*. This is then at once the Balinese word for "poetry" and the Malay for "to marry," because the marriage songs (*hymenaea*) form a principal part of the festivity, and that which most strikes the ear.[2] Respecting the origin of the Kavi language, it would seem that

---

[1] [See the later contributions, ap. Brandes, l. l. p. 73 ff.]
[2] [It is obvious that the Malay and Javanese word *kâwin*, marriage, to marry, which is a Persian loan word, has nothing but the sound in common

some new ideas must be kept in view. The priests did not hold the Kavi but the Sanskrit as the sacred language ; this language is still found on Bali in the Vedas, the Brahmâṇḍapurâṇa and other mystic writings or *tuturs* [that is Sansk. *tantra*.—ED.]. We cannot therefore agree with Crawfurd, who considered that the Kavi was the language of the priests (Crawf. " Arch." vol. ii. pp. 17, 18).

The Hindus, and particularly the Hindu-Brahmans who came to Java, brought with them the Sanskrit in their sacred writings, and, perhaps, also a Prakrit dialect. That they knew and could speak a Prakrit dialect may be concluded from the comparatively late period of their arrival from India, which we place at the highest 500 years after Christ; at that time, however, the Sanskrit had been at least 800 years a dead language in India. On the other hand, against the idea, that they spoke Prakrit, pleads strongly the fact that we do not find a single Prakrit word in the Polynesian languages, that none of the assimilations, contractions and elisions which characterize the Prakrit appear in the Indian words of the Kavi ; but it is this very fact which points the way to an explanation of the origin of the Kavi.

In the Sanskrit words on Java and Bali we find corruptions, which have not originated in an Indian mode. To this class belong the contraction of *va* to *o*, *ya* to *e*, the indistinct pronunciation, and the permutation thence arising, of *u* and *o*, of *i* and *e*; further the permutation of *ra* and *rĕ* (*kèrrèt*, formerly recognized by me as *ṛi-vocalis*), which however, as well as the preceding corruptions, never appear in good Balinese manuscripts. To this class belong also the corruption of the prefix *pra* into *par* and *per;* the omission of the initial *a* in Sanskrit words, for example *nugraha* for *anugraha*, which are interchanged with the non-significant initial letter *a* of Javanese verbs. The pronunciation of Anusvâra as *ng*, e.g. in *ong*, should not be ascribed to a corruption ; as this pronunciation appears to stand nearest to the unsettled sound of the Indian letter. The change of the Indian *v* to *b* in *Byasa, Balmiki, Baruna*, is to be considered less as a corruption than as an accommodation of the Sanskrit idiom for the preservation of the vocalic pronunciation. I, therefore, believe that the few changes in Sanskrit words have had their origin in Java, and that not a single Prakrit word has been introduced into the language of that island.

Thus the Hindu immigrants into Java, though they certainly spoke the Prakrit, as we must presume if we consider the time of their arrival, appear to have abandoned that language at once and adopted the dialect of the country. The reason for this must be sought in the circumstance of the Hindus arriving but in small numbers and finding a large population of natives; further, in

with the Old Javanese and Balinese word *kawin*, which is a poem framed after a Sanskrit original.]

their being partly Buddhists, the adherents of which creed always adopted the manners and language of the nation to be converted, in the different countries into which they came. By the Buddhists the devotees of Brahma were likewise compelled to yield with regard to language, in order not to irritate the people whom they wished to subject to their own worship and institutions, and to give thereby full play to the Buddhists. Thus Buddhists and Brahmans lived together in Java on peaceful terms, and the worship of each became not indeed blended with, but augmented and modified by, the dogmas of the other. We have noticed this already on an earlier occasion when viewing the ruins of Prambanan and Boro Budo; in the course of this account more distinct proofs will be given of this hypothesis in different places. The Kavi works are written partly by Śivaites, partly by Buddhists; both use the same dialect, and the works of both are held in high regard by the people, though the Śiva Brahmans of Bali appear to entertain a predilection for the genuine Śivaitish works.

Those friendly relations appear to be one of the chief causes of the existence of the Kavi language. The introduction of a foreign language was not practicable on account of the Buddhists, and because the original population of Java was too large; still the necessity was felt of augmenting the dialect of the country in order to express, in the tracts written for the people, ideas relating to worship and science, for which no terms were then existing. In this way the people became accustomed to a number of Sanskrit words employed by their instructors in religion, and by gradually introducing more and more foreign words, a distinct language was formed, destined exclusively for writings and teaching. This language could not of course adopt the inflexion of the Sanskrit, for, in order to understand it, the people would have had to be made acquainted with the entire Sanskrit grammar, which would have been too troublesome for a nation like the Javanese to acquire, and moreover the imparting of it was not for the interest of the priests, whose secret writings, containing unadulterated Sanskrit forms, remained unintelligible for the rest of the people.

The fact that the Buddhists formed the Kavi without the introduction of words from the Prakrit, seems also to prove that their secret writings were in Sanskrit. In Ceylon and the further Indian Peninsula the books of the Buddhists were composed in Pali (a dialect of the Prakrit); but, in China and Tibet, in Sanskrit; the promulgation took place earlier in the northern parts than in those towards the south, and, for this reason, the books were still written in the ancient sacred language of all India. If, therefore, the Buddhists brought their books to Java composed in the Sanskrit language, their introduction must have been in a comparatively ancient time. It has been observed already that this newly formed dialect[1] was chiefly intended for the converted people, while the priests preserved in the Sanskrit the religious books used by them alone (the Vedas), and whatever they wished to keep secret from the people (Brahmâṇḍapurâṇa and the Tuturs).

The Kavi contained all those works by which the religious ideas and the cherished mythology of the priests were communicated to the people. It thus became a sacred language to the people, and the holiness attached itself to all the words, principally however to the Sanskrit, which were rendered conspicuous[2] by capital letters (the *aksara g'de* or *murda*). For the priests of Bali this language is that of pleasure; they always use it for their poetical compositions; almost every one of them composes a poem of greater or less extent, which is communicated to their colleagues and scholars. But the Kavi is not sacred to them; they greatly distinguish between *Kavi* and *Śloka*. *Śloka* is the usual Epic measure of India, in which, in Bali, the *Mantras* (secret writings) and also the *Vedas* are written. The name *Sanskṛita*, as significative of the language, is unknown in Bali. It is not even of a very old date in India, having come into use to contradistinguish it from the *Prâkṛita*, the vulgar language. Śloka (the measure used in the epic poems of India) is used at present in Bali as the denomination of the works composed in that measure, the language of which is Sanskrit. Those are sacred and must be kept hidden from the people (*rahasya*). The Kavi has various epochs; in the opinion of the Balinese there are three principal ones, viz.:

1. The epoch of *Ayer Langgia;* in the compositions of his age, according to the Śiva Brahmans, the Kavi appears in the most beautiful and oldest form. He reigned in *Kediri*, and was one of the ancestors of *Jayabaya*. In his time the worship of Śiva seems to have been predominant.

2. The epoch of *Jayabaya;* of his time is the *Barata Yudda*, less esteemed than, for instance, the *Vivâha*, and indeed of a more recent style, also many works of Buddhist authors. His period cannot be ascertained from the Balinese records; according to them he reigned in *Barata Varsa* (India), but this is the India transferred by the Barata Yudda into Java. His period would appear to comprise the reigns of several rulers, since so many works are ascribed to him.

3. The epoch of *Majapahit*, where we meet with still greater admixtures of the vulgar language, and less acquaintance with the riches of the Sanskrit. This period is succeeded by a fourth one, formed by the continued poetical compositions of the priests and of some princes in Bali. These, at least the priests, have preserved the knowledge of the Kavi, and even augmented it by new

---

[1] [On the nature of Kavi and the position it holds with regard to Javanese, see the note to V. d. Tuuk's article "On Malagasy," and the references.]

[2] [See, concerning the term "capital," the note above at p. 72.]

Sanskrit expressions, which they take from the secret writings. From this we are inclined to trace their immigration into Bali, and the large stock of knowledge they are still in possession of, to another part of Java, perhaps Kediri, and not to Majapahit. The tale of Śiva Brahmans having come to Majapahit from India shortly before the destruction of that empire is altogether unknown in Bali. How is it, moreover, possible that those Brahmans should have acquired so speedily the knowledge of the Kavi and of the native language? The priests of Bali have been in Majapahit, how long is uncertain; but they descended from Kediri, and from thence probably it was that they brought their greater knowledge. These accounts can be brought into accordance with the account in question of the arrival of Śiva Brahmans at Majapahit, if we here, likewise, bear in mind the transfer of Baratavarsa into Java,—Kediri with its king Jayabaya lay in Baratavarsa; Majapahit seems not to have been comprised in it.

The literature of Bali from its nature is divisible into

1. Sanskrit works, with Balinese paraphrase; they include the *Vedas*, the *Brahmâṇḍapurâṇa*, and the greatest part of the *Tuturs*.

2. Kavi works: (a) the epics sacred to the people, viz., the *Râmâyaṇa, Uttarakâṇḍa* and the *Parvas :*—(b) the lighter Kavi poetry, as the *Vivâha, Barata Yudda*, &c.

3. Javanese-Balinese compositions, written partly in the native measures (*Kidung*), such as *Malat;* partly in prose, as the historical narratives *Kenhangrok, Rangga Lave, Usana, Pameṇḍanga.*

Some of the works in prose, especially the law-books, cannot be classed in the third category; they exhibit the ancient language strongly intermixed with Sanskrit, yet they cannot be called Kavi works, from the absence of measure, and this alone is the characteristic of the Kavi language. From this also the *poetical language* is determined.

To the accents which are used in the writings of Bali (vid. "Tijdschrift" IX. vol. iii. pp. 254–56) must here be added a sign for the long *û* differing from the ordinary Suku, and everywhere used in good manuscripts, where the Sanskrit exhibits the long *û*. This long *û* is called *Suku ilud*, and according to this, "Tijd.," *ib.*, p. 255, l. 3, is to be corrected; the kèrrèt (ṛi-vocalis) is called *Guung makèrrèt* (*Guung* is chakra, *makèrrèt*, joined to *kèrrèt*). The long *î*, with a small point in the common figure, is called *ulu mija*. The Balinese have very indistinct notions respecting long and short vowels; however, they, at least the learned priests, use the long *î*, the long *û*, and the têdung as signs for the long *â*, precisely following the tradition where they must stand according to the Sanskrit.

The priests are also in possession of a work on the euphonic laws, called *Sroyanchana*.

In earlier accounts it has been noticed that in Bali no inscriptions on stone or metal are met with, nor any older characters than the present current writing. This is naturally explained from the letters only having been introduced since the fall of Majapahit or a very little before. Although we meet with no modes of writing of a more ancient date, yet in the new writing all the richness is preserved which ever was possessed by the Sanskrit writing in Java. It is only in the Balinese manuscripts that we find reproduced, with the greatest purity, the numerous signs of the Sanskrit, which were superfluous and unpronounceable in Polynesian idioms. Nearly all doubt which may be entertained of the proper powers of the Sanskrit letters, as they have been received in Java and Bali, will be removed by the examination of the writing of such manuscripts as the Vritta Sanjaya, and principally of the numerous Sanskrit words occurring there; any possible faults will be corrected and excused by those who are conversant with the subject, if they consider the many transcriptions of such manuscripts which are made in Bali, and how easily some corruptions and inaccuracies might find their way into them among a small nation, shut out from the source of their civilization, and for 400 years dependent on themselves.

Sacred Writings newly Discovered.

The first rank in the Balinese literature, as in that of the Hindus, is occupied by the *Vedas*. According to the communications of the priests, they are not complete in Bali, but only fragments, although, to judge from appearance, tolerably large ones, of all the four Indian Vedas—viz., 1, of the *Ŗig-Veda;* 2, *Yajur-Veda* (commonly inaccurately spelt *Yayur Veda*); 3, *Sâma-Veda;* 4, *Artava-Veda* (a corruption caused merely by the transposition of the *r*, easily explained by the mode of writing the Indian-Balinese *r* above the line; the Indian name is *Atharva-Veda*). The author of the Vedas is *Bagavân Byasa* (*Vyâsa* in India).

The Vedas contain the formulas of prayer as well for the private worship of the Panditas, performed in their houses, as for the feasts, great offerings and cremations of the people, when the Panditas mumble them inwardly. They are a mystery to all except the Brahmans, and the Panditas instruct the younger Brahmans in them in secret. The metre appears to be the epic *Śloka*, as further illustrated in the Article on Metre, and the language a pure Sanskrit. From their being written wholly in Ślokas, we may suppose either that the Vedas were brought into that metre in ancient times, and in that form introduced into Java and Bali, or that the knowledge of forming Ślokas existed in Java. If the names of the Vedas were not well known, I should rather incline to suppose that they never had been in possession of the genuine Vedas, since in India the metre of the Vedas is guarded by ample commentaries, and must be regarded as an integral and sacred part of those ancient scriptures. The whole of the *Brahmândapurâna* has been communicated to me on the condition of my not making any uninitiated person acquainted with it. In the same way, I may hope to obtain, also, further information about the rest of the mystic writings, and about the Vedas themselves.

The *Vedas have also been in Java*, since the priests of Bali are of Javanese derivation and had their abode in Kediri and Majapahit. Any direct arrival of Brahmans from India is not known in Bali, and even the immigrants into Majapahit, shortly after the destruction of that empire, appear not to have adopted the Vedas of *India* but of *Java*, and it is even doubtful whether they arrived directly from *India*, or only from some other part of *Java*, since the Panditas know nothing of such an arrival from India, while they nevertheless trace their genealogy through Kediri to India. From the tenor of the *Brahmândapurâna* in Bali we may draw conclusions as to the character of the *Vedas*. The genuine Indian pieces in the Vedas, which appear to be written in *Slokas*, are, probably, accompanied by a Balinese or Kavi comment, which, after the lapse of some time, became necessary even for the priests, in order not to lose the true sense of the original texts.

It is an object of the greatest importance to get possession of the remains of the Vedas in Bali. The religion can only by their means become thoroughly intelligible; they further give the standard for the determination of the state of Hinduism when it spread to the islands, and, if compared with the antiquities of India, especially through a more intimate knowledge of the history of the Vedas in that island, will be of service in ascertaining the age from which the Indian influence, and the civilization of Polynesia consequent on it, may be dated. *Sûryasevana* (worship of the sun) signifies not only the religion of the priests, but also the book containing those parts of the Vedas which are used for that worship. I saw the outside of the manuscript; it contained about eighty lontar-leaves. In respect of contents the Brahmândapurâna come nearest to the Vedas; it is also called shortly Brahmânda. We find in India eighteen Purânas, among which is the Brahmândapurâna. These eighteen are the sacred writings of all the different Indian sects. Six are especially holy to the votaries of Vishnu, six others to those of Śiva, and six keep the mean. The more special sects have embraced chiefly one Purâna, as representing the abstract of their worship, as the worshippers of Krishna the Bhâgavatapurâna. In this way it is easily explained how, in Bali, the Brahmândapurâna only should be in use, and how the Panditas should not have preserved even the slightest recollection of the other seventeen Purânas, so little indeed that the names mentioned by me were altogether unknown to them. We find in Bali but one Śivaitic sect, and the adherents of it have acknowledged the Brahmâṇḍapurâṇa, perhaps already in India, as the only book of instruction. The Purâṇas are, as we know, the sacred books of the sectaries, and the priests in India did not trouble themselves much with the sects and their controversies, but, adhering to the more purified worship of the Veda, held the religion of the other people in contempt. Hence it is that the Purâṇas in India are, chiefly, in the hands of the people. In Bali, on the contrary, they are guarded by the priests like the whole of the holy scriptures, and even hid from the people. In Bali, everything relating to religion is in the hands of the priests, and on the great ignorance of the people in all that is necessary according to the sacred literature for their temporal and celestial happiness, is founded the unlimited power of the priests, who are the organs of the Deity for the blindly believing people.

The contents of the Brahmâṇḍapurâṇa are: the creation, the ancestors of the world under the various Manus, the description of the world according to Indian notions, the history of the ancestors of old dynasties, besides mythology and mythic chronology; it is composed by *Bagavân Byâsa* (the holy Vyâsa). He is also known in India as the author of the *Vedas*, of all the *Purâṇas* and of the *Mahâbhârata*; his name signifies [expansion, amplification, in contradistinction to *samâsa*, i.e.] composition, and Prof. Lassen is of opinion that it is a personification of the *recension* of those holy writings. (In what period did this take place?) It is worthy of remark, however, that in Bali he (as the compiler of the said works), as well as *Vâlmîki*, the author of the Râmâyaṇa, are known, since from this we may complete the traditions from India.

The Brahmâṇḍapurâṇa is written in Ślokas like the Indian Purâṇas; and it is to be lamented that we cannot get possession of the Indian Brahmâṇḍapurâṇa; a comparison of both of them would furnish us with a large amount of revelations on the progress of the literature, as well as on the relation of the Balinese to the original Indian worship. The Ślokas seldom follow each other unbroken; generally, we meet with only a fourth or the half of a Śloka, followed by an extended paraphrase in the Balinese language. Under the head of Religion we shall give a few examples.

Epic Poetry.

Râmâyaṇa.—This is the oldest Indian epos, composed by Vâlmîki, who is also in Bali acknowledged as the author of it. Here, however, it exists as a Javanese elaboration by *M'pu Raja Kusuma*, also called *Jogisvara*, or prince of the penitents, father of *M'pu* (*Hempu*) *Tanakung* and of another poet *M'pu Dharmaja*, composer of the *Svaradahana*. The language is pure Kavi, with a peculiarly large number of Sanskrit words. The Indian Râmâyana contains seven *Kândas*, large divisions, again divided into *Sargas*, chapters; in Bali we find no *Kândas*, but the whole narrative of the first six Kândas is placed together and divided into twenty-five *Sargas*.[1] The 7th, the *Uttara Kânda*, is no part of the narrative, but forms a separate work in Bali, the author of which, however, is accounted to be the same Vâlmîki. The separation of this *Kânda* from the rest of the Râmâyana is a proof that it was introduced from India as a different piece, not forming part of the large work, in favour of which position the contents also speak, the *Uttara Kânda* giving an account of the history of the family of Râma after his death. From this we conclude that in India, at the period when the Râmâyana was communicated to the Javanese, the *Uttara Kânda* was not yet annexed to this work. We, likewise, do not find, in the Java-Balinese *Râmâyana*, the long stories of the *Bâla Kânda*, the history of *Râmâ* as a child, where Vasista, the priest of the house, tells him tales of the time of old. Those narratives, partly very beautiful, such as that of the *Sagarides* and the descent of the river-goddess *Gangâ* on the earth (*vide* A. W. von Schlegel's "Indische Bibliothek"), are episodes not forming part of the Râmâyana; they have, however, so many charms, especially for a people like the Javanese and Balinese, who take every story for truth, that the absence of those tales in the Java-Balinese *Râmâyana* is surprising. We ascribe their absence to the same reasons as the separation of the *Uttara Kânda* from the Râmâyana; at the time when the Râmâyana found its way into Java, it was not so voluminous as at present in India, and comprised exclusively the history of *Râma*. As to the *Mahâbhârata*, it has long since been discovered by European scholars from the contents, and the form of different parts, that in this work, as it at present exists, we have before us a conglomerate of Indian myths, which have been interpolated, partly in recent times. The same seems to be the case with the *Râmâyana*, though the interpolations are not met with so repeatedly, and are not spread through the whole work. For a careful critical comparison of the Indian Râmâyana with that of Bali I am at present in want of an edition of the Indian one. In Java, up to this time, there is only known a Javanese elaboration of the Kavi composition, the *Romo;* this is far behind the Balinese *Kavi* work both in language and style, and is looked upon by the Balinese as a corruption. The Romo probably was not composed until the Muhammedan era, and probably when, on the cooling of the religious zeal, the beautiful ancient literature was still remembered, while the knowledge of the Kavi was forgotten.

I have borrowed a good manuscript of the Râmâyana from the highest and most learned priest in *Badong*, the *Padanda Made*

[1] [Kern, in "Bijdragen" for 1883, i. p. 1.]

ALENG KACHENG in *Teman Intaran*. It contains the Râmâyaṇa complete on 210 lontar-leaves, and is written very fairly, with great care in the use of uncommon signs, and with attention to the euphonic laws. Of this manuscript the last leaf with the signature is wanting, so that it cannot be ascertained how old it is. For my use the little that was deficient has been transcribed from the text of another manuscript. This latter was written in the year (of *Śaka*) 1693, corresponding to the year of Christ 1771; and in *Bali* at *Bandharapura* (the Sanskrit name of Badong). Badong signifies as well the small kingdom of that name, as the residences of the princes of Badong, situated at no great distance from each other. We may translate *Bandharapura*, "the town of union," or "the united palaces of the princes," *pura* meaning a town and a royal palace. The Balinese word *badong* has also the same meaning. It is written with *alpaśâstra* (small letters), which makes us think of capital (Kavi and Sanskrit) letters. The usual Balinese letters may indeed be said to be small ones (*alpa*), if compared with old writings still existing in Java. However, we find no other letters in Bali than the common recent current writing, and even the learned priests have lost every recollection of more ancient letters. Inscriptions on stone (as noticed already) are not found, and the letters of the Sanskrit shown by me to them were perfectly unknown to them. We can thus make nothing more of *alpaśâstra* than that the writer humbly acknowledges that he makes use of the *imperfect* letters, since the want of greater knowledge does not permit him to write better and more correctly.

The last words contain an invocation of the Deity, and we find them with slight variations at the end of several manuscripts; they are pure Sanskrit, and correspond to the invocations at the beginning of Sanskrit works: *Siddir astu, tatastu, ong Sarasvati namah, ong t'mung Gaṇapataye namah, ong sri Gurubyo namah*, "Be this the accomplishment, be it thus (?): *Ong* adoration to *Sarasvati*, *Ong* adoration to *Gaṇapati*, *Ong* to the gurus adoration!" The word *t'mung* is not very clear nor Sanskrit. The invocation of *tat-astu* (let this be) appears also superfluous; if we explain it by *tathâ astu* (may it be), the sense becomes no better. *Sarasvatî* is the goddess of letters, the consort of *Brahmâ*. In every Balinese year she has a feast, where the whole of the manuscripts are brought forth and consecrated in the temple. *Gaṇapati* or *Gaṇeśa*, the son of *Śiva* and *Parvatî*, is the god of arts and cunning, the Indian Mercury. His cunning is invoked in India as well as on Bali, in order to overcome the obstacles which are likely to be met with in the composition of an important work. The *gurus* are on earth the parents and spiritual teachers; here, however, are meant the *celestial gurus*, the *Pitaras*, or "spirits of the departed members of the family," who receive a daily worship.

The Râmâyaṇa is divided into twenty-five sargas or chapters. It begins with the incarnation of the god Vishṇu in the family of the king *Dasarata* of Ayodhya (the present Oude); he becomes the son of *Dasarata* by his wife *Kosalya* (Sanskrit Kauśalyâ); his half brothers are *Barata* by *Kekayi* and *Laksmana* by *Sumitra*. His teacher is the *Muni Vasista*, who instructs him above all in the *Danurveda*, "the art of arms." At an early age, the pious king *Visvamitra*, the *rajarsi*, royal *ṛishi* (*vide* the Rajarsis in Bali, his successors), when he was recognized as an incarnation of Vishṇu, invoked his aid to deliver his hermitage from the *Rakshasas* who had made war against it. This he accomplished, and bent the bow of Parasu Râma. From this the tale turns to his nuptials with the fair Sita, and to the intrigues of his stepmother *Kekayi*, who forms the design to raise her son to the throne. After that he voluntarily retires into a hermitage, and subsequently into the forest of Daṇḍaka, accompanied by Sita and Laksmana. Laksmana mutilates the *Raksasi Surpanaka* who wooed for his love, and by this excites the hatred of *Râvaṇa*, the prince of Langka (Ceylon), and brother to *Surpanaka*, against Râma and his companions. *Râvaṇa* ravishes the beautiful Sita, and *Râma* seeks for her in vain. He makes an alliance with the monkey-king *Sugriva*, and his son the swift *Hanuman*. *Hanuman* discovers the hidden spot where Sita was concealed, and then begins the war of Râma and his monkey-warriors against the Raksasas of *Langkapura*. A large part of the work is filled with instructive conversations between the monkey-princes and Râma, and their relations, especially between *Vibisana*, the brother of *Râvaṇa*, and the latter. Finally *Râvaṇa* is slain by Râma, who with his supernatural weapon *chakra* cuts off his ten heads. Sita is purified by *Agni* (the god of the fire), and disappears in mother earth. Râma becomes king of Ayodhya, and retires in old age to the forest hermitage, where he dies.

The *Râmâyaṇa* and the *Parvas* are to the Balinese a sort of pattern for princes. The *adat* of the princes, and of the second and third castes, is contained in those works, holy to them, whilst the Vedas and other secret writings furnish the rules for the Brahmans. The princes and the chiefs of Bali are to regulate their lives in accordance with the Epic writings, and as long as they do so peace and quietness shall prevail and increase in the country. In the present time, however, many princes are charged with indifference to the sacred precepts, and with being, thereby, the cause of the diminution of the fortune and prosperity of Bali. A virtuous prince, before undertaking the smallest matter, examines first the conduct of the old *Kshatriyas* and demigods, as it is described in the ancient holy literature. The conduct of those ancient heroes is ever in the recollection of the princes of to-day, in order to regulate their actions according to the holy patterns, wherever they may find themselves.

A king is to have the accomplishments of the eight gods of the points of the compass—viz., *Indra*, *Yama*, *Surya*, *Chandra*,

Anila, Kuvera, Baruna, Agni (according to Râmâyaṇa, lontar-leaf 181).

Uttarakâṇḍa.—This, as we have seen, is the last (seventh) division of the Indian *Râmâyaṇa*. The author is likewise *Balmiki* (*Vâlmîki*). Up to this time I have not had access to it; it is, however, the history of the brothers of Râma, and contains also stories altogether unconnected with the family of Râma. A more recent Kavi work is the *Arjuna-vijaya*, which borrows its subject from the Uttarakâṇḍa; of which hereafter. *Kâṇḍa* (compare the "Kâṇḍa" of Raffles, vol. i. p. 373 *et seq.*), *division* in India, is used in Bali like *Parva* for all sacred writings; those Kavi works, however, whose names are *Kâṇḍa* and *Parva*, are chiefly destined for the princes and nobles of the second and third caste in Bali, whilst the works written in *Ślokas* are confined as holy to the priests and Brahmans. The *Râmâyaṇa* and the *Parvas* (of the Mahâbhârata) have not been long known to the whole people; they were a secret of the priests and chiefs, and contain rules for the latter in their government and for every action during their temporal life. In every undertaking and in every event, persons of rank are bound to conduct themselves in accordance with the precepts contained in those works. Contempt or indifference in following those sacred writings would bring disaster on princes and people alike, and the entire happiness of the country is indissolubly dependent on the imitation of those holy works.

Parvas (of the *Mahâbhârata*).—The second great Indian epos is the *Mahâbhârata*, composed by the *Muni Vyasa* (Bal. *Byasa*). The name of *Mahâbhârata* is not known in Bali, but its eighteen divisions or *Parvas* are known. The names of those eighteen are correct. Six exist entire and two are incomplete. From the name of *Mahâbhârata* being unknown, it would appear *that this work at the time it was brought from India to Java did not bear this name, nor perhaps any general name at all,* but that its divisions were already regarded as sacred writings. In that case, the name *Mahâbhârata* is only applicable to a small part of the whole work, since the war of the Bharatas, that is, of the Paṇḍavas and Kurus, occupies not more than 20,000 Ślokas, whereas the whole work contains above 100,000. The rest consists of interpolated narratives of various descriptions, which, as occasion admits, are inserted loosely or annexed. How much the Balinese Parvas did contain of the Indian ones, it is impossible for me to decide, without being in possession of the Indian *Mahâbhârata;* the pieces contained in them stand, however, in high esteem, and are faithfully copied. They have:

1 *Adiparva*
2 *Virataparva*
3 *Bismaparva*
4 *Musalaparva*
5 *Prastanikaparva*

6 *Svarga-Rawanaparva* and parts of
7 *Udyoga Parva* and
8 *Asramawasaparva.*

The names of the remaining ten they give as follows:

9 *Saba Parva.*
10 *Aranyaka Parva*
11 *Drona Parva*
12 *Karna Parva*
13 *Salya Parva*

14 *Gada Parva*
15 *Svatama Parva*
16 *Soptika Parva*
17 *Stripalapa Parva*
18 *Asvamedayajnya Parva.**

Along with them they mention also the Santika-parva, although they expressly said there existed no more than eighteen *Parvas:* this can, therefore, be nothing but another name for one of the above eighteen *Parvas*.[1] *Vyâsa*, the author, whom we have already mentioned in speaking of the *Brahmâṇḍapurâṇa*, is the son of *Parasara*, the grandson of *Sakri*, who is the son of *Vasista*, the domestic priest in Ayodhya, teacher of *Râma*, and supposed progenitor of one of the most distinguished castes of the Brahmans. This family was nearly extirpated through Sakri, the son of Vasista, being devoured by one of the *Raksasas*. Vasista was ready to immolate himself by the flames, but was prevented on hearing from out of the womb of the mother, the cries of his grandson, who afterwards was called *Parasara*. He then resolved to spare his life for the education of the child. Upon this he performed his domestic worship, and while muttering the *Veda* a fire broke out, into which all the *Raksasas* were drawn down by an irresistible force and destroyed. This furnished the subject of a painting in the private temple of the râjâ Kassiman of Gunong Rata, where we see the holy Vasista performing his worship in the manner still observed to-day by the *Panditas*, and hosts of *Raksasas*, by the power of his words, falling into the self-existent fire.

The Balinese maintain that the family of Vasista lived in *Baratavarsa* (the eldest holy name of the Brahmanical India, which, however, comprised only a part of the valley of the Ganges between *Ganga* and *Jamuna*). Vyâsa, the writer, is also called *Hempu* or *M'pu Yogisvara*. This is a name of frequent occurrence, and signifies even the highest divinity *Siva*. It is, however, explainable by the fact that a saint or *Padanda*, who retires from the world, becomes identified with the Deity, and is himself called *Siva*. In a certain sense, the Deity is himself the author of all the holy scriptures, since he enters into the composer and speaks and acts by him.

* These are, especially, the works whose deficiency the Brahmans, who spoke with Crawfurd, regretted. They requested me to communicate them to them, which I did as far as my pieces extended, with the promise to provide, also, the large remaining part. The Indian books themselves are of no use to them, since they do not know the writing. I was thus obliged to dictate them word by word.

[1] [See, on this specification, Weber in his "Indische Studien," vol. ii. pp. 136-9. Also van der Tuuk, "Notes on the Kawi Language and Literature," (1881), p. 7; and Kern, "Over de Oudjavaansche Vertaling van't Mahâbhârnta," (Amsterdam, 1877), pp. 2-4].

The *Bismaparva* contains 102 lontar-leaves. The *Adiparva* is nearly of the same size. The *Prastanika-parva*, which I saw, contained only sixteen lontar-leaves, but was not complete. The names are all Indian ones with the exception of *Svatamaparva*, which seems to be a corruption of *Aśvatthâmaparva*, thus called after a hero of the *Mahâbhârata*, a son of Droṇa. *Stripalaparva* is called in the Sanskrit only *Strîparva* ; *palapa* seems to be formed in the Polynesian manner from *alapa* (harangue).[1] The language of the *Parvas* is, like that of the *Râmâyaṇa*, pure *Kavi*, and more difficult to be understood than the other important Kavi works. In addition we have a *Kapiparva*, containing the history of *Sugriva*, *Hanuman* and their ancestors in the monkey-dynasty. There exist also the *Chantaka* or *Khetaka-Parva ;* this is a sort of dictionary, where all the synonyms are classed together after the manner of the Javanese *dasanama ;* it was compiled by Kavidasi, the follower of Byâsa ; it commences with the numerous denominations of the gods, and is for that reason of great importance for the mythology. It is, however, written in prose, and, like the *Kaviparva*, strongly separated from the eighteen holy *Parvas*. An *Agasti* (or *Anggasti*) *Parva* came also to my knowledge, in which the holy *Agasti* (the star *Canopus* and leader of *Râma* in his campaign against the south of India) gives instruction to his son *Dredasya ;* this work is not to be confounded with the *Parvas* of the *Mahâbhârata*.

To the ancient Indian literature pertain further the books of the laws, especially that of Manu. The Balinese law-books are, likewise, drawn from them, although they are written neither in *Slokas* nor in *Kavi*, and we shall, therefore, speak of them after the Kavi literature. The original law-book of *Manu*, *Mânavadharma-śâstra*, is not known in Bali either by that name or by that of *Menava Sâstra* (as the name is said to be on Bali by Raffles, vol. i. p. 991). *Prabu Manu*, however, is mentioned as the founder of the law, and the Indian origin of the Balinese law and law-books is thus certain. The *Purvâdigama* or *Siva Sâsana*, especially, is said to have *Manu* for its author. (*Vide infra*.)

COMMON KAVI LITERATURE.

1. *Bârata Yudda.*—With respect to its contents, the Bârata Yudda stands nearest to the Parvas. For a considerable time it has been regarded as the only version of the Indian Mahâbhârata in our islands. But we have now found on Bali the original pieces of that epos. The Bârata Yudda is formed after four of the Parvas—viz., after the *Bisma*, *Drona*, *Karna*, and *Salya-Parva ;* the author is *Hempu* (or *M'pu*) *S'dah*, who lived in the time of *Sri Paduka Batâra Jayabaya*, Prince of Kediri, and wrote his works.

---

[1] [Or, rather, to be a corruption of *pralâpa*.]

by the order of the latter; the design of the Prince was to obtain by the composition of the work a *kadigjayan*, a *subjugation of the world*. In this also an Indian idea is conspicuous; by the performance of great offerings, by sumptuous works of architecture, and by works of literature, the prince thus engaged becomes not only famous, but he also acquires extraordinary power, by which he is enabled to subject the universe to his will. Such was also the aim of the great offering of the prince of Lombok (in September, 1846), who, not being recognized by all as the legitimate chief, sought, by offerings and abundant alms, to prove his royal right and to strengthen himself for warlike enterprises. The time at which the manuscript of which I made use was composed is the year of Saka 1724 (corresponding to the year of Christ 1802). To judge from its outward appearance, I should have taken it to be much older; in forty-six years the lontar-leaves have already become much injured, and it seems to prove what is said, also, of Indian manuscripts, that they cannot survive a hundred years. This, probably, is also one of the causes that in Java, in so short a time, almost the whole of the ancient literature was lost, and that, when the desire for the old literature was revived, hardly any of the old manuscripts could be discovered. In Bali, also, we must not look for very old manuscripts; however, those which are guarded and transcribed in the families of the priests may almost be considered as original, since in these families the knowledge of language and religion is preserved with the minutest care. Some faults are, of course, also possible here.

The place where the manuscript was written is *Svechchanagara*, also called *nagara Sukavati*, situated in the kingdom of Gyanyar. I have noticed above that *Badong* has also a Sanskrit name (*Bandanapura*); this is the case with all distinguished places in Bali; this place has even two nearly accordant Sanskrit names. *Sukavati* is the city abounding in pleasure; *Svechcha-nagara*, the city of well-being. We perceive here, again, how far the Indian element, and thereby the Indian language, has penetrated into Bali. However, all those places have also Polynesian names for the populace—the Sanskrit ones are frequently known to the princes and priests only.

The name *Bârata Yudda* was formerly translated "penance, combat," and commonly written *Brâtâ Yudda*; *brata* (Ind. *vrata*) is *penance*, and the heroes of the combat acquiring perfection by penance, the explanation had appearance in its favour. But we find in the manuscripts of the priests of Bali constantly *Bârata Yudda*, with the capital *b* (according to De Groot), corresponding to the Sanskrit *bh*, and followed by the *t'dung* (or *tarung*), representing the long *â*; the name cannot, therefore, be brought into accordance with *brata*, which originated in *vrata*. Bârata, as we find it written, signifies, however, "a descendant of *Bharata*" (the old Indian ruler of the universe), and we have thus in our work "*the combat of the descendants of* Bharata." Now the *Kurus* and the *Pâṇḍavas* are descendants of that ruler, and nothing can be more appropriate than such a title for the work. This explanation has already been offered by Raffles, but the reasons which render it irrefutable we first learned from the good Balinese manuscripts.

The conclusion of this work agrees much with that of the *Râmâyaṇa*, and is Sanskrit: *Ong sri devyebyo namah, ong t'mung Gaṇapataye namah, ong siddir astu, tat-astu hastu, ong dirgayur astu.* " *Ong* adoration to the happy gods ! *Ong* adoration to *Gaṇapati !* *Ong* may the accomplishment be, may that be ! *Ong,* may there be long life ! " *Devyebyo* must be *devebyo.* What gods, however, are meant is not clear. *Sarasvatî* and *Gaṇeśa* cannot be intended, since the latter is invoked separately ; *tat-astu* is here made more forcible by the addition of another *astu ;* the word *t'mung* here likewise precedes *Gaṇapati.* *Dirgayus,* " long life," is a thing for which the Indians and Balinese, and especially the composers of literary works, always supplicate the Deity. It is not necessary to draw the attention of those who are acquainted with Sanskrit to the inflected Sanskrit forms, and to the proper observance of the difficult euphonic laws of that language, occurring here and at the conclusion of the Râmâyaṇa. In an enumeration of the Kavi works of a less sacred character, the Bârata Yudda is placed at the head, because the contents are closely connected with the holy *Parvas.* It stands, however, in less esteem, and is more recent than some other Kavi works—*e.g.,* the *Vivâha.* The language is also not a very pure Kavi, but more intermixed with the common *bhâsâ.*

2. *Vivâha.*—This is known from the Javanese paraphrase of *Gericke,* published in the twentieth volume of the " Transactions of the Batavian Society." The contents and arrangement of the narrative in the Kavi Vivâha is the same as in the translated paraphrase. The language is a very pure and beautiful Kavi ; it is likewise not composed in the common Javanese song-form, but in the metres derived from India (to be afterwards described). The author is *M'pu Kaṇva,* not *Kanno,* as we find in the Javanese Vivâha, which word has been formed by the usual Javanese corruption of *va* into *o.* Kaṇva is the name of an Indian *Muni* or Saint. Our *Kaṇva,* however, we may be sure, was a Javanese, perhaps of an Indian descent. He, too, lived in *Kediri* under *Ayer Langgia,* the ancestor of *Jayabaya.*

Hempu S'dah and *Hempu Kaṇva* seem to have been adherents of the Śivaitic sect. We find here few or no traces of Buddhism in the *Bârata Yudda* and *Vivâha.*

3. *Smara dahana,* the burning of *Smara* (the god of love): a well-known Indian myth. The god Śiva is interrupted in his penance by Smara (or Kâma), that is to say, he loses the fruits of his penance by falling in love. Enraged by this, he burns the

god of love in flames which issue from his body. The god of love is therefore also called *Anangga* (the bodiless), because his body was burnt by *Siva*. This work, too, is of the time of *Ayer Langgia*, Prince of Kediri. The author is called *M'pu Darmaja*, son of Raja *Kusuma*, the composer of the *Râmâyana Kavi*.

4. *Sumâna Santaka* comprises part of the Indian *Raghuvansa*. *Raghu*, the ancestor of *Râma*, begets the *Adia;* she is permitted to chose her consort after the Indian royal custom (Svayamvara, also so called on Bali). Her husband *Devindu* died, and she then gave birth to *Dasarata*, the father of Râma. This work also is composed in Kediri or Daha under *Ayer Langgia*; the writer is *M'pu Monaguna* (the name signifies "whose prominent attribute is silence, mauna"). The writers of the three latter works bear Sanskrit names, and belong to the Śivaitic sect; the names of the Buddhist writers are in the language of the country, and, in this circumstance, likewise, the characteristic of that religion is conspicuous, which made its way chiefly by yielding to and adopting the manners of the numerous and widely different countries into which it was propagated; whilst Brahmanism, rigidly adhering to the ancient traditions, and holding in contempt all that is foreign, is nowhere found beyond India except in Java and Bali, and perhaps in parts of Sumatra and Celebes.

All the three above-mentioned works are in a peculiarly good style, and highly esteemed, and this chiefly because they are of Śivaitic authorship.

5. *Bomakăvya;* the song of *Boma* (or Bhâuma)*, "the son of the earth;" he is begotten by *Vishnu* from *Pritivi* (the earth), and has, as son of the earth, a demon form and disposition. He is a *Dânava* (that is, like the Grecian Giants and Titans). He waged war against *Indra*, the god of (the lower) heaven, and triumphed over him. (*Indra* is also overcome by *Ravana*, the giant-king of Ceylon, and his power appears everywhere as secondary, against which the evil spirits are proof.) One of the higher gods (Vishnu or Śiva) must subject his adversaries in order to restore peace and order on earth. Here it is *sang Krisna*, the well-known (eighth) incarnation of *Vishnu*, who kills Boma, and delivers Indra from his distress. *Boma* is killed by being lifted up from the earth, which constantly re-invigorates him. The author is *M'pu Bradah Boda*, that is, "a *Bauddha*, a *Buddhist;*" he wrote in the time of *Jayabaya* of *Kediri*. Under that king Buddhism seems to have found its way for the first time into *Kediri* (the largest empire which existed in Java before *Majapahit*).

6. *Arjuna Vijaya* ("the triumph of *Arjuna*") is formed after the *Uttarakânda* in like manner as the *Bârata Yudda* after the

---

* Buma Kalantaka, by Raffles; the name Anraka Sura has not yet come to my knowledge in Bali. (Raffles, vol. i. p. 388).

four above-mentioned *Parvas*. It contains the combat of *Arjuna* with *Râvaṇa* and his victory. *Râvaṇa* is here bound, but not yet killed, because his time has not yet arrived. He is to be destroyed by *Râma*. Whether we are warranted in supposing, here, an expedition of the Brahman Hindus against the South of India and Ceylon, previous to that of Râma (who is considered to be a personification of the subjugation of those regions), further research must show. The composer is *M'pu Tantular Boda*, likewise a Buddhist in Kediri under *Jayabaya*.

7. *Suta Soma.*—The *ratu Detia* (*Danawa*, Demon). Purusada had made captive all the kings of *Baratavarsa* and conquered the *ratu Darma*. He is overcome by *Suta Soma* and his relative *Prabu Maketu*. It contains many episodes, and also the history of *Râma*. The subject is said to be taken from the *Ketaka Parva* (*vide supra*), although we should not have expected it from the nature of that work. The author is the same who composed the *Arjuna-Vijaya*—viz., the Buddhist *M'pu Tantular* of *Kediri*.

We have thus compositions from older works in the epoch of Jayabaya, or at least of the successors of the King of Ayer Langgia; it appears that the older Kavi language then began to be difficult of comprehension, and that the favourite subjects of literature were, therefore, translated into a more comprehensible language. The influence of the Buddhists in this innovation is not to be mistaken.

8. *Harivangsa.*—This likewise is an Indian poem, commonly joined to the *Mahâbhârata* (the Indian one is translated by Langlois in Paris and obtainable in Calcutta); this piece, too, invites us to a comparison between *India* and *Java*, the Kavi and the Sanskrit. The contents, according to the priests, are: the conduct of Kṛisṇa towards Rukmini (his wife), and the war against the two princes *Jarasanda*, father-in-law of *Kansa*, ruler of *Magada*, and *Chedi* or *Sisupala*. This work was written in *Majapahit*,* and is thus of later origin than the preceding; the author is *M'pu Penulu Boda*, likewise a Buddhist. The King of Majapahit at this period was *Brayang V'kasing Suka*, father of *Bra Vijaya* (*Brovijoyo*), who, according to Javanese records, was the last (Hindu) prince of Majapahit.

These are the most important works of the Kavi literature, so far as I am yet acquainted with it.[1] With these, however, we are far from having exhausted Balinese literature. We have besides

---

* Majapahit is the literal translation of the Sanskrit *Vilvatikta* (corrupted Vilatikta, Us. Java), the bitter *vilva* (aegle marmelos); this then at least is not a fictitious fruit, and the name of Majapahit not unmeaning, as it was formerly considered (*vide* Raffles).

[1] [See also R. van Eck in the Introduction (pp. vi.–viii.) to his edition of *Megantaka*, in the Batavian "Verhandelingen," vol. xxxviii.]

them, first, the *law-books* written in prose; further, the *Tuturs*, or "instructive writings," of which nothing can as yet be ascertained, since they are for the most part secret writings. Further, the Babads, or historic-genealogical works, partly written in Kidung—*i.e.* the newer (Javanese) measure, partly in prose. Moreover, we have pure Polynesian myths; above all, those of Panji, which are likewise written in Kidung. Then there also exist little essays on the transmigration of the soul, on erotic subjects, &c.; and finally there is the Balinese "Kalendar," a work of the utmost importance.

BABAD, OR HISTORICAL ESSAYS.*

1. *Kenhangrok.*—He is a son of *Brahma* and progenitor of the rulers of *Kediri*, *Majapahit* and *Bali*. It has not as yet been ascertained in what epoch he must be sought for. His residence was in the Kampong *M'dok*, whose situation is not known in Bali, but is supposed to be in *Baratavarsa*. It is written in prose, and contains forty or more lontar-leaves. I am only in possession of the first part, which has no more than seventeen leaves. His mother is called *Kenhendok*. The god *Brahma* met her, much in the same way as the Greek Zeus knew how to win his numerous loves, whilst she, as a married woman, was amusing herself in the field.

2. *Rangga Lawe.*—*Siva Budda* (N. B.), ruler of *Tumapêl*, is made captive for misgovernment by the King of *Daha* or Kediri, and his empire *Tumapêl* is overthrown. The chief minister of Kediri is *Rangga Lawe;* he at a later time disagrees with his sovereign, and is finally vanquished and put to death. The work contains a minute description of the Court of Kediri and the position of the grandees of the empire, and may serve as a pattern of the constitution of the old empire in Java. It is, especially, maintained on Bali that the Court of Majapahit was altogether in the same style, and that all the rules of the Court of Kediri were carried to Majapahit. For this reason it would be desirable to have this work published (text and translation), accompanied by the necessary notes; this, however, can only be usefully done in Bali. The manuscript in my possession contains sixty-seven lontar-leaves, each of four lines front and back, and is written very neatly. It was written in *Garogor* (*Glogor*) in *Badong*, on the day of *Saneschara Kaliwon Landep*, in the month *Kasa*, the thirteenth day of the increasing moon, in *rah* 9, *tênggêk* 6, corresponding with the year of Christ 1847, Saturday, the 26th

---

* The name *Babad* is also met with in Java (*vide* Raffles, "Literature," vol. i. p. 393), and it also comprises, following him, all the historic works and new chronicles. Raffles spells it *Babat*. In Bali I find the word written *Babad*. [See also J. J. Meinsma, "Babad Tanah Djawi," vol. ii. pp. 1–15.]

of June. It commences with a metre of fifty-two syllables in each line, the stanza as usual of four lines.

3. *Usana Java.*—"The ancient institutions of Java," a work containing the subjugation of Bali by the Javanese of *Majapahit* and the settling of the *Deva Agung* in *Gĕlgel*, with the distribution of the lands amongst the grandees of the Court. One manuscript of it had twenty-nine lontar-leaves, and was derived, as they told me, from *Pasuruang;* it, however, probably, came from Bali to this place, and seems to be little or not at all known in Java. It is written in prose. In that work a predilection for *Arya Damar* and his family is plainly manifested, whilst it passes over the *Patih Gaja Madda,* the founder of *Mengui* and ancestor of the powerful family of *Karang-Asem,* almost in silence. For this we may find reason in the circumstance that it was originally composed by a follower of the dynasty of *Arya Damar.* According to the postscript it was written in *Galogor* by *Pam'chuttan* (in *Badong*), on the day *Rediti Pahing* (Sunday), in the week *Dungulan,* in the month of *Kanam* (the 6th), on the *thirteenth day of the dark half,* in the year 1 (*rah*), of the *tĕnggĕk** 6. This would be the year 51; if we take the eighteenth century, we should have 1751 of *Saka,* corresponding to the year 1839 of the Christian era.

4. *Usana Bali.*—The contents of it are known from the "Tijdschrift voor Nederlandsch Indie," 9th year, vol. iii. pp. 245–373. There I have said that it is a work exclusively intended for the people, and not esteemed by the priests. It is otherwise with the *Usana Java,* which is held in honour by all castes, at least in Badong.

5. *Pamendanga.*†—A sort of chronicle of more recent times. It contains sundry confused histories of priests and kings, of the distribution of Bali amongst the original *Pungavas* of *Gelgel,* and genealogies of kings, of *Karang-Asem,* for instance. Respecting the division of the vice-regencies among the *Pungavas,* this work widely differs from the *Usana Java,* and its value and style are far inferior to those of the latter. It is also written in prose. Other *Babads* are found in the family of every prince; if it were possible to gather the greater part of them from the different States, they certainly would spread much light on the history of Bali, if carefully compared with each other.

TUTURS, OR DOCTRINAL WRITINGS.

These are divided into two classes: the secret writings of the priests, and such as are also current among the other castes, espe-

---

* *Tĕnggĕk* is a period of ten years. *Rat,* a single year of that time. Supposing the era to be known, we find from it the year of *Saka.*

† From the Pamendanga a play is derived, performed by a single person in *topengs* (masks); [it represents the more ancient history of Bali—viz., of the *Deva Agungs.*

cially the second and third. The former are extremely numerous, but since they are kept secret, we can only mention the names of a limited number of them. They seem to be written, like the *Vedas*, in *Slokas*. The names I obtained are the following :—

1. *Buvana Sangksepa* (the shortening or contraction of the world or of men).
2. *Buvana Kosa* (the treasure of the world).
3. *Vrihaspati Tatva* (the Tatva, truth, the essence of *Vṛihaspati*, the star Jupiter, teacher of the gods).
4. *Sarasa Muschaya* (*sârasa* is explained by *isi*, the contents; it is, however, probably *sârâsa*, the *lotus; muschaya* is not very clear, but is explained by *kumpulan*, "accumulation," "gathering;" this is one of the works enumerated by Crawfurd.[1]
5. *Tatva Jnâna* (knowledge of substance, *essentia*).
6. *Kandampat*.
7. *Sajotkranti*.
8. *Tutur Kamoksa* (*vide infra*). Under this denomination exist numerous works; it means, "instruction for blessedness, or for delivery from the transmigration of the soul."

The second class of the *Tuturs*, current, also, among the other castes besides the Brahmans, are, for instance :

1. *Rajaniti* (wisdom of kings); it contains rules for the policy and the government of kings, and it is in many respects analogous to Machiavelli's "Princeps."
2. *Nitipraya* or *Nitisastra* (superabundance, or manual of wisdom): it is of a similar character with the former.
3. *Kamendaka Niti* (rules of wisdom of the sage *Kamendaka*).
4. *Naranatya* (*nara* "men," *natya* "the mimic").
5. *Ranayajna* (the sacrifice of the battle).
6. *Titi dasa guṇita ;* this belongs properly to the first division, but has been made by *Padanda Vahu Ravuh* into Kavi under the name of *Nitisara* (compendium of wisdom).

LAW-BOOKS.

These are written in prose. They comprise most of the Balinese books which are mentioned by Crawfurd and Raffles. The accounts of them, however, differ from each other. Raja *Kasiman* names them :—

1. *Âgama*. 2. *Adigama*. 3. *Devâgama* (somewhat difficult to understand).
4. *Sârasamuchchaya* (the same we have just met with among the secret writings).
5. *Dustakalabaya* (the fear of the malignant Kala), a law-book, in which in particular the faults committed by children are punished.

---

[1] [It should be *sâra-samuchchaya*, the aggregate of truth.]

6. *Svara Jambu* (the voice of Jambu), that is, "the command, the law of India," *Jambu-Dvipa*.

7. *Devadaṇḍa* (in very old language), it comes in use when *Vishṇu* appears incarnated upon earth.[1]

8. *Yajñasadma* (*yajña* "sacrifice"—*sadma ?*)

The *Pandita* in *Taman Intaram* mentions only

1. *Âgama*.* 2. *Adigama*, the two law-books mentioned by Raffles as the basis of the law for the common people. Raffles calls the latter *Degama*.

3. *Pûrvâdigama* or *Sivasâsana*, the above *Adigama*, or "the command of *Siva*," of value exclusively for the Brahmans.

4. *Devâgama*, the *âgama* of the *Devas*.

5. *Svajambu—Svarajambu;* the meaning is doubtful; perhaps *svara*, "voice," "command," and *jambu*, in lieu of *Jambu Dwipa* (*India*), thus, "the voice of the law of India."

The principal law-book from India (ap. Raffles' *Menava Sastra*, Ind. *Mânava-dharma-śâstra*) is wanting, according to all inquiries for it which I made among several priests and persons of rank. They, however, are aware that all their laws have been derived from *Prabu Manu* (the ruler of Manu), who, in different ages, under different names, holds the government of the world. I found it mentioned only in the *Śivaśâsana*, the law-book of the Brahmans, under the name *Dharma-śâstra Kuṭara-Mânavâdi;* *âdi* has here, it would seem, the true Indian sense "*and so forth*," so that the translation will be "*the law-books, that of Kuṭara Mânava and the others.*" Kuṭara† is also mentioned by Raffles as "a law-book," and is not explained by Humboldt. *Kuṭara* appears to me to be the same as *Uttama*—viz., the name of the third in the line of *Manus*. The conversion of Uttama into Kuṭara is quite possible, and supported by a passage of the *Brahmâṇḍa-purâṇa: Uṭara Manu*, lont. 11. *Uttara* is the comparative, "*the higher,*" and *Uttama* the superlative, "*the highest*" degree. The

---

[1] [A Dutch translation of this short code (35 sections) appeared in the Batavian "Tijdschrift," vol. xviii. pp. 295-309.]

* Âgama is explained by Wilson, Sanskrit Dict., "a Śâstra or work on science and of divine origin." In the Malayan and common Balinese language signifies religion ; in the names *Âgama, Adigama, Devâgama*, it has evidently more the old Indian meaning, and especially that of *law-book*. Adigama seems to have originated in *Adhi* and *Âgama*, with the omission of the first *â* of *âgama*, a carelessness which is frequently met with among the Sanskrit words in the Kavi—*e.g., Svatamaparva* for *Aśvatthâmaparva*. The *a* in Polynesian words is a euphonic prefix, which was then omitted in the Sanskrit words likewise.

† Kutara is, following Wilson, "the post round which the string passes that works the churning-stick." This explanation is here in no way applicable. [The whole question as to the existence, on Bali, of a Mânava-śâstra and a Kuṭara-śâstra has been fully treated by Dr. J. C. G. Jonker in his work, "Een Oud-Javaansch Wetboek" (Leiden, 1885), pp. 11-20].

k before *Uṭara* I am inclined to regard as the Polynesian prefix, added through ignorance. Opposed to this conjecture, it is true, is the fact that the law of India must have been framed by the first *Manu, Svayambhuva Manu;* but we have various law-books, and these are even yet not all known. Possibly the original Balinese law-book has been derived from another Indian one, although the contents are upon the whole the same as in that of Svayambhuva.

This *Dharmaśâstra Kuṭara Mânava* is either now in Bali and kept secret, or it is one of the works which existed in Java, but were lost and were not brought to Bali. It is mentioned along with the *Sârasamuchchaya*, which we learn to be one of the *Tuturs;* further, along with the *Kamandaka,* a *Tutur* for obtaining advantage or intrepidity. A learned Brahman is expected to be acquainted with all these works. It was not without the greatest difficulty that I got the *Sivasâsana* into my hands; however, I may hope to obtain in the like way insight into the remaining law-books and the *Tuturs.* The *Sivaśâsana* was borrowed by me on the same condition as the Brahmâṇḍapurâṇa— viz., not to show it to any one of the people. The manuscript of the *Sivaśâsana* in question was written on the day *Mahulu Pahing Anggara* (Tuesday), of the week *Sungsang,* in the year of *Saka* (*Sakawarsa*) 1682 (A.D. 1760), in the month *Sravana*, on the eighth day of the white half, in *Vilatikta.** After this the writer makes his excuses in the customary manner for the bad and careless writing, and he has great need to do so, for the manuscript abounds in faults; he pleads his inexperience (*muda*) and inferiority (*hina dina*). He adds further that the work is a secret writing (*rahasya*), and concludes with the well-known invocation :—

> Siddir astu, tat' astu astu
> Ong Saraswatie namah
> Ong g'mung Gaṇapataye namah
> Ong sri Gurubyo namah
> Ong ong Kâmadevaya namah

Respecting these invocations, we refer to what is said under *Râmâyaṇa* and *Bârata Yudda.* Here only is added " *Ong* adoration to *Kâmadeva!*" He, the god of love, would thus appear to be peculiarly the favourite deity of the writer. The god of love is indeed highly honoured and praised in many of the newer poems, a circumstance the analogy of which we find

---

* Where this *Vilatikta* is to be sought for in Bali remains uncertain; it is (Vilvatikta) the Sanskrit name for *Majapahit.* It is possible that the work was originally written in *Majapahit,* and that the copyists in succession retained the name of the city where it originally was composed, although they themselves were in Bali.

again in India. We give here the prologue, the text and the translation of the *Śivaśâsana* :—

"This is the *Pûrvâdigama—Śâsana-śâstra-sâro-drêtta*,* first composed by the accomplished old teacher, the raja *Purohita*, who knows all qualities, who resembles the rays of the sun, who dwells in the hearts of all mankind; *Miśraharaṇa*, who, as the highest precious stone, outshines all the divine teachers of *Śiva* (of the Śivaite sect), the lowest, the middle, and the highest; further is he named the first *Guru*, the great saint. The same asked for *ashes*, after he had obtained permission to ask for *ashes* of the children and grandchildren of *Sang Basmangkura*(?); the same commanded him thereupon to compose the *Śâsanâdigama Śâstrasarodrêta* for all priests, as many as hold the religion of ͺiva; for the Panditas of Śiva as well as who live in the cities, the perfect ones, as also those who choose to dwell partly in cities, partly in the country, also for the host of the learned, who take care of processes, who settle disputes between all men, at the Court and in the country, this is *their number*. Assuredly the Adigamaśâstra sarodrêta must contain the laws for the conduct of them all."[1]

There further exists in *Bali* a law-book, called *Svara*, issuing from the *Deva Agung*, and in force for all princes and persons of rank. It cannot, as yet, be ascertained whether it is the same work as the *Svarajambu* (or *Svajambu*), but it seems to be a different one, since the addition of *Jambu* in the latter points to its Indian origin.[2]

Tatwa or *Tutur kamoksa* (*vide* above) contains rules for a religious life, with special directions from the birth of a man up to his death. It frequently prescribes fasting (Ind. *vrata*, *brata*, votum). In accordance with those writings not only the *Padandas* regulate their lives, but also the princes and those of rank who aspire to the condition of holiness; they attain, thereby, the

* This word must be divided, it would appear, into two parts; *Purvadigama sasana*, "*the command, law of the Purvadigama*," and *Śâstra Saro dreta*, "in which is contained the essence of holy works." The *Saro* is inserted instead of *Sara*, and we thus find the nominative case in place of the theme in a composition. This seems to be an error founded very likely in the want of acquaintance with the meaning of the Sanskrit terminations and inflexions, but offering at the same time another proof of the preservation of the inflexions in the memory of the Panditas. [*Sâro-drêtta*=*sârodḍhṛita*, "gathered from the essence of the *Ś.-ś.*"] The *Śivaśâsana* or *Pûrvâdigamaśâsana* is the law-book for all the Brahmans, in the cities as well as in the country, and for those in whose hands the jurisdiction is deposited as well as for the rest. It is not, however, applicable in the decision of the lawsuits of persons belonging to one of the three lower castes.

[1] [The transliterated Kavi text, with Friederich's explanatory notes, is here, for obvious reasons, omitted.]

[2] [See P. L. van Bloemen Waanders in the Batavian "Tijdschrift," vol. viii. (1859), pp. 201-27, and the Introduction to Jonker's work previously mentioned.]

dignity of *Resi* (a saint, without sin), and the priests become *Brahmarsi*, the princes *Rajarsi*; the latter, of course, as it is natural, in consequence of their birth, rank below the former. Every prince must properly aim at this dignity, and the *Abiseka*, "the anointing" of the chief prince, is dependent upon it. By becoming *Resi* and by the *Abiseka*, not only the dignity of the prince is raised, but he is, thereby, as it were, received into the caste of the Brahmans—the like rule is also observed in India. The predecessor of the last sovereign of Pam'chuttan was *Resi*, and had received the *Abiseka*; even as the former *Deva Agungs*. At present there is no prince of Bali who has received the *Abiseka*. The *Râjâ Kassiman*, however, aims at the dignity of *Resi*.

MALAT.

The Malat[1] contains the history of the celebrated hero *Panji*, who had his adventures on Bali also. The work is as voluminous as the *Râmâyaṇa*; it is, however, not written in the *Kavi* measure or language, but in *Kidung*, which means the newer Java-Balinese measure. The subjects contained in it are exhibited to the public in the *Gambuh* (dramatic performances by men, who speak themselves). The same is the case with the *Râmâyaṇa*. The *Bârata Yudda* and *Vivâha* are represented in the *Vayang Kulit* in the same manner as on Java. Of the Indian drama nothing seems to have found its way into this island. The names of the most famous of the Indian dramas are unknown there. The tale of the Sakuntala is known from one of the Parvas, and the original narration we find also in India in the *Mahâbhârata*. But the magnificent drama *Sakuntalâ* of *Kâlidâsa* is not known. The reason of this is, probably, that most of the Indian dramas are of late times, and, perhaps, at the time the Brahmans came to Java, were exclusively found at the courts of the princes of *Ujjayini*, *Kâshmir*, *Ayodhyâ*, &c., so that the Brahmans could not be acquainted with them. Besides, the drama forms no part of the sacred literature, and the Brahmans might have neglected it for that reason.

RELIGION.

The religion of Bali, as is well known, is the Hindu, and in fact the two great Indian creeds, the Brahmanical and the Buddhist, exist there. The adherents of the latter are few in number, and live in *Karang-Assem* in the dessa of *Buddha Kling* (Crawfurd) and in *Gyanyar*, in *Batuan*. These Buddhists, whom no European has ever visited, appear, however, to hold a modified form of religion. Crawfurd remarks that the people of *Boleleng* had

[1] [R. van Eck, in "Bijdragen," III. vol. ii. pp. 3-5.]

spoken rather contemptuously of the Buddhists, but I have not noticed this in the southern part of Bali. It is true they are said to be allowed to eat all kinds of animals, cows for example, which the worshippers of Śiva are forbidden to eat, and dogs and other unclean things, but they are not accused of actually eating them. As for the relations between Śivaism and Buddhism, the Panditas state that Buddha is Śiva's youngest brother, and that the two sects exist peacefully side by side, although the Buddhists do not worship Śiva, and the Śivaites do not adore Buddha. In the form of worship, however, an intermixture of the two religions is apparent, for, on great feasts, *e.g.*, the *Panchâvalikrama*, a priest of Buddha is invited to join the four Panditas of Śiva, and performs his devotions *sitting towards the south*, while the other four throughout the service sit towards the remaining cardinal points, and in the middle. At the cremation of princes, moreover, the holy water from a Śivaitic Pandita is mingled with that of a Pandita of Buddha, and is used in this form by the worshippers of Śiva. The intermixture of the two religions is also shown by the frequent mention of Buddha in the Kavi writings, and by the Buddhist composers of these writings, these works being also held in honour by the Śivaites. This, however, applies more to Java, whence all those writings came, but it is partly applicable to Bali also. So much is certain, that the Buddhists in Bali (and in earlier times in Java) were not fanatics, and that they left the Hindu Pantheon undisturbed, whilst they worshipped Buddha as the only true God.

Śivaites.

The great majority of the Balinese hold the Brahmanical belief, and belong to the sect of Śiva. There is no trace of the other sects (Vishṇuítes) in Bali, and the worship of Śiva has absorbed, as it were, that of all other gods of the Hindu Pantheon. The religion may be divided into the *private worship of the priests* and the *public worship of the people.*

The Domestic Worship of the Priests.

The domestic rites of the Panditas remind us of the ancient Veda-worship of the Indian Brahmans, and in fact owes its origin to it. In old times the Brahmans in India did not worship *the gods of the people;* Brahma, Vishnu or Śiva, and all the rest of the gods connected with them, had no existence for those men—they adored the celestial bodies, especially the *sun,* and *fire (Agni)* and various stars. The domestic worship of the Brahmans in Bali has also the sun for its object, and is called *suryasevana* (worship of the sun); it is performed without temples or idols and with but few offerings. Upon asking what the sun meant, I was told that it was Śiva, and therefore we may presume that the Brahmans no longer hold the ancient faith, and have adopted the ordinary service of Śiva. Śiva, however, has become so idealized, at any rate by the Brahmans, that he may very well be identified with the supreme (solar) deity, and in the popular creed of India Śiva is also the representative of fire, and bears the sun as the third eye in his forehead. We, therefore, adhere to the hypothesis, that *the Brahmans in Bali have preserved the ancient worship of the Indian Brahmans, which is based on the Vedas alone, and takes but little or no notice of the gods of the people*, and that, although they conduct and regulate the worship of the popular gods, they do not themselves take part therein.

I have been permitted to see the domestic devotions of a Padanda. They are performed between nine and eleven o'clock in the morning, on a fasting stomach, and are obligatory at least at full and new moons, in addition to which most Panditas perform them on every fifth day (*Kalivon*, according to the Polynesian week of five days). Especially holy priests, and those of high rank, such as the *Padanda Made Alêng Kachêng* in *Taman Intaran*, observe them daily. On ordinary days, however, the service is not so long as on *Kalivon*, and on this day again it is shorter than at full and new moons. On the latter occasions, too, the priest is arrayed in his full vestments. The place of worship is a *Bale*, in one of the priest's inner courts. The portion of the *Bale** where the ceremony takes place is surrounded on three sides with a lattice-work of bamboo: that of my Padanda was only open to the west. The Padanda is clothed in white, with the upper part of the body naked, after the Balinese-Indian manner. He sits with his face to the east, and has before him a board upon which stand several small vessels containing water and flowers, some grains of rice, a pan with fire, and a bell. He then mumbles, almost inaudibly, some words or prayers from the *Vedas*, dipping the flowers into the water and waving them and a few grains of rice before him (towards the east) with the forefinger and thumb of his right hand, whilst at the same time he holds up the pan containing fire. After having proceeded with his prayers for some time, during which he makes all kinds of motions with his fingers and turns his rosary, he appears to be inspired by the deity; Śiva has, as it were, entered into him; this manifests itself in convulsions of the body, which grow more and more severe, and then gradually cease. The deity having thus entered into him, he no longer sprinkles the water and flowers towards the east alone, but also towards his own body, in order to pay homage to the deity which has passed into it. The bells are not used in the ordinary daily worship, but only at the full and new moons and cremations.

* The names of the *Bale* are: *Yasa, Mahantên, Mahari, Boat;* the holy water is called *Sevamba, i.e., sêiva* and *ambhas,* "water of Siva."

By this ceremony the Padanda is completely purified; all his actions, even the partaking of earthly food, are holy. He then eats (but only once in the day); while he is doing so no one but his children, who wait upon him, may approach, and they keep silence. The remains of his food are like *Amrita* Ambrosia), and are eagerly solicited and consumed by those present—including the princes, if they have a Pandita in their house, or happen to be in his house. The water which the Pandita has used during his devotions is looked upon, in accordance with the *Vedas*, as holy; it is called *toya tirta* (water of a holy place), and is bought by the people for their purifications, for sprinkling corpses and for offerings. This is one of the sources of income to the Panditas. In addition to his domestic worship, he performs the public religious ceremonies (see below), and conducts the cremations and the offerings for the departed. In his own house, moreover, he occupies himself with the *Vedas*, with the sacred and the common Kavi literature; he teaches his children and those (chiefly princes and men of rank) who come to him as pupils. He is also the people's astronomer and astrologer, and alone knows how to regulate the calculation of time according to the different divisions of the year (see the Balinese Calendar). Finally, he consecrates the weapons. Every new weapon to be wrought is brought to him before the operation: he places some mysterious signs upon it, especially the word *Ong* (*om*), and until this has been done, the weapon is of no value or power. When the weapon is quite finished, the owner makes offerings and the Pandita reads the *Vedas* over it to insure its effectiveness.

RELIGION OF THE PEOPLE.—PLACES OF WORSHIP.

The chief places of worship are the *saḍ-kahyangan* (the six temples)—so-called κατ' ἐξοχήν. They are all dedicated, under various names, to Siva. The principal and oldest temple, the founding of which is narrated in the *Usana Bali*, is (1) in *Basuki*, at the foot of the *Gunung-Agung*, the holy mountain in *Karang-Assem*; the name of the deity is *sang Purnajaya*, and his weapon *tuak* (a sword-like creese).

(2). *Vatu Kahu*, in *Tabanan*, at the foot of the peak of *Tabanan*, called *Barattan* or *Vatu Kahu*; the name of the deity is *sang Jayaningrat*, the weapon *panah* (bow).

(3). *Uluvatu*, on the point of the table-land (*bukit*) in *Badong*, picturesquely situated above the sea, over which the rock on which the temple stands projects. This temple is the *prahu* of *Devi Danu*. The deity worshipped here is *sang Manik Kumavang* (the brilliant precious-stone); his weapon is *tumbak* (lance). The access is difficult, through rocks and wild places. The temple can only be approached with the Sovereign.

(4). *Yeh Jeruk* (*Jeruk*-water), in *Gyanyar*, in the interior, in the Kampong of *Narangkana*; the deity is *sang Putra Jaya* (the prince of victory); the weapon *pedang* (sword).

(5). *Giralava*, in *Klongkong*, on the coast; the deity is *Sanging Jaya* (the triumphant one); the weapon is *sambuk* (whip).

(6). *Pakendungan*, in *Tabanan*, on the coast. The name is *sang Manik Kaleba* (*kaleba* = *dumilah*, brilliant); the weapon *duung* (sword-like creese).

These are the principal temples, in which the rulers make offerings for the whole people. In *Uluvatu*, the feast-day is the twenty-first of the Balinese year; in Basuki, on the full moon of the month *Kapat* or *Karttika* (in September or October). A few other places, although of less consequence than those already mentioned, are of special importance.

(1). *Sakennan*, on the island *Serangan*, belonging to *Badong*. The deity worshipped is *sang hyang Indra*; his weapon is the *bajra* (Sanskrit *vajra*), which really means lightning, but according to the drawing corresponds to the so-called thunderbolt. His feast is on the eleventh day after the Balinese new year.

(2). *Jempul*, in *Bangli*, also with *Indra* as its deity.

(3). *Rambot Savi*, in *Jembrana*, near the frontier of *Tabanan*.

(4). *Samantiga*; and (5). Kêntêl *Gumi*, both in *Gyanyar*. It is not known what deities are worshipped in the last three. These places are sacred through the supernatural power which issues from the gods adored there.

We have besides in each *dessa* one or more *Panatarans* (*natar*, a court; the offerings to *Durgâ*, *Kâla* and the *Bhûtas*, are placed upon the ground, in the court). In these *Durgâ*, the wife of the malignant *Kâla*, and the chief of the *Bhûtas* or *Râkshasas* (evil spirits), is worshipped. The worship of these latter occupies the people almost more than that of the beneficent gods, for the pernicious influence of these beings must be guarded against in all sorts of ways, whereas the beneficent gods are more easily propitiated. Other temples are called *Puri* and *Pangastanan*; the former are, principally, for persons of the highest rank, and the latter for the people; here Siva is worshipped with his family. Another name is *Parâryangan*, an assemblage of temples for all the gods and *Pitaras* (the shades of the dead). The small temple-houses are called *Kahyangan*, place for a deity (*Hyang*). To these belong also the *Sadkahyangan*. Finally, there is in every house a number of small temples, called *Sanggar* (in Crawfurd, *Sangga*). Among these there is *Meru*, a temple with several roofs one above the other, rising up in the form of a pyramid, dedicated to Siva. The rest of the small temples are mostly devoted to the service of the *Pitaras*. The house-temples of the princes are of some importance and costliness, but they are not built in the best taste. Among these, besides the *Merus*, which are of wood, we find also the pyramidal erections of stone. *Padmâsana* (the *Padmâsana* must be dedicated to the sun; Siva is the sun), the apex of which is truncated and provided with a sort of stool, upon which incense is burnt to Siva, in his three forms—viz., *Sadâ-Siva*, *Parama-Siva* and *Mahâ-Siva* (the incense being of three sorts: *M'nyan*, *Madyagawu* and *Chandana*); and *Chandi*, a complete pyramid, not truncated. Besides these buildings, one finds several *Bales*, partly of masonry (*G'dong Chantêl*) inlaid with Chinese porcelain and glass-work and ornamented at the back with pictures, and partly of wood (*G'dong Tarik*), upon which the offerings are placed. The *Meru* and *Padmâsana* are chiefly regarded as the seats of the supreme deity; the *Merus* are also provided with *lingas*, which however are, usually, merely of pointed wood and are fixed in great numbers in the roofs. The extremity of the *Merus* and also of the other small temple-houses is generally covered with an inverted pot or sometimes a glass, a circumstance that reminded me at once of Buddhism, since this seems to represent the dome (or *bubble*) which is the distinguishing feature of all Buddhist temples. The Sivaites, however, will not admit this, but they give no explanation of this ornament. The *linga* is also found in great numbers on the walls surrounding the temples, and here is of stone, shaped like the specimen which I have sent from *Boleleng* to the Batavian Genootschap. The original signification of the *linga* is almost lost; the word now means simply "the most excellent one." In addition to the above, we have temples on the sea-coast, dedicated to the god of the sea, *Baruṇa;* and further, small houses in the *sawahs* and on the roads, dedicated to *Srî*, the consort of *Siva;* in the latter the passers-by strew a few grains of rice, if they have any with them.

The Gods Worshipped.

In India, according to the popular belief, Brahmâ, Vishṇu and Siva, or the *Trimûrti* (Trinity), are the supreme gods. It is well known that the Brahmans, originally the first caste, pay but little honour to these gods, and that the *Vedas* place other deities above them—Vishṇu and Siva, indeed, playing a very subordinate part therein. The *popular* creed is further subdivided into two great sects, the one worshipping Vishṇu, and the other Siva, as its principal deity. In India, also, Brahmâ is not made the object of any special worship; as creator he is neutralized, as it were, for his work of creation is accomplished, while the attention of mortals is absorbed by Vishṇu, the *preserver*, and the dreaded Siva, the *destroyer*. It is certain that no Vishṇuites ever came to Bali, nor probably to ancient Java. The only idols in Java which undoubtedly represent Vishṇu are mostly found in conjunction with Siva, and, it would appear, are merely added to make the retinue of the latter god larger and more splendid. It may be safely asserted that Vishṇu has nowhere been the chief object of worship.

In Bali all the characteristics, names and attributes of Vishṇu are given to Śiva; he combines in himself the power of all gods, all others being as it were but other forms of himself. Śiva is the highest invisible firmament (*âkâśa*), or dwells alone in the heart; Brahmâ, *fire, which through smoke becomes water, or Vishṇu*. Hence it is also that a Padaṇḍa is called Śiva; if Śiva were not the all-comprising deity, completely idealized, that designation would not be applicable to these holy men, whose power, through the study of the *Vedas*, is greater than that of the common gods. Śiva's heavens are, the *Meru, Kailâsa, Gunung Agung* (*Svarga* or *Indraloka; Vishṇuloka* or *Brahmaloka*, and *Śivaloka* are the three heavens rising one above the other).

In the Indian mythology we find several gods (*Vishṇu, Durgâ, Gaṇeśa, Skanda*, &c.) provided with many arms, to indicate their power. In Bali, *four arms are given to Śiva alone*, while all the other gods, unless they assume a demoniacal (*Râkshasa*) shape, have but two arms. Śiva also has a third eye in his forehead (signifying in India the sun, but not recognized as doing so here) (*mata trinetra*) His names are: *Parameśvara* (the supreme lord); *Maheśvara* (the great lord); *Mahâdeva* (the great god); *Śrîkanda* (the throat of eloquence?); *Sudasina* (with pure throne); *Givaka* (meaning uncertain); *Sangkara, Garba* (the fœtus); *Soma* (the moon); *Vrekanda* (?); *Kṛittivâsas* (clothed in a tiger-skin); *Garbadûta* (*garbha*, fœtus, and *dûta*, messenger); *Ganggâdara* (he who carries the river *Gangâ* in his hair); *Hara* (he who grasps); *Kâmâri* (the enemy of *Kâma*, the god of love); *Vṛishaketana* (he who has the bull in his standard); *Durjadi*, probably more correctly *Durjaṭi; Triambaka* (he who speaks the three *Vedas*); *Kawandi*, Sarvajña (the omniscient); *Viskandi, Pisnaki; Bâma* (*Vâma*, the left-handed); *Mrêdda, Ugra* (cruel); *Śûli* (he who bears the trident); *Gaṇasara, Gaṇâdipa* (the lord of hosts); *Îśa* (the lord); *Îśâna* (ditto); *Kandali, Matsya-durita* (*matsya*, fish, and *durita*, sin); *Paśupati* (the lord of creatures); *Tripurâri* or *Tripurântaka* (the enemy and destroyer of the demon *Tripura*; also *Vishṇu's* name). *Vṛikshaketu* (he who has a tree in his standard); *Sambu, Śrava*, ear, and *Bava*, nature; *Dara* (the holding one); *Kṛisnarsa, Kuśâdi* (he who has the *Kuśagrass* as his first attribute); *Saddakaripu* (the enemy of the *Saddaka*); *Sima* (*sima*, whole, or *sîma*, boundary); *Prameṣṭi* or *Parameṣṭi* (the highest); *Nandakavahana* (he who rides on the *Nandi*); *Kâmadahana* (he who has burnt the *Kâma*); *Girîśa* (the lord of speech); *Pravesada, Sâli* (domestic?); *Jîvâtma* (the soul of life); *Îśvânukara, Pitambara* (covered with a yellow garment); *Berava* (*Bhairava*, the terrible one, also a subordinate deity in the demon-shape). *Nîlakaṇṭa*, and Nila-lohita (with a dark blue throat, from drinking the poison that comes forth from the troubled sea); *Śani* (*śani*, the name of the planet Saturn, and *sani*, worship); *Îśvara* (the lord); *Dṛiṣṭaketu* (with plainly-visible standard); *Umâpati* (consort of the *Umâ*); *Chaturbuja* (with four arms).

Part of the manuscript of the *Chantaka-Parva* was wanting here, but many more names were mentioned to me from memory. Śiva appears to have in all not less than a thousand names in Bali, as in India. The following are further names: *Bîma* (he who is to be feared); *Rudra* (also a special class of eleven gods of this name); *Bava* (nature); *Kapâlabṛit* (he who wears a skull-chain); and finally *Jagannâta* (the lord of the world). This last name always means Vishṇu in India, but, in Bali, Śiva is the supreme and almost the only god, and thus Vishṇu's principal name is given here to Śiva.

Śiva's Attributes.*

These are different in his various forms and temples. He has the rosary (*guduha genitri*, Sansk. *akshamâlâ*); the *fan* (*ubas-ubas*, Sansk. *châmara*). These two symbols represent him as a penitent. He has further the *triśûla* (the pointed trident, to be distinguished from the trident without points, which, *e.g.*, the *Bagavân Tṛiṇavindu* in the Batavian Society's Collection carries, and which the Balinese call *Tekan*. Both tridents stand with their points upwards; the inverted trident (of *Vishṇu*) I have not yet met with. Śiva also has in Bali, as in Java, the *Padma* (the lotus), which in India belongs to Vishṇu; this, however, is not regarded as the lotus-flower, but as a weapon. We have already mentioned other symbols of Śiva in the *Saḍkahyangan*, namely, *Tuak*, a sword-like creese; *panah*, the bow; *tumbak*, the lance; *p'dang*, a sword; *sambuk*, a whip; and *ḍuung*, a sort of creese. With the exception of the creeses, all these symbols are also Indian, and belong to Śiva in India; the creese, however, is purely Polynesian. The bow and the sword proper are not used in Bali, and which are only known there from the religion and the writings.

From Śiva is to be distinguished *Kâla;* originally they were one and the same, but Śiva is the bright (white) god of light, while Kâla is the dark (black), terrible and destroying one. Kâla is worshipped, with Durgâ and the *Bhûtas*, in the *Panatarans* and in the houses. The feast of *Bayakâla*, the day before

---

* Śiva became incarnate as *Arjuna Vijaya*. His wife, *Devî Yajñavatî*, commits suicide upon hearing a false report of the death of her husband, and at the prayer of the holy *Pulastya* is called to life by *sang hyang Sagara* (the ocean) by means of *Mṛitasanjîvana* (life-giving Ambrosia).

the Balinese new-year, is dedicated to him, and he must be propitiated by bloody offerings. The offerings placed daily before the houses and in the niches of small pillars, or in the walls, are also intended for him and the *Bhûtas*.

Śiva's consort is *Umâ*. This is one of the many names of this deity, but not the principal one in India. In Bali it is used more commonly than *Pârvatî;* she is also called *Giriputrî* (daughter of the mountain; *Pârvatî* has the same meaning). Durgâ is distinct from her, as Kâla is from Śiva. (Durgâ in conflict with Mahishâsura does not appear in Bali.) She is also called *Devî Gangâ* and *Devî Danu* (the goddess of the mountain lake; this great mountain lake lies in the midst of the great Balinese range of mountains) [Us. Bali, p. 274]; in this character she is worshipped on the *Gunung Batur*, which rises from the middle of a mountain lake (*Danu*, Jav. *ranu*), and she is regarded as the cause of eruptions and of the overflowing of the waters which is indispensable for the cultivation of rice. As goddess of the rice-fields she is called *Srî* (in India *Vishṇu's* wife is called *Lakshmî*, who here is also Śiva's wife) and has her temples on the *sawahs* and on the roads between them. She is also worshipped along with Śiva. The same applies to *Gaṇeśa*, who possesses no temples and but few images in Bali. On account of his misshapen form, he is not beloved.

Brahmâ, like Vishṇu, has no special temples; on great festivals, small-temple houses are erected for both deities, when offerings are made to all the gods, but after the festival these are taken down again. The following are other names for Brahmâ: *Chaturmukha* (provided with four faces); *Prajâpati* (the lord of created beings, the creator); *Padmayoni* (born out of a lotus; he is supposed in the Indian Mythology to have come forth out of a lotus which rises to the surface of the sea out of the navel of *Vishṇu* as Nârâyaṇa, resting upon the bottom of the sea). According to the Balinese conceptions, he has only one head; if he is represented with more than one head, with four arms and other extraordinary limbs, he is to be regarded as *Brahmamûrti*, or as a Râkshasa (*mûrti*, the body, form, figure, does not precisely express this idea). The same is true of *Vishṇu* and other gods. Brahmâ, the creator, has been deprived of all his distinguishing features; he has no temples either in India or in Bali, and he is entirely subordinated to Śiva, the supreme deity, and although he appears in the Brahmâṇḍapurâṇa as the creator of the latter, Śiva, when once created, possesses far greater power than Brahmâ the creator. Brahmâ and Vishṇu are looked on in Bali as emanations or forces of Śiva, and as related to each other; Brahmâ represents fire, Vishṇu water; the fire through smoke is changed into water, and so Brahmâ's force passes into that of Vishṇu. Siva himself has the *âkâśa*, the highest firmament, as his element, and he dwells in the hearts of the purified.* (See as to *Sadâ, Parama, Mahâ, Śiva,* Us. Bali, p. 307.) Brahmâ's symbol is the *daṇḍa* (staff); a staff is carried by the Brahmans, if they become Panditas and hence it is that they are called Padaṇḍas "provided with a staff." The *daṇḍa,* however, is also regarded as a weapon, and includes the idea of punitive justice.

Brahmâ's wife is *Sarasvatî,* the goddess of eloquence; she, too, has no special temples, but she has a feast-day in each Balinese year, in the week of *Vatu Gunong,* on the day of *Saneśchara Manis* (Saturday). On this day all the manuscripts are brought into the house-temples and consecrated; the old prince Kassiman brings his in procession to *Gunong rata* (his country residence); a *Pandita* is called upon, and reads the *Vedas* over the manuscripts, whereby their holiness is renewed. At the same time offerings of rice, kwe-kwe, *sirih,* &c., are made to the goddess, and the floor of the temple is sprinkled with holy water. Sarasvatî's names, according to the *Chantaka-Parva,* are: *Bagi* (bhaga, knowledge); *Bâsa* (language); *Giva, Givasa, Veda* (Science); *Vidâyana* (vidyâ, knowledge, *ayana,* road); *Baradi, Yani, Sâstravid* (the learned in writings); *Sudevî* (the good goddess); *Dârî* (the holder); *Sumari, Ganggadari* (she who holds the *gangga*); *Prajñadari* (she who holds learning); *Kastavit, Darjimandari, Nilasiki, Satradana.*

Vishṇu is scarcely worshipped at all in Bali; as god of water less honour is paid to him than to *Baruṇa,* although the latter is a sea-god of inferior rank. The principal temples on the sea-coast are dedicated to Śiva; we have already spoken of the erection of a temple for Vishṇu on festivals. Vishṇu is nevertheless an important personage to the Balinese; in his various incarnations he is the hero of most of the Kavi works; it might be said that *Śiva is the high and invisible, Vishṇu the incarnate god,* who has acquired infinite fame by his deeds on earth, and whose conduct serves as an example for all the actions of princes and people. His names, although better known from the Kavi writings than from religious worship, are as follow: *Nârâyaṇa* (he who floats upon or in the waters); *Sori (Sauri,* also a name for the planet *Saturn); Chakrapâṇi* (he whose hand is armed with the *Chakra); Janârdana* (he who is plagued by men with prayers); *Padmanâbha* (he who has a lotus-navel; see Brahmâ *Padmayoni);* (the holy) *Kêśi; Kesa* (the fine-haired); *Vekuṇṭa (Vâikuṇṭha,* the careless one); *Vistara* (collection?); *Srava* (srava, the ear?) *Indrâvaraja* (the younger brother of Indra); *Govinda* (a name for Kṛisṇa as a *cowherd); Garuḍa-dhvaja* (he who has the *Garuḍa* in his standard); *Keśava* (Kesa); *Puṇḍarîkâksha* (the lotus-eyed); *Kṛisṇa, Pîtâmbara* (with a yellow garment); Śiva also is so named above); *Viśvaksena* (*visvak,* everywhere, *sênâ,* an army; whose army reaches

* *Sadâ-Śiva* (the eternal Śiva) is a well-known name for Śiva in India, not for Brahmâ.

THE ISLAND OF BALI.

everywhere). *Svabû* (self-born); *Sangkhi* (he who has the *Sangkha*, shell-trumpet); *Danavara* (perhaps *Danavâri*, the enemy of the Danavas, the demons); *Hanoksaja* (?), *Vriksa* (this must be *vrisha*, the bull, also a name for Vishṇu); *Kapi* (the ape); *Basudeva* (*Vasudeva*, the father of Krisṇa, literally "the god of riches," or *Vâsudeva*, Krisṇa); *Mâdava* and *Madusûdana* (the conqueror of the demon *Madu*). These names are given in the *Chantakaparva* in *slokas*; with a few slight alterations we obtain pure inflected Sanskrit:—

Visṇu Nârâyaṇa Sori, Chakrapâṇi Janârdanah
Padmanâba Resi Kesah, Vekuṇta Vistara Srawa
Indrâvaraja Hupendrah, Gohvinda Garuḍadvaja
Kesavah Puṇḍarîkâksah, Krisnah Pîtâmbarochatah
Visvaksenah Svabû Sangkhî, Danavara Hanoksajah
Vresah Kapi Basudevah, Mâdava Madusûdana.

Besides these, his *avataras* are well known—viz., *Matsya*, fish; *Varâha*, wild pig; *Kûrma*, tortoise. To these must be added two local ones, not known in India—viz., *Pati Gaja Madda*, founder of the *Karang-Asem* family, and the cock *Silingsing*, the apotheosis of cock-fighting. *Parta* and *Maruta* also are incarnations of Vishṇu, slain by *Râvaṇa*. The following are yet other names for Vishṇu: and *Vâmana* and *Tripurântaka* (the *dwarj* and the *conqueror* of the demon *Tripura*; the latter name we have also found to belong to Siva, and it has reference to the fifth *Avatâra*); *Narasingha*, *man-lion* (in the fourth *Avatâra*); *Râma* (in the seventh *Avatâra*); *Purusottama* (the most excellent of men, with reference to his numerous incarnations). His symbols are, in the first place, the *chakra sudarsana* (the disc, which, being well slung by him, penetrates everything, and returns to him); and then the *sanghka* (the shell-trumpet), the *gadâ* (club), *daṇḍa* (the staff, also belonging to Siva and Brahmâ); the same applies to the *tuak* (a sword-like creese, which in one of the *sadkahyangans*[1] belongs to Siva as a distinguishing symbol). In images of Vishṇu and Brahmâ we also find a circular mark on the forehead; this is a third eye, but appears to point to the Indian *tilaka*, the mark of the sect. No other remembrance, however, of this *tilaka* (which name is unknown here) has been preserved, and the Balinese seem to draw the mark on the foreheads of the gods in accordance with a tradition which is no longer understood, or endeavour to keep secret the origin of this sect-mark, in order that the form of religion, at present existing, may be regarded by every one as the only and true form. According to the statements of the

---

[1] [*I.e.*, the six heavens. Sanskrit linguals are often represented by the corresponding (unaspirated) dentals in Kavi and Balinese; while, on the other hand, Sanskrit dentals frequently pass into linguals in those languages. Thus, *sad* = Sanskrit *shaḍ*; but *daṇḍa*, from which *paḍaṇḍa*, = Sanskrit *daṇḍa*.]

priests, Vishṇu and Brahmâ are invoked in the *Vedas*, and do indeed appear in the Indian *Vedas*, although as gods of a very inferior rank; if they play a higher part in the *Vedas* of Bali, we should again be compelled to entertain some doubts as to the authenticity and originality of these *Vedas*.

Vishṇu's wife is *Srî*. We have already met with Siva's consort under the name Śrî, as protector of the rice-fields and goddess of fertility. According to Indian ideas, this is always Vishṇu's wife; but just as many of the names and attributes of Vishṇu are in Bali given also to Siva, so Śrî, originally the consort of Vishṇu, appears in Bali as one of the names of Śiva's wife. We have already said that Vishṇu and Brahmâ are but other forms of Śiva; and so also their wives belong, as special forces (Śrî, goddess of fertility, of abundance; Sarasvatî, goddess of eloquence and learning), to Śiva, the supreme deity. *Lakṣmî* is unknown as a name for Vishṇu's wife. As Vishṇu's consort, she has no special temples. The mark on her forehead, and on that of Sarasvati, is called *peryasan*, derived probably from *yasas*, Jav. *yasa, fame*, and in that case meaning *excellence*. The signification of this word, however, is not clear; and upon asking whether this were the sectarial mark (*Tilaka*), I was answered in the negative.

We have thus found that the three supreme gods of the popular creed of the Hindus are looked upon as expressions of one and the same force, are worshipped together, and regarded, as it were, as one being. Śiva in the popular belief also is almost the sole god; the inferior gods, with Indra at their head, are his lesser forces. The different names of the gods mean for the ignorant people, it is true, as many different gods, but the priests hold other views.

We will here say a few words respecting Indra and the inferior gods, and will then give an enumeration of the gods, as, according to the *Brahmâṇḍapurâṇa*, they were created.

Indra.—This deity, the prince of the *Devas*, that is, of the subordinate gods, who require the *Amṛita* to keep them alive, and who are often brought into danger and vanquished by doers of penance and giants, has, singularly enough, special temples in Bali. *Sakennan*, in the island of *Serangan* in *Badong*, and *Jempul* in *Bangli*, we have already become acquainted with as such. The explanation of this we think is, that our Śivaitic sect has succeeded in making Vishṇu (and Brahmâ) of little importance, and in causing him to be regarded as a part, an emanation or force of Śiva, but did not find it necessary to deprive of his worship the popular Indra, the example of princes, who is glorified in so many poems. Indra could never be inimical to the consequence of Śiva, and was therefore harmless to the imported Śivaism, and, by allowing him temples, the prejudices of his devotees were perhaps spared from a blow. His temples and attributes are even of considerable importance. He has also the third eye. The following are among his names: *Satakratu* (worshipped with 100 offerings); *Trinetra* (provided with three eyes, like Śiva); *Sahasranetra* (provided with a thousand eyes; these are the stars, Indra himself the visible heavens, while the higher, invisible firmament, *âkâśa*, represents Śiva;) *Devarâja* (the king of the *Devas* or subordinate gods); *Sachîpati*, the husband of *S'achî*.

His weapon is the *bajra* (*vajra*, lightning; here, however, represented as a kind of weapon in the form of a thunderbolt).

Indra's wife is *Sachî*, only remarkable on Indra's account.

The eight gods of the cardinal points (*Lokapâla*) are named very frequently in the writings; in the religious worship they are less prominent. In the *Râmâyaṇa*, lont, 181, these eight gods are enumerated as follows: *Indra, Yama, Sûrya, Chandra, Anila, Kuvera, Baruṇa, Agni*. We meet with the same names again in India, only *Nirriti* appears there instead of *Sûrya*, and *Íśânî* instead of *Chandra*. The order in which they stand, beginning with the east and going round by the south, is however different; and in India is tolerably fixed: *Indra*, in the East; *Agni*, N.E.; *Yama*, S.; *Sûrya* (or *Nirriti*), S.W.; *Varuṇa*, W.; *Vâyu* (or *Marut, Pavana*, and in Bali *Anila*, all meaning *wind*), N.W.; *Kuvera*, N.; *Chandra* (or *Íśânî*), N.E. "Usana Bali," p. 261, gives the eight cardinal points thus: (1) *Pûrva*, East; (2) *Gneha*, S.E.; this is *Âgneya* ("Wilson," "the South-East quarter"), to be derived from *Agni*, fire and the god of fire, whose throne is in the south-east; (3) *Dakṣiṇa*, south; (4) *Neriti* (Sansk. *Nairriti*, belonging to the south-west quarter, to *Nirriti* ; *Nirriti*, according to some, *Sûrya*, according to others, presides over that point of the compass), S.W.; (5) *Paśchima*, behind or west; (6) *Vayabya* (Sansk. *Vâyavya*, belonging to *Vâyu*, the wind, compare *Anila, Pavana*), N.W.; (7) *Uttara*, north; (8) *Esania* (not *Resania*), answering to the Sansk. *âiśanya* or *âiśani*, "belonging to *Íśânî*," N.E. Here, therefore, we have the names of the cardinal points accurately preserved by adjectives derived from the names of the guardian deities; even the less-known *Nirriti* and *Íśânî* are not forgotten. It cannot surprise us, however, that in Bali all the cardinal points are attributed to various forms of Śiva, although this alteration seems to be of later date.

Yama and *Baruṇa* are the only gods besides Indra of any note in the religious worship; they also are, to some extent, identical with Śiva. With Indra in his heaven we find the *Varâpsaras* (the most excellent *Apsaras*), and the *Vidyâdaras* and *Vidyâdarîs* (male and female spirits), as well as the *Resis ;* the last are the human beings who have become gods, after having attained, through a holy life, to Indra's heaven; his heaven is called *Svarga*, or *Indraloka*, and is the ideal of a royal dwelling; the descriptions of it agree with the Indian accounts. Even this heaven and its inhabitants are not safe from the attacks of foes (see the *Viváha*, the combat between Indra and Râvaṇa [the latter is called *Indrajit*, the vanquisher of Indra]; and other myths); its inhabitants are also liable to become human again, at least they require the *Amṛita* in order to preserve their divine power. Indra's heaven lies beneath that of Vishṇu (and Brahmâ), and the latter beneath that of Śiva. It is not until it reaches Śiva's heaven that the soul attains the repose and release of transmigration (*Moksa*). But little is heard in Bali of Vishṇu's heaven; it is known rather from tradition than from religious doctrine. Every man endeavours to reach Śiva's heaven (which is to be sought on the *Kailâsa*, the *Meru*, or the *Gunung Agung*, in Bali, at its highest point); but only a *Paḍaṇḍa* appears to have a right to immediate entry therein. The rest of the people have to be satisfied with *Svarga*, Indra's heaven, where they hope to live for ever, entirely after the Balinese manner of living, but without care and with greater splendour. The attainment of the *Svarga* is in some cases immediate; a *Belâ* or *Satia* who follows her husband into the fire, passes into that heaven at once; a prince, who sacrifices himself and his adherents in defence of his country, goes with all his followers to Indra's heaven, where, probably, they fall again to fighting. Cremations also, if they be accomplished according to rule—which is difficult, as the priests can very easily discover a fault, if they have not been consulted as to all ceremonies, however insignificant—are considered to bring the subject of the cremation to *Svarga*. But this last means of entry is not looked upon as so certain as the two others; the Balinese say of several princes that, although they were burnt with all proper ceremony, they still wander upon earth in the form of animals (frogs, snakes, &c.). Another obstacle is the judicial power of *Yama*, who judges the dead with strict impartiality in the lower world (*Naraka*). Perhaps the postponement of cremations for two months, and sometimes for several years (up to twenty), has reference to this preliminary judgment by *Yama*, and the punishments imposed by him; here, however, as is the case in most religions, there is a palpable inconsistency: it is believed that *the souls of the dead, provided that no outward observances have been neglected, pass immediately into Svarga;* it is at the same time believed that *the soul must first be judged by Yama* (the Indian *Pluto*, and the lord, *Jehovah*, who, according to the Old Testament, will punish Jewish sinners), and must, for all sins, perform penances which will last millions of years, and which hinder them from reaching *Svarga*. *Doceant theologi meliora!*

Baruṇa (Sansk. *Varuṇa*) is the god of the sea; the temples on the sea-coast are dedicated partly to him and partly to Śiva. Vishṇu also is stated to be a sea-god, or god of water (represented in India on this account with the inverted *triśûla*), but he has no temples either in this or in his other capacities. The subordinate *Baruna*, however, for the same reason as Indra, is not erased from the list of the gods who are worshipped. Baruna is sometimes represented as a youth, in the same manner as Indra. He is then distinguished by the *pâśa*. This should really be a sling, with which he catches up the dead bodies, &c., and Yama the souls; in Bali, however, the *pâśa*, contrary to the meaning of the word, is a long dart, round which a serpent winds, and which ends in three teeth (like the triśûla). Baruna has usually a monstrous figure with the head of a *Râksasa*, from which a serpent's tongue projects, and a huge serpent's tail turning upwards, the rest of the body being human. This serpent-form indicates his nature as sea-god. The *deva agun sagara* (*agun* must be *agung;* Crawfurd, On the Island of Bali, " Asiat. Res." vol. xiii{) is the same as Varuna.

Yama, the god of death and of punitive justice, is identified with Śiva (and *Kâla*); he has no special worship, but Śiva is also worshipped under the name of Yama. He is called *sang hyang Darma* (justice); and *Prêtarâja* (the prince of the departed). His severe punishments (*e.g.* the boiling of a soul in a copper kettle for thousands of years) are very well known. He is regarded as a god, not as a *Râksasa*, although he has teeth on his cheeks and his forehead (*dangstra*, comp. *Ganeśa*), and, besides this, the well-known tusks of the *Râksasas* (*siyung* or *chaling*); his symbol is the *gadâ*, club.

The rest of the gods of the cardinal points have, as it were, no worship. *Sûrya* is the same as Śiva, and the worship of the priests is addressed to him; *masuryasevana* (worship of the sun). *Chandra*, the moon, in India an attribute of Śiva, did not become known to me as such in Bali, but all principal feasts are regulated according to the full and new moon. To insure success, all great undertakings (offerings, cremations) must be carried out in the first, or white, half of the moon. *Anila* or *Vâyu* (Bal. *Bayu*) has no worship at all, but is regarded as the vital principle; in fasting (*brata*) the doer of penance shall live by the *vayu* alone. The *vayu* in its various forms come also under notice in the healing of the sick. The physician causes his *vayu* to pass into the sick man's body. The Padandas are, therefore, in great request for curing sick people, because their *vayu* is particularly holy.

Kuvera, the god of riches (Bal. *Kubera*), known only from the myths. Still less is known of *Nirriti* and *Íśânî*. *Agni*, finally, the god of fire, is frequently invoked in the Veda-worship in Bali, as in India, but has no temples, and is not worshipped by the people.

To the family of Śiva, but still as subordinate gods, belong *Ganeśa* and *Kârtikeya* or *Skanda*, his sons. I have not yet become acquainted with the latter in Bali; of Ganeśa (commonly called *Gana*), on the entrances, there are images of stone (Ganeśa images are introduced into Bali by *Kabu Ayu*; compare *Abdullah* in the *T. v. N. I.*, 2, 161 *seq.*) and paintings, all tolerably rude. The stone images are sometimes to be found in the temples of Śiva, and Gaṇeśa then appears publicly as a subordinate, attendant deity, very much resembling the *Rāksasas* that keep watch. Special worship and offerings for him are unknown. In literature, however, Gaṇa is as important in Bali as in India. He is the god of learning and of cunning (also of the *orang dagang* and of thieves). He is called *Gaṇapati*, lord of hosts (he is the leader of the yet inferior gods); *Vināyaka* (the leader, in reference to the same idea); *Sarvāvigna* (from *sarva*, all, and *avigna*, without obstacle—*i.e.*, he who overcomes all obstacles); *Vignakarta* (*vigna*, obstacle, *karta* probably from *kṛit*, to cut, to solve—he who removes all obstacles). In the drawings which are made of him, he holds in his right hand the *pustaka*, a book of lontar leaves as a symbol of learning. Of the rest of his (Indian) attributes, with the exception of the moon, I have seen or heard nothing. He has an elephant's trunk (*tulali*) and elephant tusks (*gading*), and also the *dangstra* (which we have found in Yama), on his cheeks and forehead. It is only in Gaṇeśa and Yama that these misformed parts do not indicate a demoniacal nature; they belong otherwise only to the *Bûtas* and *Rāksasas*, and to gods who by choice assume demoniacal forms. All the rest of Gaṇeśa's body is entirely human, and he has only two arms, the reason of which we have already seen above in Śiva's case. Independently of the preference given to the worship of Śiva, the sole and supreme god, the absence of homage to Gaṇeśa may also be explained by his shape. Everything monstrous is regarded in Bali with a certain repugnance; it is true, the numerous representations of demons conflict with this statement, but then these are the hostile spirits, which are overcome in great measure by the beneficent gods. It is especially remarkable that the form of an elephant is looked upon as unlucky, although I cannot assert that this was always the case. A former prince of *Boleling* kept an elephant and used to ride out upon it; his conduct was universally condemned, and to this is ascribed the fact that this prince was punished by the gods with the loss of his kingdom. The abhorrence of the tiger is more natural; if tigers make their appearance in a kingdom of Bali, it is believed that that kingdom will speedily fall (come under the dominion of the evil spirits).* The rhinoceros, on the contrary, enjoys great honour, although not in life. The *Deva agung* and also the prince of *Lombok* have asked the Netherlands Govern-

---

* In the greater portion of Bali tigers do not occur; they swim over to *Jembrana* from *Banyuwangie*, and remain in that nearly uninhabited district and in the mountains of *Tabanan* and *Boleling*. The high cultivation of the country prevents them from spreading further. Their appearance is a sign that men must depart.

ment for one of these animals for great sacrificial festivals; they use the blood and fat for the preparation of various offerings, and the excrementa as medicine.

Kâma, the god of love, and his wife *Rati*, have, so far as I know, no special temples, but yet are much honoured among this very erotic people. Kâma also is again, as it were, a form of Śiva (see "Us. Bali," p. 275). Other names of Kâma are *sang hyang Smara* (about equal to the Latin *cura*, for "to be in love"); also *Anangga*, the bodiless, for, according to a myth, Śiva has burnt his body; and *Manobu*, born in the heart.

Vasuki, the Indian serpent-king, nearly coincides here with *Ananta* (eternity), or *Antabhoga*, the serpent upon which Vishṇu rests. Vasuki also belongs here to Śiva's retinue; he dwells in the various principal temples in which Śiva is worshipped (in the *sadkahyangans*). After the time of worship in Basuki, at the foot of the *Gunong agung* (which place is named after the same serpent), it is supposed that he goes through the air to *Uluvatu*, the sanctuary on the point of the table-land (in *Badong*), and so round to the other *Kahyangans* as well. He is then to be seen as a fiery streak in the sky. The brightness comes from the precious stones with which his immense head is adorned. Many apparently meaningless fables exist about *Vasuki* (in Bali always called *gasuki*). As yet I have not succeeded in extracting the "sachen aus diesen sagen." I have long thought of a former serpent-worship, especially as a Padaṇḍa is also called *Bujangga* (serpent), and in the "Usana Java," Śiva, Buddha, and *Bujangga* are called sons *Sang* of *Haji* (*adia*, as it seems to me, "the first"), a circumstance which indicates very strongly the existence of three different forms of worship—viz., the purely Śivaitic, the Buddhistic, and the serpent-worship (?). Of purely Indian myths, that of a former destruction of the serpents, in which *Taksaka, Vasuki,* and a third, at the prayer of a penitent, alone were spared, is known in Bali from the books. This sacrifice of serpents (*Sarpayajña*) was accomplished by king *Janamejaya,* the great-grandson of *Arjuna Vijaya* (compare the *Râksasa-Yajña* of *Bagavan Vasista*). The bird of *Vishṇu Garuḍa* is frequently represented in Bali, always in monstrous *Râksasa* shape, with a beak and wings, but at the same time with tusks; in other respects it has a human body. His parents are *Kaśyapa* and *Vinaṭa; Aruṇa* is his brother. The most inferior persons of the Indian mythology, such as *Kinnara, Kimpurusha, Uraga* (serpents), *Detya, Dânava, Piśâcha,* and others, are known in the literature of Bali. For the most part, however, we meet only with the *Gandarvas,* the *Vidyadars,* and *Apsaras,* in Indra's heaven, and the *Detyas* as giants of antiquity; the *Râksasas* and *Bhûtas* (real beings, evil spirits) as enemies of mankind and opponents of the beneficent gods, dreaded, yet always to be propitiated.

In the last-mentioned we clearly recognize the principle occurring in all religions, of a good and an evil supreme power, the conflict between which in the Hindu doctrine, it would seem, is never, and never will be, decided. A union, however, of the two powers is clearly apparent in the fact that *Kâla* and *Durgâ*, the heads of the *Râksasas* and *Bhûtas*, are regarded as no other than Śiva *and his wife,* since the gods possess the power to change the latter into *Râksasas*.

The accounts relating to the *Bhûtas* are confused; there are a great number of names for a few of them—*e.g., buta Vilis, buta Lavehan;** they are also named after the shape which they assume—*e.g., butu hulu asu,* "the buta with a dog's head" (*asu,* Sansk. *śvâ,* dog), *buta hulu lĕmbu,* "the buta with the head of a cow." A collective Balinese name is *dagan;* their haunts are chiefly burial-grounds and unclean places, and at night they break into the houses which are not protected from them by means of offerings. With the people in general the *Liaks*[1] are still more common than the Bhutas. The former are human beings, who, by the knowledge of certain *mantras* (magic formularies), can alter their shapes and also render themselves invisible, a bright light, proceeding from the place of the tongue, alone remaining; they are obliged to feed on carcasses, and chiefly haunt burial-grounds and the places where corpses are kept for cremation. They also take out the entrails of sleepers, so that the person thus robbed must die in a short time. Their mistress is *Rangda ning Gira,* the widow of *Gira,* whose history is found in the *Chalon-Arang* (a *Babad*); she lives on the *Gunung agung,* where the Liaks hold their assemblies. Fire-flies, which are very numerous and of large size in Bali, are sometimes said to be Liaks; moreover, the accusation of being a Liak often affords reasons for declaring a person to be innocent.

The Creation.

According to the *Brahmâṇḍapurâna,* where the world is created from an egg (*aṇḍa*), four beings come first into existence, through the penance performed by Brahmâ; two of these are *Sânanda* and *Sanatkumâra,* and the other two are not named. Then the heavens, the rivers, the sea, the mountains, plants, shrubs, time, &c., come into existence. He (Brahmâ) further creates the *Devarshi* (the divine *Ṛishis*), *Marîchi, Bṛigu, Anggira, Pulastya, Pulaha, Kratu, Daksha, Atri, Vasishṭha*. It is not till he has done this that he creates the *Parameśvara,* the Supreme Lord, a name for Śiva; the latter is at once regarded as Brahmâ's grandfather! He is called *Bava,* nature; *Sarva,* all; *Iśa,* lord; *Bîma,* the terrible one; *Mahâdeva,* the great god. His body

---

* Also *Klika,* servant of *Durgâ* (in India *Kâlikâ* is another name for Durgâ). Klika was probably originally the same person as Durgâ.

[1] [Wilken, l. l. p. 22; and R. van Eck, "Balineesch Woordenbock," *s. v. lejak.*]

consists (1) of *Âditya-Śarîra*, sun-body; (2) *Veśarîra*, water-body; (3) *Bâyuśarîra;* (4) *Agniśarîra*, fire-body; (5) *Âkâśa*, the higher invisible heaven; (6) *Mahâpandita*, the great Pandita; (7) *Chandra*, the moon; (8) *Batara Guru*, the teacher. He is therefore called *Ashtatanu*, with eight bodies. He must be worshipped through the *Sâdhaka*, the full priest, or the performer of the ceremonies. *Kalpa*, form, and *Dharma*, justice, are children of Brahmâ, sprung from his spirit. It is stated here from which parts of the body of Brahmâ the *Devarshis* came forth.

The lord then created the *gods* (*Devas*), the *Asuras* (evil spirits), the *Pitris* (shades), and man. He also creates out of his own body the *Yaksha*, a sort of demon; *Piśâcha*, lemures; *Uraga*, the serpents which are worshipped; *Gandharva*, heavenly musicians; *Apsaras*, the heavenly female dancers; *Gana*, the hosts, whose leader is Ganapati; *Kinnara*, elves; *Râkshasa*, demons; and, finally, the animals, *paśu*.

Then the four castes are created: the *Brâhmans*, out of Brahmâ's mouth; the *Kshatriyas*, out of his arm; the *Veśyas* (*Vaiśyas*), out of his thigh; and the *Śûdras*, out of his foot. Then *Dharma* (the Dharma already mentioned above), and *Ahingsâ* (husband and wife), *justice* and *the sparing of everything that is alive;* these are the two principal virtues of the Buddhists. It appears, therefore, that in the ancient combination of Brahmanism and Buddhism in Java, Buddhistic doctrines crept even into the *Brahmândapurâna*. I cannot say for certain, however, whether these are not found in the Indian *Brahmândapurâna* as well, this work being hitherto but little known to Europeans. (There are many repetitions in the manuscript.) Then *Svayambhuva Manu*, ("the first *Manu*,"—the Manus govern the world during a certain period, *kalpa*, "from the one creation to the other") and *batâri Śatarûpa* are created; they beget the *batâri Rati*, the wife of *Kâma*, the god of love. Then follows the genealogy of the race of *Svayambhuva Manu* and their relationships with the nine *Devarsis*. The descendants include twelve *Yamas*, and *Lakshmî* (in India, Vishnu's wife). Buddha is the son of *Buddhi*, the understanding. The rest of this race are attributes of nature, of the mind, the heart, and also the body. *Nilalohita* (Śiva) has a thousand children, the *Sahasra Rudra*. *Śrî* is the daughter of the *Devarshi Brigu*, married to Vishnu; their children are *Bala* and *Buddana*. *Sarasvatî* is the wife of *Pûrnamâsa*, the full moon. *Agni* is the son of *bagavân Anggira* and *Smriti*, tradition; among his descendants is *Parjanya*, the god of rain. The holy *Pulaha* is the ancestor of the *Kshatriya Dahâ*, the warrior-caste of *Daha* or *Kediri;* this royal family, represented in Java in *Majapahit*, and in Bali in the race of the *Deva Agung*, thus derives its origin from a *Devarshi*, and ought properly to belong to the Brahman caste. They are the grandchildren of *Kâmyâ* and *Priyabrata*.

The 60,000 Bâlakhilyas, who are all Brahmachâri—*i.e.*, students of the Vedas (compare the 60,000 *Sagarides* in the *Bâlakânda* of the Indian *Râmâyana*), are children of *Kratu* and *Sannati*. Besides a great number of other mythological personages who do not appear in the religious worship, but are sacred to the Brahmans, we find here the seven *Rishis*, who existed in the time of *Uttama Manu*, the second successor of *Svâyambhuva Manu;* they are *Râja, Batra* (Badra), *Urddabâhu, Lawana, Anaya, Satapa,* and *Saka,* and are descended from the *Devarshi Vasishtha*.

We give here a few examples from the original:

Agre sasarjja bhagavân mânasam âtmanah samam.

"In the beginning the holy one created the soul, which was like unto himself." This is explained thus: mayoga batâra Brahmâ m'tu tang Resi patang siki sang Nandana Sanatkumâra. "*Batâra Brahmâ* held the *yoga* (was sunk in meditation), thereby originated the *Resis*, four in number: *sang Nandana* and *Sanatkumâra*." The other two are not named; according to the Indian tradition, however, *Sânanda* (*sic*) and *Sanatkumâra* are two of the four first-born sons of Brahmâ. It still remains to be investigated whether the sons of Brahmâ are representatives of the (world-) soul, which, with the means at present at my disposal, I am not in a position to do.

Tatwasrijat punah Brahma.

"After that Brahma created again." Here follows in the Balinese commentary the creation of Śiva, and an enumeration of his different characteristics and bodies. *This, then, appears to be an interpolation into the original work;* the Sanskrit text says nothing about it, and this creation is certainly not in its proper place. *But with a sect such as that in Bali, Śiva could not be created later on without losing importance;* therefore advantage was taken of the Sanskrit words, which scarcely any one understood, to glorify Śiva by means of an incorrect commentary. *Tatwa* has been formed here out of *tato-asrijat;* the *a* has not been elided, but has been altered with the preceding *o* into *wa;* in the Sanskrit the word should be *tato-srijat*. This *Tatwa* occurs again in the next half-śloka, but there it can only be explained by *tathâ* "so," "in the same manner."

Tatwa devâsurapitrîn manushyako-srijat prabhu.

"So also the Lord created the gods (*Deva*), the *Asuras*, the *Pitaras*, mankind."

In *Manushyako* (see above) there must be an error; mânusyaka is a "multitude of men," but this does not suit either the sense or the metre in this passage; had it to be brought into the metre, it would be *manushyakam asrijat prabhuh*, which gives a syllable too many; moreover the *t'dung* (the sign of the long â) is wanting in the manuscript. We have altered the Sanskrit text into *manush-yânścha* "and the men (mankind)," which agrees admirably with the sense, and leaves the metre undisturbed. Our passage is reproduced in the Balinese commentary thus:

Muwah mayoga baṭâra Brahma, mijil sang deva sura pitrê manusâ, tuhun sangkanika mijil saking manah hikang deva, ring lambung sangkaning pitrê, ring pasva sangkaning manusa, jagana sangkaning Asura.

"And further was *baṭâra* Brahma sunk in meditation; thereby came into existence the *Devas, Asuras, Pitaras,* and mankind; the place whence they sprung (out of his body) was: the *Devas* came forth out of his mind (manas); the *Pitaras* out of the hollow under his arm; man out of his side (for *pasva* we must read *parśwa*); his thigh was the place whence the *Asuras* came forth."

The time also when they came into existence is stated, and this certainly has an astronomical meaning, since in India also the *Devas* and *Asuras* play an important part in astronomy (see Bentley on the Indian Astronomy). The *Asuras* are born at *noon*, *man* in the *morning*, the *Devas* at *midnight*, and the *Pitâ-Pitarah* (the worshipped shades of the departed) in the *evening*.

We will add a brief sketch of the survey of the world as it appears in the *Brahmâṇḍapurâṇa*.

The world is divided into seven *Dvîpas* (islands): *Pushkara-dvîpa* (the lotus-island), *Kronchadvîpa, Kuśadvîpa, Sangkadvîpa* (Skt. *Sâkadvîpa*), *Sâlmalidvîpa, Plakshadvîpa, Jambudvîpa*. The last, the island of the *Jambu*-fruit, is India and the adjoining countries. All these islands are surrounded by the ocean, and lie round about *Meru*, the centre of the earth, like lotus-leaves. The islands are under the rule of the grandsons of *Svâyambhuva Manu*, the first of the seven *Manus*, who govern the earth for the space of a *kalpa*, a long period of time (see below). They are named *Savana, Jutiman, Vapushmanta, Medhâtithi, Gomeda, Avya* and *Agnîdhra*. The last rules over *Jambudvîpa. Jambudvîpa* itself is divided into nine *varshas*, more or less distant from *Meru*, which is sometimes to be regarded as the North Pole, and sometimes as the centre of the earth; great ranges of mountains, mostly fabulous, divide these *varshas* from each other. The children of *Agnîdhra* are (1) *Nabi*, (2) *Kimpurusha*, (3) *Harivarsha*, (4) *Ilâvṛita*, (5) *Ramyaka*, (6) *Hiraṇyaka*, (7) *Kuru*, (8) *Bhadra*, (9) *Ketumâla*. Most of these nine also give their names to the *varshas*, over which they preside. (1) The land (the *varsha*) of *Nabi* is to the south of the *Himavân* (*Himâlaya*); this is therefore India proper. (2) Between *Himavân* and *Hemakûṭa* (the golden peak) is *Kinnaravarsha*, under the prince *Kimpurusha*. The *Kinnaras* or *Kimpurushas* (literally "what sort of man") are barbarous nations in the north of India, represented with horses' heads; they are a sort of centaur, and indicate the nomadic equestrian nations of the north (in *Tartary*). The *Hemakûṭa* is a mountain range to the north of the Himâlayas, in Tibet; it is not loftier than the Himâlayas, but is represented as being so. In this range also is the fabulous Kailâsa, Śiva's seat. (3) *Naishadavarsha ; Naishadha* is a range of mountains to the east of *Hemakûṭa* and south of *Ilâvṛita*. A country in the south-east of India also bears the name of *Nishadha*, well known through its prince *Nala* (*Naishadha*, in the *Mahâbhârata*—the episode is published by Bopp). Here, however, we have to do with the northern *Nishadha*, of which *Harivarsha* is prince. (4) *Ilâvṛita* (or Hilâvṛita) the name of prince, country, and mountain range. This is the highest and most central range on the earth, according to Indian ideas; *Meru*, the highest mountain and the seat of the gods, is situated in it. (5) The region north of *Ilâvṛita* and *Nîlaparvata*, called *Ramyaka* or *Nîlavarsha*. *Nîlaparvata*, the blue mountains, are as mysterious as *Ilâvṛita* with *Meru*; we do not find either in the position indicated by the Indians, but we may perhaps suppose the Aryans (*Ârya*, the Indian), who descended to the plains of India from the mountainous regions of the north-west, to have brought with them some knowledge of the ranges (Altai, Caucasus) of northern and western Asia. (6) *Hiraṇyakavarsha* to the north of *Svetaparvata*, the white mountains, northwards of *Nîlaparvata*. (7) *Kuruvarsha* to the north of the *Śṛingavân* range; this is the *Uttara-Kuru*, the most northern and the coldest land, but the land whence the Aryans appear originally to have come. According to the Zendmyth, it was in ancient times a fertile, inhabitable land, and was changed into a cold wilderness by *Ahriman* (the evil spirit). In this may, perhaps, be recognized a trace of a remembrance of the changes which have taken place in the climates of our earth, such as that to which the fossil bones found in Siberia bear witness. (8) *Bhadravarsha*, to the west of the *Mâlyavân* (the flowery mountain), which itself lies to the east of the *Meru*. *Bhadravarsha* is thus by the side and to the eastward of the great chains of mountains. (9) *Ketumâla* dwells to the east of mount *Gandamâdana* (delightful to the smell). This is the country lying to the west of the other *Varshas* (Persia?). We, therefore, have (1) India proper, as far as the Himâlayas; (2) the region between the Himâlayas and *Hemakûṭa* (Tibet); (3) the region between *Hemakûṭa* and *Ilâvṛita* (with *Meru*); in our enumeration this is No. 4 (Tartary, Mongolia?); (4) the region to the north of *Nîlaparvata*, north-east of the *Meru* (Eastern Mongolia, Manchuria?); (5) the region to the north of *Svetaparvata*, north of the previous country (Eastern Siberia?); (6) *Uttara-Kuru* (northern and western Siberia to the Arctic Ocean). These six form almost a continuous series from south to north, with the *Meru* as a centre. Then come to the east *Nîlavarsha* (China?) and *Bhadravarsha*, and to the west *Ketumâlavarsha* (Persia and the western regions). Concerning the rest of the *varshas* nothing further is mentioned; the narrative proceeds to enumerate the princes who ruled in India proper, descendants of *Nabi*, the eldest son of *Agnîdhra*. *Nabi* is an Emperor, the universal ruler; he is also a *Kshatriya*. From *Nabi* and his wife *Manudevî* are descended successively (1) *Rishaba*, (2) *Bharata*, who dwells south of the *Himavân* in *Bharatavarsha*, (3) *Sumati*, (4) *Tejasa*, (5) *Indradyumna*, (6) *Parameshthi*, (7) *Pratihara*, (8) *Pratiharsha*, (9) *Unnata*, (10) *Bhava*, (11) *Mudgita*, (12) *Prasastavi*, (13) *Vibhu*, (14) *Prithu*, (15) *Nakta*, (16) *Gaja*, (17) *Jara*, (18) *Virât*, (19) *Dîman*, (20) *Mahan*, (21) *Bochara*, (22) *Toshta* (*Tushta*), (23) *Viraja*, (24) *Raja*, (25) *Tus* (!). These are the *Kshatriyas* (princes) in the second great period of the world's existence, *Tretâyuga*. Several of these names are those of the *Jaina* deities; the *Jainas* are disguised Buddhists, who still exist in India. These names give us a hint towards the comprehension of Buddhism in Java. Were the Buddhists of Java *Jainas;* and have we to attribute to that sect the union of the Buddhistic and Sivaitic religions and doctrines in Java and Bali? The *Jainas* at any rate worship the Brahmanical gods besides the *Jinas*, and have even retained the institution of the castes in order to protect themselves from the persecutions of the followers of Brahma.

Under *Svayambhuva Manu* there are further eleven *Rudras* (see the feast of *Ekadasarudra*), twelve *Âdityas* (the twelve solar months), eight *Basus* (Sanskrit *Vasu* or *Vasudeva*), twelve *Sadhyas*, ten *Visvadevas*, two *Sanggis* (?), twelve *Bârgawas*. And further there are the *Devas, Asuras, Gandharvas, Yakshas, Pisâchas, Râkshasas;* these are immortal, it is true, but yet are born again. Their lifetime and that of man varies according to the different *yugas* (*Satya*, or *Krita-, Tretâ-, Dvâpara-, Kaliyuga*), and gradually decreases. In the *Tretâyuga* man attains the age of 188 years, at the close of the *Tretâyuga* 147, in the *Dvâparayuga* 126, at the close of the same 105, and in the *Kaliyuga* only 84. The lifetimes of the inferior gods differ in the same proportion. The *angulas* (inches) are given as the measure of time, but at present I am without any explanation of their astronomical meaning. Hereupon the work speaks of the *Manvantaras*, the periods of time in which a *Manu* governs; these are also called *kalpa*, and they contain seven *chaturyugas;* according to the work this appears to be the time of one *Manu*, but the latter is really but one *chaturyuga* (a combination of the four *Yugas*, a *Kalpa*); there are, however, seven *Manus*, and the seven *chaturyugas* are, in fact, the time of the duration of the world. After each *kalpa* or *chaturyuga* the world is destroyed and created again.

Here follows a description of Chaos. *Manu* alone was in existence. He (not Brahma) then creates a series of beings; *Deva, Rishi, Asura, Pitri, Manusha, Bhûta, Pisâcha, Gandharva*,

Yaksha, and *Rákshasa*. Manu is called here *Sumantia* (?) and *sang Sista* (the instructor) He instructs* the beings who through his penance have come into existence, in the *Sadáchára* (the right conduct); this consists of *lobhádeya* (*lobha*, "greedy desire," sensuality, covetousness, and *ádeya*, probably from *ádá*, sumere, tollere; thus "the putting away of greedy desire")[1]; *kshamá* (patience), *satya* (truth, truthfulness), *vidyá* (knowledge), *ijyá* (the making of offerings), *dána* (alms-giving). The attributes of the *Sadáchára* are seven in number (*Saptakáni charitráni*).

The stages in the life of a Brahman are also given: (1) *Brahmachárí*, he who lives as a pupil with his *Guru*; (2) *Grihastha*, the head of a family, the married man, whose duty it is to exercise the *dharma* (right); this consists principally in rearing a son, who must make offerings for his forefathers (*Pitarah*), and in hospitality; (3) *Vaikhánasa*, the hermit in the forest-hermitages (áśrama); (4) *Yatí*, an ascetic, who has brought into subjection all that is sensuous, and only occupies himself with *yoga* (meditation). They are also called in India *Sannyásí*, and are saints. The *Yatí* is further called *Sádhaka*; this word, which is also used as a title of the *Padandas*, is not found in Wilson; but *Sádhana* means, among other things, *accomplishment*, and *good works*, or the moral doctrine and the ceremonies of the Hindu religion, as a means for attaining purity and release from the transmigration of the soul. *Sádhaka*, then, is "some one who performs these good works." In our work the name *Sádhaka* is explained as "he who exercises the *áśramadharma* (the right or custom of the hermits)." We have, moreover, explanations of *Dharma* and *Adharma* (right and wrong). Further, *Śruti* (revelation) and *Smriti* (tradition) are mentioned. The former is like *Dharmaśástra* (the book of instruction in right), and is said to be *dhírágnihotravíjya* (*víjya*, derived, beginning from; *dhíra*, *agni*, *hotra*, the maintenance of a continual fire); it thus has reference also to the fire-worship. The *smriti* is the *varṇáśrama-áchára* (*varṇáśrama* is here perhaps an error for *vanáśrama*, forest-hermitage); thus "the mode of life, the example of the forest-hermitages." To these hermitages the ancient tradition was handed down. The seven *Rishis* shall teach the *Dharmadvaya* (the double right; *Dharma* and *Adharma* (?) or rather *Śruti* and *Smriti*) on the earth in the time of *Púrva Manu* (= *Svayambhuva*?). The *Dharmadvaya* is the contents of the *Chaturveda* (the four Vedas), according to which the *Sádhu* (the good man) regulates his life. It contains also the *Daṇḍanîti* (the regulation of punishments), the *Trayí* (the three Vedas without the *Atharvaveda*; we had just now all four Vedas, but these inaccuracies often recur), and the *Varṇáśrama* (here also *varṇa* takes the place of *vana*). Does *varṇa* perchance convey the idea of a caste? and

---

* He is here the *Guru*; the deity (Śiva) appears in Java and Bali chiefly in this character. [1] [?].

the *varṇāśrama* mean the regulation of the life (the four periods) of all castes?[1] In general the passage before us speaks only of the Brahmans.

The word *Śruti* is explained by: "ri denian kinatuturan," *because she is learned, she is called Śruti*. *Smṛiti*, makanimitta ri kangên-angênira matangian Smṛiti ngarania, *on account of her amiableness she is named Smṛiti*. The name *Smara* (love, the god of love) and a signification of the root *smṛi*, "desiderare, to desire, to like," have obviously led to the latter explanation.

The characteristics of the *Satya-Brahmachâri* (of the true Brahman pupils) are: *Tapah* (penance), *Mona* (Sanskrit *mâuna*, to be silent), *Yajna* (to make offerings), *Dâya* (the receiving of alms), *Kshamâ* (patience), *Alobha* (freedom from desire), *Dama* (subjugation, *i.e.*, of sins), *Sama* (repose of the soul), *Jitâtmâ* (victory over the *âtmâ*, the passions), *Dâna* (almsgiving), *Anamah* (not to greet; this is forbidden to the Brahmans, because they would lower themselves by bowing their heads, &c.), *Advesha* (freedom from hate), *Arâga* (freedom from affections). He is *virakta* (freed from sensuousness), *tyâga* (relinquishes all earthly power and gives them away), *vijnâna* (knows the differences, has things to discriminate, or shrewdness). These characteristics are called *dharmapratyangalakshaṇa*, the names (or signs) of the organs of the *Dharma*.

Iti-uktang tatvancha sarvang, dharmapratyangalakshaṇang.

So is the whole *Tatva* (dogma) related, which contains the names of the organs of the *Dharma*.

This is not the place to speak more fully of the contents of the *Brahmâṇḍapurâna*; it is to be hoped that in a short time they may be fully worked out. We will conclude with a note on the contents of the Vedas.

The *three Vedas* (here also the fourth is not mentioned), *Ṛig*, *Yajuh*, and *Sâma*, contain four *Stotras* (*stotra* is praise), namely, (1) *Dravya-* (Wilson, "elementary substance;" there are nine kinds); (2) *Guṇa-* (the three qualities which penetrate all beings, viz., *Satva*, reality, truth; *Rajas*, passion; *Tamas*, darkness, ignorance, badness); (3) *Karma-* (the works, actions, the practical part, the offerings); (4) *Bijana-Stotra* (this must be *abhijana*, "family, race" (Wilson). It is thus the genealogical part).[2]

RELIGIOUS CEREMONIES AND OFFERINGS.

The five daily offerings which the head (*gṛihastha*) of every Indian family has to make, are not found in Bali. The Paṇḍitas read (or mumble) the Vedas once a day; the people make their offerings and say their prayers on certain days. The religious

[1] [The duties concerning the castes and stages of life are meant.]
[2] [Probably meant for *vijnâna*, discernment, or the intellectual part.]

ceremony consists in bringing offerings, which are offered with a *sembah* and deposited in front of the small temple-houses; in the ordinary temples this is mostly done by women, to whom is also entrusted the preparation of the various offerings. The act of offering is connected with *mantras* (forms of prayer), which, however, are not said aloud. On great feasts the offerings are presented by "*tandakking*" persons inspired by a deity, *wawalen* or *prakulit* (see "Us. Bali," p. 335, *balian = wawalen*). These offerings are coupled with "*tandakking*"[1] with the creese, which indicates that the offerer is ready to offer up his life. The offerings are very numerous, and are specially appointed for each feast and each deity; one usually sees various preparations of rice, cooked meats, fruits, sirih, kwekwe, money (Chinese "cash"), clothes, and also drinks.

Bloody sacrifices are made to *Durgâ* and the Bûtas; they are usually confined to hens, ducks, and young pigs, although in great sacrifices, buffaloes, goats, deer and dogs are slaughtered. The persons offering the sacrifice eat the flesh of the three first-mentioned animals, and only offer the skin and bones and portions of the flesh, boiled or roasted; they also dress the flesh of the dogs (*sasate*), but, according to their own statements, they do not eat any of this, the whole animal being intended for the *Bûtas*. On the feast of *Bayakala* every family kills a pig, and the skin and blood are deposited in the courtyards of the houses for *Kâla* and the *Bûtas*.[2] The flesh, however, is in this case also used as food by the persons making the offering. Besides these offerings the temple is sprinkled with holy water (*toya tîrta*). This water is bought from the Panditas, who consecrate it by reading the Vedas. The persons offering also use this holy water to purify themselves, to rinse their mouths and to sprinkle their faces. We have in Bali, it is true, the *toya Sindu* (water of the Indus), at the foot of the *Gunung agung* in Basuki, and also a *Gangga* in *Tabanan*, but the priests do not regard this water as holy. They know that these rivers are in *Kling* (India), and that they cannot obtain the water thence, but this want is supplied by mumbling the Vedas. Besides the *Gangga* and *Sindu*, all the great Indian rivers are known in Bali: the *Yamunâ*, *Narmadâ* (*Nerbudda*), *Kâverî* (near *Seringapatam*), the *Sarayû*, the river of *Ayodyâ* (*Oude*), and others. The holy water produced by the Panditas is called *Mṛita* or *Amṛita* (*Ambrosia*, immortal, life-giving food). This water has *Kuśa*-grass soaked in it. The Padanda also strews *Kuśa*-grass soaked in holy water over the persons who make the offerings. The *Kuśa*-(or *Darba-*)grass is also used to lay the offerings upon. *Ghṛita* (*Ghee*) is likewise known here, but, for want of milk, is made of gooseberries. The Panditas, however, also use sometimes the milk of cows to prepare this; it ought

---

[1] [*I.e.*, dancing with gesticulation.]   [2] [Sanskrit *bhûtas*.]

really to be made of the milk of a *lembu putih*, a white cow with a hump; these animals are sacred; the common Balinese cow is not sacred, although it may not be eaten by the faithful. In *Badong* the Balinese are forbidden to kill cows, although it is done secretly, but in other States they are slaughtered openly. In order to be able to use the milk of these Balinese cows for *Ghṛita*, the beast is tied up for a fortnight, and is given nothing but *Kuśa*-grass to eat; this food renders the milk sacred, and especially purifies it from the smell of musk which the Balinese cows have. *Tila*-grass is also used, but is not known to the ordinary Balinese (see a passage in the *Râmâyaṇa*). *Madhu* (honey) also occurs in the offerings, and likewise perfumes, such as *m'nyân, maja gawu*, and *chandana* (see "Us. Bali").

The bloody sacrifices, as we have said, are chiefly dedicated to Kâla, Durgâ and the Bûtas, seldom to Śiva. In India Śiva demands blood almost entirely, but in Bali, as supreme deity, he has taken rather the mild form of Vishṇu (and Buddha). The offerings, which on great feasts are numerous and of some value, do not remain in the temples, nor are they all given to the priests. The Padandas who conduct the service receive part of the clothes and money, and the offerings of eatable things, after being presented, are taken back with prayers and eaten at home as *Amṛita*, life-giving food, by the persons presenting the offering.

The Panditas besides this receive considerable sums of money for cremations and for being present at the offerings made by the princes; this money is presented to them as an offering itself (this also characterizes the Panditas as a kind of god upon earth). Most of the Padandas return a large portion of the offering made to them. The Panditas do not take any active part in the offerings; they indicate from their books, before the ceremony takes place, all the usages to be observed—the quantity and preparation of the offerings, and the way in which they are to be presented; but during the ceremony they sit motionless, as they do in the domestic worship, mumbling the Vedas. By mumbling the Vedas they draw the attention of the gods to the offerings made by man, and cause the gods to look graciously upon them. The place where the Pandita sits is a high framework of bamboo, under a roof, and he has all the utensils for the *Sûryasevana* by his side. To the form of worship belongs also the *Pradakshiṇâ*, the marching round the temple towards the right hand, which is done three times; it is only performed by the Panditas in the spirit, while their bodies remain all the time motionless. I have not yet observed this custom at offerings either, and it seems not to have penetrated to the popular worship of Bali, the *Polynesian tandakking** appearing to have taken its place, while the priests

---

* *Taṇḍak*, however, appears to be an Indian word; *taṇḍu* is one of Śiva's doorkeepers, and *master of dancing and mimicry; tandaka* is a *juggler; tâṇḍava* "dancing with violent gesticulation," as executed by Śiva and his followers.

have retained a remembrance of the original form of worship with *Pradakshiṇā*.

DRESS OF THE PANDITAS.

At the great festivals of the princes, at the cremation of persons of high rank, and at the domestic worship on full and new moon, the Padanda has a special dress, very much resembling the articles with which the Javanese idols are adorned. They are clothed in the ordinary Balinese manner, the upper part of the body being naked (see the idols of the Bataviaasch Genootschap van Kunsten en Wetenschappen); the garment which hangs from the hips is on these occasions *white*. On his head he wears a *red cap*, which, however, may also be *white;* this is called *Jatâ* (see the catalogue of Indian Antiquities, p. xxv.); *Jatâ* is otherwise the head-dress of Śivaites, but not a covering for the head. This *jatâ* has some resemblance to the head-dress of *Bagawan Trinawindu* (No. 145), and still more to the *Glung Kurung* of the Balinese representations of Śiva. It is wider at the top than at the bottom, and goes down lower at the back of the head than in front. I counted thirteen annular divisions, formed from the bottom upwards by narrow stripes of gold, which run round the flannel covering of the top. Upon asking whether these divisions and the number of divisions had any meaning, I was answered in the negative; but nevertheless I am disposed to believe that they have some connection with those which I have observed in the *Merus* (see above) in the temples. In the *Merus* I have never as yet counted more than eleven roofs; can it be that the Panditas assume still greater sanctity by having a greater number of storeys in their *Jatâ*, which I venture to regard as a kind of *Meru?* This, added to their name (Śiva), does not seem altogether improbable; their own *Meru*, the *Meru* of the Brahmans as it were, would then be higher than that of the gods adored by the people.

Along the edge of the *Jatâ*, across the forehead, runs a band, called in Bali *Keśâbharaṇa*, ornament of the hair, and in India *Mukuṭa;* it is covered with gold, and ornamented at short distances with *Sûryakântas** (according to Balinese ideas a sort of precious stone). In the centre of this *Keśâbharaṇa*, over the forehead, there is a *Linga*, in the form usual in Bali, and of crystal (or glass). At the extremity of the *Jatâ* there is a ball, supporting a *Linga* (ball and *Linga* being of the same material as

---

* *Sûryakânta* (beloved by the sun), a precious stone, often meaning crystal, but really said to have proceeded from the rays of the sun. The Balinese *Sûryakânta* are of crystal or glass, and will be formed of *pusakas* of *Majapahit*. The fact that this precious stone is used for the *Sûryasevana*—*i.e.*, the worship of the sun—is a further indication of the importance of this heavenly body. Another precious stone of fabulous origin is the *Chandrakânta*, proceeding from the condensed rays of the moon.

above). The fact that we here find the ball ornamented with the *Linga* is perhaps again a sign of the intermixture of Buddhism and Śivaism, in which, however, the Śivaitic symbol has the upper place. The Pandita wears in his ears the *Kuṇḍala;* these are shaped like an egg, and are attached to the ear by a gold ring; it is sometimes of crystal.

For nearly all the remaining articles of his attire the name *âbharaṇa* is used, whereas in India each article has its particular name. We must not confound *Karṇâbharaṇa* (ear-ornaments) with the earrings; they are fastened behind the ear. *tmâbharaṇa* (ornaments of the *âtmâ*, the soul or the breath), a short band, worn round the neck, and on the breast on each side, with gold clasps of considerable size. *Vâyubharaṇa* (ornaments of the wind; *vâyu*, the wind, is the vital principle; the form *vâyubharaṇa* is incorrect, and should be *vâyvâbharaṇa*). These are double; they are worn round the neck, and are longer and fall lower down on the breast than the *Âtmâbharaṇa*. *Hastâbharaṇa*, as the name indicates, are worn round the wrists.

The *guduha* (or *guduha genitri*) is a kind of *rosary;* we find it in several of the Javanese idols; it is called in India *akshamâlâ* (string of beads). The name *guduha* does not appear to be Indian. The Pandita has two or three of these, and uses them on great festivals while he mumbles the Vedas, telling them after the manner of the Roman Catholics. All these ornaments, including the Brahman-band, which is called *sampat, sawit, silimpit-* are strings of the fruit of the plant *genitri* (black balls about half an inch in diameter); their interstices are inlaid with gold, and at intervals they are set with *Sûryakântas.*

The *Brahman-band* (not called here by an Indian name; perhaps it would be a profanation of this sacred ornament to make known to the people the Indian name *Upavîta* or *Yajnôpavîta ?*) is threefold, but is not formed of three cords interwoven, and not of *Munja*-grass, which name is unknown here. There are three strings, passing over the left shoulder and under the right arm, and fastened together on the shoulder. At the place where they are joined there are three *lingas* (again of crystal). The ends hang down, and are ornamented with large precious stones—one with a red stone, *Puala* (doubtless *Upala*, opal); the second with a large (white) *Sûryakânta;* and the third with a black transparent stone, found in the mountains of Bali, and called *manik girang-girangan*. These three colours have reference to the three gods of the *Trimûrti*, Brahmâ, Vishṇu, and Śiva (or *Sadâ-Śiva, Pramâ-Śiva* and *Mahâśiva*). Red is the colour of Brahmâ, white of Śiva, black or dark blue of Vishṇu (and also of Kâla). Besides this *Brahman-band*, the Pandita has also a band of white cloth, six yards long by three inches wide, which, like the other, is worn over the left shoulder and under the right arm. This band is also called *sampat, sawit,* or *silimpat.*

The Pandita, finally, wears on his hands several gold rings with costly rubies. The ruby is the favourite stone in Bali, almost more prized than the diamond; seven kinds are known in Bali, each possessing a special supernatural power. On the upper part of the arm and on the ankles the Pandita wears no ornaments, but the gods do. The gods also have many of these ornaments in the form of serpents, which is not the case with the Panditas.

Dress of the Gods.

The head-dress is very complicated, especially that of Śiva. Śiva alone of all the gods has the *Glung kurung,* a nearly spherical cap, much resembling the *Jatâ* of the *Panditas,* whose example Śiva is. This cap covers the back of the head. On the forehead is the *Glung chandi,* a round, lofty head-dress, nearly in the shape of the *chandis* in the temples. *Papudukan* are ornaments next to the *glung chandi; Garuḍa mungkur* above the *papudukan. Patitis* (among the Panditas *Keśâbharaṇa*) is the forehead-band, set with precious stones; in front is the *chûḍâmaṇi. Mangle wijaya* (perhaps *mangala vijaya,* happy victory), the plain stripe above the *Patitis. Kuṇḍala,* the earrings. *S'kar taji,* the pointed ornaments immediately behind the ear. *Ronron,* the ornaments behind the *s'kar taji. Apus kupak,* the ornaments on the shoulders. *Glangkana,* the bands on the upper part of the arm. *Glang,* the bands on the wrists. *Glang batis,* the bands on the ankles. *Bapang,* the small garment which hangs in two capes from the shoulders on to the upper part of the arms. *Kalung,* a short collar ornamented in silk with serpent-heads. *Sampat, Silimpat* or *Sawit,* also *Genitri* (after the name of the plant of the seeds of which it is made), the Brahman-band, worn, like that of the Panditas, over the left shoulder and under the right arm. *Babêdatti,* the breast-band, worn round the breast under both arms, and fastened in the middle with a jewel; this is also found on many Javanese idols. *Nâga wangsul* (the serpent of Bali), a large band hanging from the shoulders to the stomach, formed of a serpent, worn in this way as the Brahman-band. *Babaḍong (baḍong,* the name of a kingdom, means, like *bandhana,* the Sanskrit name of it, "connexion"), the upper band round the hips. *Tambeḍana,* two other bands worn round the body, below the *babaḍong. Kamben,* the cloth (not a *sarong*), unsewn, and fastened above the hips by the bands just mentioned. *Samir,* an end of the cloth, rolled up and sticking out above the *Tambeḍana. Jawat,* the end of the cloth which hangs down in front between the legs. *Linchêr,* two ends of the same hanging at the side. *Chalêr,* short breeches (these are never worn by the Balinese, and are only seen in representations of mythological personages). Śiva and all the real gods sit or stand on a lotus-bed, *padmâsana* (see, above, the *Padmâsana* in the temples as a seat for Śiva). They have also a glory, surrounding the whole figure, called here simply *trang teja,* "the bright lustre." All these ornaments can only be clearly explained by means of drawings, and I therefore caused the principal Balinese gods to be drawn by a Brahman; the first of these drawings which I sent were lost on the journey; those which I sent on the second occasion at any rate reached Batavia.

The costume just described is that of nearly all the gods; Śiva wears only the *Glung kurung* in front. This monotony also indicates that all the gods are merged in the one Śiva. In the female images we find other ornaments for the ears, and the cloth hangs down lower, as it is worn by the Balinese women. *Umâ,* Śiva's wife, has ornaments stuck through the lobe of the ear, named *Subong;* they are similar to those of most Balinese girls, which are made of lontar-leaves rolled together. She also has the *Glung chandi* of Śiva. *Śrî,* Vishṇu's wife, has the same ornaments, but a simple head-dress, called *Mengure glung.* Vishṇu's earrings are called *rumbing,* and are round and without a cavity.

It is especially to be remarked here, that the names of the articles of the Panditas' dress are Sanskrit, while the names of those of the gods themselves are Balinese. The gods are thus less sacred than the priests! But the deity may not and cannot really be represented; drawings and images have no value but for the ignorant.

FEASTS.

These are partly *feasts of the various gods and temples,* and partly *expiatory feasts.* Those of the first kind are dedicated to the more beneficent gods, the others to the *Bûtas* and *Râksasas,* with *Kâla* and *Durgâ* at their head. Especially grand feasts are celebrated in the *sadkahyangs,* the six most sacred temples in Bali. In the temples of *Bâsuki* (or *Besaki*) at the foot of the *Gunung Agung,* the feast-day is every lunar year *on the full moon* (*Pûrṇamâ*) *of the month Kapat or Kârttika.* This feast-day is really valid for all Balinese ("Us. Bali," pp. 273 *seq.* and 346); but on account of the existing hostilities, *Badong* and *Tabanan* have not for a long time performed their worship, because the temple is in *Karang Asem.* In *Basuki, Mahâdeva* or *sang Pûrṇa Jaya* (Śiva), whose seat is the *Gunung Agung* (or *Meru*), is worshipped.

In *Badong* the feast-day in the great sanctuary of *Uluwatu* is on the 21st day of the new (Balinese) year, *anggara kaliwon,* in the week *Madang Siha.* On this day the princes of *Badong* worship there, and to do this have to travel over the mountains to that holy place by wild and rocky paths. The holiness of this temple is ascribed to the fact that the ship (the *prahu*) of *Dewî Danu, Mahâdeva's* sister when she came from India, stopped at that place and turned into stone. This temple, however, cannot be so old as that of *Basuki;* it is not named in the "Us. Bali," p. 320; and it must further be taken into consideration that the feast day *is fixed, not according to the Indian, but according to the Balinese year;* while, on the contrary, in *Basuki* it is fixed according to the Indian calendar, and this seems to indicate that the temple of *Badong* is of later date. The same thing applies also to the temple of *Sakennan* or *Serangan*, dedicated to *Indra*. Here the feast is on *Rediti Manis*, in the week *Langkir*, the twelfth day of the Balinese new year.

Each temple has likewise a feast on the date of its foundation. This is called *wedalan*, commonly pronounced *odalan*, or anniversary. General feasts of the gods and *Pitaras* are celebrated on *Galungan*, and in the five succeeding weeks (see "Us. Bali"). At this time the gods are supposed to dwell on the earth, and the *Pitaras* especially return to the bosoms of their families; hence the constant offerings and the incessant games and amusements which are regarded as necessary less for the living generation than for the *Pitaras* and *gods* sojourning among them; hence also the cessation from work and the disinclination to intercourse with foreigners during this period. Trade and foreigners are not agreeable to the *Pitaras*, who desire to see old institutions and usages faithfully preserved. The princes also have feasts on their birthdays, and on the anniversaries of their temples. The number and the preparation of the offerings is minutely prescribed for each deity and each temple.

The *expiatory feasts*, however, are those most worthy of attention. They are, in great part, celebrated, not in the temples, but in the inner portion of the houses (*natar*), or in places arranged for the purpose. We have already mentioned two great feasts: *Bayakâla* (see "Us. Bali," p. 323 *sqq.*) and *Panchâvalikrama*. This feast is not kept on fixed days in the year, but on great occasions. It occurs after the conquest of a State, for the sake of the conquered population, who are thereby delivered from the evil influence of the demons, who have power over conquered places; it also takes place before the *abiseka* (anointing) of the Sovereigns, and it is celebrated by all the princes and the men who bear arms. It is further observed after a contagious disease—*e.g.*, the smallpox. It is necessary that five *Padandas* should be present, four seated facing each of the cardinal points and one in the middle: one of the five must be a *Padanda Buddha* (a Buddhist priest), who sits facing the south. We have drawn attention above to this phenomenon, and may here observe that although Buddha is also represented at this feast, he plays but a subordinate part. To the north is Vishṇu, whose colour is black; to the east *Maheśvara* (white), to the south Brahmâ (red), to the west *Mahâdeva* (yellow), and in the middle Śiva, with mixed colours. (The offerings are of corresponding colours.) In the middle is the *Padanda* of the supreme Śiva, and he naturally has the chief place. There are three other priests of Śiva besides, but only one Buddhist.

Another expiatory feast is called *Ekadaśa Rudra* (the eleven *Rudras;* Rudra is a subordinate form of Śiva; eleven Rudras are also mentioned in Wilson). The origin of this feast, however, seems to be known to but few Balinese. (See "Tijdschrift van N.I.," VIII. vol. iii. p. 242, in which passage the name *yajna*, through a printer's error, is written *jadjoeja*.) The offerings enumerated there are the greatest known in India, but, according to the descriptions which I have obtained, they are not organized in Bali and Lombok precisely in the Indian manner. I was told that there were no bloody sacrifices in the feast in Lombok (September 1846); simply large sums of money were distributed among the priests and the people, and the ordinary offerings were presented.*

It appears, therefore, that only the names of these feasts have survived in the memory of the Balinese, and that the latter, in a spirit of vain-glory, apply these sacred names to their curtailed feasts, which they have not the means to make very grand.

It is a surprising fact, however, that by indirect inquiries I have convinced myself that a few *human sacrifices* have actually taken place in Bali! A former prince of *Karang Asem*, who was defeated in war, put one of his slaves to death in a forest, and then placed his body, concealed by clothes, among the other numerous offerings, as a means of imploring the gods to restore his power. The deed was discovered, for while the Pandita was mumbling the Vedas, a wind arose and uncovered the body. A curse fell upon the presumptuous prince, and he never regained his power. Another instance is known from *Gyanyar*, where the prince (probably the first *Deva Mangis*, said to have been changed into a serpent on account of his atrocious acts) had set aside a slave † to be sacrificed; he intended to murder him in the darkness of the night, but killed by mistake his own son, and roasted and offered him as a sacrifice.

These two facts cannot well be gainsaid, for I have obtained the accounts of the former not only from *Badong*, but also from *Mengui*, which is allied with and has long been friendly to *Karang Asem*. The people of *Karang Asem* utterly deny it. Of *Gyanyar*

* For the reader's convenience I will repeat the names:— 1. *Aśvamedhayajna*, the horse-sacrifice; 2. *Gomedhayajna*, the cow-sacrifice; 3. *Manushyayajna*, human sacrifice; 4. *Râjasûyayajna*, the sacrifice of the universal prince (*i.e.* offered by him); 5. *Devayajna*; 6. *Ṛishiyajna*; 7. *Mutayajna*; 8. *Kauyasayajna*; 9. *Râjabusaṇayajna*.

† *Guling buntut* is the name for human sacrifices.

it is a common saying. How far this barbarity has gone, and, perhaps, still goes on in a thickly populated country, where the common man is a slave and of no value, I will not venture to say. The burning of widows, and also the *amok* on the fall of a State, must be classed among the human sacrifices.

The general name for these expiatory feasts is *prâyaśchitta*, commonly pronounced inaccurately *prayas-tista*. The word means, according to Wilson, expiation, penance; and thus is very appropriate. The *Panchâvalikrama* is expressly included under this term. To these also belong the purification of a house in which a corpse has lain. The feast of the *Sarasvatî*, on *Saneśchara*, in the week of *Watu gunung*, has something in common with this; on that day the collective books of the princes are carried into the temple and purified for the coming year, through the priest reading the Vedas. Another feast is *for the weapons*, the ceremony being the same as in the previous one, and at this a bloody sacrifice to the Bûtas is also necessary. Yet another feast is observed for the welfare of domestic animals, cows, horses, pigs, fowls, &c. Among the feasts belong also the cock-fights, not only as an amusement of the people, but also as a religious ceremony. At the feasts of the great temples—*e.g.*, the temple of assembly of the *Gusti Pam-chuttan*—every one belonging to the congregation must send at least one cock, and must make it fight, either himself or through a deputy. This custom is based on the supposed incarnation of Vishṇu as a cock (*Silingsing*) in Bali, but we can explain Vishṇu's assumed incarnation more satisfactorily as an apotheosis, not derived from India, of the cock-fights which are so popular in all these islands.

Further Details of the Religious Worship.

The *mangku* (see "Usana Bali," p. 267 *sqq.*) is the guardian of the temple, who superintends the edifice, and partly performs, partly conducts the presentation of offerings; he must know certain *mantras*—e.g., *patikelaning genta sapta* and *sâstra sangha*, and must employ them when offerings are made. Both men and women can fill this post. (The Brahmanic women—those sprung from the Brahmanic caste, not the concubines from the lower castes—are likewise acquainted with the Vedas, and perform some religious functions instead of the men.) The *mangkus* can further be of various castes, and not *Sûdras* alone; I know several *Gustis* (*Veśyas*) in *Badong*, who fill the office of *mangku*; usually, however, these latter hold the post in the chief temples, such as, for instance, the domestic temples of the princes. I have not yet found a Brahman acting as a *mangku*; although perhaps there are some who do so. The Brahmans generally aspire to the dignity of a *Padanda*, and therefore look down upon the position of a *mangku*. In order to become a *mangku* it is necessary, or at any rate usual, that a deity should pass into, and thenceforward speak from the body of the person selected. Two cases have become known to me in which young *Gustis* appeared for a time almost to have lost their reason, speaking an incomprehensible language, performing none of their actions in the ordinary manner, and sleeping in the temples. These *Gustis* were thereupon observed by the persons who had been longer inspired by a deity (*wawalen* or *prakulit*), and after due inquiry, acknowledged as also inspired. Such individuals are supposed to be either *wawalens* or actual madmen. When they are thoroughly penetrated by the deity, and have become calm again, they are true *wawalen*, and are able to state what deity it is that inspires them. They are then regarded as the most devoted servants (*mangku*) of the said deity. They become madmen if their minds do not become calm again—or rather if their deception is not properly carried out; for, of course, these *wawalen* must be regarded as idle impostors, who choose to lead an easy life, chiefly at the expense of the credulous populace. (Compare on this subject " Usana Bali," pp. 268 and 335.)

These temple-servants, however, detract nothing from the importance of the *Panditas*. The latter, by their life and the study of the Vedas, are identified both spiritually and materially with the supreme Śiva, whereas the *wawalen* have merely, as it were, given their bodies to be dwelling-places of the deity. In the *wawalen* an unconscious, in the *Padandas* a conscious, unity with the deity has commenced. In the great temples, therefore, the *mangku* and *wawalen* are of little consideration; all ceremonies at the feasts are regulated by the directions given from the books by the *Padandas*, and the latter mostly use for this purpose *mantras* which are unknown to the *mangku*. Moreover, the *Pandita* alone (and not the *wawalen*) is able *to call down the gods by mumbling the Vedas*. The sayings of the *wawalens*, when, at the offerings in the temples, they give utterance to the voice of the god which dwells in them, are compared with the statements of the sacred writings of the *Padandas*, after which a decision is arrived at as to what must be done in important cases (sickness, wars, &c.). Thus, in these cases also, the Padandas have an opportunity of exercising their power; in the first place, they can counteract, by quotations from their sacred works, the utterances of the *wawalens*, if they do not meet their views; in the second place, they can easily make known to the *wawalens*, whom we are disposed to regard as deliberate impostors, what they must say, and, by their approval, elevate these utterances into laws for the guidance of the people.

Archâ (Sanskrit *archâ*, an image) is an idol, usually of stone, in Bali always of rude workmanship. Sometimes it is supposed that the deity passes into such an image, and this fact then induces the faithful to bring their offerings. (See " Us. Bali," p. 274.) This belief, however, is for the most part held only by the common people. The priests, and also a large portion of the people, attach little value to the images. "Does not the deity dwell in heaven?" was an idea expressed by a common man in *Boleling*. The idols, as we have already said, are called *togog* or *tongkok*, which means neither more nor less than "doll." We find them principally as watchers, in the form of *Râksasas* and *Bûtas ;* for the same purpose there are also small watch-houses, called *Tugu*, before the temples, in order to prevent the evil spirits from entering. We also find images, such as those of *Ganeśa* and *Vâsuki*, and also of *Hanumân* and *Garuḍa*, in some of the small temple-houses, representing as it were the retinue of Śiva. *Garuḍa* is always monstrous, with *Râksaśa* tusks. The *Nandi* is very well known to the Balinese, but I do not remember to have seen representations of it. The worship of images therefore has, upon the whole, penetrated but little into the belief of the Balinese, and we have here an obvious contrast to the creed now existing in India, where the highest value is attached to idols. I have not yet seen any representations in stone of Śiva, although I have met with some rude images of Vishṇu (the subordinate incarnate deity). In pictures we also see Śiva as *Îśvara* and *Mahâdeva* (when he appears as a youth), and as *Arjuna*, but these pictures are not worshipped, and, like those of Vishṇu, as *Râma*, &c., have reference rather to the myths in the Kavi works, than to religion.

The offerings are called *banten, charu,* or *aturan*. Religious fasting, which the priests and those who desire to become *Rishi* practise daily, is called *mavinten*. The cap of the *Pandita, jatâ,* is also called *bawa*. The flowers which he uses in his domestic worship are *chempaka putih, chempaka kuning* (Sanskrit *champaka ;* the *a* is here also altered by the nasal pronunciation into a short *è*), *Jepon, Kenyeri, Ergani, Jenpiring,* &c.

The *vilva fruit* and the *śâlagrâma stone*, which play so important a part in the Indian worship, I have not yet met with in Bali.

The lotus has really no worship, but it is found planted in pots in the *Padandas'* houses, and also in the ponds which the princes are accustomed to have in their palaces.

The *Brahman-band* (*upavîta*) belongs in India to the three upper castes, which are called on this account *dvija*, "born twice" (the second time through adopting this band). In that country it is of different kinds, according to three different castes. In Bali it is found only among the *Padandas*, and then only if they are in full dress. But the *Kshatriyas* and *Veśyas*, and even *Śûdras*, who have obtained permission from the *Padandas*, also wear a protective band, a sort of amulet, in war, called by the same name (*Sampat*); they only wear it, however, in time of war. In *Badong* I have never met with it. *Chandra* or *wulan tumanggal* (the waxing moon) is in the head-dress of *Gaṇeśa*, as in the Javanese images of that god. The *skull* (*muṇḍa*) above the *chandra* is not known to the Balinese! They have a milder form of religion, with which skulls and chains of skulls (found with the Indian Śiva and *Gaṇeśa*, and also in Java) are incompatible. Śiva's name, *Kapâlabhṛit*, "he who wears a skull," seems to be no longer clearly understood in Bali. The mark on the forehead found in some gods (*e.g.* Gaṇeśa)—not to be confounded with the third eye of Śiva and Indra—is called *chuundung;* it is also marked on the foreheads of the princes when they adorn themselves for a religious service; its meaning is unknown.

The King Śiva-Buddha is named in the *Rangga Lawe* as ruler of *Tumapèl*. His kingdom was overthrown by the people of *Daha* (*Kediri*). This King's name cannot well be anything else but an indication of the state of the religion. *At that time Buddhism and Śivaism must have been completely blended together.* The fall of the kingdom, then, appears to represent a reaction, brought about by the Śivaites; and it is the more remarkable that this kingdom, with a mixed religion, was conquered by that of *Kediri*, where the flower of the Śivaitic priests and learned men were to be found under *Ayer Langgia* and *Jayabaya*, although the latter (*Jayabaya*) especially also tolerated the Buddhists (see under the article *Literature*). From *Kediri* also the orthodox Śivaitic Brahmans in Bali trace their descent. We have already drawn attention in various places to the intermixture of Śivaism and Buddhism. We will give here a few facts bearing on this point. We found an image of Buddha in a temple of Śiva in *Boleleng;* on the *jatâ* of the *Padandas* there is a *ball* under the *linga;* and, further, inverted pots or glasses are found on the small temple-houses; in the "Usana Bali" we have among the gods, and also in *Jayabaya's* retinue (in the *Bârata-Yudda*), the *Risi Seva Sogata* (Śaiva belonging to Śiva, and *Saugata* to *Sugata* or Buddha), *Risis* (holy beings partly in heaven, partly on earth) of the worship of Śiva and of Buddha; in the "Usana Java" we have Śiva, Buddha, and *Bujangga* as sons of *sang Haji* (the original one).

The Buddhists, the Balinese assert, came later than the Śivaites, and if this refers to their arrival in Java, it agrees with the accounts given in Java, where the Buddhists are also said to have come later than the Brahmans. What has happened in Java is very often confounded, even by the priests, with occurrences in Bali. These nations are particularly weak in chronology and geography. In Raffles, Appendix K, p. ccxxxix., there is an account of Bali by a Muhammedan: it states: "The religion of Buddha (under which he evidently includes the entire

Hindu religion) is divided into *Sakâlan* and *Niskâlan*. The first division will include all earthly things, and the second the religion." This division exists in the writings (*tutur*) of the Balinese, but it has no reference to religion; *sakâla* is that which belongs to time, and *niskâla* that which belongs, not to time, but to eternity, to the period after death.[1] The former, therefore, is correctly interpreted by the narrator, but the latter has a wider meaning.

The following are names of the ornaments of the gods:

Anting-anting, like *kuṇḍala*, earrings.
Glang Kupak, instead of *alang*, bracelets.
Guduha pawilangan, the rosary (*wilang*, to count).
Parmata, a golden girdle (Ind. *mekhalâ*).
Kilat bahu, the necklace (with the *Padanda âtmâbharaṇa*).
Babandong, the longest band round the neck (*vâyubharaṇa*).
Chechandian, Chandi repeated (the *glung chandi*).

The *chakra* is also to be found in the place of the *genitri* (*guduha genitri*), a substitution which in some cases can easily occur with the Javanese images as well.

The *temples* in Bali are of the same class as those of *Majapahit*, or of the third period: in Crawfurd, "Ind. Arch.," vol. ii. p. 205, "temples constructed of brick mortar." The bricks of which they are built are not of first-rate manufacture, and consequently not very durable. Stone carvings, which are plentiful in the ruins of *Majapahit*, are only to be found rarely in a few ancient temples and palaces (the best in *Mengui;* and in *Klongkong* and *Gyanyar*). This art has evidently not advanced in Bali, and there are now very few men who can work in stone, and even these no longer produce anything of beauty. The art of carving wood, ivory, and whalebone has been tolerably well preserved; neat images of gods and *Râksasas* are carved out of the last material.

Crawfurd and Raffles maintain that the religion of the people in Bali cannot be called Hindu; but, from all my inquiries into the worship of the common people, which at first I was inclined to regard as a remnant of the purely Polynesian age, I have convinced myself that this also is Hindu, and that the low estimation in which the temples of the *Sûdras* are held by the priests has merely obscured the objects and corrupted the mode of this worship. These small temples are regarded as *punggawas* (substitutes) for the large and principal ones, just as the *Sûdras* who pray in them are vassals of the men of rank who pray in the great temples.

Another difference finds expression in the saying, that not only in such temples, but also in the small *sanggars* of the upper

---

[1] [R. van Eck in "Tijdschrift voor Nederlandsch Indië," 1879, i. p. 57.]

classes, "*Śiva's children*" are worshipped. Who these children are, however, is not clear; some Balinese names—e.g., *sang Kasuhun Kidul* (meaning he who is "worshipped in the south"), *Brahmâ* or *Mahâdeva*—do not afford us any explanation. It would appear that here also we must have recourse to the difference of the castes; as the insignificant temples alone belong to the *Śûdras*, so they have no claim to the worship of the Supreme Śiva. *Only the subordinate manifestations of Śiva*, called for want of a better word, "Śiva's children," are intended for them.

Besides these *children of Śiva*, the *Pitaras*, the shades of the dead, are also worshipped in the small temples, and we shall show that these may be regarded as identical, as it were, with "Śiva's children." We have already seen in connexion with *Indra*, that it is not easy to reconcile the decrees as to becoming a *Pitara* with the punishments to be imposed by *Yama*. According to some, all the persons who have undergone cremation dwell as *pitaras* in *Svarga* or *Indraloka*, and there enjoy eternal happiness; according to others, they wander about for a long time before reaching that place, and assume various forms upon earth; and finally it is also said that, although they enter *Indraloka*, they are obliged to descend again to the earth as human beings; it is not said when this obligation ceases, and their state in heaven is called indiscriminately *deva*, *hyang* (god), or *pitara*. According to the popular belief, *Brahmaloka* or *Vishnuloka* (which are identical and higher than *Indraloka*), and *Śivaloka*, the highest of all, are not attainable. The Brahmans, however, appear not to share this belief, and lay claim also to these supreme worlds and the *moksha* (deliverance from the transmigration of the soul). Among the "children of Śiva" we have also to include such ascended souls, dwelling in *Śivaloka*, although it is surprising that they have not become identical and one with Śiva (who here is the same as the Indian *Parabrahma*), as the word *moksha* indicates.

According to the accounts of men of the lower castes, it is supposed that, in the worship of the Panditas, not Śiva himself, but *Bagawân Byâsa*, enters into the *Padanda;* the latter then becomes like *Byâsa*, and possesses the divine power of the *Devarshi*. Upon the whole, this statement is almost identical with the opinion which we have already expressed. *Byâsa* is, as it were, the same as the deity (Śiva), and, as we have already seen (under *Literature*), is called *Yogîśvara*, a name for Śiva himself.

Into the *wawalen*, to whom we have before alluded, there passes, according to the same accounts, a *Bûta kaparagan* (an embodied *Bûta*), who is said to be the confidant of the god and to know his secrets. This spirit, therefore, and not the deity itself, speaks from out of the *wawalen*. We may be surprised that a *Bûta* should be called here the confidant of the deity, yet the conceptions of a *Bûta*, a *Râksasa*, and a *Deva* are so mixed up in the minds of the lower orders, that we cannot attach much importance to this fact, and, besides this, the *Bûtas* and *Devas* were originally as closely related to each other as *Kâla* to *Śiva*, and the Elves to the Fays.

The *wawalens* are also the physicians (*balian* = *dukun*);[1] when they act in this capacity, they recite *Mantras* (*mayoga*), moving their bodies as the Panditas do when they mumble the Vedas. In addition to the *mantras*, the *bâyu* (the wind) is the remedy employed by the *balian;* he causes his breath to pass into the bodies of the sick.*

He who performs *tapa* lives only on the *vâyu*, without any other food. In the "Usana Bali," however, we have seen that *tapa* (penance) is now no longer performed in Bali.

Rishis.

Religious rites analogous to the domestic worship of the *Padandas* are performed also by certain princes and other *Devas* and *Gustis*, in order to attain the dignity of a *Risi*. These persons also perform a service every morning on a fasting stomach, using, however, not the Vedas, but the *Mantras*, namely the *Mantra pasuchian* (the purifying *Mantra*). They perform ablutions with holy water, wash out their mouths, purify their teeth, and wash their hair; not until they have done this do they dress and appear in public. When, by means of this daily service, which must be coupled with a very regular mode of life (they may not lie, nor say or do anything degrading, &c.), they have attained a certain holiness, they become *Risis*. This state of *Risi* has much in accordance with the third period of the lifetime of the Indians according to *Manu*, where they live for meditation alone, and, withdrawn from all earthly affairs, pass a peaceful life, pleasing to God, in the forest hermitages. In Bali, also, a prince who has become a *Risi* must relinquish his kingdom to his children, and, intent alone upon his heavenly state, separate himself from all human companionship. It seems, however, that at present love for earthly things is of more weight than care about heaven. The last prince but one of *Pam'chuttan* in *Badong, Ngurah G'de Pam'chuttan* had become a *Risi*, yet he retained his kingdom until his death. The old *Râjâ Kassiman* has performed the said service (which is incorrectly called also *maveda* or *masuryasevana*) for a series of years, and yet he has not become a *Risi*, and seems to keep that dignity in reserve, in case the princes of *Pam'chuttan* and *Den*

---

[1] [The Javanese *dukun* applies to both sexes, the Dayak *balian* to females only. See Hardeland's "Grammatik," p. 209.]

* In the body are *bâyu*, wind; *śabda*, sound; and *idêp*, understanding, the faculty of learning, the three properties which the *triśakti* (or *trimûrti*) form out of it.

Passar will no longer acknowledge him as their guardian. The wife of a *Ṛisi* can alone follow him into the state of separation, provided that she, too, has performed the daily service, and, like him, has remained free from all misdeeds and sins.

This service makes the Brahman (*Iḍa*) a *Padanda* (where, however, other regulations also come in), and the *kshatriya* and *Wesya* a *Ṛisi* (*Râjarshi*, royal *Ṛisi*, to be distinguished from the *Devarshis*, divine *Ṛisis*, and the *Brahmarshis*, the Brahmanical *Ṛisis*). A *Śûdra*, finally, becomes through this service a *Dukuh*.

Trimûrti.

The *Trimûrti* or *Triśakti* (trinity) is contained in the word *ong* (really Indian *om*), which is formed of three letters, *a, û, m*, or, as the Balinese say, of *ang, ûng, mang*, meaning *Sadâ-Śiva, Parama-Śiva*, and *Mahâśiva;* or *Brahmâ, Vishṇu*, and *Śiva*, also represented as *agni* (fire), *toya* (water), and *angin* (air). In this combination Śiva is co-ordinated with Brahmâ and Vishṇu, but he is called *Mahâśiva*, the great Śiva, and the other two gods bear his name, and must be regarded, as it were, as *expressions of himself*. Śiva, also, is represented hereby as being in the centre, with Brahmâ on his right hand and Vishṇu on his left.

This trinity (also called *triśakti*) repeats itself throughout Nature. We have the *tribhuvana* (the three worlds), consisting of *bhûr, bhuvah*, and *svah* (earth, air, and space). And further, *langit, pṛithivî*, and *naraka* (heaven, earth, and hell). Three kinds of human beings: *parampuwan, laki*, and *banji* (woman, man, and hermaphrodite). The last kind also appears in Śiva as *Arddhanareśvarî* (Śiva with his wife in one body).

In the month of *Kasanga*, in which the lunar year of months begins, all the Balinese keep the feast of *Matawur* or *Labu guntu; Kasanga* is also called by its Indian name, *Chetra*, and, as in India, begins the year.

Cremations.

One of the most important religious ceremonies is the cremation of the dead. Only through the burning of the body is it possible for the soul to enter the heaven of Indra (*Svarga*), and, thence, that of Vishṇu and the supreme heaven of Śiva (*Vishṇuloka* and *Śivaloka*). The doctrine of the transmigration of the soul exists in Bali, although the Balinese do not speak of its details; the *âtmapraśansâ* is a work on this subject (explained as *kumpulan badan*, the assumption of various bodies; according to the Indian words it seems to be "glorification of the soul," a point which its contents leave in uncertainty). This work, however, is a popular one, written in *Kidung*, but it does not appear to contain the whole of the purely Indian doctrine of the transmigration of souls. Other writings of the Brahmans exist on this subject, but they are secret; it is according to these that the ceremonial at cremations is regulated.

It is believed that cremation, and the offerings which precede and follow it, exempt a man from any further change of shape—at least he remains for a certain time as a *pitâ* in the heaven of the *Devas*, and as such demands the worship and offerings of his surviving relations. Cremation requires a considerable outlay,[1] and therefore every family is not in a position to show this honour to its dead. Instead of being burned, they are in that case buried, the body being inclosed in a case of bamboo, which completely conceals it, and covered with a number of clothes; it is carried out upon a bier amid the singing of *naenia*, which, among the common people, are trivial compositions. Arrived at the grave, the body is stripped of its clothes, and let down with the bamboo covering; a few small coins are then thrown into the grave (in order that the dead may provide himself with food), and it is closed. By the side of the grave a bamboo is fixed in the ground, on the top of which there is a sort of three-cornered hutch of lattice-work, in which offerings of small value, chiefly rice and flowers and fruit, are deposited immediately after the funeral, and subsequently at certain intervals. These offerings are for the purpose of propitiating the *Bûtas* (the demoniacal beings who infest places of burial especially), lest they should attack the soul of the deceased. The grave is then surrounded with a fence or hedge.

Those who are buried in this way cannot enter heaven; they then assume all sorts of shapes, and it seems that the Balinese especially believe that the numerous dogs which wander about half wild are metamorphoses of *Sûdras* (the lowest caste); for this reason they hardly ever kill a dog, and these ugly animals increase and multiply enormously, and are a pest to the European. It is now the duty of a member of the family (son, grandson, &c., sometimes even the third generation, if he has become rich enough to afford a cremation) to cause the bones of all his relations who have been buried to be exhumed and to burn them together. At most cremations, therefore, one sees a number of bodies at once, each in a special coffin, many of which have usually been buried for years. In times of general calamity, contagious diseases, &c., all bodies, even those of princes, are buried and not burned; it is not permitted then to keep any corpse above ground, for in such times no work pleasing to the gods can be undertaken, and the influence of the demons is in the ascendant. At these times, also, the *Galungan* is not celebrated.

[1] [According to Jacobs, l. l. p. 49, from 800 to 1,500 florins, in the case of princes 10,000 florins.]

The long periods that corpses are kept is also noteworthy, although I have discovered that Crawfurd's statements ("As. Researches," vol. xiii. p. 136; "Ind. Arch.," vol. ii. p. 253) as to the length of time are inaccurate. The duration of the impurity of a house in which a dead body has lain is more precisely fixed, being more than a month for a *Sûdra*, only eight days for a Brahman, and an intermediate time for the second and third castes. The time during which corpses are kept varies very much, and the day of the cremation does not at all depend upon the date of the death.

There are bodies in *Badong* which have been kept twenty years; on the other hand, the body of the prince of *Gyanyar* was burned about forty days after his death. But the statement (Crawf., "Hist. Ind. Arch.," p. 244) that a month and a week is the time that bodies must be kept for cremation is also inaccurate, for this reason, that it is not every day that is suited for a cremation; it must be a lucky day, and in order to obtain such a day all good omens must concur; it must also be in the first half of the lunar month (with a waxing moon), and thus can hardly ever happen at one and the same interval of time after the date of the death.

A series of ceremonies belong to cremation. Immediately after death the body is embalmed by the relatives, and in the case of a prince, also by the junior *râjas* of the friendly States; for this purpose spices are used, with which the body is entirely covered, and these again are covered on the principal parts of the body with small coins—over these come clothes, mats, and a covering of split bamboo. This sort of embalming[1] does not protect the body from partial decomposition; the emanations[2] from it are collected in a vessel underneath the *Bale*[3] on which the body lies, and are poured away every day. If the body remains so long unburnt, it becomes dried up in about six months. It is watched the whole time, and if emanations still run from it, they are caught in the vessel referred to; offerings and holy water are also presented. In its mouth the corpse has a gold ring, set with a ruby; this protects it from the power of the demons, and it is the most heinous sin to steal such a ring (a thing, however, which happened not long since). Three days before the cremation the corpse is stripped of its coverings, and the relatives look upon the dead for the last time. Meanwhile, the spices have penetrated into the body; the latter is then washed and again enveloped in split bamboo, mats, and clothes. Instead of a ruby, five small metal plates inscribed with the word *ong*, and with mystic formulas, are

---

[1] [Called *nglělět* in the high dialect, corresponding to the Javanese Ngoko, and *nggulung* in the low or Krama form.]

[2] [Called *banyěh*, and in the case of a Brahman corpse, *pringět*.]

[3] [The *Bale*, or more correctly *bale pandung*, is a bier or kind of tent, often of considerable dimensions, for the reception of the body until its cremation.]

put into the mouth; the five plates signify the five principal gods (Śiva, Brahmâ, Vishṇu, Indra, and Yama?), comprised in the words *Sa, ba, ta, ha, i* (*Sa* = *Śiva, Ba* = *Brahmâ, I* = *Indra ; ta* and *ha* are not clear to me, but *ha* seems to indicate *Hari*, one of the principal names of Vishṇu);* the plates are of *gold, silver, copper, iron,* and *lead.* These plates, which keep the body, as it were, under the protection of those five gods, are taken away immediately before cremation, when this protection appears to be rendered unnecessary by the reading of the Vedas and the pouring out of holy water. Houses in which dead bodies are kept are unclean, and, in the case of princes, the palace is not occupied by the successor until after the cremation, and is merely guarded by the people belonging to the deceased. This is occurring, at the present moment, in *Den Passar* (one of the three residences of princes in *Badong*), where the bodies of five illustrious princes are kept in the great palace, and the reigning prince lives for the present in a small house of little pretension. The first ceremony mentioned above, that of washing before cremation, is called *pangâskaran* or *pabrissian* (purification); *âskara* seems to be Sanskrit, but it is not found in Wilson (first edition).[1]

The preparations for cremation take much time and much money. A bridge is built on each side of the wall of the palace for the conveyance of the body to the *Bade*.[2] The *Bade*, or funeral pyre, is, in the case of princes, very gorgeous. It rests on a basis of bamboo, concealed by handsome hangings, under which the bearers place themselves, to move the structure along. On this foundation there is a pyramid of woodwork or bamboo, in from three to eleven storeys. I have only seen the latter number at the cremation of *Dewa Mangis* in *Gyanyar*, and this agrees with the number of storeys in the *Merus* of the temples; it certainly has a religious meaning, reminding us of the Buddhist pyramidal buildings and of the philosophical ideas connected therewith. This pyramid is ornamented with more or less splendour, according to the means of the relations of the deceased; the covering is made of little balls of cotton, fastened on to the wooden framework in fringes, and forming heads of elephants and *Bûtas* round the bottom and at the corners of the different storeys. These balls are of all the colours mentioned in the "Usana Bali": *white*,

---

* According to Wilson, *Tha* is Śiva; *J*, Kàma; *Ha*, Śiva and Vishnu. See also "Usana Bali," p. 328. These letters are called *Panchâkshara*, the five (sacred) letters.

[1] [*Âskara* is a mutilated form of the Sanskrit *sanskâra*—i.e., the ceremony κατ' ἐξοχήν. See v. d. Tuuk in "Bijdragen," III. vol. v. p. 212. *Pambresihan*, from *bresih*, "pure," = *bĕrsih* in Malay and Javanese.]

[2] [More correctly *waḍah*. In Javanese and Sundanese the word means any receptacle. Jacobs, l. l. p. 227 ff., gives a full account of two of those gorgeous structures he saw at Tabanan.]

red, dark blue, and *yellow.* The whole of the lower portion, as well as the corner of the pyramid, is covered in this way. The outer sides of the different storeys are ornamented with tinsel and red, and inside they are fitted up as rooms with mirrors and furniture. Persons are stationed on each storey to attend to the regular progress of the machine and to keep the little rooms clean. The corpse is laid in the highest storey, and covered with a great number of white cloths, which hang down the sides of the pyramid.

Special places are made ready for the cremation of distinguished persons. In *Gyanyar* a square of about 400 paces in length and breadth, surrounded by a wall of pillars of masonry with trellis-work between them, was prepared above the palace, on the summit of the hill up which the *dessa* extends. In the centre there was a *Bale* of masonry inlaid with a sort of mosaic of glass-work and boards, after the manner of the *Bales* used for offerings in the temples. The *Bale* consisted of two storeys, and was surrounded with trellis-work. Above it rose, on four pillars, another chamber and a roof, the chamber ornamented with mirrors, and the whole covered with tinsel. The pillars were covered in red. This place was intended for the cremation, and upon it stood a figure of a lion (*singha*). This figure is only used at the cremation of reigning princes (*chokorda*);* other distinguished persons are burnt in the figure of a cow—men in that of a black, and women in that of a white *lembu*. The common man, generally, has only a simple square wooden coffin to be burnt in, but figures are sometimes used also by the lower orders—*e.g.*, *Gajamina*, a monster, half elephant, half fish. These figures of beasts are ornamented to a certain extent (in *Gyanyar* very splendidly); the erect tail and the back are taken off, like a lid, when the body is let down into the figure, and are replaced after the ceremony of letting down the body. In *Gyanyar*, outside the square, in the centre and at the sides, there were several large and ornamental *Bales* for the distinguished spectators, and especially for the very numerous women. In addition to these, there were the places for the cremation of the three *Belas*, on the left. For several days before the cremation of people of rank, one or more Panditas reside with the relatives; they manage all that has to be done, indicate the mode of making the offerings, prepare the metal plates, and invoke, by means of the Vedas, the success of the important ceremony about to be undertaken. It is they also who conduct the *Bade* to the place of cremation. If the deceased belongs to the second caste, the *Kshatriyas*, the *Bade* is fastened to a serpent (*nâga* or *nâgabandha*, serpent-band); this serpent is

---

* It has been said, however, that this custom did not come from *India*. [*Chokorda* in Balinese = pâduka.]

ornamented in the same manner as the foot-piece of the *Bade*, and has wings; the body is quite thirty fathoms long, and is carried by men. Before the procession starts, the *Padanda* descends from his palanquin and shoots from the four cardinal points at the head of the serpent, whose evil influence is thereby destroyed. He uses for this purpose wooden arrows with white flowers attached to their ends, the flowers alone being discharged at the serpent.* This peculiar custom of fastening a serpent in front of the *Bade*, and of the killing of this reptile by a Pandita, points to a fable of former quarrels between the earthly gods (the Brahmans) and the princes. A *Deva agung* was in the habit of ridiculing the Brahmans; he especially threw doubts upon their supernatural power. Once upon a time, when a powerful Pandita was at his palace, he caused a goose to be put into a well or pit, and the latter to be closed. He then asked the Pandita what animal was in the well, and the Pandita replied, a *nâga*. Thereupon the prince wished to ridicule him, but when he opened the well, a terrible serpent came indeed forth. The king then, astounded and terrified, was rescued in his need by the good Pandita, who slew the serpent, and ever since that time, at the cremation of all *Kshatriyas*, a serpent has been fastened to the *Bade*, killed by the Pandita, and burnt with the corpse. When this serpent has been figuratively slain, it is wound round the Padanda's seat, the tail remaining fastened to the *Bade;* in this manner the Padanda conducts the corpse (or, in reality, according to their notions, the soul) to the place of cremation, and so to heaven (*svarga*), where it (the soul) is admitted among the *pitaras*.

The procession at cremations is very long, even with the lower orders. In *Gyanyar*, where the princes and many armed men, besides the bands of musicians and actors from all States of Bali (excepting *Bangli*), were present at the celebration of the feast, the procession extended for upwards of a "paal." First came always the coolies bearing the wood for the cremation. In *Gyanyar* they carried pieces of wood of uniform shape, coloured black and gold. It is said to be customary to use sandal-wood for princes; but this did not appear to me to be the case, for the pieces were too large, and would have been too costly for the means of a small Balinese prince. Then came the music and the men armed with muskets, then all the articles of personal use belonging to the deceased, and then holy water and offerings for the *Bûtas*, carried by women on their heads. The order of march is: twenty or thirty men armed with lances, and then the bearers of the *Upachâra*, walking two and two (*upachâra* means in Sanskrit *service* and also *present;* to be understood here as *the articles*

---

* This is almost the only case in which a *bow and arrow* are used in Bali; with this exception, we only meet with their use in some dramatic representations, where they appear in accordance with the Indian myths.

belonging to the service of the deceased.* These include everything of domestic use in Bali: clothes, rings, and other jewellery, mirrors, and articles of the toilet, the sirih-box (in the case of princes, of gold), the water-bottle (also of a precious metal), the umbrella (*payung;* umbrellas are also held over the jewellery by those walking nearest); and, finally, the horse of the deceased, richly caparisoned, led in the procession by men, and sometimes ridden by a young son or grandson of the deceased. All these are again followed by armed men and musicians; the bands of music separate the divisions of the procession. The second part is devoted entirely to holy water (*toya tirta*); † more than a hundred women carry small vessels of water on their heads; this water comes from the most sacred places in Bali, and is solicited and bought from the Padandas who stand in especially high esteem. Here, again, the intermixture of Buddhism is noteworthy; we have here not only *holy water from the Padanda of Siva,* but also from the *Buddhist Padanda, and these waters are mixed together.*‡ It appears, therefore, that the Sivaites also require the help of Buddha, and that Buddhism is still, as it were, an integral part of the religion of all Balinese. This water is called *toya* or *toya tirta,* "water of a holy place;" *tirtha* is Ind. "a holy bathing-place," and also "a chapel;" our holy water comes from both such places, from the sacred waters (see *toya Sindu* in " Us. Bali," p. 337), from the temples, and from the houses of the Padandas, who have consecrated it by mumbling the Vedas.

The offerings for the *Butas, bantĕn dagan,* form the third division of the procession. *Dagan* is the Balinese name for *Bûta,* although the latter word is used quite as often. These offerings consist of all sorts of meats, cooked and half-cooked, of rice, fruits, flowers, leaves; all these vegetable offerings must be of five different colours: *white* (the colour of Siva or Mahâdeva), *red* (Brahmâ), *yellow* (Buddha and also Siva in Bali,§ *black or dark blue* (Vishṇu; also Kâla), and *brumbu,* a mixture of the four colours; the last is the colour of the supreme Siva, who combines in himself the natures of the four already named. These offerings are made to propitiate the *Bûtas,* who are supposed to haunt the burial-grounds. The offerings for the gods and *pitaras* (the shades), which are offered the same day, are left at home.

* According to Gericke's Javanese Dictionary, which has reached me too late, *hupachara* means tokens of distinction and of honour, state-decorations, insignia, ceremony, pomp, splendour. This agrees with our explanation.

† This water is as holy as that of the Ganges.

‡ The mixed holy water is called *toya pangĕntas,* and is especially purifying and a protection from danger; leaves of gold (*mas pripi*) and a costly gold ring (which the Pandita keeps) with a ruby are placed in it; and also flowers, *balung-balung,* or ground sandal-wood; powdered rubies; whole rice (*bija*); cut flowers and leaves (*samsam*).

§ Comp. *Pitâmbara,* "with a yellow garment."

Here usually follows the Padanda, carried in a palanquin, and drawing after him, when a *Kshatriya* is burnt, the dead *nâga* with the *Bade* attached to it. At several points, especially at the corners of the road, before the house of the deceased, and before the place of cremation, the *Bade* is turned three times, the *Padanda* being carried before it and leading the movement. The lofty structure of the *Bade* sometimes renders it necessary to employ more than 400 men to perform these manœuvres. In *Gyanyar* the prince, the son of the deceased, preceded the *Bade*, followed by a great number of other princes and the armed men of *Gyanyar* and *Badong*. In other cases I have always seen the relatives following the deceased; the reason why the prince preceded the corpse was this, that the *Belas* with their procession followed the *Bade*, and that the princes considered it beneath their dignity to go behind the Belas, who in this case were all *Guṇḍiks* (concubines from the fourth caste). During the whole march *Kavi*-songs are sung, chiefly by those who carry the Bade; they were not songs of mourning, however, but favourite portions of the *Râmâyaṇa, Bârata Yudda*, and other works well known to the people.

When the procession has arrived at the place of cremation, and the *Bade* has turned round thrice for the last time, the body is carried down from the top of the *Bade* by a staircase made for this purpose, and up by another small staircase to the place of burning, where it is laid in the coffin (the lion or cow). The corpse is then only in the covering of bamboo referred to above; the clothes and ornaments remain on the *Bade*, and some of them are taken home again, the remainder, as well as all the ornaments of the *Bade*, being given up to the people as plunder after the cremation. The Pandita then, mumbling the Vedas, sprinkles on the body the different kinds of holy water—a ceremony which generally lasts more than an hour. At last, after all the vessels of holy water have been emptied, the Padanda quits the spot, and the bearers of wood now kindle a fire under the figure of the animal, which is consumed but slowly, on account of the copious wetting which it has received. Sand is strewn on the foundation of wood or masonry, to prevent the fire from spreading. When the corpse is consumed, the bones are collected by the watchers, laid on the purified place of burning, and covered with clothes, to which are added also the utensils for adornment and small offerings. These are carried the next day with great state to the sea and thrown into it, together with money and offerings. Before this is done the *Padanda* again reads the Vedas on a lofty erection, making frequent use of the bells, which stand by his side. Opposite the Padanda stand rich offerings of all kinds, and especially quantities of clothes and money. The *Padanda* receives these offerings. He is also offered a tolerably large sum, up to £50, for performing the ceremonies, but most priests take only part of this and return the rest to the relatives of the deceased. Other ceremonies follow at intervals of a fortnight, of some months, and of a year after the cremation. At these we have again a procession, as at the cremation itself; there is a *Bade*, upon which the corpse is represented by flowers; these flowers (*puspa*) are also thrown into the sea. During the whole of this time numerous offerings are made for the deceased. After the ceremony, which takes place a year after the cremation, the deceased is regarded as actually admitted among the *pitaras* (the shades) in *Indra's* heaven, and as sharing in the offerings which are presented to the latter in the domestic temples. Great princes sometimes celebrate a feast to the memory of the dead even after the lapse of some years.[1]

The *burning of widows* has attracted most attention from Europeans. Wonder is expressed at the great number of women sacrificed in this way in Bali in former times (Crawfurd, "As. Res." vol. xiii. p. 135); yet it should be borne in mind that in Bali *polygamy* is carried further than in any other country—that, *e.g.*, the great-grandfather of rája *Kassiman*, prince of *Ngrurah Sakti Pam'chutan*, had 500 wives—and thus it cannot surprise us to see so many women burnt, particularly since the women who offer themselves gain the highest distinction, and the sacred writings, from the *Parvas* (divisions of the *Mahâbhârata*) downwards, represent this act as praiseworthy and almost necessary. That in India but one wife follows her husband in death, is naturally explained by the fact that very few Hindus have more than one wife. But little is yet known of the burning of widows among the princes of India, and as but few independent princes now exist who are worshippers of Śiva, the silence on this subject is easily accounted for.*

In Bali *the burning of widows is confined almost entirely to the princely families*. The princes are now either *Kshatriyas* or *Veśyas* (*Devas* or *Gustis*), and so far Crawfurd is correct in saying that only the second and third castes observe this custom. The true reason of this, however, lies in the outlay which is requisite. The *Śûdras* are seldom rich enough to bear the expense of a splendid cremation; their women, also, are less under the influence of the priests, who do not trouble themselves much about such common people; and finally, the wife's respect for the deceased husband is not so great, because he was of the same rank as herself. Among

---

[1] [Greater details concerning cremation are given by R. van Eck in "Tijdschrift voor Nederlandsch Indië," 1879, vol. i. pp. 104-24. See also Jacobs, l. l. pp. 49-53.]

* A man of high rank in *Nipal, Bhugtee Thapa*, was followed into the fire by his *two wives*.—H. T. PRINSEP, *Transactions of the Marquess of Hastings*, vol. i. p. 170, note.

the Brahmans the burning of widows is still rarer, but yet a case which occurred some years ago in Badong has come to my knowledge. The Brahmans do not regard it as necessary; it is not prescribed in the *Vedas*, nor is it practised in India by the Brahmans, who have remained free from the worship of the sect.

The names given to the burning of widows are known from Crawfurd: *Satya* and *Bela*. This explanation of them must be modified. *Satya is the burning of a wife*, who from a platform erected for the purpose, *throws herself into the same fire with her husband, committing suicide with the creese at the same time*. These may be either lawful wives or concubines, and the latter is not unfrequently the case. *Bela*, on the contrary, is the burning of a wife, *who is burnt in a separate fire*, not with her husband, *jumping into it alive*, without using the creese. This latter method is not thought so much of, but is the more common. These women, who are also called improperly *Belas*, are mostly concubines, but I have also been told of cases in which lawful wives have chosen this method of self-immolation.

The names *Satya* and *Bela* are Indian—the former unmistakeably, the second in all probability. *Satya* is *truth, fidelity;* the wife who dies in this way is called *Satyavatî*, a true, faithful woman, who has performed in all things her duty to her husband. *Bela* is explained by Crawfurd as "retaliation," but so far as I am able to reconcile the Balinese explanations with each other, it is rather the Sanskrit *welâ* "sudden and easy death" (Wilson).[1] This is rendered clear by the way in which it takes place; and further by the fact that the *sacrifice of the followers of a prince* defeated in war, who then die together in an *amok*, is also called *Bela*. In general it means in Bali "dying with the man of higher rank" (the wife with her husband, the slave with his master, the followers with the prince).

That female slaves were murdered by men appointed for the purpose, and were afterwards cast into the fire, which would seem to be a compulsory human sacrifice, must have been a fact 200 years ago, and was observed by Mr. Zollinger in *Lombok*,* but I have not found any trace of it in Bali. The women who sacrifice themselves are indeed, as a rule, slaves, for they are mostly from the fourth caste (the *Sûdras*), at least all the concubines are; but

---

[1] [The meaning given in R. von Eck's "Balineesch Woordenbock" is "faithful unto death." In Javanese, the word conveys the meaning "to die or suffer with or for another." See the numerous examples in Vreede's edition of Roorda's Dictionary, p. 1093. For other explanations of the terms *satya* and *wela*, see Wilken, "Het Animisme," p. 85. *Satya* is evidently an abbreviation of *Satyavatî*.]

* See the report of the Dutch envoys to *Gelgel*, in Crawfurd, "Ind. Arch." vol. ii. p. 244 *sqq.*

their immolation is voluntary,[1] and neither in the *Satya* or the *Bela* are they touched by a man. From the moment that they declare themselves ready to be burnt alive, they are holy persons; they enjoy all the honours of the Pitaras. They may no longer tread the ground, but must always be carried. Offerings are even made to them, and all their wishes are satisfied. Nevertheless, the successor of the deceased simply regards such concubines as the servants who will be required by his father after his cremation. The women themselves are excited by religious ideas; a female priest always accompanies them till the moment of death, and describes to them in glowing colours the happiness of life in *Svarga*, the rise to a higher caste, and how they will thereby become the lawful wives of the deceased. To these deceptions must be added the honour and the advantages which the woman's relations expect to receive from the prince's successor; the men of her family have a claim to offices; they are made chiefs of *Dessas, Pamb'kèls*, &c. They are therefore the only persons who sometimes use means of compulsion to prevent the women from retracting. They accompany the victim of the family; they keep up the fire, and, if the woman hesitates, tip up the plank on which she stands above the fire, so that she falls in against her will. These cases, however, are of rare occurrence. Deception of the imagination and the use of opium have generally made the victims quite indifferent, and they jump into the fire as if it were a bath.

Eight days after the death of a prince or noble his wives are asked whether any of them wish to follow him into the fire; those who then state their willingness are accepted, and, during the interval before the cremation, are shown the above honours. They cannot easily change their minds; the opposition of their relatives, and the shame which would attach to them, as well as

[1] [In reference to this we quote an appropriate passage from the work of Dr. Julius Jacobs ("Eenigen tijd onder de Baliers," Batavia, 1883, p. 230), whose account of the inhabitants is at the same time the most recent and the least biassed: "It is perhaps too much to say that a wife does not follow her husband to the funeral pyre *of her own free will*. There are actually women who, to all appearance, voluntarily throw themselves into the fire, or, in the case of the husband having fallen in battle, stab themselves on his corpse (*bela*). A mother may also follow her child to death; a betrothed, her lover; a child, its mother; nay, even a friend his friend. Supposing that there exist, to some extent, a genuine sorrow, a holy attachment for the beloved one, it is also in a great measure a fact that those who sacrifice themselves are heartily convinced that in requital of that noble deed they are immediately after death received into the *Satyaloka*, where they are made partakers of unutterable joys, so that thereby at once their sins are wiped out and they attain to eternal bliss. Add to this the influence of the priests who here, as elsewhere, are powerful agents with women, and try to induce them to self-sacrifice by holding out to them all sorts of promises, and who bring them by dint of fasting, prayers, and stupefying drinks, to a state of mental imbecility that makes them no longer accountable for their actions, and you will know what is meant by their sacrificing themselves *of their own free will*."]

the deceptions of the priests, hold them back. The women who may wish to give in their names after this period of eight days are not accepted, perhaps in order to avoid the appearance of compulsion. The women who have offered themselves to be burnt lead thenceforward a life of pleasure, and enjoy much greater honour than they ever knew before. This again is a reason why they should not change their minds during the interval, sometimes a long one, before the cremation.

We will here add some details of a cremation, at which women were burnt, in *Gyanyar*, of which we were eye-witnesses. On the 20th December, 1847, the prince of *Gyanyar*, *Dewa Mangis*, was burnt; we have already spoken above of the way in which his body underwent cremation. The corpse was followed by *the three wives* (concubines), who became *Belas*. A procession went before them, as before the body: (1) *Upachâra*, (2) *Toya*, (3) *Banten dagan*. They, like the body, were seated in the highest storeys of the *Bades*, which, like that of the prince, were carried by men, but had only three storeys. After the body of the prince had arrived at the place of cremation, the three *Belas* in their *Bades*—each preceded by the bearers of the offerings destined for her, with armed men and bands of music—were conducted to the three fires.

Their *Bades* were also turned round three times, and were carried round the whole place of cremation. The women were then carried down steps from the *Bades*, and up the steps of the places erected for their cremation. These places consisted of a square of masonry three feet high, filled with combustibles, which had been burning since the morning, and threw out a glowing heat; the persons appointed to watch them fed the fire, and at the moment when the women leaped down, poured upon it a quantity of oil and arrack, so that it flared up to a height of eight feet, and must have suffocated the victims at once. Behind this furnace stood an erection of bamboo, in the form of a bridge, of the same width as the square of masonry, and about forty feet long, and from sixteen to eighteen feet high; steps of bamboo led up to it in the rear. In the centre there is a small house, affording a last resting-place to the victim, in which she waits until the ceremonies for her husband are finished and his body has begun to burn. The side of the bamboo scaffold nearest to the fire is protected by a wall of wet Pisang-stems. Upon the bridge lies a plank smeared with oil, which is pushed out a little over the fire, as soon as the time for the leap draws near. At first there is a door at the end of the bridge, and this is not removed till the last minute. The victim sits in the house on the bridge, accompanied by a female priest and by her relatives. They all speak to her of the happiness which she will now shortly enjoy with her husband. She then makes her toilet; her hair especially is combed, the mirror used, and her garments newly arranged; in short, she arrays herself exactly as she would for a feast. Her dress is white, her breasts are covered with a white *slendang;* she wears no ornaments, and after all the preparations to which it has been subjected, her hair at the last moment hangs quite loose. When the corpse of the prince was almost consumed, the three Belas got ready; they glanced one towards another, to convince themselves that all was prepared; but this was not a glance of fear, but of impatience, and it seemed to express a wish that they might leap at the same moment. When the door had been opened, and the plank smeared with oil and pushed out, each took her place on her plank, made three *Sembahs* by joining her hands above her head, and one of the bystanders placed a small dove (*titiran*)[1] upon her head. When the dove flies away, the soul is considered to escape. They then immediately leaped down. There was no cry in leaping, no cry from the fire; they must have been suffocated at once. One of the Europeans present succeeded in pushing through the crowd to the fire, and in seeing the body some seconds after the leap—it was dead, and its movements were caused merely by the combustion of the materials cast upon the flames. On other occasions, however, Europeans have heard cries uttered in leaping, and in the first moments afterwards.

During the whole time, from the burning of the prince till the leap of the victims, the air resounded with the clangour and noise of the numerous bands of music. The soldiers had drawn up outside the square, and contributed to the noise by firing off their muskets. Besides these, some small cannon were discharged. There was not one of the 50,000 Balinese present who did not show a merry face; no one was filled with repugnance and disgust, except a few Europeans, whose only desire was to see the end of such barbarities. The Balinese look upon this cremation simply as the consummation of their religious and domestic duties; no one sees any cruelty in it. Yet, as the all-powerful priests attach little importance to it for their own caste, with their aid the diminution and abolition of these human sacrifices among the other castes might be effected. The priests' interest in maintaining it is, alas! a monetary one—and therefore no help can be expected from them.

The number of women burned in Bali itself is not considerable; in Lombok, however, where only 9000 Balinese reside (the rest are the Mahomedan *Sesakers*), this ceremony is more frequent."[2]

---

[1] [It is called *Katitiran* in Malay, and a kind of sacredness attaches to it.]
[2] [A full and interesting account of the self-sacrifice of the wife of a *Gusti* is given by Zollinger in his article on *Lombok*, "Journal of the Indian Archipelago," vol. v. p. 529 ff. The Journal of the Dutch Embassy to Bali ("Bijdragen," II., vol. i. p. 52 ff.) gives a description of the funeral ceremonies

During the time I spent in Bali, five or six cremations of *Gustis* took place in Lombok, and on each occasion from four to seven women offered themselves up. This preciseness in following the ancient usages also shows itself in great offerings, which cost considerable sums, but at the same time add greatly to the fame of the prince who makes them, and strengthen him for war (*e.g.*, the offerings in September 1846). The explanation of this lies in two circumstances : first, the Balinese of Lombok, and especially their prince, are much richer than those of Bali, where even the reigning princes, through the great extension of their families, possess but little means; and secondly, the Balinese of Lombok, and particularly the present prince, are looked down upon, and said to be ignorant in their religion and their customs, by the Balinese of Bali, and especially by the *Deva agung*, whom the people of Lombok do not acknowledge. Now to refute these unfavourable opinions, they show themselves to be much more precise in the performance of their religious duties than the majority of the Balinese in Bali. *During the two years* of my stay in Bali, I only knew of *one case of widow-burning* in *Gyanyar*. In all the southern States also none took place; intelligence from *Karang-Assem* and *Boleleng* is uncertain and irregular, but I heard nothing of the practice in these States either. It cannot be asserted, however, that the custom has entirely disappeared. Widow-burning is considered a necessary adjunct to the cremation of a great prince, and in the last thirty years a large number of women have actually been sacrificed in *Badong*.

Nine *Belas* were burnt with the prince of *den Passar*, Ngrurah Made Pam'chuttan, Kassiman's father, and three with the last prince but one of *Pam'chuttan*, Ngrurah G'dé Pam'chuttan (the father of the principal wives of the present *Râja* of *Pam'chuttan*). One very young wife, who threw herself *tandakking* into the flames, was burnt with the last prince of *Pam'chuttan*, Anak Agung Lanang (father of the present prince).*

Râja Kaleran Kanginan was followed by two wives; one killed herself and became *Satyavati* (see above), after the example set by the wife of the *râja Salya*, one of the heroes of the *Mahâbhârata*, known here from the *Salyaparva*. *Râja Kaleran Kawan* was followed by three wives. A young wife followed *râja Halit Kassiman*, a nephew of the old *Kassiman*, who died very young. Some women also followed *Kassiman's* brother in *Belaluan*. If the dead bodies in *Den Passar*, which have already lain unburied

at the burning of the king's mother on March 21, 1633, at which many of her female slaves were stabbed and burnt. At the funeral of the two royal princes, forty-two and thirty-four of their wives respectively threw themselves into the fire. Princesses of royal blood are not previously stabbed.]

* *Tandakking* on this occasion does not permit another person to *tandak* also.

for fifteen or twenty years, are burnt, it is doubtful whether women will follow them. The principal wives seldom follow, and in this case the deceptions cannot have the same effect upon the concubines as when they are practised upon them shortly after the death. *Râja Kassiman* prevents this burning for political reasons, as it might possibly deprive him of his prestige; another reason is the poverty of the present prince of *Den Passar*, whose revenue has been very much diminished by *Kassiman*, and who will not for years be able to amass the sum required for such a grand cremation.[1]

CASTES.

We know from Crawfurd that the four Indian castes exist in Bali; we will hereafter give reasons which seem to show that *caste has also existed in Java*.

The names given by Crawfurd are—*Brâhmana, Satriya, Wisiya, Sudra*. The names *Brâhmana* and *Sudra* are correct; *Satriya* is the corrupt pronunciation of *Kshatriya*, which is found in good manuscripts (*Brahmâṇḍapurâṇa, Râmâyaṇa*, &c.); *Wisiya* has arisen, through an oral mistake, out of *Vesya*, as the Balinese call the third Indian caste; the Sanskrit *Vâiśya* cannot be rendered otherwise in Balinese; in the Balinese letters the four words correspond closely with the Sanskrit names. We have shown in the "Usana Bali" (l. l. p. 254) that the Balinese *taling* has a mark above the line in words where it represents the Sanskrit *âi;* in the word *Wesya*, however, the idea that this *taling* answers to an *âi*, which is unpronounceable, appears to have been lost. I have never yet found the mark in the word *Wesya* in any manuscript.

The Indian names, however, are not those in common use in Bali to indicate the difference in caste. The three upper castes have names with meanings, which are used both in speaking to and speaking of each member of the caste.[2] These titles are:—

1. *Iḍa* for a Brahman; this is the Balinese pronoun of the second and third person in the high language. It is also used for the titles of *Deva* and *Gusti;* but when it stands alone, it always means a Brahman, who is called *He* or *Thou*. A male Brahman is called *Iḍa bagus*, a female Brahman, married or single, *Iḍa hayu*, or, contracted, *Iḍayu* (see below as to the word *Padanda*).

2. *Deva* is the title of a *Kshatriya*, both for men and women (e.g., *Deva agung putri*). *Deva* means in Sanskrit *god*, and in the language of the stage *king* (Wilson); but in the lists of names of royal houses in India which we meet with in Tod's "Annals of Rajasthan," and in several inscriptions published in the "Journal

---

[1] [According to R. van Eck, the last widow was burnt at *Klongkong* in 1862 (see "Tijdschrift voor Ned. Indië," 1879, vol. i. p. 124); but this is doubtful.]

[2] [See Jacobs, l. l. p. 36. P. L. van Bloemen Waanders, l. l. p. 125.]

of the Asiatic Society of Bengal," we find also the title of *deva* (or, corrupted, *dew* or *deb*) added to all the names, and we thus discover that the title of *deva* is used for all *Kshatriyas*, not only in Bali, but also in India, for every one in that caste can become king, and they are also all called *Râja* in India.

3. *Gusti** is the title for the *Wesyas*, or third caste ; this name is not Indian, at least not clearly. In India the third caste is not of much importance, and we are therefore not surprised that it has not a special title.† It is quite otherwise in Bali (and Java); but few *Kshatriyas* have come here from India; there were more *Wesyas*, originally merchants, agriculturists, and artificers. Since the *Kshatriyas* alone were too insignificant in number, greater honour naturally fell to the more numerous *Wesyas*. They even became kings probably in Java, and certainly in Bali, although they are always regarded as subject to the *Deva agung*, a pure *Kshatriya*. For this reason a title of honour was also given to the *Wesyas*, and this is "*Gusti.*" *Gusti* is never interpreted by the Balinese as anything but a name for a *Wesya*. In Java it is now used before the name of God, "*Gusti allah*," and before the names of princes of royal blood ; *Gusti*, used before *allah*, indicates that the word is equivalent to *tuwan* (lord). The fact, however, that the princes of *Solo* and *Jokyokarta* are called "*Gusti*," seems to indicate that this family is also of *Wesyan* descent, and that they retained this title of honour, although the name of the caste, through Mohammedan influence, had been almost lost.

4. The fourth caste, very naturally, has no title of honour. They are the born servants, and can make no claim to marks of honour. Courtesy, however, assigns to them in address the hypocritical name of "father" and "mother" (*bapa* and *meme*). In speaking of them, the term which is also applied to all foreigners (Buginese, Chinese, and Europeans) is used—*kahula*, slave, dependent, or *wang* (= *orang*), man ; they represent the *ordinary man*, while the three superior castes trace their descent from gods and demi-gods.

Mixed castes do not exist in Bali, whereas, even in the very ancient Indian law-book of *Manu*, a large number of mixed castes are enumerated. This is to be explained by the fact that too few people of the three principal castes came over to Java and Bali,

---

* *Goshṭhî* is in Sanskrit "assembly, meeting ; *conversation*, discourse ; *family connexions*, but especially the *dependent or junior branches.*" [This derivation appears very doubtful in spite of Favre's qualifying concession ; see his "Dictionnaire Malais," *s.v.* If tenable at all, it could only come through a supposed adjective, *goshṭhin.*]

† *Arya*, it is true, is the name for a *Wesya* in India ; but what does it mean ? The name *Arya* for the *Kshatriyas* of *Java* (and Bali) is to be read with a long *â* (*ârya*), and then means "*one of the nation of the Aryans* (an *Indian*, a *Persian*). According to Wilson: *Arya*, "a master, a man of the third tribe ; adj. *excellent ; ârya*, of a good family ; respectable, venerable ; apposite, proper ; a master, an owner."

and that these probably brought with them too few women, to maintain the purity of their descendants, and therefore, to prevent the extinction of the chief families, all the children remained in the caste of their father, although the mother may have been of common extraction.

In India the mixed castes arose in two ways: first, through the marriage of a man of a higher caste with a woman of a lower one; secondly, through the marriage of a woman of high caste with a man of inferior birth. The first case is not considered a disgrace to the mixed caste; the second degrades the offspring, because this union is a disgrace; and thus we have the most despised of all Indian castes—the *chaṇḍâlas* (*Parias*), the offspring of a marriage of a female Brahman with a *Sûdra*. In Bali the first kind of marriage causes no mixture of caste; the children follow the caste of the father, but are inferior to the children of high-caste women, and in matters of succession and inheritance are dealt with as of lower standing, even though they be older than their more noble brothers and sisters. The second case cannot occur, for, in Bali, all marriages of high-caste women with men of lower birth (provided they are acknowledged) are punished with death. The guilty woman is burnt alive—a hole is made in the ground and filled with combustibles, into which the woman is cast; this punishment is called *labuh gni* (to fall or be cast into the fire). The man is weighted with stones and drowned in the sea; this is called *labuh batu*.[1] This penalty, however, especially the burning of the woman, is not always carried out so relentlessly. In several cases which came to my knowledge, both the man and the woman were drowned; in another case, where the guilty man had escaped vengeance by flight, the woman, at the command of her father (a *Gusti* in *Kutta*), was killed with the creese by a relation, her mother's brother, after having been adorned with flowers and fine clothes, and rendered fearless by opium and strong drink.

There are, then, no mixed castes in Bali. In the "Usana Bali" (l. l. p. 262) different classes of Sûdras are mentioned—viz., *Mandesa, Gaduh, Dangka, Batu-haji, Pasek, Kabayan, Ngukuhin, Talikup;* these, however, are not different castes, but are all *Sûdras*, some of whom have been degraded to this caste from that of the *Wesyas*, and still maintain, in a political sense, a higher position than the common *Sûdras*.[2]

Chaṇḍâlas, nevertheless, exist in Bali, but they are not *chaṇḍâlas* by birth; there can be none such in Bali. They are afflicted with malignant and contagious diseases, and especially *leprosy*. Such diseases are ascribed to the curse of some deity or of a *Padanda*. These persons may not reside in the *kampongs*,

---

[1] [Jacobs, l. l. p. 34.]
[2] [R. van Eck in "Tijdschrift voor Ned. Indië," 1859, vol. i. p. 129.]

and are found in such places as the frontiers of two hostile States (*Mengui* and *Tabanan*), where they live in misery and without intercourse with the rest of the people. I have seen others on the high roads; their employments are named by Crawfurd.

BRAHMANS.

All Brahmans in Bali trace their descent from *Padanda Wahu Rawuh*, who, according to the Brahmans of the present time, lived in or was descended from Kediri; his descendants went thence to *Majapahit*, and from *Majapahit* to Bali. According to the Javanese accounts, a number of Śiva-Brahmans made their appearance in *Majapahit*, shortly before the fall of that place, from India, and fled upon the destruction of that kingdom to the East and to Bali. The statements of the Balinese upon historical and geographical subjects are extremely inaccurate. According to some, Kediri was situated in *Baratawarsa* (the holy land of India). If we accepted this as true, we should be able to reconcile the accounts of Java and Bali respecting the arrival of Śiva-Brahmans at *Majapahit;* but there are many reasons against this. *Jayabaya* is said by some Balinese to have been a king in *Baratawarsa;* undoubted Javanese accounts, however, state that he ruled in *Kediri* in Java, and all the Kavi works of most importance were composed under him and his predecessor, *Ayer Langia*. The Brahmans, who composed these works, must therefore have come from India at an earlier period and acquired the Kavi language in Java. We must bear also in mind here the localization of Indian places in Java.

Wahu or *Bahu Rawuh* means "the newly-arrived" (*bahu* is the Malay *bahru ; rawuh*, Jav.-Bal., is equal to the Mal. *datang*). He is also named *Bhagavân Dvijendra*, the holy Brahman prince (*dvija* is a Brahman, one born twice—the second time through initiation into religion and sacred literature, and through assuming the sacred band, *Upavîta*). *Indra* is generally king, prince; thus we have *Gajendra*, prince of elephants, *Râkshasendra*, prince of the Râkshasas, namely, Râvana. His two names, therefore, are not family-names, but merely indicate his position; he was the leader of a colony of Brahmans which came from India. Concerning his sojourn in *Kediri* or in *Majapahit* and Bali, the accounts, as we have seen, are uncertain; but, according to the accounts of the priests themselves, the five existing subdivisions of the Brahmans in Bali are descended from him and his five wives. We have:

1. *Brâhmaṇa Kamenu*. (Kamenu is in Gyanyar.) They are descended from Wahu Rawuh and a Brahmanic woman (Brahmaṇa-Brahmanî); according to Indian notions, these alone would have the full rights and dignities of Brahmans, yet we find that, in

spite of their purer descent, they do not enjoy greater honour than their brethren who are of inferior birth. The rank of the Brahmans depends upon their ability, their personal appearance, and their conduct, so that even in youth the qualities of a powerful Pandita may be recognized. The supernatural power attributed to them, and not their descent, therefore, determines the choice of the domestic priests of the princes. Political reasons also have their weight. Brâhmana Kamenu are found in *Boleleng*.

2. *Brâhmaṇa of Gelgel.* (*Gelgel* is the ancient seat of the Deva-agung, already mentioned in the account of the Dutch envoys in 1635, in Crawfurd, "History of the Indian Archipelago," vol. ii. p. 244 seq.; it is also referred to in the Malayan Manuscript of Abdullah—"Tijdschrift voor Nederlandsch Indië," Jaargang 7, 2de Deel, p. 166—where it is erroneously written *Gila gila* in the translation.) They are descendants of Wahu Rawuh and a Kshatriya woman; they are called *Brâhmana-geniten*, and include most of the Brahmans in *Klongkong, Mengui, Bangli*, and those of *Sanor* in *Badong*. The last-mentioned place is chiefly inhabited by Brahmans; none of those at *Badong*, however, are of high rank, but the *Padanda Agung* of Somawati, and the Padanda Made Aleng Kacheng in Taman Intaran, both belonging to other subdivisions of the Brahmans, are the domestic priests of the princes. Some Brahmans in *Boleleng*, also, came originally from Sanor.

3. *Brâhmaṇa-Nuaba.* These are descended from Wahu Rawuh and a Kshatriya widow (*Balu manis*, that is, "a short time married"). Their original seat is the kampong *Nuaba* in *Gyanyar;* hence came those of *Sindhu* in *Karang-Assem*, and of this family is the *Padanda Agung* in Sindhuwati, near Taman Intaran, who, some twenty years ago, left Karang-Assem for political reasons, and was received with gladness in *Badong*.* He is the chief domestic priest in *Badong*, and his brother or cousin in *Gyanyar*.

4. *Brâhmaṇa-mas:* descended from Wahu Rawuh and a Wesya woman.† Their original seat is the kampong *Mas* in *Gyanyar*. The family of the Padanda Made Aleng Kacheng in Taman Intaran came from that place. He is also a domestic priest, and although he is younger than and became a Padanda long after the Padanda Agung was already a domestic priest, still,

---

* He had correspondence with *Gyanyar* at a time when *Gyanyar*, allied with *Badong*, was at enmity with *Karang-Assem;* he therefore lost his position in Karang-Assem, and, together with his brother, was invited by the princes of *Gyanyar* and *Badong*, received with much ceremony, and appointed to the office of domestic priest.

† In general, the Brâhmaṇa-geniten, descended from a Kshatriya woman, seem to be sought after by the princes in the States governed by Kshatriyas—and the Brâhmaṇa-mas, descended from a Wesya woman, where the Wesyas rule—on account of their connection with these castes.

on account of his learning, his morals and the sakti ascribed to him, he is held in the highest honour in *Badong* and *Gyanyar*. There are also *Brâhmaṇa-mas* in Tabanan.

5. *Brâhmaṇa kayu śûnya* (*kayu śûnya* is literally *empty tree,*—this seems to be an allusion to the position of the woman from whom they are descended, for she was a slave, and was therefore without education and learning). They trace their descent to Wahu Rawuh by a slave. To this subdivision belong part of the Brahmans in *Mengui*.

The Brahmans are very numerous in Bali; their position as regards the prince depends upon whether they are ordinary Brahmans (*Iḍas*) or *Padandas*—*i.e.*, learned priests. The former are dependent upon the prince, must follow in war, may be employed as envoys, and may be banished from the country, if they do not strictly obey the prince's commands. Nevertheless, they are of higher rank than the princes, and can marry daughters of princes, while the princes may not marry Brahmanic women. On account of their large number, a considerable portion of them live in extreme poverty, and they do not disdain to cultivate the rice-fields, to engage in the fisheries, and to do manual work for money.

The *Paḍaṇḍas* are Brahmans who have received a complete education from another *Paḍaṇḍa* (their *Guru*). They must be thoroughly acquainted with religion and with literature.

In order to become a Padanda, they undergo all kinds of tests, to show their knowledge and their submission to the Guru. Thus, for instance, they place their heads under the Guru's foot, and drink the water that runs off his feet during his ablutions. Many other ceremonies precede their consecration, and a certain amount of wealth is required to defray the expenses, so that the dignity of *Padanda* mostly remains in a family which has already grown rich by means of this position. Others are supported and helped to become *Padandas* by the *Rajas*. The mark of the dignity is a staff, *daṇḍa*,[1] which they receive from the Guru, and which gives them power to guide and to punish men in all things relating to religion. After this staff they are called *Padanda*, that is, "bearing a staff." Their other name, *Paṇḍita*, merely indicates their knowledge; *Paṇḍita* is "learned," and is explained in Bali by *prajna*, Sanskrit, and *pintar*, Mal.

The domestic priest, *Purohita* (Sanskrit idem), is chosen from the Padandas by the prince; or sometimes the prince helps an Iḍa whom he thinks clever and upright to become a Padanda, and then makes him his domestic priest. He is then the spiritual teacher (Guru) of the prince, who becomes his *śishya* or pupil, makes the *sembah* * to him, and thereby shows his inferiority to the priest; he always sits on a raised seat (see Crawfurd, "Asiatic

---

[1] [The Sanskrit *daṇḍa* is written *ḍaṇḍa* in Javanese and Balinese.]

* The *sembah* is not an ordinary token of courtesy in Bali. The upper

Researches," vol. xiii. p. 110). The domestic priest is consulted in all religious and political matters, and even in the ordinary affairs of life, in taking up arms, in choosing wives, &c. He alone teaches the worship of the Pitaras and conducts the cremations of the princely families. In all offerings, both domestic and for the State, the advice of the domestic priest is acted upon; he is present in his elevated place *opposite the offerings*, and blesses the ceremonies by means of prayers from the Vedas.

Sometimes the word *Purohita* is applied generally to all priests who carry the staff (Padandas). It is these whom Raffles heard spoken of under the name of *Maperwita* or *Mapurwita*. *Purwita* is the corrupted pronunciation of Purohita, which latter word I first recognized in good manuscripts; *mapurohita* (or *mapurwita*) means the being a *purohita*, or the *collective Purohitas*.*

Guru loka, "teacher of the world," is a name applied only to a few chosen Purohitas or Padandas, who present offerings for an entire kingdom; there are one or two of these in each of the different States in Bali. They are the special *Gurus* and counsellors of the chief prince, and are also the *Gurus* of the *loka*, of the world, or the subjects of a State.

The prince can also call other Padandas to perform less important religious functions, and the smaller *râjas* (who are of inferior birth) can likewise choose a Guru out of the rest of the Padandas.

The present *Guru lokas* in the southern States, who exercise great influence upon the actions of the princes, are:—

In *Klongkong*—
1. Padanda *Wayahan Pidada*, who is a *Brâhmaṇa-nuaba* (*balu*-manis).
2. Padanda *K'tut Ngrurah*, a *Brâhmaṇa-gĕniten*. He lives in the kampong of *Dawan*.

In *Gyanyar*—
1. Padanda *Wayahan Kakeran*, a *Brâhmaṇa-nuaba*, cousin of the Padanda *Agung* in *Badong*. He lives in the kaḍaton of *Sindhuwati*, in the kampong of Kramas.

In *Budong*—
1. Padanda *Agung, Brâhmaṇa-nuaba*. He resides in *Sindhuwati* (or *Somawati*), near *Taman Intaran*, and is the father-in-law of
2. Padanda *Made Alêng Kacheng*, *Brâhmaṇa-mas,* in *Taman Intaran*.

castes only make it to the prince, and to the Padandas who are *Guru loka*. The reason of this is, that to the sembah is added an inward formula of reverence out of a Mantra or the Vedas; by making them to other persons of rank they would humble themselves too much.

* The explanation formerly given ("Tijdschrift voor N. I.," Jaarg. 8, Deel 4) of *Purwita*, by means of *purva* and *ita*, thus falls to the ground.

In *Tabanan*—
1. Padanda *Jumpung*, *Brâhmaṇa-gĕniten*, in *Pasekan*, to the north of the kaḍaton in *Tabanan*.

In *Mengui*—
1. Padanda *Putu*, *Brâhmaṇa kayu śûnya*, resides in *Kabakaba*. On account of their low birth the *Brâhmaṇa kayu śûnya* appear to receive much less respect than the rest; yet we find a *Guru loka* among their number, although the men of Badong assert that the people in *Mengui* are grossly ignorant. But Badong and Mengui are old enemies.

The Brahmans also have many wives from among the people, but the children always remain Brahmans.* There is not a single one of pure blood, but, at any rate, care is taken that a Brahman does not have too much Śûdra blood among his ancestors. If, in three generations, no woman of high birth has married into the family, the descendants lose all rank, and are treated by the princes as Sudras, and are obliged to perform service as vassals. It is the same with the other two upper castes.

The Brahmans' wives of low extraction, especially if they have children, are ennobled by the husband; their rank in life, it is true, is much inferior to that of women of high birth, and their husbands give them nothing (they have to maintain themselves and their children), but, after death, they are burnt as Brahmanic women, and enjoy the honour of the Pitaras.

The women of high birth share in all the privileges of their husbands. They are also instructed in the Vedas, *themselves present offerings with the mumbling of the Vedas*, and assist the Belas at cremations. They are also called *Padanda*, with the addition of *istri*, which is the highest title for women in Bali. (In the Sanskrit *strî* only means "woman," in Bali "princely woman," compare *putrî*.)

KSHATRIYAS.

In India the *Kshatriyas*, the second caste, are, according to law, those who, alone, bear arms and defend the country. The princes are of this caste. But, in the present day, there are no longer any pure Kshatriyas in India; even the Rajaputras of Râjasthan are not regarded as of pure extraction. The profession of arms has thus come into the hands of the whole people. The same thing has occurred in Bali. The râjas and their fami-

* Raffles, App. K., p. 238, says that the children of a priest by a woman of lower rank are called *Bujangga*, but this nowhere came to my knowledge. See below respecting the word *Bujangga* [the note in the section on Caste in Java]. In the "Tijdschrift v. N. I.," Jaargang 7, vol. ii. p. 172, subdivisions (*Pomah*, *Anggana*, &c.) of Brahmans are mentioned, whose existence I did not discover, in spite of my repeated inquiries.

lies, at least, are said to be Kshatriyas, but this is but partially the case. The highest prince, the Deva Agung, is a Kshatriya, but most of the other princes are of the third caste, the Wesya. The Kshatriyas no doubt came to Java only in small numbers. In Java the Usana *Jawa* enumerates Kshatriyas of *Koripan* (Panjis-seat), *Gaglang, Kediri*, and *Janggala*. The chiefs of the court of *Jawa* or *Kediri*, who were Kshatriyas and Wesyas, are mentioned in the *Rangga Lawe*. This, the largest kingdom in Java, did not contain many Kshatriyas; they are called *Mahisa* or *K'bo* (*buffalo*, to indicate their strength), and *Rangga* (*Jav. ronggo*); their names are as follow: *Mahisa Bungalan, K'bo Wilalungan, K'bo Siluman, K'bo Jerang, K'bo Kanigara, K'bo Chaluk, K'bo T'ki, K'bo Taluktak, Ki Mahisa Sapati, K'bo Mundarang*, and further *Rangga Smi, Rangga Mayang, Rangga Palana, Rangga Ralengsong, Rangga Pasung, Rangga Wirada, Rangga Rabete, Rangga Sumbi, Rangga Sampana*, and *Anurangga Sunting*. These are all the Kshatriyas who existed in the largest kingdom of Java. A particular sort of creese is attributed to each of them, and these creeses have crossed over to Bali through Majapahit. The Kshatriya families themselves, however, have not crossed to Bali, with the exception of the Deva Agung and his half-brothers, Arya Damar and six others. The pure Kshatriyas were probably exterminated in the numerous Javanese wars, and in the destruction of Majapahit, and the royal family of the Deva Agung also seems to have once (either in Bali or Java) been on the verge of extinction, for the reigning prince *Taruna* (a youth, unmarried) had no children. Here, however, a new race was raised by a priest, *Dang hyang Kapakisan*, out of a stone, *batu henggong* (see "Us. Bali," p. 344). The race thus sprung from *batu henggong* reigns in Bali at the present time, and from it the Kshatriyas are descended. The descendants of the half-brothers (Arya Damar and the others) were in later times degraded to Wesyas. Thus all the Kshatriyas now existing in Bali trace their descent from the Deva Agung—a fact which would surprise us, for their number is considerable, were it not that there are but few of them in Badong, Tabanan, Mengui, and Karang-Assem; and the rest can have descended from the one Deva Agung (who lived 400 years ago) just as well as 800 Gusti Pam'chuttan in Badong, counting only the heads of families who have houses of their own, and are married, may have sprung from the Râja Ngrurah Sakti Pam'chuttan (who four generations ago was prince of all Badong, excepting *Jambe*). At the present day the Kshatriyas are still reigning only in Klongkong, Bangli, and Gyanyar; formerly there was also a Kshatriya dynasty in Boleleng, descended from the Deva Agung, and its descendants now live in Badong. This dynasty was expelled by Wesyas seven generations (?) ago. The same thing took place in earlier times in Karang-Assem.

Two hundred years ago (1633) the Kshatriyas and all the princes of Bali seem still to have been subject to the Deva Agung, who is called *prince of Bali* by the Dutch envoys of that time. The authority of the Deva Agung was very much weakened by a war with Karang-Assem about a hundred years ago, in which the ancient seat of *Gĕlgel* (to the east of Klongkong, near the sea) was destroyed. Since that time Karang-Assem and Boleleng, which was conquered by it, have no longer paid homage to the Deva Agung. Soon after this, also, an insignificant Deva in *Gyanyar* raised himself to the rank of a great prince by expelling the relatives of the Deva Agung from the various provinces which form the present Gyanyar. The new dynasty of Gyanyar, however, returned to the sovereignty of the Deva Agung. *Bangli*, where a Kshatriya prince also rules, acknowledged the Deva Agung until recently, but now has no connection with Klongkong. *Tabanan* has withdrawn from the supremacy of the Deva Agung, because Karang-Assem and Boleleng do not pay him homage. Thus there remain only *Mengui*, *Badong*, and *Gyanyar* which acknowledge the Deva Agung as Sovereign of Bali. Karang-Assem and Boleleng use the name of the Deva Agung as their Sovereign whenever it suits their purpose, but they pay him no homage (*sembah*) and send no presents (or tribute) to Klongkong. Badong also yields him but little, and, in fact, has always been opposed to his interests, although openly it pays him homage, sends envoys to him, and contributes a little to great offerings and feasts in Klongkong.

Dessak, *Pradeva*, and *Pungakan* are names of Kshatriyas who have much Śûdra blood in their veins.

Wesyas.

This caste, from a political point of view, is at present the most important in Bali. To it belong the princes of *Karang-Assem*, *Boleleng*, *Mengui*, *Tabanan*, and *Badong*, and also the prince of *Lombok*. It is much more numerous than the Kshatriyas. The race of the princes of *Karang-Assem*, *Boleleng*, *Mengui*, and *Lombok* is descended from *Patih Gaja Madda*, the second general of Majapahit, who, together with Arya Damar, conquered Bali; he was a Wesya of Majapahit, while Arya Damar, the chief conqueror, was a Kshatriya, and a half-brother of the prince. Arya Damar was the ancestor of the princes of Tabanan and Badong; these, however, are now Wesyas, having apparently been degraded to this caste, about 300 years ago, by the Deva Agung. The reason of this degradation is said to have been that these Kshatriyas wore their hair after the manner of the Wesyas. In the present day there is no perceptible difference between the Kshatriyas and Wesyas in the mode of wearing the hair; the Deva Agung wear it exactly as the ancient Kassiman did, and the young Kshatriyas and Wesyas both wear theirs sometimes loose and sometimes bound up (in the Sivaitic manner) at the back of the head. The true reason was no doubt political; it was desired to humble the powerful race of Arya Damar, and the rest of the Kshatriyas, who were descended from the Deva Agung, and were already very numerous at that time, endeavoured to obtain more power. This object was not attained, but the princes of Tabanan and Badong have remained Wesyas.

We have seen above that the Kshatriyas of Daha and Majapahit bear the titles of *Mahisa* or *K'bo* and *Rangga*. *Patih, Demang,* and *Tumenggung* are given as names for the Wesyas. *Mantris,* who in Java now occupy the lowest position among the native chiefs, can, according to the Balinese, be of either caste; this is explained by the original meaning of the word *Mantri;* in Sanskrit it means "*Minister,*" and is thus applicable to any one who fills this position, whether he be Kshatriya or Wesya. *Patih* also was a much higher rank in ancient Java and Bali than it is in Java now: *Gaja Madda,* who is stated to be the ancestor of four princely families in Bali, and is regarded as the incarnation of Vishṇu, bears the title of *Patih.* And further, the first Deva Agung (see "Usana Java") appoints the conqueror of Bali and governor of *Tabanan, Arya Damar,* to be Patih or first Minister, who must be consulted on all occasions. Of the Javanese titles we also find that of *B'kel* in Bali; it belongs, however, not to members of one of the three upper castes, but to Sûdras, and is equal to *mandur* in Java. In Bali they are called *Parb'kel, Pamb'kel,* or *Prab'kel;* the original name is *Prab'kel,* which, like Pragusti and Pradeva (usually pronounced Pergusti and Perdeva) means the assembly of the *B'kels* (Gustis and Devas).

Of the principal Wesyas of the Court of Daha (Kediri), the following are named in the "Usana Java": *Mantri Bawong, Kala Mudong, Tumenggung Parungsari, D'mang Drawalika, Gebob Basah, Lobar* (the creese of this man's shape is still used by the princes in *Karang-Assem,* according to the Pusaka in *Ngalihan*), *Kala Limpung, Buta Wilis, Bubar Baleman, Jalak Katengeng.* From such Wesya families, as well as from the real brothers of Arya Damar, a great number of Balinese have sprung; but all, except the descendants of Arya Damar and Patih Gaja Madda, are of no importance, and most of them have become Sûdras. A few still bear the title of Gusti and have followers, but the rest are, in all respects, like the Sûdras. The reason of this is, that their forefathers in Bali were conquered and displaced by the races of Arya Damar and Patih Gaja Madda.

The Wesyas were originally intended for commerce, agriculture, and the exercise of arts and handicrafts. This is known in Bali, but the principal Gustis despise these occupations, and they are only disposed to carry on trade for the sake of obtaining the money required for opium-smoking and cock-fights. Trade, however, is not solely in the hands of the Wesyas; all the other castes, also, take part in it.

In order to become better acquainted with the present position of the Dewas and Gustis in Bali, we shall give here an account of the princely families and their descendants.

THE PRINCELY FAMILIES.

We have already referred briefly to the fact that all the Kshatriyan princes, and all the present Kshatriyas, trace their descent to the Deva Agung. The princes and Gustis of *Tabanan* and *Badong* are descended from Arya Damar; and, finally, the princes and Gustis of *Mengui, Karang-Assem, Boleleng,* and *Lombok* derive their pedigree from *Patih* Gaja Madda. This carries us back to the time of the conquest of Bali by the Javanese of Majapahit.

An ancient connection between Java and Bali is indicated in the "Usana Bali." Bali was in the possession of evil spirits, or giants, that is, the Balinese were not yet Hindus (comp. Abdullah, in the "Tijdsch. voor Neêrlands Indië," Jaargang 7, vol. ii. p. 160, *sqq.*). A few Hindus from Majapahit had settled in Bali, and had a temple in *Bazuki* (so-called after the Indian serpent-king *Vâsuki* who, in the Indian and Balinese mythology, accompanies Śiva and plays an important part. They were oppressed, however, by the infidel princes and people. The account of the descent of the gods and the defeat of the Maya Danawa and the demons indicates the triumph of Hinduism. The "Usana Bali" does not tell us by what earthly means this religion was established, and the reason of this seems to be, (1) *that, in order to attain its full sanctity, the religion must be introduced by the gods themselves;* (2) *that it was desirable or necessary to spare the feelings of the conquered people* (*the original Balinese*) *by representing them as conquered, not by men, but by gods.* The "Usana Bali" is intended only for the people.

In the "Usana Java," however, we find traces of the true conquest. It is represented, here, as taking place immediately before the crossing over of the Deva Agung, the chief of Majapahit; but at that time Bali (according to the same "Usana Java") had already become a province of the kingdom of Majapahit, and is merely subdued a second time after a revolt of the governor. The institution of castes and the Hindu religion evidently existed in Bali previously to this, as is clear also from the narrative of Abdullah; but the revolt and the defeat of the Governor of Bali afforded an opportunity of dividing the land among the nobles of Majapahit, and the prince of Majapahit, or his son, came to reside in this island after the fall of the kingdom of Majapahit. This destruction of Majapahit was effected, according to the Javanese accounts, by Muhammadans; according to the Balinese, the kingdom and city were deserted in consequence of a disease caused by a buta (demon).

According to the "Usana Java," Arya Damar and Patih Gaja, Madda were sent from Majapahit in the capacity of generals against the rebellious Bali. Arya Damar conquers the north, while Patih Gaja Madda remains inactive in the south; but, on the approach of Arya Damar, the latter portion also submits to this victorious general. The crossing over of the prince of Majapahit is caused, according to the "Usana Java," by the appearance in Bali of a demoniacal king, *Mraja Danawa* (another infidel, therefore!); the latter is of the family of *Maya Danawa* in the "Usana Bali," and refers to the event that forms the subject of that writing. At that time *Arya Damar* was in Majapahit, and on the receipt of the intelligence that this Raksasa Mraja Danawa is exercising his power in Bali, the prince of Majapahit himself sets out against Bali with Arya Damar and his whole army; after defeating the Raksasa prince, who, when he can resist no longer, flies away through the air, the prince of Majapahit establishes himself in *Gelgel*. This account is obviously improbable, and was perhaps invented to conceal from the original Balinese the manner in which, and the reasons for which, the prince of Majapahit, or his son, left his kingdom to settle in Bali.*

What would seem nearest the truth in these accounts is this: *Arya Damar had subdued rebellious Bali, and again compelled respect for the prince of Majapahit; a short time afterwards the kingdom of Majapahit fell to the ground (through war or other disasters), and the surviving prince, or one of his sons, came over to peaceful Bali.* The Balinese naturally regard this arrival as an honour, and look upon the loss of Majapahit as of little moment, for they say that place (and all Java) became infested with evil spirits. The princes do not seem to have so easily forgotten the loss of their great kingdom in Java; hence their continual wars with *Blambangan*, and even in *Passuruan* (Raffles, vol. ii. p. 200, *sqq.*, "History of Java"), whence, however, they finally had to withdraw. *Blambangan* (the country near *Banyuwangi*) for a long time still belonged to Bali. The wildness of this country is partly owing to the wars with the Balinese, who were unable to hold it. It is remarkable that the opposite side of Bali, *Jembrana*, is also, to a great extent, desolate; here, as in Majapahit, the reason of this desolation is said to be that the dwelling of a king of demoniacal form made the land unsafe. But both *Jembrana* and *Blambangan* were really laid waste by the long wars between Java

* The "Usana Java" does not give the name of the prince who became the first Deva Agung in Bali. According to other accounts, his name was Deva Agung K'tut, and this is given by Raffles and confirmed by the Balinese.

and Bali, and, even now, are little cultivated, more for security's sake than from fear of the demoniacal king. The longing of the Balinese to regain their lost country has shown itself in the expedition of the Bolelengers against *Banyuwangi* under the English rule. They have also attempted to gain in the East what they have lost in the West—hence the conquest of Lombok and the attack on *Sembawa*, where they were stopped by the Dutch Government.

After the settlement of the Deva Agung in Bali at *Gelgel*, the land is divided among the chief men in the army and the Court. Arya Damar received the great land of Tabanan, and became a *Patih*, first Minister of the Deva Agung. The prince could not undertake anything without consulting him, and this privilege descends to his offspring, and forms the ground of the present grievances of the princes of Tabanan and Badong, who never forget this ancient privilege, and, as the Deva Agung does not keep the old promise, no longer consider themselves bound to him. Badong, however, preserves, for political reasons, the appearance of subjection. Arya Damar also obtains the title of *Arya Kencheng* (*Kenjeng* or *Kengjeng* is the title for princely Javanese invested with authority, and is also given to the Resident, the Government, &c.). The number of his men is said to have been 40,000. Smaller governorships were also given to Arya Damar's brothers; to *Arya Sento*, the countries of *Pachung*, the present *Marga*, belonging formerly to *Mengui*, but now to *Tabanan;* to *Arya Beleteng*, the country of *Pinatih*, since conquered by the princes of Badong, but still a separate kingdom; to *Arya Waringin*, that of *Kapal* in the present *Mengui;* to *Arya Blog*, that of *Kabakaba* in *Mengui;* to *Arya Kapakisan*, that of *Habiansĕmal* in *Mengui;* to *Arya Binchaluku*, that of *Tangkas* in *Klongkong*. Besides these brothers of Arya Damar, *Arya Manguri* is mentioned as governor in Dawuh in Karang-Assem, and the three principal Wesyas, *Tan Kuber, Tan Kawur*, and *Tan Mundur* (names, really, symbolical), also receive a domain. In the "Pamendanga," a sort of history of the princes and priests, however, of little value, the governorships allotted to these nobles are somewhat different, but, at any rate, this work mentions Patih Gaja Madda as governor of Mengui, a fact confirmed by all Balinese, but omitted from the "Usana Java."* We thus see Bali, at the very outset, divided among governors; these could soon change from governors into independent princes, such as we now find. In the year 1633, according to the Dutch Envoys, the Deva Agung seems still to have been the only prince in Bali, and it is probable that he was regarded as such and had influence over the whole of Bali until about 100 years ago, when Gelgel,

---

* The "Usana Bali" betrays partiality for the race of Arya Damar.

his ancient seat, was destroyed. The countries adjoining Klongkong, *Bangli, Gyanyar,* and also *Boleleng,* seem to have been immediately under the Deva Agung, and were then, in course of time, given as governorships to members of his family. Here also, after the degradation of the race of the Arya Damar, were the only remaining Kshatriyas, but even these were partly expelled by the Wesyas. The history of Arya Damar's descendants is remarkable only on account of the conquest of Badong and the founding of this kingdom. The race of Patih Gaja Madda has much more influence upon the history of the whole of Bali. This chief, the second general of the princes of Majapahit, had his seat in Mengui. The palace of Mengui is one of the oldest. Abdullah (p. 163) even makes the Deva Agung reside in Mengui from the first; the information I have obtained as to this point, however, agrees with the "Usana Java," where the Deva Agung has his first seat in Gelgel; proceeding subsequently to Klongkong. To Mengui belonged, besides the present country of that name, the greater portion of Badong (the smaller, eastern portion of Badong, formed the kingdom of Pinatih, which in later times was subject to Mengui); and, further, a portion of the present Gyanyar, *Kramas,* and the land of *Marga,* which now belongs to Tabanan. It was thus a considerable domain, and as large, if not larger, than Tabanan. Arya Damar's brothers had, it is true, various portions of the present Mengui, but they all appear to have been speedily subjected to the power of Gaja Madda and his successors; the kingdom of *Pinatih* alone remained under the descendants of Arya Damar, but it became tributary to Mengui. The position of Bali at this period (about 250 years ago) may therefore be thus described: *Klongkong, Gyanyar* (with the exception of *Kramas*), *Bangli,* and *Boleleng* belonged to the Deva Agung and to *punggawas* (governors) of his family; *Tabanan* to the descendants of Arya Dama; *Mengui* with *Badong* and parts of *Gyanyar* and *Tabanan* (*Kramas* and *Marga*) to the descendants of Gaja Madda. *Karang-Assem* was probably still under the descendants of *Arya Manguri* (at least partially). A change in this state of affairs was caused by the princes of Mengui conquering Karang-Assem, and a Gusti of Tabanan establishing himself and his descendants in Badong, and forming a separate independent kingdom, after being for a time subject to Mengui.

Another and a more important change began about one hundred years ago, in consequence of the war of Karang-Assem against Klongkong. The cause of this war was the putting to death of a prince of Karang-Assem, by command of the Deva Agung. The prince in question did penance after the manner of the Indian *yogis;* he gave himself up entirely to contemplation, and, thereby, neglected all outward worldly things so much that he grossly transgressed decorum—*e.g.,* he allowed his excrement to fall where he happened to be sitting. When he was in Klongkong, he conducted himself in the same manner, and thus offended the Deva Agung and the nobles of the court of Gelgel. On his return journey, he was killed from an ambush by command of the Deva Agung. He left three sons, who immediately resolved to avenge his death. The penance performed by their murdered father rendered their power irresistible in the eyes of the Balinese; the real fact is, however, that the race of Gaja Madda, which then possessed all the extensive country of Mengui and Karang-Assem, was the most powerful in Bali. They defeated the Deva Agung and destroyed his royal seat in Gelgel. The Deva Agung retained his territory, however, and seems, from this time forward, to have fallen into the state of dependence under the Karang-Assem family in which we now find him. Peace was restored by marriages, and Klongkong was held in subjection. The wife of the Deva Agung last-deceased was a princess of Karang-Assem, and governed the whole land for him so completely that she even dared to murder another wife of her husband, a princess of Badong. From this time the decline of the power of the Deva Agung is principally to be dated. He was a conquered prince, and, although he retained his territory, and the conqueror remained in outward appearance his inferior, yet his prestige among his own people was seriously lowered. In addition to this, the princes of Kareng-Assem no longer performed feudal service in Klongkong, but simply conceded to the Deva Agung the title of *first ruler of Bali*, without paying him tribute.

This victory had yet other important consequences for the family of Karang-Assem. The conquerors of Klongkong could without much difficulty also attack Boleleng, where dynasties had already changed several times, and which at that time was certainly in a weak state. They took this country also, and one of the brothers became king of Boleleng. At that time the most ancient dynasty of the Kshatriyas had already ceased to exist in Boleleng;[*] the statements of the people of Badong asserting that it was driven from the throne seven generations ago, retiring to Badong, where it still lives, subordinate to the ruling Wesyas, but yet of some distinction. (Its head is the Deva Made Rahi in Kutta, who has obtained the chief command of that place from the râjas of Badong.) One of the succeeding princes of Boleleng, also of Wesyan blood (being descended from Arya Beleteng in Pinatih), was *Panji;* he, however, did not hold the kingdom long. Whether he expelled the Kshatriyas is not certain, nor is it known whether the family of Karang-Assem immediately succeeded him.

[*] This is open to doubt. In that case how can Kshatriyas have ruled in Boleleng in Crawfurd's time (1812)?

The last exploit of the victorious brothers of Karang-Assem was the conquest of Lombok. Here, also, one of the brothers remained as prince, keeping five thousand Balinese families with him, from whom the present Balinese population of Lombok have sprung.

In the south, the Gusti family from Tabanan had, in the meantime, subdued the whole of the western portion of Badong, namely, Pinatih : the eastern portion was conquered somewhat later.

About the same time (three generations ago) the family of the Deva Agung was also robbed of its possessions in Gyanyar, and an inferior Deva (*Pungakan*), named Deva Mangis, founded the present kingdom of Gyanyar.

A hundred years later, therefore, we have the following state of affairs in Bali :—(1) The *Deva Agung* in Klongkong, only in name still prince of all Bali, and with his territory reduced to Bangli and Klongkong. Bangli, however, had its own princes, who were also Kshatriyas and descended from the Deva Agung, but of lower birth than the Kshatriyas in Klongkong. In Gyanyar the relations of the Deva Agung were conquered by a Deva of insignificant rank. (2) *The family of Gaja Madda* ruling in Mengui, Karang-Assem, Boleleng, and Lombok. Mengui, their original country, had, however, already lost a large piece of territory to the newly arisen Badong. (3) The family of *Arya Damar* in *Tabanan* and in the newly founded *Badong*.

Since that time there have still been quarrels without end among the eight States which we have mentioned. We say eight, for *Pahyangan* was not a separate State, but belonged formerly to Bangli, and now to Mengui, and *Jembrana* has also, always, or for a very long time, been subject to Boleleng—it was conquered twenty years ago by Badong, but retaken by Boleleng.

The most frequent wars have been between Badong and Mengui, with its allies Karang-Assem and Boleleng; and between Gyanyar and Mengui, allied with Bangli. The new kingdoms of Badong and Gyanyar soon became allies, although they have had a few small wars with each other, when one has been for and the other against the party of the Deva Agung. In general, they maintain friendly relations with the Deva Agung, pay him homage, and send him a few presents. To show the present condition of Bali, we will now speak of each State in particular.

1. *Klongkong*, governed by the Deva Agung, is the smallest, and is not a rich country. His men are said to number 6000. Formerly there were members of his family in Nagara, Sukawati, and Pejeng (all in the present Gyanyar); the family also had Boleleng, but it was driven out thence and went to Badong. In Bangli, also, the Kshatriyan family is no longer related to the Deva Agung, but, down to the most recent period,

the Kshatriyas of Bangli were always true followers of, and paid homage to, those of Klongkong. At present, Bangli and Klongkong are bitter enemies. Gyanyar, Badong, and Mengui acknowledge the authority of the Deva Agung by presents and envoys. Karang-Assem and Boleleng acknowledge him as supreme prince, but pay him no homage, and, although they act in full harmony with Klongkong, they do so as an entirely independent State. Towards the Dutch Government, however, they make use of the pretended power of the Deva Agung, in order to represent their acts as controlled by the Deva Agung, and to take refuge behind him. Tabanan, Bangli, and Lombok do not even acknowledge the superior rank of the Deva Agung, much less give him presents.

The name of the present Deva Agung is G'ḍe Putra;* his sister, the daughter of the above-mentioned princess of Karang-Assem, is named Deva Agung Istri. The Deva Agung's mother was a Sudra woman, but the deceased Deva Agung had no male children by noble wives, and thus the son of a Sudra woman was obliged to succeed him.

2. *Gyanyar.*—This State is governed by *Deva Pahan*, a son of *Deva Mangis*, who died in October 1847. The family is Kshatriyan, but of low descent (on account of too much intermixture with Sudra blood), and is called *pungakan* (*pungakan* means *fallen*). Deva Pahan's great-grandfather, named Deva Mangis, was the founder of this State. He was commander of 200 men in the *dessa* of Gyanyar, and was under the Punggawas of the Deva Agung, who were governors in Nagara, Sukawati, and Pejeng, and relations of the ruling Deva Agung. By deceit, violence, and poison he gained the mastery over these punggawas, and conquered from Mengui the country of Kramas. On account of his infamous deeds, his poisoning, &c., he is said to have changed after death into a serpent, which was kept for a long time in the palace at Gyanyar, but disappeared in the last few years. His success in all his undertakings was probably owing to the fact that he began in a time when Klongkong was defeated by Karang-Assem, and deprived of all power. Gyanyar, however, has submitted to the Deva Agung as the supreme ruler, and sends

---

* *G'ḍe* means the oldest son or daughter of the same mother among other than royal persons, and among Brahmans the usual word for this is *Wayahan* (old); *Made* is the second (really the middle one, Sanskrit madhya); *Nyoman*, the third, if there be a fourth; *K'tut*, the third or fourth (really the youngest). If there are more children, the same expressions are used, but are placed before the name instead of after it. Thus we have in *Den Passar* a râja *Ngrurah K'tut*, and a *K'tut Ngrurah*, both sons of the deceased prince, the brother of Kassiman. *Putra* is prince, but ought properly to be applied only to those of purely noble birth; in this case, however, the Deva Agung is the son of a Sudra woman, but, as the only one who could succeed to the throne, he was ennobled.

him numerous presents, which cause him to forget that his nearest relatives are disgracefully oppressed—for the former punggawas are still living in Gyanyar, but they are under the command of a Pungakan. It thus appears that, all over Bali, noble birth is not sufficient to protect a family. Here, too, the stronger conquers, even though he be of the lowest extraction. Such a victorious family is then again elevated by noble marriages. Gyanyar is stated to contain 35,000 men, but not more than half this return can be taken as true. It is one of the most fertile and best-cultivated districts of Bali.

Gyanyar is allied with Badong, and acts as mediator in the disputes between this State and Klongkong. Its attitude towards Karang-Assem is neither friendly nor hostile. In the last Dutch expedition against Boleleng, Gyanyar, by command of the Deva Agung, sent 5000 men to assist; they arrived too late, however, and were not the best soldiers, but, on the contrary, the refuse of the kingdom.

Gyanyar has had many quarrels under the three princes bearing the name of Deva Mangis, chiefly with Bangli and Mengui, but also with other States. At the conquest of Mengui by Badong, Gyanyar was allied with the latter, and received a piece of territory on the frontier, *Kadewatan.* Gyanyar's friendship towards Badong is not to be relied on; hence the new campongs built by the raja Kassiman on the frontier of Badong.

3. *Bangli.*—The reigning prince is *Deva G'de Putu Tangkeban.** His family also is descended from the first Deva Agung in Klongkong, but in rank it stands lower than the line of the Deva Agungs. Formerly this family ruled over two States—*Bangli* and *Taman-Bali.* This close relationship was not sufficient to prevent the prince of the former State from seizing the latter and extirpating its princes. The same thing has, however, occurred to the families of Karang-Assem and of Lombok. Until about ten years ago, Bangli was attached to Klongkong; the prince of Bangli, the most warlike in Bali, was commander-in-chief (*Senâpati*). Its enmity with Klongkong was brought about by the influence of the princess of Karang-Assem, who was married to the deceased Deva Agung. In its many wars with Karang-Assem, Boleleng, and Gyanyar, however, it lost part of its territory in the north, and lately also Pahyangan, which lies south of Bangli, and is now divided from Bangli itself by a strip of territory acquired by Gyanyar. Pahyangan has been won by Boleleng and ceded by this State to the Deva Agung, who again has handed it over to the government of the prince of Mengui, his Punggawa.

Bangli no longer acknowledges the Deva Agung, and has entered into friendly relations with Tabanan and Badong, which,

* *Putu* is applied to a person at whose birth the grandfather or grandmother is still living.

however, the surrounding hostile States render of little account. The war with Gyanyar has recently been stopped through the influence of Badong. The country has also suffered nothing from Karang-Assem and Boleleng since the first Dutch expedition; now, however, it is in great danger from the union of these two States and of Klongkong and Mengui. The men of Bangli are the bravest in Bali, and it is only by virtue of this quality that they have been able to hold their own against so many powerful enemies. Women also bear arms in this country. There are only fifty firearms in Bangli.*

4. *Mengui*.—The reigning prince is *Anak Agung K'tut Agung*. He murdered his elder brother, who was the first prince; the widow of the latter, *Byang Agung*, however, still has much influence. The families of Karang-Assem, Boleleng, and Lombok are of Menguian extraction. *Patih Gaja Madda* was governor of Mengui. According to some accounts, this Patih Gaja Madda was an incarnation of Vishnu, who has thus also assumed the body of a Wesya. The story probably originated when the family had subdued nearly the whole of Bali and Lombok. Another account says that Patih Gaja Madda vanished from the earth and left no children, the house of Mengui being descended from *Ki Yasak*, who married the granddaughter of Arya Damar against the will of her father, *Arya Yasan*. In ancient times Mengui included the whole of western Badong, while the eastern portion, the State of Pinatih, also acknowledged the supremacy of Mengui among the descendants of Arya Beleteng. Besides this, Kramas and Kadevatan of Gyanyar and Marga, in the mountain range of Tabanan, formerly belonged to Mengui. Kramas was conquered by Gyanyar, as we have seen;

* The above, like all the rest of this account, was written in 1848. The third expedition despatched by the Dutch Government against the hostile States in Bali in 1849 has very much altered the position of several princes. The author has thought it desirable, however, not to alter his work on this account, but to describe Bali in the state in which it was when he left it. Now that Boleleng, Karang-Assem, and Bangli are better known, the public will of course have fresh information regarding them; hitherto, however, but little that is authentic has come to the author's ears, and he therefore gives the information which he gathered, to serve as far as possible as historical data. It is well known that the prince of Bangli, the faithful ally of the Dutch Government, has now, in addition to his own country, received from the Government the State of Boleleng, to be ruled under the sovereignty of Holland; also that Karang-Assem has been given to the prince of Mataram-Lombok, who believed he had a well-founded claim to it. The authority of the Deva Agung has also been still further lessened, both because he has been compelled to acknowledge the sovereignty of Holland, and because two princes, who previously did not recognize his authority, have now become his powerful and dreaded neighbours, who will always be ready and able to hold him in check. To avoid repetition, we need here only allude to the fact that the princes hitherto reigning in Boleleng and Karang-Assem, and the still better-known Gusti Jelanteg, have fallen in the struggle.

we shall speak of the rest in connection with Badong. Mengui was for some time, about twelve years, under the dominion of Badong, but is now again free from that kingdom and stands as a separate governorship under Klongkong. The house of Mengui is not only of the same origin as that of Karang-Assem, but is also allied to it by a very recent marriage between the prince of Karang-Assem and a princess of Mengui. Mengui must obey blindly the orders of the Deva Agung; it is, however, hostile to Badong and Tabanan, and is nearly neutralized by its position between these two States. The small piece of territory belonging to Mengui on the sea-coast is very much coveted by Badong, which, by obtaining it, would touch the frontier of its ally Tabanan. This piece of territory, however, is strongly defended by its rocky coast, which only leaves open a small path.

The hostility which exists among the Balinese is shown by, among other things, the diversion of water; Mengui, for instance, has dug a new bed on its territory for a river which formerly flowed into the sea in Badong, and by this means has left dry the rice-fields of Grobokkan on the borders of Badong.

5. *Karang-Assem.*—The reigning prince is *Ngrurah* G'de Karang-Assem.* The family is that of Gaja Madda, and the country was conquered by Mengui more than two hundred years ago. A list of the names of the princes of Karang-Assem is given in the "Pamendanga," a work which we have mentioned above, but nothing is stated as to their acts. In the "Usana Java," the governorship of Dawuh in Karang-Assem is held by Arya Manguri; it is not certain whether that family had the whole of Karang-Assem—possibly part of it was in the possession of the Deva Agung. By the conquest of Karang-Assem by the house of Mengui, Klongkong was cut off from Boleleng, and the powerful royal family in the conquered State afterwards found it an easy matter to subdue Boleleng by itself.

No State has waged so many wars as Karang-Assem. We have spoken above of the victory over the Deva Agung and the destruction of *Gelgel.* The consequence of this was the subjugation of *Boleleng* and *Lombok*, and the family would perhaps have ended by making itself master of all Bali, Lombok, and Sĕmbawa (Sĕmbawa was actually attacked, but was spared through the intervention of the Dutch Government) but for its numerous civil wars. Many of the princes of Karang-Assem and of the conquered Boleleng were expelled by members of their own family. In

---

* *Ngrurah* means something that overshadows, *palindongan*, a payong, and also the vault of heaven. The princes of the Wesyan race nearly all bear this title; they overshadow and protect the land. The prince of Mengui has not this title, for his country belongs to Klongkong, and is merely entrusted to the present prince as a fief of Klongkong: *Ngrurah, Angrurah, Anglurah,* is in Java *Lurah*, a chief of the fourth rank.

Lombok, also, the two princes of the house of Karang-Assem were at war with each other nine years ago, with the result that the chief prince, that of Karang-Assem-Lombok, was defeated by the prince of *Mataram*, and committed suicide. Of the Karang-Assem-Lombok family two children were saved, a son and a daughter of the last prince, and they are now living in Karang-Assem-Bali.* The rest of the family, including the women murdered each other in true Indian fashion, in order not to survive the shame of defeat. They even wished to murder also a European who had sided with them, in order to go to heaven (Svarga) all together. This method "of quitting life by the members of the family murdering each other" is also regarded in Bali as a *Bela*, and here also the Indian meaning of the word *wela* ("sudden and easy death," see above) is applicable. Since the fall of Karang-Assem-Lombok, the princes of Karang-Assem-Bali, of Boleleng, and the Deva Agung, who is independent of them, have been enemies of Lombok, and do not acknowledge each other as lawful rulers. The prince of Lombok, which is also called *Selaparang*, is *Ngrurah K'tut Karang-Assem*.

Karang-Assem is the most mountainous country of Bali, and grows little rice, but the dense population is very skilful in manual work, especially in wood-carving, whereby they gain their livelihood. According to the statements of the Balinese, it contains 50,000 men able to bear arms.

6. *Boleleng.*—The prince is *Ngrurah Made Karang-Assem*. The family comes from Karang-Assem, and thus is originally descended from Mengui and Patih Gaja Madda. The present prince is a brother of the prince of Karang-Assem. Many dynasties have ruled in Boleleng. Seven generations ago the Kshatriyan princes of Boleleng, relations of the Deva Agung, were expelled by a Wesyan family; to the latter belonged Ngrurah Panji, a descendant of Arya Beleteng. The surviving Kshatriyas of Boleleng now live in Badong. Boleleng was finally conquered four or five generations ago by Karang-Assem, but this did not put a stop to the wars, for the members of the Karang-Assem family could not agree together. The most profound peace reigns now, since two brothers have filled the thrones of Karang-Assem and Boleleng. According to Balinese statements, Boleleng has but 12,000 men capable of bearing arms; perhaps so few are returned in order to represent its conquest by the Government as of little importance.

The well-known *Gusti Jelanteg* is a cousin of the prince; his father was murdered by the late prince; yet the son now reigns, whilst the lawful king is but a shadow.

* Perhaps these sole descendants have now been killed by the prince of Mataram-Lombok; at all events he was formerly in constant dread of these lawful heirs of Lombok.

7. *Tabanan.*—Prince *Ratu** *Ngrurah Agung.* The family is that of *Arya Damar*, which is said to have remained pure, although here this is at any rate improbable, and in Badong is untrue. Tabanan does not engage in many wars; it has suffered defeat a few times from Boleleng, but has never been entirely conquered. In the war with Mengui, in which the whole of that State was conquered by Badong and its allies, Gyanyar and Tabanan, Tabanan received the mountain-district of Marga. The more recent quarrels with Mengui are of no importance and never result in anything. The men of Tabanan understand the art of war much less than the other Balinese. Two men of Tabanan are calculated to be no more than a match for one of Mengui, and the people of Badong add to this that one man of Badong is equal to two of Mengui.† The men able to bear arms are stated to be 100,000 in number (?). Under the prince of Tabanan stands that of *Kediri*, a relation of the former, ruling over a tolerably large territory.

Another Punggawa of Tabanan is the prince of the Marga already mentioned; the latter is not a Wesya, but a Sûdra. His ancestor was a seller of palm-wine (tuak), who managed to gain the favour of the prince of Mengui, and by him was made Punggawa. When the territory was transferred from Mengui to Tabanan, the prince of Marga retained his position. (His district grows most of the coffee in Bali.) This instance is the only one which has come to my knowledge of a Sûdra prince, but it indicates the decay of the institution of caste. One often hears the nobles say that Bali must go to the bad now that the Sûdras or children of Sûdra mothers become kings. Compare *Deva Agung, raja Pam'chuttan.*

8. *Badong.*—The three princes who together rule this State are—(1) *Ngrurah G'de Pam'chuttan*, (2) *Made Ngrurah* in *Den Passar*, and (3) *Ngrurah G'de* (*Kassiman*). This State has been formed gradually. The western portion formerly belonged to Mengui, and the eastern, the State of Pinatih, to the descendants of Arya Beleteng, who acknowledged the supremacy of Mengui. Pinatih lies to the eastward of Kassiman, from the frontier of Gyanyar to Tanjang, opposite Serangan (at the place where the roadstead is on the eastern side). It comprises Gunung Rata, Sanor, Taman Intaran, Soong, and the island of Serangan, and is a very fertile district. The poorer western portion with Grobokkan, Legian, Kutta, Tuban, Jembaran, and the southern corner of Bali (the point of the table-land called by the Balinese

---

* The title of *ratu is always used in addressing* princes, but it is only used before the name in speaking of especially distinguished princes. The raja of Tabanan has lately adopted it, and also *Sagung-Adi* in Pam'chuttan.

† Recent experience during the third Dutch expedition does not confirm this assertion, Badong having, as is well known, been defeated.

bukit, the mountain-range), were immediately under Mengui, to which State also belonged the *P'kên Badong*, a much-frequented place of trade. The founder of the State of Badong was a Gusti of the royal house of Tabanan. In a manuscript which was lent to me, and in which a brief enumeration of the names and marriages of the princes of Badong was written at the end of another work, he was called *Gusti Ngrurah Bola;* he had settled in Tabanan in the kampong of *Buahan* (*Buah* and *Jambe* mean the betel-nut, pinang), and is therefore called—(1) *Anak Agung ring Buahan bumi Tabanan* (the prince in or of Buahan in the land of Tabanan); he was the younger son, and sought for a place. From him to the raja Kassiman, who now has the supreme government, there are ten generations, but until we come to the great-grandfather of this man, their history is little more than a list of names).* He went from Tabanan to the P'ken Badong, and lived there in the house of Hi Sedahan, a Sûdra (the name *S'dah* means *sirih;* this name renders the matter somewhat open to suspicion; was it necessary exactly that the pinang (bush) should come to the sirih?). He thus had no palace, nor does he seem to have had a governorship, nor a fixed residence in Badong, for his son or grandson again comes from Buahan to Badong. His sister married the Gusti Agung, the prince of Mengui, but left no children. The reason of his departure is said to be that he went to seek a governorship in Mengui, an object which his son or grandson seems for the first time to have attained.

2. *Anak Agung K'tut Mandesa:* this prince, the son or grandson of Ngrurah Bola, went from Buahan, in Tabanan, to the Gunung Batur, the mountain which vomits fire, on which Dewi Danu or Gangga is worshipped. This was evidently a pilgrimage; he did penance on the sacred mountain, in order to obtain earthly power. Thence he came to Badong and lived in the house of the *M'kel* (*B'kel*) *Tinggi*, to the south of the place of cremation of the present Pam'chuttan, in the dessa of *T'gal*. His surname, *Mandesa*, is said to have been given him because he resided at first in the house of a mandesa (it is possible that he himself was nothing more than a *mandesa*, a kampong-chief). With the aid of the M'kel Tinggi he soon managed to gain a large number of followers, the result of his penances, and became a Punggawa of Mengui.

3. *Anak Agung Pededekan*, son of the last mentioned; he also appears to have been a Punggawa.

---

* The date of a war with Sideman (1582, corresponding with 1660 A.D.) is found in the manuscript of the Wriga Garga, which was lent to me; in that year the men of Karang-Assem (Sideman) with their allies, Mengui, &c., had attacked and invested Badong, but had not conquered it. This is the only historical fact chronologically determined which came to my knowledge in Bali. It appears to have occurred in the time of Gusti Nyoman T'geh.

4. The three sons of the last are *Gusti Wayahan T'geh*, *Gusti Nyoman T'geh* and *Gusti K'tut K'di*. The second, *Gusti Nyoman T'geh*, is the ancestor of the succeeding princes, and increased the power of the house. He married a woman of noble family (*prami*) of *Buahan*. He was brave and cunning, and had a body of picked troops. One of his wife's sisters was married at Klongkong to the Dalem (Deva Agung), and died as a Satya; and the other married in Mengui the Gusti Agung, and became the ancestress of all the Gusti Agungs (princes) of Mengui. These noble alliances and his personal qualities added to his influence, and he seems to have possessed the whole of ancient Badong from *Abian-Timbul* to *Glogor*, *Pam'chuttan*, and *Kassiman*. It is not certain when the wars with Mengui began, but probably he and his son, and grandson after him, were Punggawas of that State.

5. *Gusti Ngrurah Jambe Mihik* (he is named Jambe, because his mother was from Buahan, or Jambe, in Tabanan).

6. The two sons of the last mentioned, by one mother, are *Anak Agung G'de Galogor* and *Anak Agung T'las ring batu Krotok*. Their mother was from *Panataran*, a place in the present Pam'chuttan; the *Aryas Panataran* were at that time still Wesyas, but afterwards they were degraded to Sudras. His wife was also from Panataran, and he seems to have founded Pam'chuttan, or to have made it his residence. *Pam'chuttan* is derived from *p'chut*, an ox-whip; the descent of the race of Pam'chuttan from an ox-driver is found in Abdullah ("Tijdschrift," vii. 2, p. 166 *sqq.*). It is admitted in Badong that the wife of one of the ancestors was of humble origin, the daughter of an ox-driver, but it does not appear that the wife of Anak Agung T'las ring batu Krotok was of such low birth; had she been so, her son Ngrurah Sakti Pam'chuttan would not have attained such great distinction and power.

At this time there were princes' capitals in *T'gal*; this is the most ancient, and was founded by the second prince. T'gal lies to the south of Pam'chuttan—the principal family, of course, resided here; thence was descended the family in *P'ken Badong*, which had palaces both here and in *Kshatriya*, north of Den Passar. *Galogor*, to the north of Pam'chuttan, was also a capital, founded by the elder brother of Anak Agung T'las ring batu Krotok; the family still exists, and has probably been spared on account of its near relationship with the line of Pam'chuttan. The descendants became Punggawas of Pam'chuttan, and afterwards of Den Passar.

Pam'chuttan, finally, the capital of Anak Agung T'las ring batu Krotok, was at that time the seat of the younger line, which, however, was soon to unite the whole of Badong.

7. The sons of *Anak Agung T'las ring batu Krotok* are called *putras*, princes. They are—(*a*) *Anak Agung ring Pam'chuttan*, also called *Ngrurah Sakti Pam'chuttan*, (*b*) *Gusti Made T'gal*, (*c*) *Gusti K'tut T'labah*. Of the last two nothing is known.

The first is he who founded the power of Pam'chuttan. He had obtained that great power by means of a creese pussaka,[1] called *singha*—thence his name *Sakti* (supernatural power). He subjugated the most ancient capital of the princes of Badong in T'gal, and waged successful wars against Mengui, from which he wrested the territory from the present frontier of Mengui to the point of the table-land. He appears to have been the first who was regarded in Badong as an independent prince. He had five hundred wives; the principal ones (*prami*) were from *Tangkeban* (*Bangli*, thus an intermixture with Kshatriyas), *Galogor*, and *Mengui*. From this prince are descended eight hundred Gusti Pam'chuttan, who, on account of their near relationship, are regarded as the support and strength of the land. But where brother is ready to fight against brother, such a strength is imaginary. These eight hundred Gustis have a common sanctuary in Pam'chuttan, where they must appear once a month, and in case of absence have to pay a penalty.

Besides Pam'chuttan, the kingdom of the Jambes also existed at that time in P'ken Badong and Kshatriya (the last being merely a country residence of the prince). They also gained distinction by subduing the kingdom of Pinatih, the eastern portion of Badong. They were still of importance at that period, and really of nobler birth than the princes of Pam'chuttan. Galogor had transferred itself to Pam'chuttan as Punggawa.

Ngrurah Sakti's principal sons were:

8. (*a*) *Ngrurah G'de Pam'chuttan, devata di Ukiran* (who died in Ukiran); from him are descended the present princes of Pam'chuttan, of whom we shall speak hereafter. (*b*) *Ngrurah Mayun*, in the palace of *Mayun*,* on the opposite side of the river to the east of Kassiman. This palace no longer exists; all the materials of which it was built have been taken to Den Passar. (*c*) *Ngrurah Kaleran*, in the palace of Kaleran; to the north of Pam'chuttan, which position is also indicated by the name *kaleran* (northern). Little is recorded of these princes; of course they, too, had wars with Mengui and other States, but they have done no prominent acts, and are overshadowed by the fame of their father and their descendants. Pam'chuttan remained and still remains the chief seat of the family; the prince of Pam'chuttan alone can obtain the *Abbisheka*, that is, can be anointed as prince of the whole realm.

9. The most remarkable of the descendants of the three sons of Ngrurah Sakti was *Ngrurah Made Pam'chuttan*, the son of *Ngrurah Kaleran*. This chief married the daughter of Ngrurah Mayun, thereby uniting two portions of the possessions of the Pam'chuttan

---

[1] [*Pusaka*, an heirloom.]

* *Mayun* is the same as *Made*, "the middle or second son (or daughter)." This name now no longer exists in Badong; the second prince in the family of Pam'chuttan is called *Made*.

family, and founded the palace of Kassiman. Not content with this, he attacked the Jambes in P'ken Badong and Kshatriya, and conquered their territory after a severe struggle. He was supported by Pam'chuttan and Gyanyar, whilst the Jambes received aid from Mengui. Great must have been the slaughter in the palace of P'ken Badong—it is spoken of with terror to this day. The fate is also lamented of the murdered Raja Jambe, who, the people say, was entirely blameless, and had given no cause for the war. He had his revenge, however, upon his conqueror, according to the belief of the Balinese, for he was born again in the family of his foe, as his grandson, and the one of noblest birth, a circumstance which was an omen of great misfortune to that family. The conqueror began to build the great palace of Den Passar, but died before it was half finished; he had already taken up his residence, however, in the new palace, and in him began the line of the princes of Den Passar: the palace in Kassiman was still inhabited afterwards by his wife from Mayun, and was finally given up to his second son (according to birth), the still living Raja Kassiman. This prince, for the sake of distinction, is called *devata di made*, " died in the middle "¹ (*made*—the middle—is here Den Passar,† which, both from the rank of its prince and from its situation, comes between Pam'chuttan and Kassiman). His numerous quarrels with Mengui and nearly all Bali have been without result. Even Tabanan has once fought against him, at the desire of the Deva Agung, and, to save appearances, burnt a single kampong; in reality, however, Tabanan and Gyanyar have always remained friendly to Badong, but they were obliged for political reasons to assume the appearance of hostility against their ally. Badong has neither gained nor lost territory under his rule, while it has become an independent State. The quarrels with the other States were caused chiefly by the aggressions of the Jambes.

10. The sons of this prince, besides many of lower birth, were —(*a*) *Ngrurah Made Pam'chuttan* in Den Passar, (*b*) *Ngrurah Kassiman* in Kassiman, (*c*) *Ngrurah Jambe*, who lives near Den Passar. All three are by different mothers; the first is by a mother from Pam'chuttan, daughter of the *Devata di Ukiran* (*Ngr. G'de Pam'chuttan*) and a princess of Tabanan. This prince was younger than the prince of Kassiman, but as he was born of a Raja-woman he took the highest rank among the sons. *Kassiman*, the old prince who still lives, is the son of a Gusti-woman of Pam'chuttan. *Ngrurah Jambe* is the son of the daughter of the last prince of Kshatriya, who was forced to marry the conqueror and murderer of her father. By birth he would be more noble than

---

¹ [*Devata*, in the sense of dying (lit. being deified), is only used of princes.]

† *Den Passar* means, north of the Passar, or, still better, on the further side of the Passar; thus we have also *Den Bukit*, " on the further side of the mountains," as another name for Boleleng.

Kassiman, and equal to Pam'chuttan, but the descendants of a conquered prince can never again acquire rank in Bali. His noble birth is acknowledged, but he can make no claim to the throne.

The prince of Den Passar, called after his death *devata di Kshatriya*, was an ally of Gyanyar and Tabanan. These three began a fresh war against Mengui, which was carried on more by artifice than by force of arms; the Punggawa of Marga, for instance, who at that time was subject to Mengui, being induced to surrender to Tabanan. For fear that he would lose all his territory in this way, the prince of Mengui gave his land in fief to the prince of Den Passar, and remained in possession of Mengui as Punggawa of Badong; he only lost Marga to Tabanan, and Kadewatan, a small piece of territory on the frontier, to Gyanyar. After this arrangement, the four southern States were allied together against Karang-Assem and Boleleng, the old enemies of Badong and Tabanan, whilst Klongkong remained neutral. This state of affairs continued until shortly after the death of the prince of Den Passar, which took place in 1829.

The prince of Den Passar continued the building of the palace at that place, but did not finish it; we see it now in the state in which he left it. Most of the building materials had to be found by the conquered State of Mengui, where timber was obtained from the mountains, this article being very scarce in Badong. He had several noble wives, but his only son of noble birth, Ngrurah G'de Putra, died a short time before his father. This was the one already mentioned, who was considered to be the last râja Jambe born again, which belief his own father shared. He was regarded as certain to bring misfortune upon the family, and it would seem that he did not die a natural death. In the compact with Mengui, the prince of that land had declared himself a vassal of Ngrurah Made Pam'chuttan and his son Ngrurah G'de Putra. The death of both without a previous renewal of the compact enabled Mengui to regard itself as discharged from its obligations towards Badong, and it soon, in fact, withdrew from them.

After the death of Ngrurah Made Pam'chuttan, Kassiman was the only prince of importance of the family of Den Passar, and he thus gained the supremacy in Den Passar and Kassiman. During his brother's lifetime these two nearly came to blows; Kassiman had already placed his country in a state of defence, but this civil war was prevented by the intervention of Ngrurah G'de Pam-'chuttan, the then prince of Pam'chuttan.

The eldest surviving son of Ngrurah Made Pam'chuttan was *Ngrurah G'de Oka*. He would have become prince of Den Passar, but he would not acknowledge the supremacy of Kassiman. Kassiman, in conjunction with the prince of Pam'chuttan, compelled him, however, to leave the country, and banished him to Tabanan. This did not prevent him from acting against Kassiman. From Tabanan he went to Mengui, and, both here and in Bangli, gained friends who were willing to support him. To strengthen his party still further, he released Mengui from its vassalage to Badong, under the pretext of being his father's heir, and gave it to the Deva Agung. The latter hastened to make use of this gift, and was able to do so without scruple, because the prince of Mengui had only sworn allegiance in the contract with Badong to the deceased princes Ngrurah Made Pam'chuttan and his son Ngrurah G'de Putra. The Deva Agung then commanded that Ngrurah G'de Oka should be received again in Badong, and this command was obeyed, for this prince had made his appearance with a numerous army from Mengui and Bangli. Ngrurah G'de Oka afterwards carried off Kassiman's only daughter, and took her to wife. Old Kassiman again made use of this to confirm his power over Den Passar: he was now in fact the prince's father. Not long after this marriage, however, Ngrurah G'de Oka died also. The sudden deaths of this prince, his brother, and his father lead us to suspect unnatural means, but I cannot assert, nor would I willingly believe, that they were applied by Kassiman. This old man, it is true, took the best advantage of circumstances, not only in Den Passar, but also in Pam'chuttan, of which we are about to speak. The present prince of Den Passar is Ngrurah Made, who, against his will, acknowledges old prince Kassiman as supreme prince in Badong, but, nevertheless, is independent and endeavouring to increase his power.

Pam'chuttan, since the time of Ngrurah Sakti, has been the chief seat of princes in Badong. The family of Den Passar, however, has, by its wars, acquired great fame, and under Kassiman's father and brother has, in fact, held the supreme authority, notwithstanding the nominally higher rank of the prince of Pam'chuttan. We have seen above, that the eldest son of Ngrurah Sakti Pam'chuttan took up his residence in Pam'chuttan. His name was (8) *Ngrurah G'de Pam'chuttan devata di Ukiran* (Ukiran is a place in Pam'chuttan). He was succeeded by his son (9) *Ngrurah G'de Pam'chuttan devata di Munchuk;* both were always allied with their more famous relations in Den Passar, and this friendship was maintained by marriages. The last prince of noble birth was (10) *Ngrurah G'de* Pam'chuttan *devata di g'dong;* he was anointed,* and played an important part in the wars of Kassiman's father and brother. By command of this prince and Kassiman's brother, his cousin *Anak Agung Lanang* crossed the sea with an army to

---

* The anointing of a prince, *Abhisheka* (Sans.), is performed by the priests (the Guru lokas). In Badong it only takes place at Pam'chuttan. In order to be anointed, the prince must be both of noble birth and instructed in all religious duties. The prince of Pam'chuttan referred to in the text was a Rishi; he had attained the position of a saint by penances (maveda).

Jembrana, and conquered this country, which belonged to Boleleng. Anak Agung Lanang went thither because the prince of Den Passar wished to banish him from Badong. This fact also shows the supremacy of Den Passar at that time. Jembrana was soon lost again, however, and subsequently (11) *Anak Agung Lanang* (about 1830), after the death of Ngrurah G'de Pam'chuttan, who left no sons, became prince of Pam'chuttan. He was not anointed, but yet enjoyed greater renown than his son, the present prince. He had no sons of noble birth; he only had by a Gundik (concubine) the two sons now called (12) *Ngrurah G'de Pam'chuttan* and *Ngrurah Made Pum'chuttan*. These, during their father's lifetime, were his *Parakans*, who carried after him his sirih-box, &c. After the death of Anak Agung Lanang, a great portion of the Punggawas of Pam'chuttan would not acknowledge his son as prince, on account of his low birth. Kassiman, however, who in the meantime had also obtained the supreme power in Den Passar, supported the new prince. Some Punggawas (*e.g.*, Deva Made Rahi, in Kutta) submitted, and a Gusti of Legian fled the country and took refuge in Gyanyar. Kassiman then established the new prince in the ancestral palace of Pam'chuttan, and his authority, by marrying him to the daughters of Ngrurah G'de Pam'chuttan, the cousin and predecessor of his father. These women are the principal surviving members of the family, and their illustrious birth enhances that of the prince, who is himself, as it were, his wife's inferior. His principal wife's name is *Sagung** *Adi*, another is called *Sagung Made*, and a third *Sagung Oka*. Sagung Adi has now assumed the name of *Ratu*, which we have also seen was done by the prince of Tabanan.

Kassiman's intervention in the affairs of Pam'chuttan gave him the supreme authority in this part of Badong also. He is regarded as the father of the princes of Den Passar and Pam'chuttan, and uses circumstances very cleverly to keep those princes in dependence.

The prince of *Den Passar*, *Made Ngrurah*, and his brothers *K'tut Ngrurah* and *Ngrurah K'tut*, were all born of mothers of low extraction, and, had they a brother of higher birth, would not have the least claim to rule. Besides this, K'tut Ngrurah is in opposition to Made Ngrurah, and asserts that he has a better claim than the latter. He has several of the Punggawas on his side, and Made Ngrurah is therefore obliged to invoke the aid of his uncle Kassiman to maintain his position. Kassiman, however, it would seem, does not trust Made Ngrurah, who has inherited much of his father's ambitious character: he therefore does all he can to uphold the power of Pam'chuttan, and has

---

* *Sagung* means a princess, born of a princely father and mother. *Sayu*, one whose mother was only a Gusti-woman. *Sagung* is derived from *agung*, great; *Sayu* from *ayu*, good, which we have also found to be a name for the female Brahmans (*Idayu*).

enriched the prince of that country and invested him with a certain renown. The prince of Pam'chuttan, therefore, dares not dispute Kassiman's authority; he is of low birth and a peaceful disposition, and would also have to fear the house of Den Passar, which considers itself raised above so low a birth by the deeds of its father and grandfather. The prince of Pam'chuttan has not the abhisheka; although he is a man of about forty-five, he is not yet sufficiently instructed in his duties and in religion; he has performed his duties to the Pitaras, having, with all due ceremony, burnt his father, and built a new domestic temple, which was finished a year ago; yet it appears that he will not receive the abhisheka during Kassiman's lifetime, and, in the event of his death, this would also, perhaps, be prevented by the opposition of Den Passar. The prince of Den Passar has not fulfilled his duties towards his ancestors; his father and brother as well as other chief members of his family are still unburnt, and are preserved in the palace of Den Passar. On this account Made Ngrurah does not reside in the palace.[1]

This cremation must from the rank of the deceased be very splendid; the prince of Den Passar, however, has not the means to do it, and although, apparently, the whole population of Badong works for him, this produces very little visible result. He has to complete the palace which his father left unfinished, and in which much work has still to be done, and further to improve the roads of his country, which have fallen into a very bad state of repair since the death of his father, the last prince of Pam'chuttan who had the abhisheka. And, finally, he cannot easily raise the funds for a great cremation, and is opposed in his undertakings by K'tut Ngrurah, and, in secret, by Kassiman. In Den Passar also, therefore, it is probable that the position of affairs will remain unchanged till Kassiman's death. Yet another reason against the cremation of the late prince of Den Passar and his son G'de Putra appears to be the above-mentioned superstition, that prince Jambe has been born again in the family of Den Passar in the person of G'de Putra. This second birth indicates misfortune for the family, which fears either that that prince will be born a third time, or that the curse which seems to attach to the family prevents it from performing works pleasing to the gods.

[1] [The position of affairs, 35 years later, is thus described by Dr. Jacobs, l. l. p. 168: "Badung, however small, is divided among three princes, each of whom originally ruled his own portion, and contested the supremacy with the other two, so that we find there three chief cities, Den Passar, Pam'chutan, and Kasiman. The present Raja Kasiman, though still residing at Kasiman, has deputed his power to the Raja Den Passar, so that actually the latter shares with Rajah Pam'chutan supreme authority. Raja Den Passar exercises sway over the whole of Badung, or is at least looked upon by our government as exercising such sway, while also Pam'chutan is recognized as a ruling prince.]

Genealogical Table of the Princes of Badong.

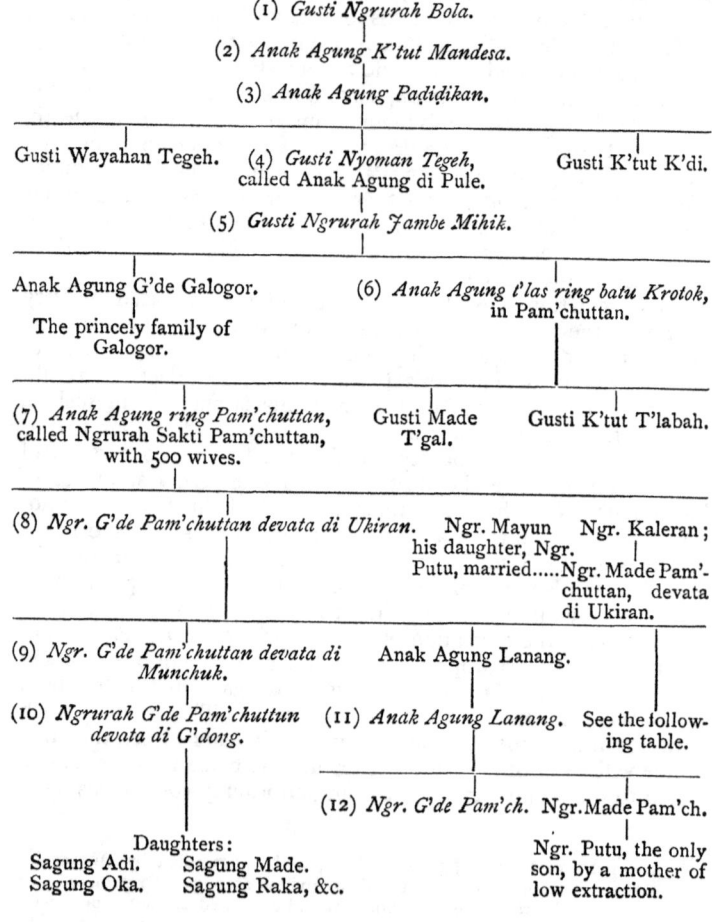

(1) *Gusti Ngrurah Bola.*

(2) *Anak Agung K'tut Mandesa.*

(3) *Anak Agung Paḍiḍikan.*

Gusti Wayahan Tegeh.   (4) *Gusti Nyoman Tegeh,* called Anak Agung di Pule.   Gusti K'tut K'di.

(5) *Gusti Ngrurah Jambe Mihik.*

Anak Agung G'de Galogor.   (6) *Anak Agung t'las ring batu Krotok,* in Pam'chuttan.

The princely family of Galogor.

(7) *Anak Agung ring Pam'chuttan,* called Ngrurah Sakti Pam'chuttan, with 500 wives.   Gusti Made T'gal.   Gusti K'tut T'labah.

(8) *Ngr. G'de Pam'chuttan devata di Ukiran.*   Ngr. Mayun his daughter, Ngr. Putu, married......Ngr. Made Pam'chuttan, devata di Ukiran.   Ngr. Kaleran;

(9) *Ngr. G'de Pam'chuttan devata di Munchuk.*   Anak Agung Lanang.

(10) *Ngrurah G'de Pam'chuttun devata di G'dong.*   (11) *Anak Agung Lanang.*   See the following table.

(12) *Ngr. G'de Pam'ch.*   Ngr. Made Pam'ch.

Daughters:
Sagung Adi.   Sagung Made.
Sagung Oka.   Sagung Raka, &c.

Ngr. Putu, the only son, by a mother of low extraction.

TABLE OF THE FAMILY OF KALERAN—DEN PASSAR.

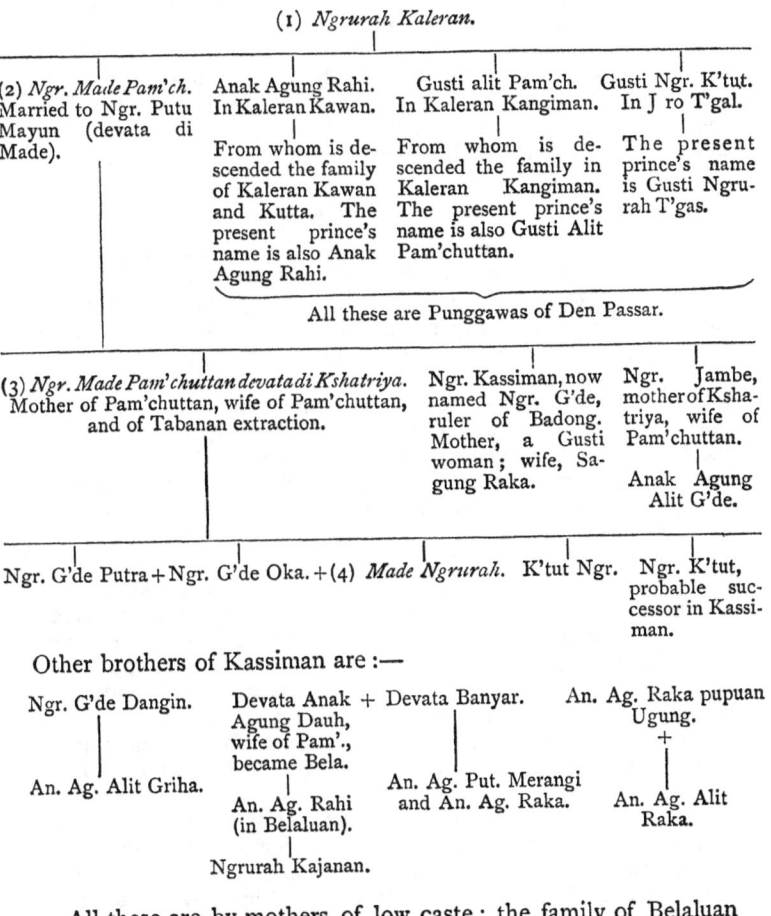

(1) *Ngrurah Kaleran.*

(2) *Ngr. Made Pam'ch.* Married to Ngr. Putu Mayun (devata di Made).

Anak Agung Rahi. In Kaleran Kawan. From whom is descended the family of Kaleran Kawan and Kutta. The present prince's name is also Anak Agung Rahi.

Gusti alit Pam'ch. In Kaleran Kangiman. From whom is descended the family in Kaleran Kangiman. The present prince's name is also Gusti Alit Pam'chuttan.

Gusti Ngr. K'tut. In J'ro T'gal. The present prince's name is Gusti Ngrurah T'gas.

All these are Punggawas of Den Passar.

(3) *Ngr. Made Pam'chuttan devata di Kshatriya.* Mother of Pam'chuttan, wife of Pam'chuttan, and of Tabanan extraction.

Ngr. Kassiman, now named Ngr. G'de, ruler of Badong. Mother, a Gusti woman; wife, Sagung Raka.

Ngr. Jambe, mother of Kshatriya, wife of Pam'chuttan.

Anak Agung Alit G'de.

Ngr. G'de Putra + Ngr. G'de Oka. + (4) *Made Ngrurah.* K'tut Ngr. Ngr. K'tut, probable successor in Kassiman.

Other brothers of Kassiman are :—

Ngr. G'de Dangin.
|
An. Ag. Alit Griha.

Devata Anak Agung Dauh, wife of Pam'., became Bela.
|
An. Ag. Rahi (in Belaluan).
|
Ngrurah Kajanan.

+ Devata Banyar.
|
An. Ag. Put. Merangi and An. Ag. Raka.

An. Ag. Raka pupuan Ugung.
+
An. Ag. Alit Raka.

All these are by mothers of low caste; the family of Belaluan has again raised itself in rank by means of noble marriages. The others, after one more intermixture with Sûdran blood, will sink into the position of ordinary Gustis.

FURTHER REMARKS ON THE CASTES.

The *Dewas, Gustis,* and *Iḍas* are much too numerous in Bali to maintain their dignity; they, and especially the first two classes, are too proud to gain their livelihood by work, and prefer unjust privileges. They rob the people without limit; they are the cause of the plundering of ships, and of the extortions to which foreign traders are often exposed. The high-caste princes are seldom guilty of such misdeeds, but they wink at the robberies of their relations, and it is difficult to obtain justice from the princes against these pests of the land. The Gustis in the countries ruled by Wesya princes, and the Devas in those where Kshatriyas reign, have properly all the official posts about the prince, but, although they derive much honour from these, they get little pay.

Feudal System.

As Raffles has observed, the condition of Bali very much resembles that of Europe in the Middle Ages; there is *a feudal system throughout the land*. The *Deva Agung* must be regarded as *the supreme feudal lord;* in ancient times he was so in reality (see "Usana Java," above). How this is modified now, we have already seen. He still calls the other seven princes, and also the prince of Lombok, his *Punggawas*,* which in Bali conveys the idea of *vassal*. The rest of the princes (*Kshatriyas* and *Wesyas*) have subdivided their land among the members of their families, and so we find in Badong the princes of *Kaleran Kawan, Kaleran Kanginan, Ngrurah T'gas*, the prince of *Galogor*, and Kassiman's brother with their children as Punggawas of Den Passar (formerly most of them were under Pam'chuttan, but they have preferred to acknowledge as their lords the two warlike princes of Den Passar, Kassiman's father and brother; unless Kassiman had interfered, even the sovereignty over Badong itself would have been transferred from Pam'chuttan to Den Passar). Now they are all under Kassiman, but only in so far as Den Passar also is under his sovereignty. The real Punggawas of Kassiman, in his small original territory, are few in number, and, for the most part, merely the descendants of his brothers, who were entirely without means.

Under these princes, who are Punggawas of the highest princes and most closely related to the royal families,† stand the rest of the Gustis, also as Punggawas; these also have an undefined authority over the men whom they rule, and have even the power to punish with death; the prince above them and the prince of the whole kingdom do not trouble themselves about their subjects further than their feudal duties are concerned. The *Diaksas* ‡

---

* *Punggawa*, "bull" and "excellent" in the Sanskrit.

† We do not find many exceptions to this rule; in Tabanan the prince is descended from Marga; in Klongkong, *e.g.*, Ngrurah Pinatih, from Arya Bleteng. In Gyanyar from Sukawati.

‡ I write *Diaksa* instead of *Yaksa* (as the judges are usually called in Bali and Java), on the authority of a manuscript, where the writing with the second *d* reveals the origin of the word. *Diaksa*, which is also found as

have merely to pronounce judgment between the Sûdras and sometimes between Gustis of equal rank; in all cases concerning the distinctions of caste and feudal duties the princes and Punggawas are judges; in spiritual matters, however, the Padandas act in this capacity.

The primary feudal duty, as in the Middle Ages, is *service in war;* and further, the Punggawas and their subordinates have to furnish assistance in all *public works and festivals* of the prince, and the lower orders also have to carry out all the works of the Punggawas. The people, under the guidance of the Punggawas, have to build the princes' palaces and places of cremation, to repair the roads, and besides this to contribute, mostly in kind, towards the expenses of all offerings, family feasts, and cremations. The direct taxes are very unimportant; the common man pays a small tax on garden land, and a little more on sawahs. The princes, therefore, cannot be rich, unless they possess considerable private means; they are powerful, however, so long as their names hold the Punggawas in subjection, and they can therefore celebrate their splendid feasts and cremations without cost to themselves, and sometimes even with advantage to their private treasuries, their faithful vassals zealously contributing to these ceremonies. (One of the reasons why the great cremation in Den Passar does not take place is, that the present prince is not in very high esteem with the Punggawas, and that not enough is contributed towards it. Besides this, Kassiman retains the revenue.) To the revenues of the princes and the Punggawas belong also the duties on commerce, the customs-duties, and the bridge or road-tolls.* Trade especially produces a considerable revenue for the prince, and has made the princes of Badong comparatively rich, above all Pam'chuttan and Kassiman. Karang-Assem also makes a great deal by it. These imposts affect only the lower orders, and the Chinese, Buginese, and Europeans. The Gustis, Devas, and Idas who carry on trade pay no duty upon it. The feudal lords, princes, and Punggawas still do something for the people—they give them water, and the making of canals and the effective irrigation of the rice-fields are their duty; in return for this, however, they draw a small revenue from the rice-growers.

Adiaksa in the MSS., is Skt.—*adhi* and *aksha*, an inspector, protector (see Wilson). *Yaksa*, on the contrary, is a sort of demon, allied to the Râksasas. [See Roorda's "Javanese Dictionary," *s.v. jaksha*, where the etymology from *adhyaksha* is correctly given.]

* I am only acquainted, however, with two bridges in Bali (excepting those over small brooks) in any way worthy of the name—one at Kutta, built by Europeans with Balinese aid, and one, very dangerous for want of planks, over a rocky chasm in Tabanan.

Śûdras.

The fourth caste, the *Śûdras*, have many duties and hardly any rights, at any rate as regards the higher castes. Their subjection goes so far that the prince or Punggawa can take out of their houses whatever he likes; when the prince goes from one place to another, the victuals, fowls, ducks, geese, &c., are usually taken by the Parakans (followers of the prince) from the houses of the Śûdras in the *dessas* through which the route lies, and the persons thus robbed may not even complain. The prince or Punggawa can even take away the wives of a Śûdra, but religious feeling is opposed to this, and still more to the murder of a Śûdra, who has committed no fault, by a noble. Both acts are done, however, although they are of rare occurrence, in Badong. The wanton young Gustis and Devas think that they prove their valour and noble birth by the abduction of women and the murder of innocent beasts of burden, such as the Śûdras are. In Badong, old Kassiman suppressed such deeds, and the fear of punishment after death also has a deterrent effect.* Nevertheless the position of the Śûdras is most miserable, and only rendered supportable by their courage and industry, and by the belief that they are born to it. An exception to the rest of the Śûdras is formed by the Parakans (the followers of the princes, &c.); these lead as idle a life as the princes and Punggawas to whom they belong, and plunder the rest of the people. These and the nobles are the chief cock-fighters and opium-smokers, for the inhabitants of the *dessas* take little part in these dissipations. Another exception to the lot of the ordinary Śûdras is formed by the *Mandesas*, *Prab'-kels*, and others, who occupy official posts.

Mandesas are the *dessa*-chiefs; they have been degraded to Śûdras by the Deva Agung, having been Wesyas by birth. Under them are the *Kabayan*, *Nguhukin*, and *Talikup*, Śûdras by birth, who carry out the orders of the Mandesas.

Gaduh are the Mandurs in the *dessas*; they are Śûdras by birth. *Dangka* and *Batu-Aji* are under these.

Pasek are also Wesyas who have been degraded to Śûdras, and still retain a certain superiority of rank above the rest of the populace.

We find all these names in the "Usana Bali" (see p. 262), where their special religion is mentioned (the "Usana Bali," as we have seen, is only of importance to the Śûdras and their chiefs of the same caste).

* Balinese superstition regards the fate of the first *Deva Mangis*, the founder of Gyanyar, and that of the wife of the last Deva Agung, the much-feared princess of Karang-Assem, as examples of such punishments; the former was changed into a serpent (*nâga*), and the latter into a frog (*dongkang*). Both had murdered many victims.

The names are not heard in ordinary life, with the exception of Mandesa. For all the rest the collective name *Prab'kel* (the collective B'kels) is used. These have a certain number of common Sûdras under them at the prince's disposal, to serve in war or on public works, and also to exercise handicrafts (as smiths, &c.). They are responsible for the presence and the work of their subordinates, just as the Mandesa is responsible for his dessa. *Prab'kel* or *Pam'kel*, also *M'kel*, has become a title for every superior among the Sûdras—the owner is the M'kel of the slave, the husband the M'kel of the wife. This exalted rank is also accorded to Europeans, but they stand below the three principal castes; they have not been born twice (*dvija*).

The Balinese Sûdras are partly of Javan and partly of Balinese origin. The former celebrate the new year (*Sugian*) six days before the Balinese new year (*Galungan*). The latter, however, is taken as the beginning of the calendar by the whole people.

In addition to the above, degraded Brahmans, Kshatriyas, and Wesyas also belong to the Sûdras. The original Wesyas, those who came from Majapahit, have all become Sûdras, and this at the same time that the descendants of Arya Damar were degraded to Wesyas. The reason given for this does not agree with that of the degradation of the Kshatriyas. All castes, indeed, are said to have descended a step, excepting the original Brahmans. The descendants of *Batu Henggong*, the Deva Agungs, who, on account of their procreation by the *Padanda Dang hyang Kapakisan*, were also regarded as Brahmans, sank back, through the curse or the anger of the Padanda who produced the Nâga from the well (see as to the *Nâgabandha*, under *Cremations*), to true Kshatriyas, and the consequence of this was the degradation of the other Kshatriyas to Wesyas, and of the Wesyas to Sûdras. This explanation is open to great doubt. Most of the descendants of the Aryas, the brothers of Arya Damar, have been degraded to Sûdras. They were degraded, as we have seen, to Wesyas, but when they had also lost their governorships and their authority, oppressed by the descendants of Patih Gaja Maja (the royal race of Mengui-Karang-Assem), they gradually sank to the rank of Sûdras. Many of them are still called Gustis by the people, but they have to give their services as vassals to the princes in whose territory they live, and no longer enjoy any honour. The conquered are always despised and degraded in Bali. Brahmans are also degraded to Sûdras if, on account of frequent intermixture with Sûdra blood, they are no longer considered capable of retaining their dignity. An instance of a Padanda being thus degraded is actually mentioned. Brahmans do, indeed, become Sûdras, but the people hold the caste in such great respect that they are still regarded and honoured as Brahmans. *Brahmana chute* are mentioned in the "Usana Java;" the Balinese explain these to be lying and thieving Brahmans, who, on account of their conduct, have sunk to the rank of Śûdras. *Chute* is, indeed, in Sanskrit, *chyuta,* "fallen."

Sangguhu is a subdivision of the Śûdras, *who are acquainted with the Vedas,* and perform the ceremony of domestic worship, as well as the priests. If they have, indeed, the Vedas (they may be only *Mantras,* formulas), it would seem that they were originally Brahmans. Now, we find in the "Usana Java" a statement that the *Sangguhus* are, in fact, descended from Brâhmaṇa-Brâhmaṇî, and thus are pure Brahmans, and that they were degraded on account of the worship of the *Dalem mur,* that is, *the god of death* (perhaps as indicating an exclusive *Kâla-worship,* which no longer exists in Bali). We have therefore had in Bali departures from the worship of the gods, not to say sects. The present Brahmans, who have suppressed the sect referred to, now tell us, to conceal the existence of any other worship but their own, that the Sangguhus are descended from a *parakan* (follower) *of a learned Padanda,* who was hidden under the *Bale* whenever the Padanda performed his domestic worship, and so came to understand the Vedas. When he was discovered, the Padanda set him at liberty, that he might perform the Veda-worship for himself and his descendants. From him are descended the *Sangguh* or *Sangguhu,* which word is explained by means of *kira : having the appearance of being Brahmans.* There is some number of them in Bali.

Byagaha are also mentioned in the "Usana Java" as a distinct class, and these appear to be of the same rank as the Sangguhu. The name, however, is almost unknown, even to the Panditas. Thus in the three classes of Sudras last mentioned, we find also no mixture of caste; but they all three point to the former existence of sects, or at least to some departures from the orthodox religion.

It would be a fortunate thing for the Śûdras to be freed from the oppression of the princes and Punggawas. The number of noble idlers increases every day, and presses more and more heavily upon the poor Śûdra populace. One means of escaping from the oppression of a prince is to flee to another State, but even this avails them little, for the prince of the State in which the fugitive seeks refuge immediately imposes upon him the very burdens from which he has fled. Besides this, a fugitive who arrives without his family is sold by the prince, in order to make some profit out of him, and to prevent his escaping again to another country. The best asylum is generally afforded by the Padandas; the prince has no right to fugitives who seek refuge with them, and there are several kind-hearted really pious men among these Padandas who consider it shameful to sell a person seeking an asylum, or even to require much work from him. Many Padandas, however, are also genuine natives, and avail themselves of these cases to enrich themselves. The chief curb upon the despotism of the noble castes over the Śûdras is, in fact, the fear lest they should run away, and the power and revenues of the nobles should thereby be diminished. The Balinese, however, are unusually attached to their country and their dessa; ordinary extortion does not drive them to flight; it is generally only some glaring cruelty or the fear of being sold out of Bali that induces them to escape. Still, the fact that there are always many fugitives in Bali shows the injustice and cruelty of most of the princes, and the degeneration of the system of caste. In Badong there are very many fugitives from Gyanyar, Mengui, Klonkong, and Karang-Assem; on the other hand, scarcely any fugitives from Badong are to be found in the other states. The reason of this is, that the government in this state is comparatively mild and humane, and this is attributable to Kassiman's higher intelligence and his contact with Europeans. For the sake of humanity it is desirable that intercourse between Europeans and the Balinese should increase, and that the position of the Śûdras should thus be improved, at any rate a little, if they could not be entirely freed from their oppressors. The character of the Balinese as a people, irrespectively of their castes, has been very accurately perceived by Raffles: *they are a manly nation*, both in body and mind, far superior to the Javanese (although outwardly less civilized), and endowed with many virtues which in Java have disappeared beneath the mire of immorality and fickleness. The Balinese (excepting those who carry on trade and are corrupted by undue gains) are *faithful* and *honest* and *can work hard;* it is only for their prince that they work reluctantly, for they receive from him neither payment nor food; and, finally, they are *braver* than all other natives, but against the European they are as incapable of resistance as all the descendants of the black Adam, and the defiant language employed to Europeans comes from a timid heart. The European is as a tiger to all natives, and they know him by instinct.

CASTE IN JAVA.

The existence of caste in Java has hitherto been denied, but what we now know of Bali appears to have placed it beyond doubt. That all the institutions of the Balinese are of Javan origin is affirmed by the manuscripts and the oral tradition of the people. The "Usana Java" enumerates Kshatriyas of *Koripan* (where Panji lived), of *Gaglang* or *Singhasari*, of *Kediri* or *Daha*, and of *Janggala*. In all the great kingdoms of Java, therefore, Kshatriyas existed. The descent of the Kshatriyas of Daha is traced in the Brahmâṇḍapurâṇa to the Muni Pulaha. In the same work the Brahmans are divided into *Siva-Brahmans, Buddha-*

Brahmans, and *Bujangga-Brahmans* (thus the Brahmans in Java were exactly like those now in Bali); these are sons of Brâhmaṇa Haji, that is to say, the various forms of worship are derived from Haji Saka, the founder of the Indo-Javanese calendar. *Bujangga* seems in ancient times to have been a distinct sect. We have spoken of the present meaning of this word; it seems formerly to have meant a particular kind of worship, in contradistinction to Śiva and Buddha.* The Wesyas are also mentioned in the "Usana Java" as existing in Java; to these belong the *Patihs*, D'mangs, and Tumenggungs. The names Wesya and Gusti (see "Tijdsch. v. N. I." 7, 2, 185) still exist in Java, although their meaning has become obscure. The *Sûdras* are expressly mentioned, and their name also is still heard in Java.

In the "Usana Java" (which really only relates to Java) the *Brahmans* spring from Brahmâ's *Sivadara*, the opening in the head which in children does not close for some years, the *Kshatriyas* from his *breast*, the *Wesyas* from his *abdomen*, and the *Sûdras* from his knee.

The nobles of the courts of Daha and Majapahit, according to express testimony, were *Kshatriyas* and *Wesyas*. To the *Kshatriyas* belong all those who bear the title of *Arya, K'bo,* or *Mahisa* and *Rangga*. The titles of the Wesyas have just been given.

The appearance of caste and the existence of the Vedas in Bali afford the strongest evidence for the existence of both in ancient Java, because all that we find in Bali was derived from Java *alone*, not a single fact discovered in Bali proving, or even indicating, direct communication between this island and India, and because the Śiva Brahmans, who, after having established themselves for a short time at Majapahit, crossed over to Bali, came, according to the Balinese, not direct from India, but from the interior of Java (*Kediri*). The real origin of all the Balinese institutions is also shown by the fact that we find nothing to remind us directly of India, and no ancient writing, Sanskrit, Kavi, or Javanese: we may well ask how could emigrants from India have so neglected and forgotten their own writing and language, and have merely preserved the modern Javanese writing and the Kavi tongue?

---

* The word *Bujangga* means a *serpent;* in India the serpent-worship has been adopted in the Brahmanical doctrine; we find it especially in Cas'mira; serpent-worship is still found in Java and Bali (Vasuki), and the Bujanggas appear to have originally been serpent-worshippers, who afterwards joined the Sivaitic sect.

The Calculation of Time in Bali.

The calculation of time is of two kinds: the *Indian* and the *Balinese*. All that we know of it is contained in a work called *Wriga Garga*.* This work is composed of Indian and Polynesian elements, and, like the rest of the literature, must be of Javanese origin, as in that island alone do we find an almost identical calendar.

We have an Indian division of time, according to the *lunar months*. These months, however, are transformed by interpolation, into the solar year, and the solar years are calculated from the time of *Salivahana* or *Saka*, as is also the practice in the greater part of Hindustan and of the Dekkan. This calendar begins on the 14th of March, 78 B.C. This calculation, however, is but little used by the Balinese, and their scanty astronomical knowledge renders it extremely difficult, although, for the sake of agriculture and a few feasts, it must be preserved. The interpolation is irregular; in India two months are introduced in five years, but in Bali, on the one hand, the month of *Kârtika* may comprise two months, and, on the other, the month of *Asada* may last till the constellation of the Pleiades (*Krittika*) is visible at sunset. The only constellations used by the Balinese in such calculations are the Pleiades and Orion. The latter is called *Waluku*, the plough, and also by the Indian name *lânggala* (in Malay *tangala*). They understand by this, however, only the three centre stars of Orion. To supplement this defective means of calculating the year, the Balinese observe certain natural phenomena occurring regularly every year at the same time, such as the blossoming of certain flowers and plants and the appearance of wings on the white ant, and also the phenomena of the sea. A man of rank informed me that the interpolation of a month had only happened three times in his life. This would give an interval of about twelve years between each interpolation; it is more probable that an interpolation is made every ten years, hence the name *tenggek* for such a division. At present the Balinese lunar months are rather more than thirty days in advance of the Indian, as fixed by Wilson. The year begins with the month of *Kasanga*; the Indian name for this is *Chetra*, and commences, according to Wilson, in March. This, then, proves that the Balinese years do indeed start from the exact date of Śaka (14th of March), and Raffles' and Crawfurd's conjectures as

---

* *Garga*, according to Wilson, is one of the ten Munis or saints; one Garga is also the author of astronomical works in India; see Bentley, "Hindu Astronomy," p. 54; his book is named Sanhitâ; he lived 550 years B.C. [See, however, Kern, in the Introduction to his edition of "Varâka-Mihira's Brihat-sanhitâ," p. 31 ff.] The Balinese Calendar, as it is, cannot be derived from him, because it contains elements never known in India.

to the difference of the calendar in Java and Bali can be solved by assuming that the Balinese have retained the ancient and true calendar, whilst the Javanese, through Muhammadan influence, have forgotten how to calculate the solar year, and have, therefore, got seven or eight years further from Śaka than they should be.

All the months but two *(Jyeshṭa* and *Asaḍa)* have both Sanskrit and Balinese names.

The Sanskrit names are :

1. Śrâvaṇa.
2. Bhâdra or Bâdrawada (Sanskrit Bhâdrapada).
3. As'uji or As'uje (derived from As'vayuj).
4. Kârttika.
5. Mârgas'ira or Mârgas'îrshya.
6. Pos'ya or Paus'a.
7. Mâga.
8. P'âlguna.
9. Mad'umasa or Chetra.
10. Wes'aka.
11. Jyeshta.
12. Asâdha.

The Balinese names for the first ten are the ordinal numbers from 1 to 10:

1. Kasa.
2. Karo.
3. Katiga.
4. Kapat.
5. Kalima.
6. Kanam.
7. Kapita.
8. Kahulu.
9. Kasanga.
10. Kadas'a.

We have no Balinese names for *Jyeshṭha* and *Âshâḍha* (vulgo *Sada*), and this leads us to suspect that the original Balinese-Javanese year, like that of the ancient Romans, had only 10 months. Now we find in the purely Balinese calendar, of which we shall speak shortly, divisions of 35 days or 5 weeks, which, it is true, do not now possess a special name, but no doubt originally corresponded with the 10 months; 10 times 35 gives about the duration of the year of lunar months, 354 days. The addition of *Jyeshṭha* and *Âshâḍha*, then, occurred at a later period, when Indian influence had led to the division of the year into 12 months, each of 29 or 30 days.

In the year 1847 the first day of the month *Kasanga* or *Chetra* was on the 16th of February; in 1848 on the 5th of February; in 1849 it will fall on the 24th of January. In 1844, on the contrary, it was on the 24th of March, almost on the day on which, according to Wilson, the Indian month *Chetra* should begin. Although in Bali, from ignorance of the calculations, the method of fixing the solar year is obscure, and is known but imperfectly to a few learned priests (who themselves cannot properly explain the reasons for it), yet we learn from the tables called *Pengalihan wulan* (the searching of the moon) how the time of the Balinese calculation is brought into accordance with that of the lunar months: 64 lunar months, of which 30 are of 29 and 34 of 30 days, give us 1890 days, which agree with 9 Balinese years of 210 days.

According to the Indian calculation, there should be one or two intercalary months next year (1849), because then the

THE ISLAND OF BALI.

difference between the solar and the lunar year will be from the 24th of January to the 20th of March, and will thus amount to 55 days; nothing, however, has yet been said to me of any such intention. In India, as we have already pointed out, there are 2 intercalary months every 5 years called *Malimlucha;* this name is unknown in Bali, nor have I heard any name which could correspond to it.

The six Indian seasons do not exist in Bali. The lunar months are chiefly important for fixing certain feasts. For all other dates use is made solely of

THE BALINESE CALENDAR.

This is formed by a combination of the *Polynesian week of 5 days* (*pahing, puan, wage, kaliwon, manis*) with the *Indian week of 7 days* (*Rediti,* Soma, Anggara, Budd'a, Vrihaspti, Sukra, Saneschara*); this combination gives us 35 days, which form the basis of the Balinese calendar; we write them thus:

Budda kaliwon,	Soma pahing,	Sanes'chara wage,
Wrihaspati manis,	Anggara puan,	Rediti kaliwon,
Sukra pahing,	Budda wage,	Soma manis,
Sanes'chara puan,	Wrihaspati Kaliwon,	Anggara pahing,
Rediti wage,	Sukra manis,	Budda puan,
Soma kaliwon,	Sanes'chara pahing,	Wrihaspati wage,
Anggara manis,	Rediti puan,	Sukra kaliwon,
Budda pahing,	Soma wage,	Sanes'chara manis,
Wrihaspati puan,	Anggara kaliwon,	Rediti pahing,
Sukra wage,	Budda manis,	Soma puan,
Sanes'chara kaliwon,	Wrihaspati pahing,	Anggara wage.
Rediti manis,	Sukra puan,	

We find these combinations of 35 days six times in each Balinese year of 210 days, but they are not called months. On the other hand, each of the 30 weeks has its own name. We find these names in Raffles, vol. i. p. 476. The order of sequence is the same in Bali, but some names must be corrected. Each division begins with *Budda kaliwon*, the day on which Galungan, the Balinese new year, falls, and not on *Rediti* (or *Diti*) *Pahing*, as Raffles asserts. The week in which the year begins is Dunghulan; *Sinta*, however, is always named as the first week in Bali, as in Java; the names are:

---

* The name *Rediti* can only be explained by *Aditya*, "sun." The substitution of *ri* for *â* may well have arisen by the uncommon initial *a* having been taken for the sign *rê*, which is very well known. *Vrihaspati* is found in good MSS. for Respati, which is the ordinary pronunciation. [Van der Tuuk, "Notes on Kawi," p. 9. On the Batah Calendar, which in many points agrees with the Balinese and Javanese arrangements, see J. B. Neumann, in "Tijdschrift van het Nederlandsch Aardrijkskundig Genootschap," II., vol. iii. p. 528 ff.]

1. Sinta
2. Landep
3. Wukir
4. Kurantil
5. Tolu
6. Gûmreg
7. Wariga
8. Warigadian, or Wariganing Wariga
9. Julung Wangi
10. Julung Sungsang
11. Dunghulan (in Raffles Galungan)
12. Kuningan
13. Langkir
14. Madang Siha
15. Julung Pujut
16. Pahang
17. Kurw'lut
18. Marakih
19. Tambir
20. Madangkungang
21. Mahatal
22. Huje
23. Menahil
24. Prang Bakat
25. Bala Muki
26. Hugu
27. Wayang
28. Kulawu
29. Dukut
30. Watu gunung.

Raffles, vol. i. p. 376 sqq., gives the fable respecting the origin of these names of the weeks. I have not yet heard anything of it in Bali. In Bali this division, like the rest of the calendar, is said to be derived from India. Its introduction was no doubt made by the priests at an early period, in order to add to the sanctity of the religious feasts and institutions, which are regulated according to this calendar.*

Of the 35 days the *first*, *eleventh*, and *twenty-first* (*Budda kaliwon*, *Saneśchara kaliwon* and *Anggara kaliwon*) are sacred. Here again, therefore, the decimal system prevails. In the first five weeks, the feast of *Galungan*, the new year, falls on Budda kaliwon, the feast of *Kuningan* (in Crawfurd Galunan and Kuninan) on Saneśchara kaliwon, and finally the feast in the principal temple of Uluwatu in Badong on Anggara kaliwon.

Some Balinese only call this year of 210 days a half-year. It is indeed, however, their civil year, and they are only disposed to regard it as a half-year to make it agree with the Muhammadan, Chinese, and European year.

Each of these 35 days has a constellation, which indicates its good or evil qualities, and is of special importance for nativities; these constellations are not the same, however, as our own, or even as the Indian, for, with the exception of the *Waluku* (Orion) and the *Krittika* (the Pleiades), the signs are somewhat arbitrary.

ASTROLOGIGAL CALENDAR.

These constellations, which decide the good or evil fortune of the day, are called *lintangan* (lintang = bintang, " star "). They are supposed to pass into the body of people born on that day.

Rediti manis has the *Ancha-ancha*, a human figure standing on

---

* *Sapta Resi* (the seven ancient saints, sages) are said to have prepared it. The *pengalihan bulan*, also, in which the lunar calendar is brought into agreement with that of thirty weeks, is attributed to the same persons.

its head and hands. People born on that day have weak bodies and weak voices, but are impertinent to their parents.

Rediti pahing, the *Gaja*, elephant. This signifies sorrow caused by other people.

Rediti puan.—*Patrem*, the creese. This signifies a predisposition to suicide.

Rediti wage.—*Waluku*, the plough (Orion). Signifying happiness late in life.

Rediti kaliwon.—*Gowang*, a body without a head. A strong propensity for stealing and robbery.

Soma manis.—*N'yu*, the gooseberry-bush. Happiness and riches, which, however, will not last long.

Soma pahing.—*Dupa*, incense. Early death of the married man or woman.

Soma puan.—*Ulanjar*, a divorced woman. One who is prone to take upon himself the faults of others, and gets into dilemmas.

Soma wage.—*Lembu*, a white bull. Happiness and riches.

Soma kaliwon.—*Padati Sunya*, the empty cart, deserted by its driver. Easily robbed.

Anggara manis.—*Kuda*, the horse. Disposed to bad tricks.

Anggara pahing.—*Juju*, the crab. Good sense and speedy acquirement of wealth.

Anggara puan.—*Asu ajak*, the wild dog. Excellence and boldness in war, esteem among the great.

Anggara wage.—*Jong sarat*, the overladen boat. Probable misfortune at sea.

Anggara kaliwon.—*Cheleng*, the hog. Success in breeding swine.

Budda manis.—*Ngerang-erang*. weeping, lamenting. Much sorrow all one's life.

Budda pahing.—*Gajamina*, half elephant, half fish. A good omen.

Budda puan.—*Lumbung*, the rice-barn. Wealth of goods and money quickly obtained; fortunate in travel.

Budda wage.—*Krittika* (the Pleiades). In marrying, will obtain many slaves. Spends much and makes many presents, is beloved by the princes.

Budda kaliwon.—*Titiwa*, the carrying away of dead bodies, or the depositing of the dead in the place of burial. Loss of children.

Wrihaspati manis.—*Sangal tikel*, the broken axe. All undertakings unsuccessful.

Wrihaspati pahing.—*Salah ukur*, discontent and constant strife with men.

Wrihaspati puan.—*Bade*, the bier (on which corpses are burnt). Many long illnesses.

Wrihaspati wage.—*Kumba*, the vessel with holy water.

Wrihaspati kaliwon.—*Naga*, the serpent. A very bad disposition.

Sukra manis.—*Banyak angrîm*, the brooding goose. Loss of property by theft.

Sukra pahing.—*Bubu bosor*, the open bow-net. Quick change, coming and going, rich and poor.

Sukra puan.—*Prawu p'gat*, the broken boat. The husband will be deserted by his wife, the wife by her husband.

Sukra wage.—*Mengrabut untang* or *glutan*, the shifting of one's faults on to another's shoulders.

Sukra kaliwon.—*Udang* or *Makara*, the sea-lobster. Poverty in youth.

Saneśchara manis.—*D'pat*, a head.. (This and the *Gowang*, see Rediti kaliwon, remind us of the head and the body of the demon Rahu, which pursue the moon.) Many members of the family will die.

Saneśchara pahing.—*Ru*, the dart. Boldness and skill in war, esteemed by princes (Sanskrit, *ru*, " war, battle ").

Saneśchara puan.—*Sengenge* (Jav. Srĕngenge), the sun. Freedom from sickness.

Saneśchara wage.—*Puhuh tarung*, a species of quail (Dutch *vecht-kwartel*, the " fighting-quail "). Much fighting.

Saneśchara kaliwon.—*Jampana*, the bier. Much misfortune. Repeated illness.

There is not much astronomical science in all this, and many of the ideas are really ridiculous, yet the Balinese attach value to them, and those who are born on a day with a good constellation often boast of it.

In addition to these astrological meanings of the 35 days, there are for each of the seven days of the week: (1) *a god*, who presides over it; (2) *a human figure*, indicating the character of the person; (3) *a tree;* (4) *a bird;* (5) *a buta* (demon); (6) *a satwa* (beast). The nature of these is supposed to indicate what the character of the person born on that day will be.

The seven gods are given, following the order of the days of the week, beginning with Sunday, as follows : *Indra, Umâ, Brahmâ, Vishṇu, Guru, Srî, Yama;* or, according to another account, *Indra, Pritiwi, Wishṇu, Brahmâ, Guru, Umâ, Durgâ*. The seven Butas are : *Hulu asu* (dog's head), *Hulu k'bo* (buffalo's head), *Hulu kuda* (horse's head), *Hulu lembu* (cow's head), *Hulu singha* (lion's head), *Hulu gaja* (elephant's head), *Hulu gagak* (crow's head). From these the man obtains his passions, and from the beasts his lower qualities.

According to the astrological notions of the Balinese, the day is divided into five parts, each of which has a separate name, although they occur in different order on different days. Raffles also mentions a division of the day into five parts in Java; but in

Bali we have different names and rules for this division. The principal part is called *Mṛita* (Amṛita); he who is born at this time of day is certain to have good fortune. The five parts of the days undergo twelve changes, and to know their order on a particular day, the number of the day of the Indian week is added to that of the day of the Polynesian week, and the result is one of the twelve combinations of the five parts of the day (and also of the night). The rest of the divisions (besides *Mṛita*) are *sunya* (empty, poor), *kala* (passionate; after the god Kâla), *pati* (must die), *linyok* (will become bad and thievish). The day is further divided, in a civil aspect, *into eight hours, dadauhan*, calculated from sunrise to sunset (their names are *dauh pisan*, stroke one, *dauh ro, dauh tiga* or *telu*, &c.). The night is also divided into eight parts in the same manner. To find the hour a sort of water-clock (clepsydra) is used, consisting of a clapper with a little hole in its bottom which rests on the water. As soon as the clapper is filled it is emptied by an attendant, and the number of strokes are given at the same time upon a drum. Contrivances of this kind are to be found in the principal palaces—*e.g.*, in Den Passar (in Badong), Mengui, &c.

The lunar month is divided into the white and the black half, *śukla-paksha* and *kṛishṇa-paksha* (literally, the white and black wing), as is the case in India. The days of the white half are called *tanggal*, and are reckoned from new to full moon; those of the black half are called *panluang*. To describe a date, the Balinese give the day of the week (of the Indian week of seven days as well as of the Polynesian of five), the name of the week (according to the Balinese division of 30 weeks), the name and the half of the lunar month (white or black), the day of that half, and finally the year, calculated from Śaka. Instead of the year of Śaka, they also give simply the year of the century, the century itself being understood. The century is divided into 10 divisions, each of 10 years; each such division is called *tenggek*, each single year *rah*. Thus we have, for instance, on the 26th of June, 1847, *Saneśchara* (Saturday) *kaliwon* (according to the Polynesian week) *wara Landap* (in the week of Landap) *masa kasa* (in the month of Kasa) *śukla paksha* (in the white half; also simply *tanggal*, with a waxing moon) *ping* 13 (on the thirteenth day) *rah* 9, *tenggek* 6 (thus 69). Adding to this the century (1700), we get the year of Śaka 1769, to which 78 must be added to arrive at the year of our Lord (1847).

Besides the *Wriga garga*, which, as we have said, is entirely of Indian origin, there are two other works upon the calendar, which, however, are no longer used; their titles are *Sundari** *trus* and

---

* The name *Sundari* is Sanskrit, and means "the fair one." *Trus* and *bungka* are Polynesian additions; the former seems to indicate that it contains *a continuous* calendar.

Sundari bungka. As I have not yet been able to get a sight of them, I cannot say much about them. The Pandita in Taman said that these works are more recent than the Wriga Garga, and were composed in Java, whereas the Wriga Garga was composed in India (Kling). They were used formerly, but the Balinese priests have given the preference to the older Wriga Garga. This also is an instance of their adherence to all that is ancient and, in their opinion, of Indian origin. The Wriga Garga appears to date from the time of the kingdom of Daha (Kediri), whence our priests are descended, and which kingdom, as we have seen, they often confound with India and call *Baratawarsa.*

We have enumerated in the "Tijdsch. van N. I.," Jaargang VIII. iv. 211, still further divisions of time, namely, a *dvivara, trivara, chaturvara, shaḍvara, astavara, sangavara,* and *daśavara,* besides the *saptavara* and *panchavara;* all these are less prominent in ordinary life. The *trivara* serves to indicate the market days, as the Panchavara does in Java; there is a market every third day (*Dvara*).

The *shaḍvara* is often found in dates added to the *saptavara* and *panchavara.* The names of the *shaḍvara* are Polynesian: *Tunggleh, Haryang, Wurukung, Paniron, Was, Mahulu.* Thus the first day of the week *Sinta* is *Tunggleh Pahing Rediti,* the second *Haryang Puan Soma,* the third *Wurukung Wage anggara,* the fourth *Paniron Kaliwon Budda,* the fifth *Was Manis Wrehaspati,* the sixth *Mahulu Pahing Sukra,* the seventh *Tunggleh Puan Saneschara.* The remaining divisions are chiefly used for astrological definitions. I have not yet discovered clearly how the *astavara* are brought into accordance with the tutelar deities attributed to each of the seven days of the week (see above). The names of the gods of the Astavara are: *Sri, Indra, Guru, Yama, Rudra, Brahma, Kala, Uma;* the tutelar gods of the seven weekdays are: *Indra, Uma, Brahma, Wishnu, Guru, Sri, Yama,* or, according to the other account, *Indra, Pritiwi, Wishnu, Brahma, Guru, Uma, Durga.*

The *zodiac (rasi)* is also used for astrological purposes. We have given the names in the "Tijds. v. N. I.," Jaargang VIII., iv. 211. In good MSS. we find them written still better according to the Sanskrit. The signs of the zodiac, which I found drawn in a manuscript, are the Indian ones; there is no aquarius, but only the water-pitcher (kumba), and instead of the ram there is a shrimp (udang = makara). *Mrechika* is Skrt. *Vṛiśchika,* the scorpion. *Rakata* should be *Karkaṭa.* What is most remarkable is, however, *the absence of the tulâ* (scales) in the manuscript referred to. This could not be an accidental omission, for the claws of the scorpion stretch over the place where the *tulâ* ought to have been, and the scorpion thus took up the room of two signs. Now it is well known that the Greeks in ancient times had only eleven signs of the zodiac, and that it was precisely the scales which were absent, and also that it is supposed that the scales originated out of the claws of the scorpion; although it is not certain whether a sign was lost in the course of transmission from the East (or from Egypt), or whether there were only eleven originally. The discovery of a zodiac with eleven signs in India now renders this question still more intricate. This zodiac cannot have come from the West, for the entirely Indian character of our zodiac excludes this theory; we must therefore suppose that in India also the zodiac once had but eleven signs, and that it was not till later times that the scales were added both in India and in Greece. In Bali all twelve signs are given by name, and thus here also a twelfth has been added; but the fact that we found in Bali the drawing referred to proves that at the time of the first intercourse between India and Java the zodiac still had but eleven signs in the former country. It is not known whether a similar zodiac has been found in India, but it would be of the highest importance to obtain further information from there on this point, and if possible to determine the age of such representations, which would furnish a date of the utmost importance both for the history of astronomy and for that of civilization in Java.

The eclipses of the sun and moon are explained in Bali, as in India, as the devouring of these bodies by a demon (*Rahu*); the eclipses of the sun are called *graha* and those of the moon *rahu*, which in India, however, is no distinction, as the former means the act of devouring and the latter the devouring demon. To help the moon on these occasions, the Balinese make a terrible noise with their rice-blocks and other instruments, as they do on the eve of Galungan and of the fast-days (*nyepi*), when the evil spirits are driven away by noise. The Panditas know that Europeans predict the eclipses of the sun and moon, and questioned me about it; they themselves, however, are ignorant of the method of calculation. They also keep this knowledge secret from the people, as the following instance will show. A European, Mr. M., lived some time in Tabanan, and was very intimate with the young prince. On the approach of an eclipse of the moon, he predicted its occurrence to the prince, who was very pleased thereat, but was compelled by his priests to banish the European from his country, for since the European knew more than the priests, it necessarily followed that he was possessed of an evil spirit from which he obtained his knowledge. Had the European first told it to the priests, they would not have driven him from the country, but would have displayed their knowledge to the people.

As I do not possess a MS. of the Wriga Garga, I cannot give here any further information as to the astronomical and astrological science of the Balinese, although it is most worthy of attention. The greater portion of the people are still utterly ignorant of the calendar. Even among the priests this science is only retained mechanically; but what knowledge they have they use especially to make the people dependent upon them. Every important undertaking requires the help of the priest as the mediator with the deity, and as astronomer and astrologer.

XI.

NOTICES ON ZOOLOGICAL SUBJECTS.

By Messrs. DIARD *and* DUVAUCEL,

Naturalists employed under the authority of the Lieut. Governor of Bencoolen.[1]

[Translated from "Malayan Miscellanies" (Bencoolen, 1821), vol. i. No. 9.]

NOTICE ON THE PANGOLING ANT-EATER OF THE EAST INDIES.

THE forms and proportions of certain animals appear to harmonize so little with their habits, that one may, so to speak, be pardoned for considering them as the accidental sports of organization, escaped from the hands of Nature and betraying, by the heteroclitic contrasts of their structure and their course of life, the imperfection of their original outline.

When one sees, for example, such large and strong quadrupeds as the tamandua, sharing a mode of living with the birds which appears unworthy of the most miserable quadruped, can we help being shocked at the part which has been theirs, and looking upon an animal more than four feet in length, feeding solely upon ants, otherwise than as a monster in creation, or at least, as a creature ridiculously degraded by the insectivorous regimen to which it has been subjected?

In vain would one search in the necessity with which, for example, the tamandua in burrowing and digging out the earth, often at great depths, to get at its prey, for a sufficient reason for excusing

---

[1] [Concerning these gentlemen, see the "Memoir of the Life and Public Services of Sir T. S. Raffles" (London, 1830), pp. 372 and 703 ff.; and more especially vol. xiii. of the "Transactions of the Linnean Society," pp. 239, 240.]

its large body; one would be forced to put aside this explanation, since other very small species of the same class execute absolutely the same manœuvres, and do not in the least appear to need an enormous force to declare war against a colony of ants. One must therefore return to the belief that Nature has not always realized, even in the most perfect relationships, that this animal must make an exception to the harmonic rules which we admire in the greatest part of its productions.

When we say that Nature in creating certain animals did not quite conceive of them in the highest sense, we are told that absolute analogy was not reckoned among their organic and instinctive faculties. Certainly, if it pleased Nature sometimes to omit placing things in harmony in some of her works, it can never have been at the expense of the creatures she has created. Whether we recognize or not some anomalous quadruped, with a mouth, without the sign of teeth, and only provided with a tongue like a bird's, protractile and almost filiform, it nevertheless still belongs to the class of the most wonderful animals, and to those most worthy of the researches and investigations of naturalists.

There are five or six species of ant-eaters to be found in America, one of which, as we have said before, has an enormous body, considering its insectivorous habits; but in the Eastern hemisphere only two species have been found as yet, one in Africa and the other in Asia: anatomically speaking, these species are exactly the same as those in America, but differing completely in the scale-like armour which covers the whole of their body. These animals, which have been transported into Europe several times, have been seen and described by naturalists who call them generically Manis, and who distinguish them by the special names of brachyura and macrura. The macrura is the phatagin of Buffon, the brachyura is his Pangoling, which he had all reason to call it, as the word Pangoling really means in Malay an animal that rolls itself up, and is one of the true names of the Manis in this country. To complete this descriptive word, the Malays generally say Pangoling sisik, the scaled animal that rolls itself up; nevertheless, it is well to observe, that along the west coast of Sumatra, the Manis is not called Pangoling, but Pangilling;[1] the Malays want to express by this the faculty which this animal has for climbing; this is what we cannot decide.

Although the Pangolings are not very rare animals, nevertheless, as they are extremely valuable to most of the Indians, an account of the wonderful medicinal properties attributed to their scales and to their nails, it is very difficult to procure them, and as yet we have only one in our collection.

The specimen we found at Pulo Pinang seems to be full-grown; its total length is three feet and a half, and its tail is only twenty

[1] [Properly panggoling, panggiling.]

inches long, while its body is very long, and its legs are very short; its little head, which is of the same narrowness as its neck, has the appearance of being sharpened into a pointed cone; its tail, on the contrary, is very thick and strong, rounded above and flat underneath, sharp at the sides, and diminishing in size from the top to its point.

This animal has a very pointed snout, little eyes, a very small mouth cleft underneath, and its round ears resemble great pads more than real conchas. With the exception of the upper part of the nose, the side and inferior parts of the head, underneath the neck, and the stomach, and the inner side of the front legs, the Pangoling is entirely covered, even to the roots of its nails, with scales strong and sharp, and of different shapes and sizes according to the parts they are destined to protect. For instance, those at the top of the head, and those which cover the limbs, get smaller as they come to the nose and fingers; it is the same with those of the tail, they are very narrow at the point and very large at the top. The largest scales are those covering the flanks and rump, they are more than an inch in diameter. Their surfaces are all marked with wrinkles and divergent flutings, and most of them have their ends divided into three lappets. Those which entirely cover the hind legs, and those which fringe the sides of the tail, are alone cut in the shape of a pointed angle. These angular scales are also divided into different classes. The first kind have a rather sharp keel, the second kind are folded into grooves angularly, according to their length, so as to be able to fit in above and below. The sharp sides of the tail have a still more wonderful shape; from underneath each scale several single long hairs are seen to appear, while there is not a single one to be seen on the parts we have indicated as being naked.

The Pangolings are not such slow animals as you might expect at first; they run fast enough, and climb quite easily, by means of their strong and sharp nails, and by helping themselves with their tail, using it as a hand or as a buttress. These animals always go along ferreting about and looking under dead leaves and under old trunks of trees for larvæ and insects, which is their staple food.

But the most remarkable faculty the Pangoling possesses is that of rolling itself up into a ball, when it is threatened with danger. To do this it stops all of a sudden, doubles itself up, puts its head between its front legs and finishes by covering itself with a complete scaly armour by putting its long and broad tail over its feet and above its head.

These animals have five fingers on each foot, armed with strong and pointed nails; but of these five fingers, pulled out to their utmost length, only the three middle ones are strong and long enough to be of service to the Pangoling in climbing and in digging, the outer ones are too short to be of any use to them.

NOTICE ON TWO SHREW-MICE OF INDIA.

These little quadrupeds have been distinguished under the name of field-mice, shrew-mice, *Sorex musaraneus*, because, owing to their common form, they are so very closely related with rats, strictly speaking *Mus*, but which in other ways differ completely in their organic characters and even in certain exterior characters, remarkable enough, even if they only existed for the purpose of preventing them from being confounded with the rats. The shrew-mice, essentially destined for an insectivorous life, have partly an organization quite fitted to this kind of life: their teeth have been armed with sharp points, and their jaws furnished on all their circumference with a scarcely interrupted series of canine sharp incisors. None the less are their exterior characters to be compared to their nocturnal and subterraneous habits. Their snout, which is formed into a movable and pointed trunk, serves them as an instrument for digging into the earth to look for food; and their eyes, reduced to two bright specks scarcely visible, suffice to guide them in their excavations underground, and at the same time by their smallness protecting them against things which would have got into them had they been larger; but what serves to distinguish the shrew-mice more than anything else, is the strong musky smell which generally all their species give out; it is a strong smell which comes from a sort of pomade secreted by a particular small matter of granular follicles, which is found on all the true shrew-mice on the lower parts of their body. These follicles, covered with little strong short hairs convergent together, are dotted about on a longitudinal line along nearly the whole of the length of the flanks of all the well-known shrew-mice. On the contrary, in the other two specimens which we have to notice as we live in India, these little glands are concentrated into one, and are round and can be seen on both sides of their body a little behind the shoulder; it is principally to note this slight irregularity in the form of an organ which seems to have some internal connection with the organization of these little animals, that we will give here the description of the two varieties which form part of our collection. Although they are one of the most remarkable species of their kind, because of their body, which is sometimes as long as six inches and more, without counting the tail, which is more than three inches long, and although it is extremely common in Bengal and in the Indian Archipelago, where it is vulgarly known under the name of musky rat, it has nevertheless as yet only been imperfectly described. The only writer who mentioned it particularly is Buffon, who indicates it, more than describes it, as a low animal brought from Pondicherry by Mr. Sonnerat: but as his description is incomplete and as he omitted, according to his habit, to give this species a

Latin name, the result was that it has been confounded with some other kind by the nomenclators; at any rate it has been impossible for us to recognize them in any of their catalogues, if we venture to give it the name of Sorex Indicus, without fear of giving the word a double meaning.

This shrew-mouse, as we have said before, is a little more than six inches long, its tail being about half the size, while its size and form are like the common rat; its fur is of a pretty light grey underneath, and slightly browny above; it may yet be distinguished by the pale pink tint of its naked parts and feet, its tail, the sides of its mouth and ears.

Its quadrangular tail is covered with tiny scaly compartments, which are very fine and furnished with spare hairs, some short and some long. Its snout, straight and flexible like a little trunk, divided at its extremity into two little tubercles, reaches more than half an inch further than the inferior snout.

Lastly, its eyes are extremely small, and its ears round and short, bare, and pressed against the head, are joined in the inside by two large valves, which can almost completely shut the auditory meatus.

The generic characters in this shrew-mouse, as we have already said, consist in a tiny moschiverous gland situated behind each shoulder, and in a digestive organ, just like that of other shrew-mice: thus they have six incisors above and four below, the ends of which are very long; it has one canine and four molar teeth in the upper jaw, and only one canine and three molar teeth in the lower one.

With the shrew-mouse as well as with several kinds of rodents and marsupialia the vulva and the anus open into one common duct.

Our second species of shrew-mouse only differs by its body from the other species we have just described; three inches and a half from the extremity of its snout to the beginning of its tail, is its greatest length, and otherwise it is exactly the same animal, with the short and quadrangular tail, the long and flexible snout, bare ears with large interior valves, tiny little eyes, the feet with five toes, and the grey colour a little darker on its back; the teeth, the intestinal duct, and the moschiverous gland are exactly the same in every respect to the preceding species, and the vulva and anus open into a common drain too.

Notice on the Viverra Mungos.

Owing to a kind of inborn pride which most of us possess, of only thinking of ourselves as the object of all the wonders of creation, and above all if they can come in for our own use, the happy instinct which renders certain animals natural enemies of some hurtful species, has always been considered as a means employed by Nature for protecting mankind from too great a multiplication of some destructive beings who have escaped from its bountiful keeping. This idea, above all with those people naturally inclined to mysticism, ought particularly to lead to exaggerate the instinctive inclinations of these little quadrupeds so celebrated under the name of ichneumon for their combats with the most dangerous reptiles. That is why the Egyptians (who worship these animals) believe that they are incessantly hunting for crocodile's eggs, which they break just for the pleasure of doing an abhorred creature an injury; and not able to attack these great amphibians openly, they try to attack them when asleep with wide-open mouth, then they throw themselves with fury at their throats and kill them by eating out their tongue and their guts: but one fact which has contributed more than anything to increase the marvellous in the history of the ichneumons is that of their deadly combat with the Cobra di Capello. It is scarcely to be believed that such feeble quadrupeds could stand up before such mighty adversaries, without supposing that Nature taught them the means of neutralizing the terrible effects of the most terrible of poisons.

To verify this phenomenon, nothing better can be found than to imagine that the ichneumons knew a certain Dyctom the power of which rendered the bite of the worst vipers harmless. If only this precious plant could be discovered, it would be pointed out as a sure specific against every kind of animal, and the botanists would consecrate its astounding properties by giving it the name of *Ophioriza Mungos*. A circumstance easy enough to explain, very probably, gave rise to this fable.

When the Cobra di Capello, attacked by the ichneumon, keep up the defence too long and vigorously, it happens sometimes that these last named, worn out with fatigue, retire from the battle-field a minute to take breath, and then return to the combat with renewed ardour. Thus this momentary retreat can easily be interpreted. But how can we be content with an explanation natural enough in a case as extraordinary as this? The most marvellous ought to seem the most likely. Besides, people were convinced that the ichneumons only disappeared for a few minutes to be able to look for a remedy for their wounds. As to what is true in all these stories, manufactured by report, is that they possess most wonderful courage and voracity, and that they are very fond of all kinds of eggs, and that they seem to prefer reptiles to any other prey; that they attack everything they have strength enough to put to death; and that if they are not even afraid of fighting the most venomous, it is because their poison has no great effect upon them, which would not be anything so extraordinary, as we know of several poisons which have no effect upon certain animals, or, rather, because they are agile enough to avoid the deadly fangs of their enemy; and we must own that this seems the most likely. If the ichneumon did not fear the poison of the cobras, why would it seize them in a way to avoid their poisoned fangs? and why, from fear of a single bite, should it prolong the attack for hours, often uselessly—an attack which would be extremely hurtful to it—if it were not kept back from ending it by the fear of a single bite?

We have ourselves no confirmed observation on this subject; but the assertions of several trustworthy persons, who have assured us of their having seen ichneumons killed by the cobras, seems to us to tend greatly to the support of this last-named probability.

The ichneumons, as well as the other Viverras, are to be found in all warm climates of the old continent. As their species are not numerous (there are not more than four kinds), and as their instinct has always attracted the attention of all travellers, it follows that there are descriptions exact enough; nevertheless, we do not think it useless to give the ichneumon of India (Viverra Mungos of Linneus) a place here. This species, which is the most celebrated for its combats with the Cobra di Capello, is not as large as the ichneumon of Egypt. Its body, from the tip of the nose to the beginning of the tail, is never longer than fifteen inches, and its slender tail, which ends in a point, is from nine to ten inches long. Its head is of quite a different shape than the other Viverras. The bones of the nose are very much arched above the nostrils, the forehead seems to end in a snout rather higher than large, and the round ears are pressed against the head, and are very far back; this gives its head a still more particular aspect; in short, this ichneumon is a very long animal and low on its legs. Its body, covered with rather long and rough fur, and shaded from four to five times with dark-brown and white, has the appearance of being uniformly quilled with the same colour. On the snout and at the extremities of the four paws, this fur is very scarce; everywhere else it is lined underneath with a woolly and russet-coloured down like the otters.

This Viverra, like the others, has five toes to each foot, but the nails are all longer, sharper, and hardly retractile; like the others it has also six little incisors, three false molars and two long canine ones in each jaw, one carnivorous one and three tuberculous above, and below four false molars, one tuberculous one, and a carnivorous one; then the anus of the Viverra Mungos opens at the end of a large bag in which certain glands exude a particular humour. Although these little animals are instinctively very cruel, and are not satisfied except with slaughter, they can be tamed nevertheless easily enough, and be allowed to run about freely in the house. But domestication does not in any way affect their sanguinary instinct, for, however well fed they may be, they kill anything that happens to resist them just as cruelly, and are always giving chase to the rats, fowls, birds, and snakes.

NOTICE ON THE PORCUPINES OF INDIA.

If there are animals who ought to be positively well known, it would be the porcupines, the numerous specimens of which are very common, and they are otherwise very curious for their sharp quills which clothe their body instead of fur; nevertheless, when we come to consult the descriptions the nomenclators have given of them, we find them so very vague and incomplete, that we cannot be positively sure of either their number, identity, or of the different varieties indicated. So, to keep to the specimens of the old continent, the common porcupines of the southern parts of Europe, Africa and India, which are certainly different, at any rate those of the last-named country, we count as one animal, while certain authors have divided them into two distinct species from the only porcupine with the long penicillegerous tail of the Eastern continent and isles; let us show them that we know more. We have said that the common porcupine of India was different to that of Italy; we will add further, that we believe there are two particular varieties in Asia quite similar in form, it is true, to the Hystrix cristata, but which differs in the way in which the black and white bands run on their quills.

During our stay in Bengal we were able to procure several specimens of this species of porcupine, which is commonly found in this country; but being ourselves led away by the general opinion, we did not give it enough attention to notice that it differed from the European species, and it was only after our first journey to Pulo Pinang that we verified this difference, having accidentally compared the quills of the short-tailed porcupine which you find in this island as well as in Sumatra, and probably throughout the Sunda archipelago, with some of those we brought from Calcutta, and we were struck with the different placing of the colours on each kind, and saw then that they belonged to a different species of animal, not only they, but neither of these species were, as people have believed till now, a long-haired porcupine; in fact, this latter kind has all its quills white at the extremities.

The quills of the Bengal porcupine, white at first, have a little above their roots a little black ring, then a white one, and then they are entirely black to their extremities, while those of the Sunda islands are quite white, with the exception of a single black ring situated a little above the middle part; this is the only real difference we can indicate as yet between these three species; but it is probable that comparing each one would lead us to find out other kinds.

The total length of the largest we have seen does not exceed twenty-eight inches: its head is nearly five inches, and its tail hardly three inches long; when it bristles up and lifts up its back, it stands about from fourteen to fifteen inches high; otherwise this species has just the same shape and proportions as the common European porcupine. Its ears are round and bare; its snout thick, shaped like a trunk; it has five toes on the hind and four on the fore-legs; one nailed tubercle serves as a thumb; its long quills only cover the posterior half of the body; the chest, the upper and lower parts of the shoulders, are covered with another kind of quill, much shorter, flat like the blade of a sword, and quite black, with the exception of some which are white at the ends, and forming under the throat a kind of half-collar of this same colour. Those on the nape of the neck are white at the tips, but they are differently shaped; they are thick round hairs, a little longer than the rest, nevertheless without being sufficient to form a mane; the thick stiff hairs which cover the feet and legs are more sturdy, shorter, and of a very deep black: the tail is short and straightens itself when the animal stands up. At the beginning of the tail are quills like those on the back, and those at the tip resemble very delicate and elastic hairs, entirely white, swollen at the ends into round tubes and ending naturally in sharp points. Although they are mostly open and hollow, when the porcupine bristles itself up these tubes rub together and produce a kind of audible dull noise: not counting the different quills we have spoken of, the porcupines have still here and there, and chiefly on the lower parts of their body, other very long and slender quills, with a single black ring on them, like the others.

To terminate the history of this porcupine we must add that at Bencoolen it is called Landah, and that we have provisionally specified it under the name of Hystrix torquatus; lastly, we must mention that, in Bengal, the one we described at the commencement of this article is called Lazaroo.

We must now speak of the long brush-tailed porcupine, and to prove (what is in fact the general opinion) that the Hystrix macrura is nothing else than the fasciculata of Linneus. In fact, the only particular character which Seba and Shreber gave to their macrura, was the twofold enlargement of the thongs of the elastic hair at the end of the tail, which several descriptions of the porcupine of Queda mention; but this character is of no value whatever; for on the same animal these enlarged hairs are always to be found. Besides this the long-tailed porcupine is well enough known; it has even been seen in Europe several times, nevertheless we believe it to be still possible to add some interesting facts to his description.

It seems that this species is never longer than from seventeen to eighteen inches, without counting the tail, which is from eight to nine inches long; it stands lower on its legs, its body and its head are longer, and its proportions are generally far less massive than those of the porquatus; its quills, the longest of which is never more than an inch and a half, are of the same shape as those covering the shoulders of the last named, that is to say, they are flat like the blade of a sword and very much fluted at the top; those on the back are of a greyish colour, with a large brown speckle in the middle; those on the lower parts of the body, on the contrary, are only white at the roots, and are quite black otherwise: imperceptibly those on the legs take the form of coarse round hairs; besides the Malacca porcupine has, like the others, on the lower parts of the body, several long black hairs, dotted about here and there among its ordinary quills: their tail is covered at the top with needles like those on the back, and is not, as some say, scaly nearly everywhere; on the contrary, it is well covered with very fine and delicate spikes which appear to be the remains of the old ones, which surround the ends in the form of a tuft: otherwise these are, as we have already said, either singly or doubly in thongs, and these thongs are naturally pointed at the tip, and are never truncated, except by accident. This singular species always carries its tail lifted up like a trumpet, and makes the tuft at the end tremble, like the others.

We have counted on each jaw, like on the preceding ones, except the two great ordinary incisors, four cylinder-like teeth concentrically striated at their crown, and it has, like the others, five toes on the hind and four on the fore-feet with a tubercle taking the place of a thumb.

XII.
DESCRIPTIONS OF MALAYAN PLANTS.
By WILLIAM JACK.

["Malayan Miscellanies" (Bencoolen, 1820–22), vol. i. Nos. 1 and 5; vol. ii. No. 7.]

ZINGIBER GRACILE.—W. J.
Monandria Monogynia.
N. O. Scitamineæ.

Foliis glabris, scapis erectis, spicis cylindricis gracilibus coloratis, bracteis ovatis acutis, corollæ labio trilobo, lobo medio bifido.

Native of Pulo Pinang.

Stem erect, somewhat recurved, round and smooth. Leaves alternate, subsessile on their sheaths, broad lanceolate, 6 or 7 inches long, acuminate, very entire, very smooth, shining above. Sheaths smooth, with a long scariose ligula, often lacerated on the edge. Scapes erect, a foot high, invested with alternate sheaths. Spikes cylindrical, oblong, imbricated with bright red ovate acute bracts, shorter than the flowers. An inner bract or involucre surrounds the base of each flower. Calyx shorter by one-half than the corolla, membranaceous, curved, cleft on one side. Corolla yellowish white; exterior limb 3-parted, longer than the inner one; laciniæ acuminate, the upper one longer and incumbent; interior limb unilabiate, lip 3-lobed, middle lobe bifid, with reflexed margins. Anther terminating in an incurved horn. Ovarium 3-celled, many-seeded. Style filiform, longer than the horn of the anther, embraced at the base by two linear corpuscules.

AMOMUM BIFLORUM.—W. J.

Monandria Monogynia.

N. O. Scitamineæ.

Foliis lato lanceolatis glaberrimis, caule ancipite, spicis bifloris. Native of Pulo Pinang.

A slender delicate species. Stem erect, somewhat recurved, 3 feet in height, compressed, double edged. Leaves alternate, bifarious, short petioled upon their sheaths, broad lanceolate, acuminate, narrow at the base, entire, very smooth, the middle nerve somewhat pubescent. Sheaths striated, slightly tomentose, with a short, round ciliate ligula. The base of the leaf-bearing stem is swelled into a tuber, which throws out horizontal shoots of some feet in length, of the thickness of a quill, and invested with membranous sheaths. These shoots, which run underground, send up from their joints a number of biflorous peduncles, or scapes, which are enveloped in bracteal sheaths. Flowers, generally two, the one appearing after the other. At the base of each flower is a single lanceolate, acute reddish bract; besides this there is a tubular bract, or involucrum, surrounding the base of the germen, membranaceous, half as long as the calyx, and deeply cleft on one side. Calyx superior, tubular, 2 or 3 cleft. Corolla white, tubular; upper part of the tube villous within; exterior limb membranaceous, 3-parted, segments nearly equal; interior limb unilabiate, lip broader above, rounded, thickened, and yellow in the middle. Filament of the stamen broad, incumbent. Anther short, thick, 2-lobed, crowned with an erect 3-lobed crest. Style filiform; stigma infundibuliform. Nectaries two, linear, at the base of the style. Ovarium 3-celled, many-seeded.

PSYCHOTRIA MALAYANA.—W. J.

Pentandria Monogynia.

N. O. Rubiaceæ.

Foliis lato lanceolatis, stipulis indivisis, paniculis terminalibus corymbosis, corollæ fauce villosa.

Byumbada. *Malay.*

Native of Pulo Pinang.

A shrub with round smooth branches. Leaves petiolate, opposite, broad lanceolate, 10 inches in length, acuminate, decurrent upon the petiole, entire, very smooth. Petioles short, thick, round, surrounded at the base by a prominent ring, from which a thick rib diverges on each side and unites with a similar one from the base of the opposite leaf to form the nerve of the large interpetiolar ovate acute stipule. Panicles corymbose, terminal. Flowers numerous. Bracts broad, membranaceous, embracing. Calyx superior, erect, quinquefid. Corolla white, with greenish limb, infundibuliform, longer than the calyx, mouth closed with dense white hairs, limb 5-parted, somewhat reflexed, laciniæ ovate. Stamina 5, erect, inserted on the tube, filaments very short, anthers linear. Style filiform, stigmata two, thick and linear. Capsule inferior, 2-celled, 2-seeded.

RONDELETIA CORYMBOSA.—W. J.

Pentandria Monogynia.

Tetrandra, pedunculis plerumque terminalibus dichotome corymbosis, floribus unilateralibus, foliis obovato lanceolatis.

Native of Pulo Pinang.

Stem erect, shrubby, from 4 to 6 feet in height, with somewhat compressed villous branches. Leaves opposite, petiolate, obovate lanceolate, acute, attenuated to the petiole, entire, punctate above with callous dots, villous below. Petioles short, thickened at the base. Stipules interpetiolar, long, erect, tongue-shaped, obtuse, villous, with a thick middle rib formed by the union of one from each axil. Peduncles terminal, and from the upper axils, supporting dichotomous corymbs, composed of unilateral spikes. Flowers erect, sessile, disposed alternately in a double series. Calyx superior, 4-cleft, with short acute laciniæ. Corolla white, tinged with red, funnel-shaped, much longer than the calyx, faux naked, limb erect, 4-parted, laciniæ sub-rotund. Stamina 4, inserted into the faux, filaments very short, anthers linear. Style filiform, exsert. Stigma bifid. Capsule crowned with the calyx, 2-celled, many-seeded, with central placentæ.

PHYTEUMA BEGONIFOLIUM.
Pentandria Monogynia.
N. O. Campanulaceæ.

Foliis semicordatis inequilateralibus serratis, spicis unilateralibus axillaribus, revolutis.

Phyteuma begonifolia. Roxb. "Hort. Beng." p. 85.

Pulo Pinang.

A small herbaceous plant. Stem procumbent, 1 or 2 feet in length, thick, villous chiefly at the summit, with fasciculate hairs. Leaves alternate, petiolate, semicordate, inequilateral, turning to one side, 8 inches long, acute, with gross subspinescent serratures, villous beneath, adult leaves smooth above, nerves generally dichotomous. Petioles thick, round, furrowed above. Stipules none. Peduncles axillary or supra-axillary. Flowers unilateral, erect, arranged in two rows on a recurved spike, nearly sessile, crowded. Bracts cuneiform, obtuse. Calyx semi-superior, ovate, villous, 5-lobed, lobes obtuse. Corolla white, campanulate, persistent, limb recurved, 5-lobed, lobes obtuse; after florescence the corolla becomes green and enlarges. Stamina 5, erect, short, inserted on the calyx and opposite to its divisions. Anthers linear, acute. Ovarium surrounded by the calyx and connected with it by five longitudinal septa or processes, from which the stamina spring, 3 or 4-celled, many-seeded, placentæ from the inner angles of the cells. Style short, thick. Stigma large, thick, 3-lobed. Capsule 3 or 4-celled, containing numerous seeds arranged on convex placentæ.

The septa which unite the calyx and ovary appear continuous with the filaments of the stamina. The young parts of the plant are densely villous, but the hairs are easily rubbed away. In drying, the plant assumes a bright yellow colour. It appears extremely doubtful whether this plant be truly referrible to Phyteuma; it does not, however, agree well with any other genus of the family of Campanulaceæ, and it will deserve consideration whether it ought not to constitute a new genus in that order.

CURCULIGO SUMATRANA —Roxb.
Hexandria Monogynia.

Foliis lato-lanceolatis plicatis glabris, spicis densis brevibus, tubo perianthii baccâ longiore.

Involucrum. Rumph. "Amb." vi. p. 114, t. 53.

Kalapa puyu. *Malay.*

Sumatra and Pulo Pinang.

Root composed of fibres proceeding from a tuber. Leaves radical, petiolate, ovate-lanceolate, acuminate, attenuated to the base, plicato-nervose, very entire, smooth. Petioles erect, channelled above, keeled beneath, sheathing at the base. Spikes radical from among the sheaths of the petioles, erect, dense, much shorter than the petioles. Flowers erect, sessile, adpressed to the rachis, each furnished with an ovate acuminate membranaceous spathe. Calyx none. Corolla yellow, superior, limb spreading 6-parted, laciniæ lanceolate acute, tube impervious, being a thick, solid column on the summit of the germen. Stamina 6, erect, opposite to the laciniæ of the corolla. Anthers linear. Style short. Ovarium 3-celled, many-seeded. Capsule baccate, ovate, 3-sided, containing from 8 to 10 ovate black seeds which are imbedded in pulp.

I found at Singapore another species, agreeing in most respects with this, but having hirsute leaves.

LORANTHUS COCCINEUS.—W. J.

Floribus spicatis tetrandris, spicis axillaribus erectis foliis subovatis glabris.

Found at Singapore.

Branches long, vimineous. Leaves alternate petiolate, oblong-ovate, subcordate at the base, attenuated towards the apex, which is obtuse, entire, smooth. Petioles short. Spikes axillary, solitary, or in pairs, erect, longer than the leaves; flowers sessile, closely pressed to the rachis before expansion. A single small, ovate ferruginous bract is situated at the base of each flower. Calyx superior, nearly entire, scarcely toothed. Corolla coccineous, 4-petaled, erect, tubular, limb spreading, petals nearly linear, broader at the base. Stamina 4, red, erect, inserted into the middle of the petals and equalling them in length; anthers oblong adnate, red. Style red, erect, scarcely longer than the stamina. Stigma obtusely capitate. Berry ovate, elongated above, 1-seeded. Seed contained in a hard shell, 4-sided, its apex immersed in gluten, into which the radicle shoots. Embryo inverse, the radicle produced beyond the albumen.

This species is nearly allied to the L. pentapetala of Roxburgh, agreeing with it in habit and inflorescence.

LORANTHUS FERRUGINEUS.—Roxb.

Ferrugineo villosa, foliis ellipticis obtusis supra glabris, pedunculis fasciculatis axillaribus 2–6 floris, floribus tetrandris extus ferrugineo villosis.

Roxb. " Hort. Beng." p. 87.

Sumatra, &c.

A parasitic shrub which attaches itself firmly to the branches of trees by means of long runners and numerous circular bands. The branches are long and hanging, and when young densely covered with reddish ferruginous wool. Leaves opposite, short petioled, coriaceous, elliptic, obtuse, entire, smooth and green above, ferruginous and densely villous beneath. Stipules none. Peduncles fascicled, from 1 to 4 in each axil, 2–6 flowered. A small scale-like bract embraces the base of the ovary. Calyx (if any) an entire margin crowning the ovarium. Corolla covered externally, as well as the peduncles and ovary, with ferruginous tomentum, green and smooth within, tubular, divisible into four petals, which commonly adhere at their base but separate at the limb, which is generally more deeply cloven on one side. Stamina 4, inserted into the tube, and nearly as long as the limb. Filaments flat, deep purple. Style as long as the corolla. Stigma sub-rotund. Berry ovate, ferruginous, 1-seeded.

NEPHELIUM LAPPACEUM.

Marsd. "Hist. Sumatra," pl. iv.
Rambutan. *Malay.*
Frequent throughout the Malay countries and islands.

A tree. Leaves alternate, pinnate, leaflets generally from 5 to 7, ovate, acute at both ends, very entire, smooth. Panicles terminal, erect. Flowers numerous, small, white, male and hermaphrodite. Calyx from 4 to 6-parted, spreading. Corolla none. Stamina from 5 to 8, spreading, longer than the calyx, inserted into a disc below the germen. Anthers sub-rotund. Ovarium 2-seeded, abortive in the male flowers. Style 1. Stigmata 2, revolute. Fruit geminate, one commonly abortive, the rudiment of which remains at the base of the perfect one, which is sub-rotund, covered with a coriaceous rind and echinate with long soft spines, 1-seeded, the seed covered with a white acid pulp.

The fruit is much esteemed, and has an agreeable subacid flavour. The parts of the flower vary much in number; six is perhaps the most frequent number of the stamina. There is but one style, not two as commonly described. The affinities of this tree seem to have been little understood. It belongs without doubt to the family of the Sapindi, and is closely related to Scytalia, as justly conjectured by the author of the botanical articles in Rees' "Cyclopædia."

SAPINDUS RUBIGINOSUS.—Roxb.

Octandria Monogynia.

Arborescens inermis, paniculis terminalibus, calicibus 5 phyllis, corollis 4-petalis, baccis tribus connatis oblongis.
Kulit layu. *Malay.*

Pulo Pinang.

Arborescent. Leaves alternate, abruptly pinnate leaflets nearly opposite, subsessile, ovate-lanceolate, obtuse, with a small mucro or point, very entire, nearly smooth, with a few scattered hairs, chiefly on the under surface. Petioles tomentose. Panicles terminal, erect, composed of numerous simple racemes. Pedicles short, generally in pairs. Bracts subulate. Calyx 5-leaved, leaflets sub-rotund, concave, the two outer ones smaller. Corolla white, 4-petalled, somewhat longer than the calyx, petals ovate, obtuse, appendiculate at the base, appendices furnished with two transverse lines of white hairs. Stamina 8, of which the 5 upper and longer are incumbent over the remaining 3. Filaments villous. Anthers oblong, yellow. Style 1, short, persistent. Stigma capitate, 4-sided, villous. Germina 3, 1-seeded. Berries 3, connate at the base, purple, oblong, 1-seeded.

MELIA EXCELSA.—W. J.

Decandria Monogynia.

Foliis pinnatis, foliolis integerrimis, paniculis coarctatis axillaribus foliis paullo longioribus.

Pulo Pinang.

A lofty tree, with straight trunk and light grey bark. Branches rough with the vestiges of the fallen leaves, foliose at their summits. Leaves crowded, disposed in a spiral manner, pinnate with an odd one which is often wanting, leaflets sub-opposite, oblong-lanceolate, inequilateral, obtusely acuminate, very entire, smooth, shining above. Petioles round, smooth, thickened, and somewhat scaly at the base. Panicles axillary, ascending, rather longer than the leaves, not diffuse. Flowers pedicellate, pedicles bracteolate. Calyx very small, 5-parted. Corolla white, 5-petalled, spreading, petals linear. Staminiferous tube erect, gibbous at the base, 10 dentate, 10 furrowed, as if consisting of 10 united filaments. Anthers 10, oblong, yellow, within the mouth of the tube. Style as long as the tube. Stigma capitate.

MICROCOS TOMENTOSA.—Smith, in Rees' "Cyclopædia."

Polyandria Monogynia.

N. O. Tiliaceæ.

Foliis trinerviis subtus villosis.

Grewia Paniculata. Roxb. " Hort. Beng." p. 93.

Native of Pulo Pinang.

A moderate-sized tree with rough bark, the branchlets villous and ferruginous. Leaves alternate, short petioled, elliptic oblong, broader above, with a short acumen, 3-nerved, dentate, serrate towards the apex, scarcely pilose above, densely villous beneath, the hairs divaricate and often stellate. Stipules linear, generally bifid. Panicles terminal. Flowers for the most part in threes, involucred with deciduous trifid and linear bracts. Calyx 5-leaved, spreading, leaflets oblong concave. Corolla yellow, less than the calyx, petals ovate, unguiculate and without nectaries. Stamina numerous, inserted below the germen. Germen stipitate. Drupe containing a nut marked externally with five lines, 3-celled, 3-seeded.

This agrees perfectly with the excellent description given by Sir J. E. Smith in Rees' "Cyclopædia," from a specimen preserved in the herbarium of the younger Linnæus, unaccompanied with any notice concerning its native country, and also deficient in fruit. Its affinity to the original species of Microcos is fully proved on actual examination of the fruit, and this exact agreement affords a further confirmation of the propriety of separating Microcos from Grewia. The terminal inflorescence and involucral bracteæ form a peculiar and distinctive character. In this species the flowers are generally three together, and are surrounded by three trifid bracteæ, within which are found three other smaller and linear ones.

MICROCOS GLABRA.—W. J.

Foliis trinerviis serratis glabris.
Found on the Island of Carnicobar.

It nearly resembles the M. Tomentosa, differing chiefly in having smooth leaves. In inflorescence and fruit it is entirely similar. The young branches are tomentose. There are frequently flowers in the uppermost axils.

MIMOSA JIRINGA.

Arbor inermis, foliis conjugato pinnatis, foliolis 3-jugis glaberrimis, paniculis fasciculatis axillaribus, capitulis paucifloris leguminibus maximis articulato-contortis nigris.

Mimosa Djiringa. Roxb. "Hort. Beng." p. 93.
Bua Jêring. *Malay.*
Pulo Pinang, Malacca, &c.

A lofty tree, unarmed, with grey bark and round smooth branches. Leaves alternate, conjugato-pinnate, leaflets 3-paired, on short thick pedicles, ovate lanceolate, obtusely acuminate, very entire, very smooth, the upper pairs larger. Petioles round, somewhat keeled above. An indistinct gland above the base of the common petiole. Capitula few flowered, panicled; these panicles are fasciculate, axillary, or in the axils of fallen leaves. Flowers white. Calyx 5-toothed. Corolla twice as long as the calyx,

5-cleft. Stamina numerous, monadelphous, long, fertile. Style as long as the stamina. Legumes solitary, very large, almost black, about a foot in length, spirally contorted, articulate, 2-valved, articulations subrotund, 1-seeded, convex and prominent on both sides. Seeds large, subrotund, double convex.

This species belongs to the genus Inga of Willdenow.

CLERODENDRUM MOLLE.—W. J.

Didynamia Angiospermia.

Caule erecto tetragono, foliis cordatis acuminatis integerrimis tomentosis, panicula terminali, tubo corollæ calycæ vix longiore, calyce fructûs ampliato carnoso albo.

Frequent in Sumatra, Pulo Pinang, &c.

A shrub from 3 to 6 feet in height, erect, little branched; stem 4-sided, villous. Leaves opposite, petiolate, cordate, acuminate, very entire, softly tomentose. Panicle terminal, oppositely trichotomous, erect, with leaf-like bracts. Calyx 5-parted, tomentose, laciniæ ovate, acute, erect, with reflexed margins. Corolla tomentose without, tube as long as the calyx, limb 5-parted, spreading, secund, laciniæ nearly equal, crisped at the margin. Stamina exsert, horizontally deflexed to each side. Style erect, as long as the stamina. Stigma bifid. Calyx of the fruit flat, enlarged, fleshy and white. Berry from 1 to 4-seeded, according to the number that abort.

This species approaches nearest to the C. infortunatum, but is abundantly distinguished by the softness of the leaves, which are larger and more deeply cordate, by the comparative shortness of the tube of the corolla, and by the white calyx of the fruit.

Besides this species, I have met with another in various parts of these islands, and particularly at Acheen, which has been figured in Andrews' "Repository" under the name of Clerodendrum pyramidale. It is a large, showy plant. A still more beautiful species, and perhaps the most elegant of the whole genus, is the C. nutans, so named by my friend Dr. Wallich, Superintendent of the Botanic Garden at Calcutta, who received it from the North-eastern frontier of Bengal. I found it not uncommon at Pulo Pinang, and this is not the only instance in which I have had occasion to observe a coincidence between the plants of these distant countries. This species is characterized as follows:—

C. nutans, Wall.—Foliis lanceolatis acuminatis glabris, paniculis longissimis terminalibus nutantibus, pedunculis remotis divaricatis paucifloris.

These panicles or racemes hang gracefully from the extremity of the branches, the flowers are white, not numerous, the peduncles, or primary divisions of the panicle being remote, opposite, divaricate, short, and seldom bearing more than three flowers. It is called Unting unting by the Malays.

GMELINA VILLOSA.—Roxb.

Spinosa, foliis rhomboideis subtus villosis, racemis terminalibus, bracteis magnis acuminatis, drupis sphericis dispermis.

Radix deiparæ. Rumph. "Amb." ii. p. 124, t. 39.
Kayo Briang.
Native of Sumatra, &c.

Arborescent. Leaves opposite, broad ovate, sometimes obscurely 3-lobed, rather obtuse, entire, smooth above, villous beneath, as well as the petioles and branchlets. Racemes terminal. Bracts large, ovate, acuminate. Calyx obliquely 4-toothed, marked externally with 6 green scutellæ or pustules. Corolla yellow, ventricose. Anthers 2-lobed. Ovary 4-sporous. Drupe with a 2-seeded nut.

VITEX ARBOREA.—Roxb. "Hort. Beng." p. 46.

Didynamia Angiospermia.

Arborea, foliis ternatis, foliolis ovato lanceolatis integerrimis subtomentosis, paniculis terminalibus, bracteis calyce longioribus.

Lĕban. *Malay.*
Sumatra, &c.

A tree, with somewhat four-sided branches. Leaves opposite, petiolate, ternate, sometimes quinate, leaflets ovate lanceolate, acuminate, very entire, rigid, covered with a very short tomentum. Petioles long, thickened at the base, pulverulent. Panicles terminal; flowers subsessile. Bracts opposite, ovate lanceolate, acute, tomentose, longer than the calyces. Calyx 5-dentate, tomentose, persistent. Corolla cœrulescent, or nearly white, longer than the calyx, contracted and almost closed at the mouth, limb bilabiate, upper lip 2-lobed, lobes diverging, lower lip larger, 3-lobed, the lateral lobes reflexed, the middle one larger, subrotund, concave, tomentose at the base, and of a deeper blue than the rest. Stamina 4, didynamous, ascending, longer than the corolla. Style longer than the stamina. Stigma bifid. Berry black, juicy, containing a 4-celled, 4-seeded nut.

The wood of this tree is very hard, and is employed by the inhabitants of Sumatra in the construction of houses, also for paddles. They consider an infusion of the bark as a useful application in cases of ophthalmia.

SPHENODESME.—W. J.

Didynamia Angiospermia.
Vitices Juss.

Calyx tubulosus 5-dentatus. Corolla 5-loba subirregularis. Stamina 4-5 exserta. Ovarium 4 loculare, 4 sporum. Bacca monosperma.
Flores fasciculati, involucrati.

SPHENODESME PENTANDRA.—W. J.

Foliis oblongo ovatis glabris, involucris 5-6 phyllis, fasciculis 6-7 floris, floribus pentandris.
Roscœa pentandra. Roxb. "Cat. Hort. Beng." p. 46.
Native of Pulo Pinang.
A climbing shrub, with 4-sided, somewhat pilose branches. Leaves opposite, petiolate, oblong ovate, subcordate at the base, acuminate (sometimes with a retuse acumen), very entire, very smooth. Petioles short, pilose. Fascicles 6 or 7 flowered, peduncled, disposed in panicles at the extremity of the branches and in the upper axils. Involucres consisting of 5 or 6 oblong, obtuse, membranaceous, reticulated leaflets, which are longer than the sessile flowers. Calyx campanulate, 5-plicate, 5-dentate. Corolla infundibuliform, faux villous, limb 5-lobed, nearly regular. Stamina 5, long, exsert. Style filiform, bifid. Ovary very hairy, 3 to 4-celled; cells 1-seeded.
There is always one leaflet less in the involucrum than the number of flowers in the fascicle, the central flower having no fulcrum. This species was sent to Dr. Roxburgh from Sylhet, and by him called Roscœa; that name, however, being preoccupied, a new one has become necessary. I have therefore given it that of Sphenodesme (*fasciculus alatus*).

STERCULIA COCCINEA.—ROXB.

Monadelphia Decandria.

Foliis oblongo lanceolatis obtusè acuminatis glabris, racemis axillaribus et lateralibus nutantibus, laciniis calycinis linearibus patentibus, folliculis coccineis.
Native of Pulo Pinang.
A large smooth shrub. Leaves at the summits of the branches, alternate, petiolate, 8-10 inches long, oblong lanceolate, obtusely acuminate, abrupt at the base, entire, smooth on both sides. Petioles thickened at both ends. Racemes lateral from among the leaves at the end of the branches, drooping; flowers alternate, pedicellate; pedicles articulate. Tube of the calyx somewhat

ventricose, limb 5-parted, laciniæ linear with revolute margins, twice as long as the tube, spreading. Corolla none. Stamina 10, sessile on the stipes of the germen. Ovarium stipitate on a column of the length of the tube, subrotund, 5-lobed, crowned with a declinate style. Stigmata 5, linear, revolute. Fruit composed of five nearly equal crimson follicles, each of which contains two or three seeds, which are enveloped in a black pulpy arillus.

Dr. Roxburgh's S. coccinea is a native of Sylhet, and is said to have panicled flowers and 4–8 seeded follicles. My plant agrees, however, so well in every other respect that I cannot consider it to be really distinct, as those differences may be merely the effect of a less favourable situation.

STERCULIA ANGUSTIFOLIA.—Roxb.

Foliis lanceolatis superne latioribus acuminatis subtus villosis, racemis extra axillaribus nutantibus, laciniis calycinis linearibus apice connexis.

Unting Unting Besar. *Malay.*
Native of Pulo Pinang.

A tree. Branches covered with ferruginous wool. Leaves at the summits of the branches, alternate, petiolate, lanceolate, broader above, acuminate, narrowing to the base and there rounded, entire, smooth (in adult leaves) above, covered beneath with stellate hairs. Petioles thickened at both ends, ferruginously villous, as well as the nerve of the leaf. Stipules linear, acute, shorter than the petiole, deciduous. Racemes (panicles?) near the extremity of the branches lateral or extra axillary, branched, lax, ferruginous. Bracts linear lanceolate acute. Calyx deeply 5-parted, tomentose, laciniæ long, linear, acute, connected at their points and gaping at the sides, greenish yellow, with a red spot at the base. Corolla none. Stamina 10, on a curved column. Ovarium stipitate, tomentose, 5-lobed. Style declinate. Stigma 5-lobed.

A great proportion of the flowers are male, and I have not seen the perfect fruit.

Dr. Roxburgh's plant was a native of Chittagong.

CALLA HUMILIS.—W. J.

Monœcia Monandria.

Acaulis, foliis ellipticis supra glabris, pedunculis 4–5 ex-axillis foliorum petiolis brevioribus.

Kladi Ayer. *Malay.*
Pulo Pinang, &c.

A small stemless plant, growing under the shade of forests, 5 or 6 inches in height. Root a leaf-bearing tuber, which sends out numerous long villous fibres. Stem none, except the above-mentioned tuber, which is everywhere invested by the sheaths of the petioles. Leaves erect, petiolate, elliptic, ovate, rather obtuse, with a subulate acumen, slightly cordate at the base, entire, with a pellucid, crisped margin, smooth and green above, somewhat hoary beneath, with villous papillæ. Petioles shorter than the leaves, channeled above, sheathing, and dilated into a waved margin at the base. The bases of the sheaths are often perforated by the fibres of the root. Peduncles 4–5 axillary, 1-flowered, shorter than the petioles, furnished with membranous sheaths at the base. Spathes of an obscure red colour, oblong, convolute, acuminate, as long as the spadix. Spadix cylindrical, entirely covered with florets, male above and female below for about a quarter of the length. Anthers numerous, subrotund, yellow, sessile. Germina ovate. Styles very short. Stigmata obtuse, peltate. A few anthers are intermingled with the pistilla. Capsules membranaceous, globose, somewhat 4-lobed (2-celled?) generally 8-seeded. Seeds somewhat kidney-shaped, arranged round the axis.

CALLA ANGUSTIFOLIA.—W. J.

Acaulis, foliis lanceolatis utrinque acutis glabris, pedunculis 4–5 ex-axillis foliorum petiolis brevioribus.

Pulo Pinang.

A small plant of the same size and nearly related to the preceding. Leaves radical, petiolate, lanceolate, acute at both ends, entire, smooth. Petioles sheathing at the base. Peduncles 4–5 axillary, 1-flowered. Flowers, &c., exactly as in the preceding.

These two are so closely allied that it is doubtful whether they might not be considered varieties.

CALLA NITIDA.—W. J.

Foliis ovato-lanceolatis acuminatis, scapis compressis foliis brevioribus, baccis monospermis.

Found at Pulo Pinang.

This is a large subcaulescent species; the leaves are from a foot to a foot and a half in length, ovate lanceolate, acuminate, very entire, very smooth, with numerous parallel nerves proceeding from a middle rib. Petioles sheathing nearly their whole length. Scapes compressed, smooth, shorter than the leaves. Spadix invested by the spathe, covered with florets, male above, female beneath. Berries oblong, large, 1-seeded.

FLACOURTIA INERMIS.—Roxb.

Arborescens inermis, floribus hermaphroditis fasciculatis axillaribus, foliis ovatis serratis glabris.

Koorkup.[1] *Malay.*
Sumatra and Pulo Pinang.

A tree of moderate size. Leaves alternate, short petioled, ovate, obtusely acuminate, with large blunt serratures, very smooth, lucid, from 6 to 8 inches in length. Peduncles fasciculate in the axils, many flowered. Flowers hermaphrodite. Calyx 4-leaved, spreading, somewhat tomentose, leaflets subrotund, sharpish. Corolla none. Nectary composed of numerous small, subrotund, orange-coloured glands, situated at the base of the calyx and surrounding the stamina. Stamina numerous (20–30), hypogynous, longer than the calyx, filaments white, anthers yellow, subrotund. Ovary superior ovate, crowned with 4–5 short, thick, diverging styles; stigmata capitate, 2-lobed. Berry reddish purple, with a juicy, acid flesh, in which are imbedded from 8 to 10 pyrenæ, according to the number of the styles.

The fruit of this, though rather too acid to be eaten in its raw state, is much esteemed in tarts and pies.

ROTTLERA ALBA.—Roxb.

Foliis rhomboideo-ovatis, subtus incanis, paniculis terminalibus laxis, fructibus stellato pilosis spinis mollibus echinatis.

Baleh angin. *Malay.*
Sumatra and Pulo Pinang.

A tree of moderate size. Branches roundish, furfuraceous, with appressed, stellate hairs. Leaves alternate, petiolate, rhomboidal ovate, often approaching to 3-lobed, long acuminate, rounded and bi-glandular at the base, where the petiole is inserted within the margin, remotely denticulate towards the apex, smooth and green above, hoary and tomentose beneath. The young leaves have stellate, deciduous hairs on the upper surface. Petioles long. Stipules none. Panicles terminal, or from the bifurcations of the branches, peduncled, lax, and drooping. Flowers small, numerous, short pedicled. Bracts small, and together with the peduncles and calyx sprinkled with furfuraceous tomentum.

Male.—Calyx 3-phyllous, leaflets ovate acute. Stamina numerous in the centre of the flower. Anthers subrotund.

Female.—Calyx 4 sometimes 5-parted, erect, laciniæ acute. Styles 3, diverging, hirsute above. Stigmata simple. Fruit tricoccous, beset with soft flexible spines, and covered with stellate hairs, 3-seeded. Seeds subrotund, attached to the superior and internal angle of the cells.

[1] [? Rukam.]

DIDYMOCARPUS.—WALLICH.

Calyx 5-fidus. Corolla infundibuliformis, labio superiore brevi, inferiore trilobo. Stamina 5 nunc 4, quorum 2 vel 4 fertilia. Capsula siliquæformis, pseudoquadrilocularis, bivalvis; dissepimenti contrarii lobi valvulis paralleli iisdemque æmuli (ideoque fructum bicapsularem mentientes), margine involuto seminiferi. Semina minuta nuda, pendula?

Herbæ villosæ, resinoso-glanduliferæ, aromaticæ.

Genus Bignoniaceis, Brown; admissa Incarvillea, adsociandum, huicque proximum, Wallich.

I am indebted for the above character of this hitherto unpublished genus to my esteemed friend Dr. Wallich, who has ascertained five species, natives of Nepaul; the four following have been since discovered in the Malay Islands.

DIDYMOCARPUS CRINITA.—W. J.

Erecta, pilosa, foliis longis spatulatis acutis serratis subtus rubris, pedunculis 2–5 axillaribus unifloris basi cum petiolo coëuntibus, staminibus duobus fertilibus.

Timmu. *Malay.*

Native of the forests of Pulo Pinang.

Root long and tapering. Stem short, erect, thick, rough beneath with the vestiges of fallen leaves. The whole plant is covered with hairs. Leaves alternate, crowded, subsessile, long, spatulate, 9 or 10 inches in length, acute, obtuse at the base, serrated, rugose, hairy, brownish green above, purplish red beneath, middle nerve strong and thick, forming a short petiole at the base. Stipules none. Peduncles 2 to 5 in each axil, 1-flowered, round, 2 inches long, uniting at the base into a short thick unilateral rachis, densely pilose, and adhering beneath to the petiole. Bracts linear, 2, alternate on each peduncle. Calyx 5-parted, hairy, reddish, laciniæ erect, linear, acute, the upper one smaller. Corolla white, tinged with purple externally, much longer than the calyx, infundibuliform; tube somewhat gibbous at the base, incurved, expanding above, limb bilabiate, upper lip 2-lobed, lower 3-lobed, larger, internally streaked with yellow, all the segments roundish, obtuse, not very unequal. Stamina inserted within the tube, 2 fertile, with the rudiments of 2 abortive ones, the former scarcely so long as the corolla, conniving at their summits. Anthers composed of 2 divaricate transverse lobes. Ovarium linear, surrounded at the base with a white tubular entire nectarial ring or cup, and produced into a tomentose style of the same length as the stamina. Stigma obtuse, truncate. Capsule long, linear, silique-shaped, cylindrical, acute, somewhat tomentose, an inch long, 2-valved, 2-celled, dissepiments contrary, with 2 lobes which are parallel to the valves, revolute and seed-bearing at their margins, and part the cells in such a manner as to give the appearance of a 4-celled siliqua. Seeds numerous, naked, small, and subrotund.

Obs.—The deep red colour of the lower surface of the leaves and the crested disposition of the flowers in their axils render this a very remarkable species. The æstivation is imbricate, the two lateral lobes of the lower lip being the outermost. The genus is nearly related to Incarvillea, but differs in having simple naked seeds.

DIDYMOCARPUS REPTANS.—W. J.

Prostrata, reptans, foliis petiolatis ellipticis crenulatis, pedunculis 1–3 axillaribus unifloris, staminibus duobus fertilibus.

Timmu kechil. *Malay.*

Found in the forests of Pulo Pinang with the preceding.

Stem prostrate, round, villous, striking root at every joint, often a foot in length. Leaves lying flat, opposite petiolate, oblong-oval or elliptic, rather obtuse, sometimes slightly cordate at the base, slightly crenate, covered with white hairs, green above, paler and sometimes reddish beneath. Petioles villous. Peduncles 1–3 axillary, 1-flowered, erect, as long as the leaves, pilose, furnished with 2 bracts near the summit. Calyx 5-parted, with erect acute laciniæ, the uppermost smaller. Corolla white, infundibuliform, bilabiate, similar to that of D. crinita but smaller, as well as the whole plant. Stamina 2 fertile conniving above, 2 sterile. Anthers approximate, reniform, 2-celled. Nectary surrounding the base of the ovarium, obsoletely 5-toothed at the margin. Style equal to the stamina. Stigma simple. Capsule long, straight, silique-shaped, pseudo-quadrilocular as in the genus. Seeds numerous, naked.

DIDYMOCARPUS CORNICULATA.—W. J.

Erecta, foliis alternis obovatis acuminatis serratis, floribus diandris fasciculatis secundis super pedunculum axillarem elongatum.

Found at Tapanooly in Sumatra.

The stem is nearly erect, from 1 to 2 feet in height, herbaceous or somewhat shrubby, villous. Leaves alternate, petiolate, obovate, acuminate, narrowing to the base, serrated, pilose above, villous below. Peduncles axillary, solitary, elongated, bearing several dense fascicles of flowers all turned to one side, depressed or bent at an angle to the peduncle, and spreading in a kind of half circle, somewhat in the manner of the Lotus corniculatus. Flowers many, white; pedicles articulate below the calyx, covered as well as the calyx with glandular hairs. Bracts linear, acute. Calyx 5-parted, segments linear. Corolla white, much longer than the calyx, infundibuliform, wide at the faux, limb somewhat oblique, bilabiate, the lower lip longer, 3-lobed. Stamina 2, connected above by their anthers, whose lobes are transverse. Style as long as the stamina. Stigma capitate. Capsule silique-shaped, 2-celled, cells bipartite (as if 4-locular), 2-valved, generally bursting at one side, many-seeded. Seeds naked.

The disposition of the flowers and fruit is peculiar, the capsules spreading horizontally like radii in a sort of semicircle of which the peduncle is the axis.

DIDYMOCARPUS FRUTESCENS.—W. J.

Caule suffrutescente erecto, foliis oppositis longe petiolatis ovato-lanceolatis acuminatis supra glabris subtus canescentibus, floribus axillaribus fasciculatis didynamis.

Native of Pulo Pinang.

Stem generally simple, suffrutescent, densely covered with ferruginous appressed scales or chaffy hairs. Leaves opposite, long petioled, ovate-lanceolate, acuminate, attenuated to the base, slightly serrated, 8 or 10 inches long, smooth above, hoary and tomentose beneath, with appressed hairs. Petioles 3 inches long, furrowed above, thickened at the base, villous. Stipules none. Peduncles axillary, fascicled, 1–3 flowered, shorter than the petioles, purplish. Bracts lanceolate acute. Calyx tomentose with glandular hairs, tubular, 5-parted, laciniæ linear, spreading above. Corolla white, tomentose without like the calyx, much longer than it, infundibuliform, incurved; all the laciniæ subrotund obtuse. Stamina 4, didynamous, arcuate, approximate at their summits, each pair connected by their anthers. The filaments of the upper pair are thickened below their middle. Anthers white, adnate to the filaments, consisting of two lobes nearly parallel. Style of the length of the stamina. Stigma truncate. Capsule long, linear, silique-shaped, 2-valved, 2-celled, cells 2-parted by the septiform lobes of the dissepiments, which are revolute and seminiferous at their margins. Seeds numerous, naked.

SONERILA ERECTA.—W. J.

Triandria Monogynia.

Erecta, ramosa, foliis lanceolatis serratis, racemis terminalibus paucifloris, floribus sessilibus.

Summow. *Malay.*

Native of the forests of Pulo Pinang.

Root fibrous. Stem erect, from 6 inches to a foot in height, oppositely branched, round, tinged with red, fringed with 2 opposite longitudinal lines of hairs (like that of the Veronica chamœdrys). Leaves opposite, petiolate, ovate-lanceolate, acute at both ends, serrated, villous with erect hairs, 3-nerved, green above, reddish beneath. Petioles nearly smooth. Stipules none. Peduncles terminal, springing from the centre of a 4-leaved verticil which terminates the branch, and of which two opposite leaves are smaller. The spike is unilateral, about 4-flowered, recurved, smooth, each flower sessile on the upper sides of the clavate peduncle, which is there thickened and as it were scooped out to receive it, and is attenuated downwards to the point of insertion into the branch. Bracts none or very minute. Calyx smooth, trifid, laciniæ acute. Corolla of a light flesh colour, composed of 3 lanceolate-ovate acuminate spreading petals. Stamina 3, alternating with the petals, erect, scarcely so long as the corolla. Anthers 2-celled, acute, cordate at the base. Style erect, equal to the stamina. Stigma obtuse. Ovarium long, linear, inferior. Capsule oblong, obtusely 3-angled, 3-celled, 3-valved, many-seeded, the dissepiments opposite to the valves. Seeds attached to a central columnar 3-sided placenta.

Obs.—This plant differs considerably in habit from the other species of Sonerila in having an erect slender brachiate stem, and small lanceolate leaves, not oblique at the base as in most of the genus.

The uppermost leaves are quatern, forming a kind of involucre to the slender peduncle which springs from their centre.

SONERILA MOLUCCANA.—Roxb.

Subcaulescens, villosa, foliis oblique cordatis integris oppositis altero minore, pedunculis axillaribus, racemis unilateralibus.

Roxb. "Fl. Ind." vol. i. p. 122.

Pouh. *Malay.*

A native of the moist shady forests of Pulo Pinang.

A small herbaceous plant whose root is fibrous, and whose stem does not exceed a few inches in length. Every part is thickly covered with red hair. The leaves are petiolate, opposite, one much smaller and rounder than the other, unequally cordate, acute, very entire, of a deep green on the upper surface, red beneath, with quintuple nerves. Petioles round, and hairy. Stipules none. Peduncles generally from the axils of the smaller leaves, erect, bearing from 1 to 3 unilateral somewhat recurved racemes, and furnished about the middle with 2 small opposite bracteolar leaflets. The racemes are at first revolute, but unroll themselves as the flowers open. The flowers are unilateral arranged in 2 rows upon short pedicles, and each supported by a linear ciliate bract. Calyx superior, covered like the rest of the plant with red hairs, 3-parted, laciniæ lanceolate, acute. Corolla white, composed of 3 petals inserted between the divisions of the calyx, ovate, acute, with a few red hairs along the middle of the under surface. Stamina 3, alternating with the petals; filaments linear, ascending; anthers linear, bending towards the style, yellow, 2-celled. Style declinate in an opposite direction to the stamina. Stamina simple. Capsule ovate, crowned by the calyx, hairy, 3-celled, 3-valved, many-seeded, the dissepiments opposite to the valves, the placentæ peltate, pedicellate, affixed to the axis of the capsule.

RHOPALA ATTENUATA.—W. J.

Tetrandria Monogynia.

Proteaceæ. Juss and Br.

Foliis alternis ovatis acuminatis, racemis axillaribus foliis longioribus, pedicellis geminatis calycibusque glabris.

Native of Pulo Pinang.

Arborescent, with round smooth branches. Leaves alternate, petiolate, ovate, acuminate, attenuated to the base and decurrent on the petiole, 10 or 11 inches long, entire, sometimes with 1 or 2 toothlets near the point, very smooth. Petioles short, thickened at the base. Stipules none. Spikes rather longer than the leaves, axillary, cylindrical, flowers geminate, short pedicled. Perianth 4-leaved, leaflets linear, dilated and staminiferous at the summit, revolute. Stamina 4, inserted near the apex of the perianth; filaments scarcely any; anthers linear, 2-celled. Style filiform, as long as the corolla. Stigma clavate. Ovarium 1-celled, containing 2 erect ovula.

RHOPALA MOLUCCANA.—BR.

Foliis alternis obovatis obtusiusculis integerrimis, racemis plerumque lateralibus, pedicellis bifidis calycibusque glabris.

Found in a garden at Pulo Pinang.

Arborescent with grey bark. Leaves alternate, petiolate, 6 or 7 inches long, obovate or cuneately ovate obtuse, very entire, very smooth, yellowish green. Petioles an inch long, flattened above, thickened at the base. Spikes lateral, generally below the leaves. Flowers geminate on a bifid pedicle. Bracts very small. Perianth 4-leaved, leaflets revolute, dilated and stamen bearing at the summit. Stamina 4; anthers linear, nearly sessile. Style filiform. Stigma clavate. Ovarium 1-celled, 2-sporous.

Obs.—In the preceding the leaves are acuminate and the

flowers in pairs, each with its proper pedicle; in this the leaves are rounded and obtuse at the apex, and the flowers are geminate on a common pedicle.

IXORA PENDULA.—W. J.
N. O. Rubiaceæ.

Foliis elliptico-lanceolatis glaberrimis, corymbis longe pedunculatis pendulis.

Bunga yarum. *Malay.*

Native of Pulo Pinang, &c.

A shrub with smooth compressed branches. Leaves opposite, short petioled, 11 or 12 inches long, elliptically lanceolate, rather obtuse, very entire, very smooth, shining above. Petioles little more than half an inch in length. Stipules interpetiolar, broad at the base, ending in a subulate point. Corymbs terminal, long peduncled, hanging, trichotomous, many-flowered. Flowers red. Bracts 2, small at the base of the calyx. Calyx small, 4-parted, slightly tomentose. Corolla red, tube long and slender, limb 4-parted, lobes ovate-lanceolate, rather acute. Stamina spreading. Style filiform. Stigma clavate.

Obs.—This is a beautiful species, at once distinguishable by its long pendulous corymbs. Bunga Yarum is the generic Malay name of the Ixoræ.

EPITHINIA.—W. J.
Tetrandria Monogynia.
N. O. Rubiaceæ.

Calyx cylindricus superus, quadridentatus persistens. Corolla tubulosa, limbo patente quadripartito, fauce villosa. Stamina exserta. Stylus exsertus. Stigma bifidum. Bacca sulcata, dipyrena, nucibus oblongis dispermis, semine uno super alterum.

EPITHINIA MALAYANA.—W. J.

Found in mangrove swamps on the island of Singapore.

A moderate-sized shrub with brown bark and smooth branches. Leaves opposite, petiolate, obovate, obtuse, rounded at the summit, attenuated at the base into the petiole, very entire, very smooth, almost without veins, shining above, paler beneath. Stipules none. Peduncles axillary, dichotomous, many-flowered, 1-flowered in the bifurcations. Calyx cylindrical, persistent, almost entire or obsoletely 4-dentate. Corolla white, tube longer than the calyx, limb spreading, 4-parted, lobes ovate, rather acute, faux closed with white hairs. Stamina 4, exsert, spreading, inserted alternately with the lobes of the corolla, filaments short, anthers linear, acute, dark coloured. Ovary oblong, compressed, 2-celled, cells 2-seeded, the one placed over the other. Style exsert. Stigma bifid, with thick linear lobes. Fruit inferior, oblong, marked with 8 deep longitudinal furrows, crowned with the calyx, containing 2 long narrow oblong nuts, each with 2 seeds, the one placed above the other. One of them sometimes proves abortive.

Obs.—I have not been able to refer this to any known tetrandrous genus; it seems to come nearest to Malanea of Aublet, but differs in several essential characters. The position of the seeds is peculiar.

MORINDA TETRANDRA.—W. J.

N. O. Rubiaceæ.

Tetrandra, pedunculis umbellatis terminalibus, corollis quadrifidis intus hirsutis, foliis lanceolatis.

Pada vara. Rheed, " Mal." vii. p. 51, t. 27.
Mangkudu kĕchil. *Malay.*
Native of the Malay Islands.

A small diffuse shrub, with long slender branches, nodose at the bifurcations. Leaves opposite, short petioled, lanceolate, acuminate, very entire, very smooth, the nerves reddish below, and furnished with ciliated glands in the axils. Stipules interpetiolar, truncate. Peduncles from 5 to 10, umbellate, terminal. Flowers aggregate on a common receptacle. Calyx an entire margin crowning the ovary. Corolla infundibuliform, 4-parted, the laciniæ densely covered within with long white hairs. Stamina 4, shorter than the corolla, and alternating with its divisions; filaments very short; anthers oblong. Ovary inferior, 2-celled, 4-seeded. Stigma bifid. Fruit subglobose, yellow, composed of coadunate berries, angular by their mutual compression, crowned with the vestige of the calyx, 4-seeded; seeds osseous.

Obs.—Rheed describes his Pada vara to be 14 feet in height; this is the only particular in which it differs from my plant. In every other respect they agree exactly.

MORINDA POLYSPERMA.—W. J.

Tetrandra, pedunculis axillaribus et terminalibus, corollis quadrifidis intus hirsutis, foliis ovatis acuminatis, baccis bilocularibus polyspermis!

Found on the island of Singapore.

A shrub, with short subdichotomous flexuose branches. Leaves opposite, petiolate, ovate, acuminate, obtuse at the base, very entire, very smooth, coriaceous, flat, about 3 inches long. Stipules short, interpetiolar. Peduncles axillary and terminal; axillary ones opposite, terminal ones from 1 to 4 in a kind of umbel. Capitula few-flowered. Calyx an entire margin. Corolla infundibuliform, 4-parted, densely covered within with white hairs. Stamina-4 shorter than the corolla; filaments short; anthers linear. Style erect. Stigma bifid. Berries coadunate, 2-celled, many seeded! Seeds numerous, angular.

Obs.—The flowers of this species are perfectly similar to those of the preceding, but the fruit presents a singular anomaly in being polyspermous. Both differ so much from the other species of Morinda that I think they might properly constitute a new and distinct genus.

EUTHEMIS.—W. J.

Pentandria Monogynia.

Calyx inferus 5-phyllus. Corolla 5-petala. Stamina quinque, hypogyna, antheris oblongis acuminatis apice poro dehiscentibus. Stylus filiformis, staminibus equalis. Bacca 5-sperma, seminibus circa axim dispositis, oblongis, intus angulatis, arillo fibroso inclusis, albuminosis, embryone inverso cylindrico longitudine fere seminis, radicula superiore.

Frutices, foliis alternis pulcherrime striatis nervis parallelis, racemis terminalibus, demum peractâ floratione lateralibus et oppositifoliis.

EUTHEMIS LEUCOCARPA.—W. J.

Foliis lanceolatis pulchre spinuloso serratis, racemis basi ramosis, baccis niveis globosis.

Pělâwan běruk. Malay.

Native of the forests of Singapore.

A shrub of uncommon elegance and beauty, erect, 4 or 5 feet in height; branchlets round, smooth, sometimes slightly angled. Leaves alternate, petiolate, lanceolate, acute, decurrent on the petiole, spinuloso-serrate, very smooth and shining, beautifully striated with fine parallel transverse nerves. Petioles margined, flat and channelled above, dilated at the base into a thick rounded prominent rim, which half embraces the stem. Stipules lanceolate, acuminate, ciliate, very deciduous. Racemes erect, with 1 or 2 branches near the base, at first terminal, afterwards lateral and oppositifolious, by the shooting up of the stem from the base of the peduncle. Flowers predicellate, generally in pairs. Bracts ovate, acute. Calyx inferior, 5-leaved, spreading, leaflets ovate, obtuse, ciliate, the 2 inner ones rather smaller. Corolla white, sometimes tinged with purple, 5-petaled, petals twice as long as the calyx, reflexed, ovate-oblong, obtuse. Stamina 5, inserted below the ovarium; alternating with these are sometimes found 5 short abortive filaments. Filaments very short. Anthers longer, erect, conniving round the style, oblong, prolonged into acumina, which are sometimes a little contorted, and which open at their summits by a pore, the cells are adnate below to the sides of the filament. Ovary oblong, acute. Style filiform, erect, equal to the stamina. Stigma simple. Berry snow-white, globular, obscurely angled, crowned with the persistent style, which is obliquely deflexed; of a spongy or farinose substance, containing in the centre 5 seeds, which are disposed round the axis, and enclosed in arilli composed of tough longitudinal fibres. Seeds (pyrenæ?) oblong, somewhat reniform, hard. Albumen conform to the seed. Embryo inverse, cylindrical, nearly as long as the seed. Cotyledons semicylindric, obtuse. Radicle superior, longer than the cotyledons.

The branches are terminated by long corniculate buds, in which the gemmation is involute.

EUTHEMIS MINOR.—W. J.

Foliis angusto-lanceolatis leviter serrulatis, racemis simplicibus, baccis rubris angulatis acuminatis.

Found at Singapore along with the preceding.

This is a smaller shrub than the former, branched, and smooth. Leaves alternate, petiolate, linear-lanceolate, rather obtuse, with a mucro, attenuated to the petiole, slightly serrulate, very smooth, shining, finely striated with transverse veins. Petioles short, thickened at the base, channelled above. Stipules linear, siliate. Racemes simple, erect, at first terminal, becoming afterwards lateral. Flowers alternate, pedicellate, often in pairs. There is a single leaflike bract and several smaller ones at the base of the pedicles, less deciduous than in the preceding. Calyx 5-leaved, leaflets ovate, ciliate. Corolla white, spreading, 5-petaled, petals lanceolate, acute. Stamina 5, erect, conniving, hypogynous; filaments very short; anthers yellow, oblong, broader at the base, 2-celled, cells adnate to the sides of the filament, prolonged above into an acumen opening at the top by a pore. Ovary oblong, acute. Style a little longer than the stamina. Stigma simple. Berry red, 5-angled, acuminate, composed of a whitish farinaceous pulp, and containing 5 seeds, each enveloped in a tough, fibrous arillus, and in structure the same as the preceding.

CELASTRUS (?) BIVALIS.—W. J.

Pentandria Monogynia.

Foliis lanceolatis acuminatis integerrimis, pedunculis lateralibus paucifloris, corollis nullis, capsulis bivalvibus monospermis.

A shrub with smooth branches. Leaves opposite, petiolate, lanceolate, acuminate, acute at the base, very entire, very smooth.

Stipules none. Peduncles lateral, divaricately dichotomous, few flowered (5-10 flowered). Bracts small. Calyx 5-parted, bibracteate at the base, laciniæ roundish, imbricated. Corolla none. Stamina 5, erect, united beneath into a 5-toothed ring or urceolus; filaments flat; anthers oblong. Style erect, as long as the stamina. Stigma truncate. Capsule ovate, green, smooth, crowned with the style, 2-valved, 1-celled, 1-seeded; valves opening from the base, and falling off from the seed, which is more persistent, and remains on the peduncle. Seed ovate, contained in a beautiful crimson arillus, which is delicately veined. Albumen cartilaginous, conform to the seed. Embryo erect, central, as long as the albumen. Cotyledons flat, foliaceous, ovate, obtuse. Radicle inferior, obverse to the umbilicus, round, much shorter than the cotyledons.

STYPHELIA.

LEUCOPOGON MALAYANUM.—W. J.

Pentandria Monogynia.

N. O. Epacrideæ. Br.

Spicis axillaribus multifloris erectis brevibus, drupis globosis 5-locularibus, foliis lanceolatis mucronatis subenerviis subtus glaucescentibus.

Měntâda. *Malay.*

Found abundantly at Singapore.

A small branchy shrub with hard dry leaves, exhibiting the peculiar character of this family. Leaves alternate, sessile, lanceolate, acute, mucronate, very entire, very smooth, shining and convexed above, somewhat glaucous below, and, when examined by the microscope, appearing to be covered with numerous very minute white dots, firm, with scarcely perceptible longitudinal nerves. Spikes axillary, erect, much shorter than the leaves; peduncles somewhat tomentose. Calyx supported at the base by two oval acute concave bracts, 5-leaved, oblong, acute, leaflets lanceolate, glaucescent, ciliate. Corolla infundibuliform, a little longer than the calyx, quinquefid, puberulent, segments lanceolate, bearded above beyond the base. Stamina 5, short, alternate with the laciniæ; filaments subulate; anthers subpendulous, marked on each side with a longitudinal furrow, simple, and bursting longitudinally in the manner so accurately described by Mr. R. Brown, "Prodr. Fl. N. Holl." p. 535. Pollen globose. Ovary surrounded at the base by 5 distinct erect obtuse scales, 5-celled, each cell containing a single oblong ovulum. Style erect, villous. Stigma subglobose. Drupe baccate, subglobose, 5-celled, cells 1-seeded.

Obs.—The discovery of this species is remarkable, as forming an exception to the general geographical distribution of the Epacrideæ, a family almost exclusively confined to Australasia or at least to the southern hemisphere. Singapore, situated at the extremity of the Malay peninsula, and forming as it were the connecting link between continental or Western India and the islands of the great Eastern Archipelago, partakes of this character in its Flora, which exhibits many remarkable points of coincidence with the Floras of both regions. I have had occasion to observe resemblances between its productions and those of the northern frontier of Bengal on the one hand, and of the Moluccas on the other, while the present connects it with the still more distant range of New Holland.

RAUWOLFIA SUMATRANA.—W. J.

Pentandria Monogynia.

N. O. Apocyneæ.

Foliis ternis quaternisve elliptico-oblongis superne latioribus glabris, floribus terminalibus umbellatis, corollæ fauce villis clausa.

Tampal bâdak or Sĕmbu bâdak. *Malay.*
Frequent in the neighbourhood of Bencoolen.

It grows to a small tree, having somewhat the habit and foliage of the Mangga laut, or Cerbera manghas. The whole plant is lactescent. Leaves verticillate, generally in threes, sometimes in fours, short petioled, about 6 inches long, elliptic oblong, broader above and terminating in a short point, very entire, very smooth, rather firm, and having nearly transverse nerves. Peduncles 3 or 4, umbellate, terminal, long, round and smooth, bearing compound umbels of small white flowers. Calyx small, 5-lobed. Corolla white, tube longer than the calyx, limb spreading, 5-parted, lobes subrotund, faux closed with white hairs which appear to form 5 tufts. Stamina 5 incluse; filaments very short; anthers yellow, sagitate, acute, conniving over the stigma. Ovary furrowed on both sides, 2-celled, tetrasporous, surrounded by an obscurely 5-lobed nectarial ring. Styles 2, united together. Stigma peltate, capitate, glutinous, papillous. Berry globose, smooth, containing 2 nuts, which are compressed, rugose, gibbous below and tapering towards the top, subunilocular with an imperfect dissepiment; generally 1-seeded. Seed compressed.

Obs.—This species appears to have considerable resemblance to Rauwolfia nitida, but is sufficiently distinguished by its inflorescence. The wood of this tree is very light, and employed by the Sumatrans for the scabbards of their swords and krises.

TACCA CRISTATA.—W. J.

Foliis indivisis lato-lanceolatis, involucro diphyllo, umbellâ secundâ cernuâ superne intra involucrum foliolis duobus involucro duplo longioribus stipatâ.

Native of Singapore and Pulo Pinang.

Root thick and tuberous, sending out a number of fibres. Leaves nearly 2 feet long, numerous, radical, erect, petiolate, ovate-lanceolate, acute, entire, smooth. Petioles sheathing at the base. Scape erect, round, nearly as long as the leaves, striated, smooth. Flowers peduncled, all drooping to one side; peduncles subumbellate, arranged transversely in 2 parallel rows, and uniting into a kind of crest, from which proceed 10 long pendulous filaments. Involucre 2-leaved, leaflets ovate, acute, broad at the base, nervose, purplish, twice as long as the peduncles, the upper one erect, the lower reflexed and bent down by the drooping flowers. From within the upper leaflet of the involucre spring 2 erect folioles, which are twice as long as the involucre, obovate, attenuated below into straight, flat, deep purple petiolar ungues, acute at the apex, pale coloured, with purplish nerves. Perianth superior, of a dark purple colour, campanulate and somewhat ventricose, rather contracted and 3-cornered at the mouth, where it is also striated, limb 6-parted, somewhat reflex, laciniæ hyaline, oblong, broad, obtuse, the 3 interior ones larger. Corolla none. Stamina 6, in the bottom of the perianth and opposite to the laciniæ. Filaments broad at the base, arching upwards into a vaulted cucullus, within which the anthers are concealed. Anthers adnate, 2-lobed. Style thick, shorter than the stamina, with 6 prominent angles. Stigma flat, umbilicate, orbicular, 6-rayed, three alternate sinuses deeper. Berry ovate, 6-angled, 1-celled, seeds numerous, attached to 3 parietal receptacles.

Obs.—This approaches to T. integrifolia, "Curt. Mag." t. 1488, but is a much larger plant, and is abundantly distinguished by the 2-leaved involucre, the long erect leaflets within it, and the flowers drooping to one side.

VERATRUM (?) MALAYANUM.—W. J.

Foliis radicalibus lanceolatis, scapis erectis verticillato-paniculatis, baccis trilocularibus.

Native of Pulo Pinang.

An erect herbaceous plant. Leaves radical, 3 or 4 feet in length, petiolate, lanceolate, acuminate, attenuated into a petiole at the base, very entire, tomentose, striated with parallel nerves, which run nearly longitudinally but diverge from a central one. Petioles canaliculate, obtusely carinate, sheathing at the base.

Scape erect, round, tomentose, verticillately panicled. Peduncles alternately semiverticillate, divaricate and spreading. Flowers sessile, on hermaphrodite or male plants fascicled, on female solitary. Beneath each semiverticil is a large floral leaf, which is ovate, acute, and contracted at the base into a flat, straight, petiole-like unguis, which embraces the stem. Perianth 6-parted, the 3 inner laciniæ petaliform, white, spreading. Stamina 6; filaments flat, dilated at the base. Styles 3, short. Stigmata 3.

In the female the calyx embraces a globular berry which is 3-celled, each cell 1-seeded.

Obs.—The true place of this plant is somewhat ambiguous, and I am doubtful whether it can be admitted as a genuine species of Veratrum. It does not, however, agree exactly with any other genus of the same family; in habit it is somewhat like Alisma.

MEMECYLON CŒRULEUM.—W. J.

Octandria Monogynia.

Foliis cordatis amplexicaulibus, pedunculis axillaribus brevibus, pedicellis appositis divaricatis brevibus, fructibus ovatis.

Kûlit nîpis. *Malay.*

Native of Pulo Pinang.

A handsome shrub, of 10 or 12 feet in height, with round smooth branches. Leaves opposite, subsessile, about 5 inches in length, cordate, amplexicaul, oblong, acute, very entire, margin reflexed, coriaceous, very smooth, deep green and shining above, lateral nerves inconspicuous, uniting at their extremities into a line which runs parallel to the margin. Stipules none. Peduncles axillary, solitary, short, few-flowered; pedicels short and thick, opposite, somewhat verticillate, divaricate, forming a kind of corymbiform head. Flowers blue. Bracts opposite, short, acute. Calyx superior, coloured, smooth, nearly entire, becoming by age more distinctly 4-toothed. Corolla deep blue, 4-petaled, spreading, petals broad, ovate, acute. Stamina 8, erect, shorter than the corolla. Filaments short. Anthers blue, attached by their middle, horizontal, shaped somewhat like the head of an axe, with a knob behind; cells parallel on the anterior edge. Before expansion the anthers are bent downwards (somewhat in the manner of the Melastomæ), and the surface of the germen and bottom of the calyx are marked with their impressions, of which the 4 inner are the deepest; the ridges between them form 8 sharp prominent rays, and there are 8 other less conspicuous lines formed by the faces of the bilocular anthers. Ovarium ovate, 1-celled, containing from 6 to 8 erect ovula. Style filiform, a little longer than the stamina. Stigma acute. Berry cortical, crowned by the persistent calyx, ovate, a little oblique at the base, 1-seeded, the rudiments of the abortive ovula surrounding the umbilicus. Seed ovate, umbilicate at the base and a little oblique. Albumen none. Embryo erect. Cotyledons membranaceous, contortuplicate. Radicle cylindrical, nearly as long as the seed, obverse to the umbilicus.

Obs.—The different species of Memecylon have not been well defined by authors; this appears to differ from M. cordatum Lamarck, and M. grande Retz., or Nedum chetti (Rheed, "Mal." ii. p. 21. t. 15) in having ovate not globose fruit, and in the flowers not being umbelled. In the latter the flowers are small, yellow and numerous, in this they are larger, blue, and much fewer in number.

LAURUS PARTHENOXYLON.—W. J.

Enneandria Monogynia.

Foliis venosis ovatis acutis petiolatis subtus glaucis, paniculis brevibus paucifloris axillaribus et lateralibus, fructu globoso calyci truncato insidente.

Kâyu gâdis. *Malay.*

Abundant in the forests of Sumatra.

This is a lofty timber tree. Bark brown and rough. Leaves alternate, rather long petioled, ovate, acute, often acuminate, and varying in breadth, about 3 inches long, entire with somewhat revolute edges, smooth, glaucous beneath, nerves lateral and irregularly alternate. Petioles round, an inch long. Peduncles from the young shoots at the extremity of the branches, axillary or lateral, terminated by a short few-flowered panicle, and generally longer than the young leaves, from whose axils they spring. Bracts none. Perianth funnel-shaped, 6-parted, yellowish. Stamina 9, arranged in 2 rows, the outer 6 naked, the inner 3 furnished at the base with 2 yellow glands; filaments flat; anthers adnate, the cells opening with a longitudinal valve or operculum. Style as long as the stamina. Stigma obtuse, 4-cornered. Drupe seated on the enlarged cup-shaped, persistent truncated base of the perianth, globose, containing a 1-seeded nut. Embryo inverse. Cotyledons hemispherical. Radicle superior, within the edge of the cotyledons.

Obs.—This species has considerable affinity to L. cupularia. The fruit has a strong balsamic smell, and yields an oil, which is considered useful in rheumatic affections, and has the same balsamic odour as the fruit itself. An infusion of the root is drank in the same manner as sassafras, which it appears to resemble in its qualities. The wood is strong and durable when not exposed to wet, and in that case considered equal to teak. Kâyu gâdis signifies the virgin tree, whence the specific name.

May this be the Oriental sassafras wood mentioned under the article "Laurus" in Rees' "Cyclopædia?"

GOMPHIA SUMATRANA.—W. J.
Decandria Monogygnia.
N. O. Ochnaceæ.

Foliis lanceolatis vel oblongo ovalibus acuminatis obtuse denticulatis nitidis subquinque nerviis, stipulis intrapetiolaribus deciduis, paniculis terminalibus.

Sibûru. *Malay.*
Sumatra.

A large shrub or small tree. Leaves alternate, short petioled, 8 or 9 inches in length, from lanceolate to oblong oval, varying considerably in breadth from 2 to 3 inches, acuminate, acute at the base, obtusely denticulate, very smooth, shining, middle nerve very strong, lateral veins numerous, transverse, somewhat reticulate, delicate, uniting near each margin into two nerves, which run parallel to it almost the whole length, and give the leaf the appearance of being 5-nerved. Petioles very short. Stipules intrapetiolar, broad at the base, acuminate, deciduous. Panicles terminal, not much branched; pedicles slender, rarely solitary, surrounded at their bases by small acute bracts. Calyx 5-leaved, persistent, leaflets ovate, acute, smooth, lucid. Corolla yellow, 5-petaled, scarcely longer than the calyx. Stamina 10; filaments very short; anthers long, linear, opening at the top by 2 pores. Style as long as the stamina. Stigma acute. Ovaries 5, surrounding the base of the style, and elevated on a receptacle. This receptacle enlarges as the fruit ripens. The number of abortive ovaries is variable; sometimes only 1 comes to perfection. The berries are drupaceous, obliquely reniform, somewhat compressed, 1-seeded. Seed exalbuminous.

Obs.—This appears to have so much resemblance to the G. Malabarica, Decand. Puah Chetti (Rheed, "Mal." v. p. 103. t. 52), that I have some hesitation in proposing it as a distinct species. The points of difference are the following: The leaves of this are much longer than those of the Malabar species, which are described as almost veinless, while in this the transverse veins unite into two very distinct marginal nerves, which it is difficult to suppose could have escaped observation had they existed in the other. The representation of the inflorescence in Rheed's figure is unintelligible, and his description of it is not much clearer; but as far as it can be made out, it appears different from this. Further examination of the Malabar plant will be necessary to determine whether this is really distinct, and whether the differences above noticed exist in the plant itself, or are mere omissions in the description.

MURRAYA PANICULATA.

Decandria Monogynia.
N. O. Aurantiæ.

Foliolis ovatis acuminatis, floribus terminalibus axillaribusque subsolitariis, baccis oblongis sæpins dispermis.

Chalcas paniculata. Lour. "Fl. Coch." p. 270.
Camunium. Rumph. "Amb." v. p. 26, t. 17.
Kamûning. *Malay.*

This is an abundantly distinct species from M. exotica, though unaccountably confounded with it by later authors. Loureiro discriminates between them very well, and his description is, on the whole, good. Rumphius's figure is bad, but preserves several of the distinguishing characters, particularly in the inflorescence and leaves, which, however, are not sufficiently acuminate. It grows to the size of a small tree, and the wood is much employed for the handles of krises, being capable of receiving a fine polish. The leaflets are generally 5, ovate, terminating in a long acumen, which is slightly emarginate at the point, shining and very entire, the terminal one considerably the largest. In M. exotica, the leaflets are more numerous and closer, obovate, blunt, and of a much firmer, thicker substance. The flowers of M. paniculata are fewer and larger than those of M. exotica, and are sometimes terminal, generally 1 or 2 together from the axils of the upper leaves. The ovarium is 2-celled; the berries are oblong, reddish, and mostly contain 2 seeds, which are covered with silky hairs. The berries of M. exotica are ovate and generally 1-seeded. The whole habit of the 2 plants is very distinct. The specific name paniculata is objectionable, as the flowers are much less panicled than in the other species.

The Camunium sinense (Rumph. v. t. 18, f. 1), which is commonly met with in gardens in all the Malay islands, is quite a distinct genus from the other 2 Camuniums, and has been described by Loureiro, "Fl. Cochinch." i. p. 173, under the name of

AGLAIA ODORATA.

It has a 5-parted inferior calyx, and 5-petaled corolla. The stamina are 5 in number, and are inserted in the manner of the Meliaceæ on the inside of an ovate nectarial tube, which is contracted at the mouth, and conceals the anthers. The stigma is large, sessile, simple as far as I have observed, not double as stated by Loureiro. The ovary appears to be 1-celled, and to contain 2 pendulous ovula. It rarely ripens its fruit in these islands, but, according to Loureiro, it bears a small red 1-seeded berry. The flowers are very small, yellow and fragrant, in small axillary panicles.

In the catalogue of the "Hortus Bengalensis," p. 18, this plant is specified under the name of Camunium sinense, after Rumphius. The Murraya paniculata above described is the true Kamûning of the Malays, and the name C. sinense is only applied by Rumphius in the manner of the older botanical authors, as one of comparison and resemblance, for want of a better of native origin; if, therefore, the generic name Camunium is to be adopted at all, it ought to be applied to the plant to which it really belongs, and cannot be admitted for one of a different family not indigenous to the Malay islands. On this account Loureiro's name is to be preferred.

RHIZOPHORA CARYOPHYLLOIDES.—W. J.

Dodecandria Monogynia.

Fruticosa, foliis ovato-lanceolatis utrinque acutis, pedunculis axillaribus trifloris, rarius dichotome quinquefloris, floribus 8-fidis, radiculâ subcylindricâ acutiuscula.

Mangium caryophylloides. Rumph. "Amb." iii. p. 119, t. 78.

Found at Singapore and Pulo Pinang.

This is a much smaller shrub than the common mangrove, and does not divide its roots so much. It is generally found in shallow sandy salt marshes, rising with a tolerably erect stem and branched nearer to the base than the common species. Leaves opposite, petiolate, about 4 inches long, oval or ovate-lanceolate, acute at both ends, sometimes slightly inequilateral, very entire, very smooth, coriaceous; the lower surface appearing under the lens dotted with minute white points. Petioles round, furrowed above, smooth. Stipules long, enveloping the corniculate buds in the manner of the Ficus, very deciduous. Peduncles axillary, solitary, 3-flowered, shorter than the petioles; sometimes they are dichotomously 5-flowered, having a flower in the bifurcation. Calyx semi-inferior, surrounding the ovary, ovate, limb 8-parted, spreading, laciniæ linear, acute, thick, rather incurved at their points. Corolla white, 8-petaled, petals nearly erect, alternate with the laciniæ of the calyx, conduplicate, enclosing the stamina by pairs, bifid, furnished with a few threads or filaments at the point, ciliated on the margin. Stamina double, the number of the petals inserted on the calyx in a double series, the inner ones shorter, erect, not so long as the petals, enfolded by them until the period of complete expansion, when they burst from their recesses with an elastic force, and disperse their pollen. Anthers linear, acute, 2-celled. Ovarium contained within the calyx, 2-celled, tetrasporous; ovula subrotund, affixed near the top of the cells. Style filiform, as long as the stamina. Stigma bifid with acute laciniæ. Fruit contained in the persistent calyx, 1-seeded, the other 3 ovula proving abortive. The seed is at first ovate or roundish, with albumen conform, the embryo inverse, in the upper part of the seed. As the fruit advances, the radicle is elongated and becomes at length nearly cylindric, obsoletely angled, and rather acute at the point. I have generally found 3 cotyledons, rarely 4.

Obs.—Rumphius's figure is by no means a good representation of the plant, but his description of it is correct. It comes nearest to the R. cylindrica, Kari Kandel (Rheed, "Mal." vi. p. 59, t. 33), which differs from this in having the radicle very obtuse and more exactly cylindrical, and the peduncles generally 1 or 2-flowered. According to Rumphius this species is rather rare, and is called Mangi Mangi Chenke, or Clove Mangrove, whence his appellation Caryophylloides, which I have thought proper to retain, as the resemblance holds good in some particulars.

ACROTREMA.—W. J.

Dodecandria Trigynia.

Calyx pentaphyllus. Corolla pentapetala patens. Stamina quindecim, erecta, filamentis brevibus, antheris longis linceribus apice biporis. Ovaria tria, distincta, 2-spora, ovulis angulo, interiori affixis. Styli tres. Stigmata simplicia. Capsulæ uniloculares.

Herba acaulis, pilosa, pedunculis racemoso-multifloris.

Genus Saxifrageis affine, numero partium inusitato distinctum.

ACROTREMA COSTATUM.—W. J.

Found on hills, and among rocks at Pulo Pinang.

Root tapering, sending out a few fibres. Stem scarcely any. Leaves alternate, spreading, short-petioled, 6-inches long, oblong-obovate, obtuse, sagittate at the base, dentato-serrate, somewhat ciliate, pilose, furnished with a short tomentum and also with more remote longer appressed hairs; the nerves are very hairy, parallel, and terminate in the denticulæ of the margin. Petioles short, sheathing; their margins dilated into membranaceous auricles which might be considered as adnate stipules. Peduncles or scapes central, erect, from 3 to 6 inches high, pilose, recurved at the summit, 8 or 10-flowered. Flowers yellow, pedicellate, racemose. Calyx 5-leaved, pilose, leaflets ovate acute. Corolla yellow, spreading, 5-petaled, petals broader above, lanceolate. Stamina 15, erect, hypogynous; filaments very short. Anthers very long, linear, 2-celled, opening by 2 pores at the top. Ovaries 3, distinct, superior, 1-celled, 2-seeded, each bearing 1 style of the height of the stamina. Ovula attached to the inner angles. Stigmata simple. Capsules 3.

Obs.—I am at a loss to determine the exact affinities of this plant; it has the habit of the Saxifrageæ, but the number of both the male and female parts of fructification is greater by one-third, and the ovaries are distinct.

LAGERSTRŒMIA FLORIBUNDA.—W. J.
Icosandria Monogynia.

Foliis suboppositis ovato-oblongis glabris, paniculis terminalibus ramosissimis multifloris ferrugineo vellosis, staminibus inequalibus calycibus turbinatis sulcatis.

Found at Pulo Pinang.

A tree. Leaves subopposite, short-petioled, rather recurved, 7 or 8 inches long, ovate-oblong, somewhat acute, entire, smooth, with strong prominent nerves and reticulate veins. Panicle terminal, much branched, spreading, many-flowered. Peduncles, pedicels and calyces ferruginous, densely villous with stellate hair. The flowers are smaller than those of L. Reginæ, but much more numerous and in much larger panicles, pale rose colour on their first expansion, and passing through various gradations of intensity until at length they become nearly purple. Calyx covered with ferruginous wool, turbinate, regularly marked with many deep longitudinal furrows or ribs, giving it a fluted appearance, limb spreading, 6-parted. Before expansion the calyx is obconical and nearly flat at the top. Corolla 6-petaled, spreading, petals inserted by short ungues alternately with the segments of the calyx, ovate, not much undulated. Stamina red, numerous, inserted on the calyx, 6 of them longer, thicker and more conspicuous than the rest. Ovary thickly covered with white hair, 6-celled, many-seeded. Style erect. Stigma clavate.

Obs.—This beautiful and splendid species may be readily distinguished from the L. Reginæ by the greater size of the panicles, and their ferruginous colour. The flower-buds in that species represent in some degree a double cone, in this a single inverted cone, being flat and even depressed at top. The L. hirsuta "Lam." is also quite distinct from this, having hirsute leaves.

TERNSTRŒMIA RUBIGINOSA.—W. J.
Polyandria Monogynia.

Foliis ovatis spinuloso serratis subtus incanis floribus lateralibus et axillaribus fasciculatis, monadelphis pedunculis calycibusque glanduloso-pilosis, fructu triloculari.

S'ingo ingo. *Malay.*
Sumatra.

A tree. Branches cinereous, young parts covered with acute

scales. Leaves alternate, petiolate, ovate, acuminate, spinuloso-serrate, smooth above, hoary and white beneath, the nerves furnished with ferruginous paleaceous scales. Flowers in fascicles, lateral and axillary. Peduncles and calyces covered with glandular hairs. Bracts small about the middle of the peduncles. Calyx 5-parted. Corolla white, campanulate rotate, 5-parted, divided about half-way down. Stamina numerous; filaments short, united at the base into a ring which is inserted on the bottom of the corolla; anthers oblong, recurved, affixed by the middle, 2-celled, opening at the top by two oblique pores. Ovary ovate, acute, covered with glandular hairs, 3-celled, polyspermous, placentæ central. Style trifid, divided to the base. Stigmata simple.

TERNSTRŒMIA PENTAPETALA.—W. J.

Foliis obovata-lanceolatis, spinuloso denticulatis glabris, floribus lateralibus fasciculatis, pedunculis glabris fructu triloculari.

Native of Pulo Pinang.

A shrub with grey bark and leafy at the summit. Leaves alternate, petiolate, 10 to 12 inches long, obovato-lanceolate, acuminate spinuloso-denticulate, smooth; the nerves are furnished with a few appressed, innocuous scale-like spines. Petioles about an inch in length, covered, as well as the summits of the branches and buds, with small ferruginous scales. Flowers in fascicles below the leaves from the axils of the fallen ones of the preceding year; they are pedicellate and white. Calyx coloured, 5-leaved, the two outer leaflets smaller. Corolla white, 5-petaled, petals subrotund, a little longer than the calyx. Stamina numerous, distinct, inserted on the base of the petals; filaments short; anthers oblong, yellowish white, didymous, truncate at the top and there opening by two pores. Ovarium ovate, 3-celled, many seeded, placentæ from the inner angles of the cells. Style deeply trifid (Styles 3?). Stigmata 3.

I have not seen the ripe fruit of this, but have been informed that it produces a white berry.

ELÆOCARPUS NITIDA.—W. J.

Polyandria Monogynia.

Foliis ovato-lanceolatis, serratis, racemis axillaribus foliis brevioribus staminibus quindecim, nuce quinqueloculari, loculis plerumque quatuor abortivis.

Bua manik. *Malay.*

Native of Pulo Pinang.

A tree of moderate size, with grey bark and round smooth branches. Leaves alternate petiolate, 3 or 4 inches long, ovate-lanceolate, acuminate, obtusely serrate, attenuated to the base, very smooth. Stipules none. Racemes simple, axillary, secund, shorter than the leaves. Flowers white, short-pedicelled. Calyx deeply 5-parted, laciniæ linear, acute. Corolla 5-petaled, fimbriated at the summit. Nectary of 5 yellow retuse glands surrounding the ovary. Stamina 15, erect; 10 are inserted by pairs between the glands of the nectary, the remaining 5 between those glands and the ovary. Anthers linear, bilamellate at the summit. Style as long at the calyx. Stigma simple. Drupe globose, containing a 5-celled nut, which is rugose and marked with 5 obtuse longitudinal ridges; in general only 1 cell is fertile and contains a single seed. Seed furnished with albumen; embryo inverse with flat cotyledons and superior radicle.

Obs.—This may perhaps be one of the smaller varieties of Ganitrus mentioned by Rumphius; it differs from E. ganitrus of Roxburgh, who quotes Rumphius, III. t. 10, in the number of the stamina, the position of the racemes, and the number of fertile cells in the nut. Compare Adenoda sylvestris, Loureiro, "Fl. Cochinch." which agrees in the number of the stamina. I suspect Gaertner must have fallen into an error in representing the embryo erect in his Ganitrus; in this it is certainly inverse.

MONOCERA.—W. J.

Elæocarpi species.

Calyx pentaphyllus. Corolla pentapetala, petalis apice laciniatis sæpe sericeis. Stamina plura, antheris apice dehiscentibus, unicornibus valvula laterâ majore. Ovarium basi glandulis cinctum, biloculare, polysporum. Drupa nuce 1–2 sperma.

This genus, whose characters appear to be sufficiently distinct, will include, besides the following new species, several hitherto referred to Elæocarpus—viz., E. Monocera cavanilles, the separation of which has already been suggested, and of which the specific name may be appropriately adopted for the genus E. rugosus, E. aristatus, and E. bilocularis of Roxburgh, probably also E. grandiflora and E. reticulata, Sir J. E. Smith in Rees' "Cyclopædia." The E. dentata, Dicera dentata, Forst., may also belong to this, if, as remarked by Sir J. E. Smith, Rees' "Cyclopædia" *in loco*, the anthers have only one of their valves awned, not both equal, as originally stated by Forster. His capsule may perhaps be only the ovary, which will then agree with the present genus.

MONOCERA PETIOLATA.—W. J.

Foliis longe petiolatus ovato-lanceolatis integris labris, racemis axillaribus foliis brevioribus, petalis medio intus incrassatis villosis. Native of Pulo Pinang.

A lofty tree. Leaves petiolate, alternate or scattered, 8 or 9 inches long exclusive of the petiole, ovate lanceolate, generally obtusely acuminate, entire, very smooth, deep green and shining above, with lucid nerves and veins which are destitute of glands. Petioles 4 inches long, smooth, thickened at the base and summit. Racemes axillary, as long as the petioles; flowers pedicellate, turning one way. Calyx white, 5-leaved, leaflets lanceolate acuminate. Corolla white, 5-petaled, as long as the calyx, petals ovate lanceolate, fringed at the point, sericeous without, thickened along the middle, and covered with white hairs within, margins inflexed. Ten thick subrotund yellow glands surround the stamina. Stamina numerous (23–30), inserted within the glands, erect, shorter than the petals; filaments short; anthers longer, linear, bivalved at the apex, the outer valve elongated, the inner short and acute. Style filiform, longer than the stamina. Stigma acute. Ovary ovate, 2-celled, many seeded. Drupe ovate, containing a smooth, 1-celled, 1-2-seeded nut.

MONOCERA FERRUGINEA.—W. J.

Foliis oblongo-ovatis acuminatis integris subtus cum pedunculis ramulesque ferrugineo villosis, racemis axillaribus foliis brevioribus.

Found at Singapore.

A tree. Branchlets rusty and villous. Leaves irregularly alternate, petiolate, oblong ovate, acuminate, 6 or 7 inches long, entire with revolute edges, smooth above, ferruginously villous below, nerves without glands. Petioles from 2 to $2\frac{1}{2}$ inches long, villous and ferruginous, thickened under the leaf. Racemes axillary, shorter than the leaves. Flowers pedicelled. Peduncles and pedicels ferruginous. Drupe oval, of the form of an olive but smaller, with a single rather smooth nut, which generally contains but one perfect seed; sometimes there is a second smaller, and the vestiges of the partition and abortive ovula can almost always be observed. Seed oblong, pointed above. Albumen conform; Embryo inverse, extending nearly the whole length of the albumen. Cotyledons flat, oblong, with a distinct nerve along their middle. Radicle superior clavato-cylindrical, much shorter than the cotyledons.

Obs.—I have not seen the flowers of this species, but its fruit and general resemblance to the preceding leave no doubt as to the genus, and its characters are sufficiently marked to distinguish it from the others.

TETRACERA ARBORESCENS.—W. J.

Polyandria Tetragynia.

Foliis obovatis integerrimis glabris, floribus paniculatis axillaribus et terminalibus, calycibus pentaphyllis.

Found near the shores of the Bay of Tapanooly in Sumatra.

Arborescent. Leaves alternate, petioled, about 3 inches long, oblong obovate, rounded at the apex and terminating in a short point, very entire with reflex edges, smooth, shining above, coriaceous and firm, veins reticulate, nerves somewhat pilose on the under surface. petioles short. Panicles axillary and terminal, many-flowered. Calyx 5-leaved, spreading, persistent, smooth, Stamina numerous. Capsules generally 3, smooth and shining, roundish ovate, opening on one side, containing a single seed attached to the base of the capsule, and enveloped in a pale yellowish laciniate arillus. The vestiges of two or three abortive ovula are observable in the bottom of the capsule.

UVARIA HIRSUTA.—W. J.
Polyandria Polygynia.

Tota hirsuta etiam calyces fructusque pilis erectis, floribus sub-solitariis, petalis patentibus subequalibus, foliis ovato oblongis basi cordatis.

Pulo Pinang.

The whole plant is hirsute with long erect hairs. Branches round. Leaves alternate, short-petioled, ovate oblong, acuminate, cordate at the base, entire, simply pilose above, hirsute beneath with stellate fasciculate hairs. Flowers lateral, almost solitary, short-peduncled. Bracts lanceolate acute. Calyx hairy as well as the peduncles and bracts, bursting irregularly, often into two segments. Corolla of a deep red colour, 6-petaled, petals spreading lanceolate acute. Stamina numerous, with long linear anthers. Germina numerous; styles and stigmata the same. Berries numerous, long pedicelled, oblong, hirsute with ferruginous hairs, many-seeded. Seeds arranged in a double longitudinal series.

CAREYA MACROSTACHYA.—W. J.
Monadelphia Polyandria.

Arbor, foliis petiolatis obovatis subserratis racemis lateralibus nectantibus densissime multifloris, floribus sessilibus multi seriatis.

Pulo Pinang.

A tree with grey bark and smooth branches. Leaves alternate or scattered, petiolate, obovate or oblong ovate, acuminate, sometimes obtuse with an acumen narrowing to the base, slightly serrated, very smooth. Petioles roundish, thickened at the base. Stipules none. Racemes or spikes lateral, hanging, thick, massive, cylindrical, densely covered with flowers, which are sessile and arranged in numerous spiral lines; the whole is 8 or 10 inches in length. Bracts none. Calyx superior, purple, 4-parted, laciniæ rounded, smooth, somewhat ciliated on the margin. Corolla purplish red, longer than the calyx, 4-petaled, petals ovate, obtuse inserted into the base of the calyx. Stamina white, very numerous, longer than the corolla, united at the base into a thick ring. Anthers yellow, didymous, the lobes bursting on opposite sides, so as to give the whole the appearance of a double 4-celled anther. Nectary surrounding the style within the stamina, hypocrateriform, red and striated within, yellow and entire on the margin. Ovarium inferior, 4-celled, many-seeded; about 4 seeds in each cell attached to its upper and inner angle. Style red, as long as the stamina. Stigma simple. Fruit a berry or pome.

Obs.—The inflorescence of this tree is very remarkable, and quite different from the other species of Careya.

CLERODENDRUM DIVARICATUM.—W. J.

Didynamia Angiospermia.

Foliis obovato-lanceolatis acuminatis glabris, paniculis terminalibus erectis elongatis, pedicellis fructus reflexis, calyce subintegro fructifero, vix aucto.

Found at Laye, on the West Coast of Sumatra.

Stem shrubby, erect, about 2 feet in height, smooth, with opposite branches, which are thickened at the joint. Leaves opposite, short petioled, obovate lanceolate, acuminate, entire, sometimes denticulate, smooth. Panicle erect, terminal, long, composed of opposite divaricate ramifications which are subdichotomous and many-flowered. Pedicels of the fruit reflexed. Bracts large ovate, acuminate, foliaceous. Calyx cup-shaped, nearly entire. Corolla tubular, limb 5-parted, secund, the lower segment longer and of a blue colour. Stamina long, exsert. Style 1. Berry deep purple, resting on the calyx, which is scarcely at all enlarged, 4-lobed, 4-seeded, from 1 to 3 seeds occasionally proving abortive.

HEDYCHIUM SUMATRANUM.—W. J.

N. O. Scitamineæ.

Spica imbricata nutante, corollæ labio bifido, laciniis oblongis divergentibus.

Gandasuli utan. *Malay.*

From Salumah, on the West Coast of Sumatra.

Stem erect. Leaves alternate, short petioled on their sheaths, lanceolate, very entire, very smooth, parallel veined; above a foot in length. Sheaths smooth, prolonged into a very long ligula. Spike terminal, nodding, short, dense, strobiliform. Bracts lanceolate, as long as the calyx; within this the ovary is embraced by a tubular bract about half the length of the other.

Flowers numerous. Calyx superior, tubular, oblique at the mouth. Corolla long, outer limb 3-parted, with long narrow segments; two segments of the interior limb much shorter and broader; the third segment or lip, which is united to the filament, bifid, the divisions narrow and diverging. Filament very long, embracing the style. Anther recurved, naked. Style length of the stamen. Stigma thick. Ovary pilose, 3-celled, several seeded. Nectarial bodies oblong.

Obs.—This is a handsome species, and though its flowers are not so large and showy as those of the H. coronarium, this is in some degree compensated by the greater number which expand at one time. It is the first wild species I have met with in the Eastern islands.

ALPINIA ELATIOR.—W. J.
N. O. Scitamineæ.

Scapis radicalibus elatis, spicis ovatis, corollæ labio integro basi mutico, foliis basi subcordatis glabris.

Bunga kenchong. *Malay.*

Found on Pulo Nias, also at Ayer Bangy on the West Coast of Sumatra.

The stems are from 5 to 8 feet high, round, somewhat compressed, smooth, striated. Leaves alternate, bifarious, petiolate on their sheaths, ovate oblong, broad, subcordate at the base, acuminate, very smooth on both sides, polished above, striated with fine parallel nerves; from 1 to 2 feet long. Ligula of the sheath rounded. Scapes, rising at a little distance from the stems, 2 or 3 feet high, erect, round, smooth, invested by sheaths which are rounded at their points and mucronate below the apex. Spikes short, thick, ovate, compact, densely covered with flowers. The lower bracts are of a fine rosy colour, large and spreading, so as to form a kind of involucre to the head; the upper bracts are shorter, imbricated, oblong or tongue-shaped, rosy with white ciliate edges, each supporting a single flower, The involucel or inner bract which embraces the ovary is tubular and irregularly bifid, being cloven more deeply on one side than the other. Calyx reddish, deeply cloven on one side, by which the three regular segments become secund. Corolla, outer limb three parted, segments nearly equal, erect, the upper one rather the largest; inner limb unilabiate, longer than the outer, lip ascending, involving the anther, deep purplish red with yellow edge, rhomboid ovate, entire, somewhat crisped at the point, without spurs or sterile filaments at the base. Stamen shorter than the lip; anther naked. Style as long as the anther. Stigma thick, triangular, anteriorly concave. Ovary sericeously pilose, 3-celled, many-seeded.

Obs.—This is a very remarkable species, easily distinguished from the other Alpiniæ with radical inflorescence by the great height of the scapes, and the fine rosy colour of the lower bracts.

ALPINIA CAPITELLATA.—W. J.

Foliis longe petiolatis supra glabris, racemo terminali composito, capitulis florum bracteis involucratis.

In the interior of Bencoolen.

Stems 4 or 5 feet high. Leaves alternate, bifarious, long petioled on their sheaths, broad lanceolate, fine pointed, entire, parallel veined, smooth above, slightly tomentose beneath. Sheaths villous near the top, terminating above the petioles in a long ciliate ligula. Raceme terminal, compound, inclining, red. Flowers in heads which are embraced by large round bracts. Calyx tubular, 3-cornered, nearly entire. Corolla, outer limb 3-parted, the upper segment fornicate; the inner limb unilabiate, of one large coloured segment. Stamen 1, anther 2-lobed, naked. Ovary tomentose, 3-celled. Style slender. Stigma concave.

Obs.—The peculiar manner in which the involucral bracts embrace the capitulate flowers and subdivisions of the panicle forms a good distinctive character. The whole inflorescence is stiff and rigid, and wants that copiousness and richness which marks the greater part of this splendid genus.

GLOBBA CILIATA.—W. J.

Foliis ovato-lanceolatis nervis supra pilosis, paniculâ terminali erectâ, antherâ bicalcaratâ.

Puar amas. *Malay.*

Stem slender, erect, from 1 to 2 feet high, somewhat compressed, spotted towards the base with purple. Leaves alternate, bifarious, subsessile on their sheaths, ovate lanceolate, rounded at the base, acuminate, entire, the upper surface furnished with erect hairs disposed in lines along the principal nerves, lower surface smooth, dotted under the lens with minute papillæ; about 4 inches long. Sheaths striated, smooth, ciliate along the margins, extending very little beyond the petioles, and there bifid. Panicle terminal, nearly erect, with alternate, divaricate, somewhat rigid branches, on which are disposed alternately several subsessile yellow flowers. Bracts lanceolate. Calyx trifid. Corolla orange-yellow, 2-bordered, the exterior 3-parted, of which the upper segment is largest and concave; the inner consisting of 2 smaller segments alternating with the outer ones. Lip elevated on the lower part of the filament and reflexed, emarginate, with a purple spot in the centre. Filament long, tubular. Anther with 2 subulate recurved horns or spurs. Style simple. Nectarial bodies long and linear. Ovary containing several ovula.

Obs.—It is a small delicate species, growing in moist hollows on the sides of the hills and among the forests in most parts of Sumatra. The ciliary lines of hairs on the upper surface of the leaves distinguish it from most of its congeners.

ARISTOLOCHIA HASTATA.—W. J.

Gynandria Hexandria. N. O. Aristolochiæ.

Foliis hastato-trilobis glabris, racemis axillaribus, perianthio basi inflato, laminâ erectâ ellipticâ marginibus revolutis.

Found at Natal on the West Coast of Sumatra.

Suffrutescent. Branches long, spreading over the neighbouring shrubs, but not twining, angulate, jointed, smooth. Leaves alternate, petiolate, from 6 to 10 inches long, hastately 3-lobed, middle lobe elongated and terminating in a blunt acumen, very entire, very smooth, 5-nerved, and strongly veined. Petioles 2 inches long, thick, round, channeled above. Racemes axillary, longer than the petioles. Flowers alternate, pedicellate, somewhat distichous; rachis flexuose. Perianth superior, purplish-red, smooth without, inflated at the base into an ovate 6-angled ventricle, from which rises an ascending infundibuliform curved tube with revolute margin; lamina erect, elliptic, revolute at the sides, tomentose on the inner surface, as is also the inside of the tube. Style short, thick. Stigma orbicular, peltate, divided on the summit into 6 conical erect lobes. Anthers sessile, regularly arranged in a circle below the stigma, 6 in number, each consisting of 2 lobes which are 2-celled and deeply furrowed along the middle. (As these are not arranged by pairs, might they not with equal propriety be considered as 12 distinct 2-celled anthers?) Ovary oblong, obtusely 6-angled, 6-celled, many-seeded.

Obs.—This is a large and very beautiful species of Aristolochia, remarkable for the size and form of its flowers. The ventricle at the base is large, and the narrow urn-like tube rises upwards with a very graceful curve. In this species the anthers might properly be considered as 12 in number, each 2-celled, as they are all arranged at equal distances round the stigma, and it seems questionable whether the genus itself ought not to be referred to Dodecandria in place of Hexandria. The arrangement of the anthers by pairs in the other species does not appear to necessitate the supposition of a deviation from the usual structure in ascribing to them 4 parallel cells in place of the more usual number of 2, nor does the analogy of other cognate genera furnish anything opposed to the inference so strongly suggested by the present species.

BEGONIA.—Linn.

The island of Sumatra abounds with Begoniæ, a tribe of plants which are chiefly found in moist shady situations at the foot of hills and in the recesses of forests. Being succulent herbs they are with difficulty preserved in herbaria, and the specimens are frequently deficient in one or other of the parts of fructification. Descriptions from the living plants in their native soil are therefore particularly desirable, and in this view the following account of the species which have fallen under my observation will not be uninteresting. They seem to differ from all those described by Mr. Dryander in the first volume of the Linnean "Transactions," and no great additions have been since made to our knowledge of the genus.

BEGONIA CÆSPITOSA.—W. J.

Subacaulis, foliis inequaliter cordatis angulatis acuminatis glabris, pedunculis dichotome cymosis, capsulæ alis equalibus obtusangulis v. rotundatis.

At Bencoolen.

Nearly stemless. Leaves petiolate, oblique, cordate at the base, with rounded slightly unequal lobes overlapping each other a little, somewhat falcate, rounded and sublobate on one side, straighter on the other, attenuated into a long acumen or point, spinulose but scarcely serrated on the margin, smooth, shining above, pale and punctato-papillose beneath; nerves 5–9, branched towards the margin. The leaves are of unequal size and vary somewhat in shape, the old ones being much rounder and more decidedly lobed than the younger ones, which have the point so much incurved as to be nearly falcate on one side. Petioles red, pilose. Peduncles often as long as the leaves, smooth, bearing a dichotomous cyme of white flowers. Bracts ovate, concave. *Male.*—Perianth 4-leaved, the inner pair smaller. Stamina numerous, collected into a head. *Female.*—Perianth superior, 3-leaved, 2 exterior large, subrotund, applied to each other as in the male flowers, and enclosing the third, which is much smaller and oblong. Style trifid. Stigmata lunato bifid, yellow and glanduloso-pilose. Capsule 3-winged, wings nearly equal, obtuse angled or rounded.

BEGONIA ORBICULATA.—W. J.

Subacaulis, foliis orbiculatis cordatis crenatis glabris, pedunculis subdichotomis, capsulæ alis subequalibus obtusangulis.

Interior of Bencoolen.

Nearly stemless. Leaves petiolate, subrotund, from 3 to 4 inches in diameter, slightly oblique, cordate at the base where the lobes overlap each other, remotely crenate, rounded at the point, smooth, except on the nerves of the under surface, beautifully and finely punctate above. Stipules scariose, acute. Peduncles erect, subdichotomous, nearly as long as the leaves—*i.e.*, about 6 or 8 inches in height. Flowers white. *Male.*—Corolla 4-petaled, the outer pair large, oblong; the inner small. Stamina numerous. *Female.*—Capsule 3-celled, many-seeded, 3-winged; wings obtuse angled, nearly equal.

BEGONIA SUBLOBATA.—W. J.

Repens, foliis cordatis subquinque-lobis vel angulatis dentato-serratis margine reflexis glabris, capsulæ alis equalibus obtusangulis.

Found under moist rocks on Pulo Penang, West Coast of Sumatra.

Repent, with a thick knotty root. Leaves alternate, petiolate, cordate, sometimes unequally, large and broad, often 6 or 7 inches long, angulate, sometimes with 5 acute lobes, sometimes nearly ovate, acuminate, dentato-serrate, edges recurved, very smooth, 5–7-nerved, finely punctate, the dots appearing elevated on the upper surface and depressed on the lower. Petioles 4–6 inches long, nearly smooth, furnished immediately below their junction with the leaf with a semiverticil of linear acute appendices or scales. Stipules large, ovate, rather laciniate towards the apex, 1 on each side the petiole. Peduncles axillary, erect, 6–8 inches long, red, very smooth, terminated by a dichotomous divaricate panicle of white flowers tinged with red. Bracts roundish. *Male.*—Perianth 4-leaved, leaflets rather thick and fleshy, the 2 outer ones much larger and subrotund, before expansion completely enclosing the inner 2, and having their edges mutually applied to each other in such a manner that they form an acute carina round the unexpanded flower. Stamina numerous, in a roundish head; filaments short, inserted on a central column which rises from the base of the flower. Anthers oblong, cells adnate to the sides of the filaments, bursting longitudinally. *Female.*—Capsules with 3 equal obtusely angled wings, 3-celled, 3-valved, valves septiferous in the middle, sutures corresponding to the wings. Seeds numerous, attached to placentæ, which project from the inner angle of the cells.

Obs.—The serratures are hard and cartilaginous, and recurved in such a manner along with the margin of the leaf that, when only observed on the upper surface, their place is perceived by an indentation. It seems to resemble the B. grandis, Dryand., which differs, however, in having oblique, doubly serrated leaves and purple flowers.

BEGONIA FASCICULATA.—W. J.

Foliis inferioribus alternis, superioribus oppositis, oblongo-ovatis basi semicordatis duplicato-serratis pilosis, perianthiis masculis diphyllis, capsulæ alis equalibus obtusangulis.

Found at Tappanuly on the West Coast of Sumatra.

Caulescent. Stem weak, jointed, thickened at the joints, round, covered with red hairs. Leaves petiolate, the lower ones alternate, the upper ones opposite, oblong ovate, inequilateral, semicordate at the base, acuminate, irregularly serrate, covered above with red erect subspinescent hairs, beneath with softer and weaker hairs. Petioles densely pilose. Stipules linear, acuminate, pilose. The flowers come in fascicles from the middle of the petioles, and these flower-bearing leaves are always opposed to another without flowers; hence it is that the upper leaves are opposite, while the lower are alternate. Fascicles composed of male and female flowers; pedicels slender, smooth, white. Bracts several at the base of the fascicles, acute, pilose, red. *Male.*—Perianth diphyllous, white. Stamina numerous. Anthers yellow. *Female.*—Perianth superior, white, cup-shaped, 5-leaved; petals ovate, acute, with a few short red hairs on the outside. Style deeply trifid; lobes convolute, infundibuliform. Capsule 3-winged, 3-celled, wings equal, obtuse-angled.

BEGONIA PILOSA.—W. J.

Foliis subsessilibus irregulariter serratis acuminatis pilosis subtus rubris, bracteis ad basin pedicellorum subrotundis ciliatis, capsulæ alis subequalibus parallelo rotundatis.

Interior of Bencoolen.

Caulescent, pilose. Leaves alternate, scarcely petiolate, ovate, inequilateral, acuminate, slightly and irregularly serrate, pilose with long red hairs, under surface of a bright red colour; about three inches long. Stipules large, lanceolate, pilose externally. Peduncles oppositifolious, subdichotomous. Bracts at the base of the pedicels, roundish, ciliate. Flowers white. *Male.*—Corolla 4-petaled, the inner pair smaller. Stamina numerous. *Female.*—Corolla 5-petaled; the two outer petals larger. Capsule 3-winged; wings nearly equal, parallel and rounded.

BEGONIA BRACTEATA.—W. J.

Foliis duplicato-serratis acuminatis pilosis, pedunculo 1-3-floro bracteis numerosis appressis vestito, capsulis basi bibracteatis, alis equalibus rotundatis.

Near the foot of Gunong Bunko, in the interior of Bencoolen.

Suberect, strong and branching, very villous, shaggy. Leaves alternate, short petioled, ovate, semicordate at the base, acuminate, duplicato-serrate, pilose, 3–4 inches long. Stipules large, pilose. Peduncles oppositifolious, generally supported by a smaller leaf, invested particularly towards the base with many pair of opposite ovate acute pilose ciliate bracts, which are pressed flat against each other; the uppermost pair is distant from the rest, and supports from 1 to 3 pedicels. Flowers white. *Male.*—Corolla 4-petaled; the outer two large, subrotund. Stamina numerous. *Female.*—Corolla 5-petaled; petals nearly equal. Styles three. Stigmata lunate, villous with yellow short glandular hairs. Capsule embraced by 2 bracts at the base, 3-celled, 3-winged; wings equal, rounded.

BEGONIA RACEMOSA.—W. J.

Foliis obovato-oblongis irregulariter dentatis acuminatis glabris, racemis erectis masculis, flore femineo axillari, perianthiis masculis diphyllis, capsulæ alis equalibus parallelo-rotundatis.

Interior of Bencoolen.

Layang-layang simpai. *Malay.*

Suberect, stem smooth, jointed. Leaves alternate, short petioled, obovate oblong, attenuated towards the base, which is unequally cordate, acuminate, irregularly and unequally dentate, smooth, 6–7 inches long. Stipules large, oblong. Racemes, oppositifolious, long, erect, bearing numerous fasciculate male flowers, and having a single female one in the axil. *Male.*— Corolla 2-petaled, petals very thick. Stamina numerous. *Female.* —Capsule with 3 equal parallel rounded wings, 3-celled.

BEGONIA GENICULATA.—W. J.

Caule geniculato, foliis ovato-oblongis denticulatis acuminatis glabris, pedunculis divaricato dichotomis, floribus superioribus masculis dipetalis, inferioribus femineis, capsulæ alis equalibus obtus angulis.

Rumput udang-udang. *Malay.*

Sumatra.

Caulescent, stems smooth, compressed, channelled, jointed, thickened at the articulations. Leaves alternate, petiolate, semicordate at the base, obovate oblong, acuminate, denticulate, smooth.

Peduncles oppositifolious, dichotomous, divaricate, many-flowered, lower flowers female, upper male. There is often a female flower from the axil. *Male.*—Perianth 2-petaled, white. Stamina numerous; anthers oblong, broader above. *Female.*—Capsules long, 3-winged, wings obtuse-angled, equal, smooth.

Obs.—The leaves of this plant are used by the natives for cleaning andtaking out rust from the blades of crises. It has considerable resemblance to the preceding species.

SONERILA HETEROPHYLLA.—W. J.

Foliis oppositis altero minimo reniformi, altero oblongo acuminato versus basin attenuato ibique semicordato, supra glabris, pedunculis axillaribus brevissimis paucifloris.

Found at Tappanuly, on the West Coast of Sumatra.

Stem creeping, round, covered with appressed scaly hairs. Leaves opposite, almost sessile, one very minute and reniform, the other about 3 inches long, oblong, broader above, acuminate, narrowing to the base, semicordate, the outer lobe forming a rounded auricle, obsoletely denticulate or nearly entire, a small spinule on the denticulations; 3-nerved, smooth above, whitish beneath, with some hairs on the nerves. Petioles scarce any. Flowers from the axils of the small leaves, sometimes nearly solitary, sometimes 4 or 5 on a very short peduncle. Pedicels reddish, seated on small tubercles, furnished with glandular hairs. Calyx superior, trifid. Corolla 3-petaled. Stamina 3. Capsule turbinate, 3-celled, many-seeded.

Obs.—This species is remarkable by the extreme difference in the size of the opposite leaves, one of which is so minute as almost to escape observation. The same peculiarity exists in the Sonerila Moluccana.

RHODODENDRON MALAYANUM.—W. J.

Foliis oblongis glabris punctatis, floribus terminalibus, pedicellis cernuis, corollâ punctatâ basi gibbâ.

Observed on the summit of the Sugar Loaf Mountain, in the interior of Bencoolen.

This is a large shrub or small tree much branched. Bark brown and spotted. Leaves alternate or scattered, short petioled, lanceolate-linear, $2\frac{1}{2}$–3 inches long, attenuated to both ends, somewhat bluntish at the point, entire, smooth, thickly sprinkled beneath with brown dots and green above with depressed points; the middle nerve is strong, the lateral ones scarce any. Stipules none. Flowers from a short terminal bud, which is at first closely invested by numerous imbricated broad bracts, which successively fall off and at length leave the short thick peduncle annulated by their cicatrices. It throws out near the point several nodding 1-flowered pedicels, which are dotted in the same manner as the leaves. Calyx very small, 5-toothed. Corolla crimson, tubular, expanding into a 5-lobed limb, sprinkled with callous dots, tube gibbous at the base and marked with 5 furrows. Stamina 10, leaning to one side, inserted on the very base of the corolla and about as long as its limb; filaments red; anthers yellow, opening at top by 2 oblique pores. Style a little shorter than the stamina. Stigma a round head marked with 5 indistinct rays. Ovary superior, oblong, 5-sided, covered with brown spots, 5-celled, polysporous.

Obs.—I found this and the following species of Vaccinium on the very summit of Gunong Bunko, a remarkable insulated mountain in the interior of Bencoolen, commonly called by Europeans the Sugar Loaf, in reference to its shape. Its elevation is not estimated to exceed 3,000 feet, yet the character of its vegetation is decidedly Alpine. This character is probably more marked than it would be at a similar height on the side of a differently shaped hill, owing to the steepness, which refuses space for large trees; and the consequent exposure and want of shelter on its sharp conical peak.

VACCINIUM SUMATRANUM.—W. J.

Racemis axillaribus foliis brevioribus, foliis elliptico-ovatis integerrimis coriaceis.

Found on the summit of Gunong Bunko, or the Sugar Loaf Mountain, in the interior of Bencoolen.

A small tree, with reddish brown bark and smooth branches. Leaves alternate, short petioled, elliptic ovate, acuminate, sometimes obtuse, entire, edges a little reflexed, very smooth, firm, stiff and leathery, pale green beneath; about 4 inches long. Stipules none. Racemes axillary, shorter than the leaves, often from the stem below them. Flowers white, pedicellate, alternate. Calyx small, cup-shaped, slightly 4-toothed. Corolla oblong ovate, contracted at the mouth; limb short, recurved, 4-parted. Stamina 8 incluse, inserted on the base of the corolla; filaments dilated at the base, pilose, tinged with red; anthers 2-lobed, between which are 2 short filaments or processes, each lobe prolonged upwards into a membranaceous horn or awn, which is bifid at top and opens by a pore. Ovary semi-inferior, 4-celled, polysporous, ovula attached to the inner angles of the cells. Style columnar, a little longer than the stamina, incluse. Stigma round, obtuse.

HALORAGIS DISTICHA.—W. J.

Foliis alternis distichis obliquis integris, floribus axillaribus subsolitariis, petalis tridentatis.

Kayo kanchil. *Malay.*

This species is not unfrequent in Sumatra, at Singapore, and other parts of the Malay Archipelago.

A shrub with ferruginous pilose branches. Leaves alternate, distichous, arranged in two series, one of large leaves and another of very small ones which resemble stipulæ, being regularly placed a little below the insertion of the large ones, so as to lie over their bases; the large leaves are subsessile, rhomboid oblong, inequilateral, acute, entire, nearly smooth above, pilose with short appressed hairs beneath; from an inch to an inch and a half long; the small leaves are similar in shape, but more acute, and little more than a quarter of an inch long; they are arranged on the anterior side of the branch and are closely appressed to it, so as to resemble stipules. Flowers axillary, generally solitary, subsessile. Calyx 4-leaved, persistent. Petals 4, shorter than the calyx, trifid. Stamina 8, as long as the petals; anthers 2-celled. Ovary inferior, 4-sided, ferruginous, 4-celled, tetrasporous. Styles 4, equal to the stamina. Stigmas simple. Drupe oblong ovate, red, containing a nut with 8 longitudinal furrows, and containing a single seed. Seed oblong oval; embryo central in an ample albumen.

Obs.—The general habit of this species is very peculiar, and has much the character of Australasian vegetation, to which country the genus principally belongs.

ELODEA.—Adanson.

Hypericinæ. Juss.

This genus, which has been revived by a late author on American Botany, appears to be abundantly distinguished from Hypericum, and to form a good natural division. It is principally characterized by having the stamina united into 3 phalanges, which alternate with an equal number of nectaries. In the following species the placentation is peculiar; I know not whether the American plants exhibit the same structure, as it is not mentioned in any description which I have seen, but if it should prove on examination that they do, it should form part of the generic character. Loureiro's Hypericum Cochinchinense, which undoubtedly belongs to Elodea, appears to be very nearly related to my E. Sumatrana, and his description of the seeds seems to indicate a structure similar to what I have observed. The Hypericum petiolatum of the same author seems also referable to this genus, and to be different from Linnæus's H. petiolatum, which is a native of Brazil. In all the species now referred to Elodea, the generic distinction appears to receive confirmation from certain differences of habit which may be remarked between them and the true Hyperica, particularly in the colour of the flowers, which in the latter is almost without exception yellow, but in Elodea is often red.

ELODEA SUMATRANA.—W. J.

Foliis subsessilibus oblongis attenuato-acuminatis glabris rigidiusculis, paniculis terminalibus foliosis, staminibus numerosis triadelphis, petalis basi nudis.

Found at Tello Dalam, in the island of Pulo Nias.

A large shrub or small tree; branchlets rather compressed, obscurely 4-sided. Leaves opposite, almost sessile, oblong, tapering to the point, acute, broad at the base, entire, smooth; nerves proceeding from a middle rib, strong; 6 or 7 inches in length; the surface appears by the aid of the microscope to be dotted with opaque points. Panicles terminal, foliose, the lower divisions being axillary; oppositely branched and rigid. Flowers dark red or purple. Bracts minute. Calyx 5-leaved, persistent, leaflets ovate, smooth, the outer ones smaller. Corolla cup-shaped, longer than the calyx, 5-petaled; petals subrotund; ungues naked, without pore or scale. Nectaries 3, yellow, inserted below the corolla and half as large as the petals, subrotund, doubled backwards upon themselves in such a manner as to form a sac which opens behind near the base. Stamina numerous, their filaments united for about half their length into three phalanges, which are inserted alternately with the three nectaries; they are a little shorter than the corolla; anthers yellow, 2-celled. Ovary oblong, 3-celled, many-seeded. Styles 3, diverging. Stigmata 3, subrotund. Capsule oblong, 3-celled, each cell containing several seeds as long as the cell and attached to the bottom of the central column; they are thin and flat, disposed regularly one within the other, forming concentric circles, which are particularly apparent in the transverse section of the capsule.

Obs.—This curious arrangement of the seeds is not a little remarkable; they lie one within the other like skins of an onion, each occupying the full length and breadth of the cell, but diminishing regularly in size from the outermost to the middle in proportion to the different radius of the circle which it describes round the common centre. They are attached one above the other to the bottom of the cell at its inner angle. The leaves are destitute of pellucid dots, and have their lateral nerves strongly and distinctly marked. The nectaries which alternate with the stamina are very peculiar, being saccate, apparently by being doubled backwards. This species differs from the following and those of America in having no scales at the base of the petals, and from the latter in having numerous stamina. It appears to be nearly related to Loureiro's Hypericum Cochinchinense, which, as already observed, belongs to this genus.

ELODEA FORMOSA.—W. J.

Foliis petiolatis lanceolatis subtus glaucis pedunculis fasciculatis axillaribus, staminibus numerosis triadelphis, nectariis acutis.

Kayo gaghak. *Lampong.* Sepadas Bunga. *Malay.*

Native of Sumatra.

A small tree with cinereous bark and smooth branchlets. *Leaves* opposite, elliptic oblong, acute, very entire, smooth, glaucous beneath, pellucidly punctate, two and a half inches long; the nerves proceed from a midrib. Petioles slender. Peduncles axillary, and from the axils of fallen leaves, fasciculate, 1-flowered, slender, smooth. Flowers white, with a slight rosy tinge. Bracts several at the base of the peduncles. Calyx 5-leaved, smooth, leaflets acute. Corolla 5-petaled, longer than the calyx; petals oblong, each furnished with a broad adnate scale a little above the base. Stamina numerous, united into 3 phalanges. Nectaries 3, alternating with the stamineous fascicles, red, acute, carinate behind, fleshy. Ovary 3-celled, each cell containing several flat ovula lying one within the other, and attached by their bases to the lower part of the axis. Styles 3, long. Stigmas capitate. Capsules oblong, crowned by the persistent styles, 3-celled, many-seeded. Seeds thin, flat, attached by their bases to a central triangular column, on which they are inserted alternately in a double series.

Obs.—The arrangement of the ovula is similar to that observed in the E. Sumatrana; they are thin, attached by their bases to the lower part of the cell, suberect, and concentrically disposed, but are inserted rather higher on the axis of the cell than in the former. This species agrees with those of America in having a scale at the base of the petals, but differs in having numerous stamina; it therefore comes nearer to the E. Egyptica (Hypericum Egypticum, Linn.).

TERNSTRŒMIA.

The Malayan species of Ternstrœmia exhibit a remarkable agreement among themselves, at the same time that they differ considerably from the rest of the genus. They have a trilocular ovarium surmounted by 3 styles, which are inserted on the same point, but are separate to the base. In some the corolla is monopetalous with monadelphous stamina, in others it is 5-petaled with distinct stamina. The anthers are 2-celled and open at the top by 2 oblique pores; this is probably the case with the whole genus, though it has been omitted in the generic character, of which it ought certainly to form an essential part. It seems doubtful whether the monogynous species with bilocular fruit and definite seeds ought to be united with those which have 3 styles, 3 cells and numerous seeds; but an examination of their ovaries and placentation is necessary to decide the question. I have met with four species in Sumatra and the adjacent islands, two of which I have already described in the first volume of the "Malayan Miscellanies." Their common appellation in Malay is Ingor-ingor karbau, or Buffalo's spittle.

TERNSTRŒMIA ACUMINATA.—W. J.

Foliis obovato-lanceolatis acuminatis spinuloso-denticulatis glabris, floribus axillaribus solitariis polyandris, pedunculis squamosis, fructu triloculari.

Found at Tappanuly on the West Coast of Sumatra.

Branches round, somewhat flexuose. All the young parts green, with a few appressed scales. Leaves alternate, petiolate, obovate lanceolate, attenuated to the base, terminating in a long acumen or point, spinuloso-denticulate, smooth, with the exception of a few appressed scales on the lower surface; about a foot in length. Petioles short, scaly. Peduncles axillary, solitary, 1-flowered, scarcely so long as the petioles, covered with small scales. Calyx 5-leaved, the 3 outer leaflets with appressed scalets. Corolla white, 5-petaled, little longer than the calyx. Stamina many, inserted on the base of the petals; anthers large, truncate and opening by 2 pores at the top. Ovary 3-celled, many-seeded. Styles 3.

Obs.—This agrees with the T. pentapetala in having the corolla divided to the base, but the leaves are more acuminate, and the flowers are solitary and axillary.

TERNSTRŒMIA SERRATA.—W. J.

Foliis obovato-oblongis cartilagineo-serratis glabris, pedunculis axillaribus binis, floribus monadelphis, laciniis corollæ emarginatis, fructu triloculari.

Frequent on the island of Pulo Nias.

A small tree. Young parts furnished with brownish scales. Leaves alternate, petiolate, obovate oblong, acuminate, serrate with irregular cartilaginous uncinate serratures, smooth, pretty strongly nerved; 7–8 inches long. Petioles brown, scaly.

Peduncles generally 2, axillary, 1-flowered, slender, about an inch long. Calyx 5-parted, whitish, leaflets unequal. Corolla white, monopetalous, quinquefid, longer than the calyx, cup-shaped, lobes bifid or emarginate, generally oblique. Stamina shorter than the corolla, and inserted on its base; filaments united below; anthers oblong, bifid, 2-celled, each cell opening at top by an oblique cucullate pore. Ovary hairy, 3-celled, many-seeded; placentæ central. Styles 3, longer than the corolla, irregularly bent. Berry 3-celled, many-seeded. Seeds angled, foveolate.

Obs.—This differs from the other Sumatran species in having firmer leaves, with stronger nerves and thickened callous serratures. The peduncles are more slender, the styles longer, and the lobes of the corolla obliquely notched.

TERNSTRŒMIA CUSPIDATA.—W. J.

Foliis obovato-ellipticis acuminatis dentato-serratis, serraturis, apice hamatis, fructibus 5-locularibus, pedunculis axillaribus 1-3 floris.

A tree, young parts ferruginous. Leaves petiolate, elliptic ovate, attenuated to the base, broader above, sharply acuminate, serrated, the narrow sharp toothlets generally curved or hooked at their points, smooth, often marked with whitish glandular dots on the nerves, veins, and serratures; 6-8 inches long. Peduncles axillary. 1-3 flowered, smooth. Calyx 5-parted, segments orbicular, Corolla white, monopetalous, 5-parted. Stamina numerous; anthers opening by two gaping pores. Ovary subglobose, 5-celled, ovula very numerous; placentæ from the inner angle of the cells. Style very deeply 5-parted.

Obs.—This species (received from Salumah during the printing of the present sheet) comes very near to the T. serrata; it differs in having the leaves more sharply acuminate, with longer tooth-like serratures, and rather shorter petioles, the peduncles frequently bearing 2 or 3 flowers, and not so slender as in the former and in the 5-celled fruit.

MILLINGTONIA.—Roxb.

Calyx 5-phyllus, foliolis duobus exterioribus minoribus. Corolla 5-petala, petalis duobus minoribus squamiformibus. Stamina quinque, quorum tria sterilia difformia basi petalorum majorum inserta; duo fertilia basi minorum adnata, filamentis apice scyphum gerentibus cui antheræ bilobæ insident. Ovarium nectario annulari cinctum, biloculare, loculis disporis. Drupa nuce plerumque monospermâ. Embryo erectus, curvatus albumine nullo aut parco.

Obs.—It will be perceived that I have made a considerable and material alteration in the terms of the generic description from that given by Roxburgh ("Fl. Ind." i. p. 102), which I conceive to be necessary towards explaining the true relations of the various parts of the flower, and thereby affording the means of tracing more correctly its natural affinities. The principal point is to determine the real nature of what Roxburgh calls the nectarial scales at the base of his petals. I have no hesitation in considering them as abortive stamina, which the examination of the flower before expansion places, I think, beyond a doubt. In that state the whole of the stamina connive over the pistil, the anther of the fertile ones is turned inward, so as not to be visible, and there is no considerable difference of appearance between them and the sterile ones. The anther-bearing hollow of the fertile stamina is applied to a corresponding hollow on the side of the sterile ones, and at the time of expansion the former separate themselves with a jerk and become erect, while the latter continue in their original position incumbent over the pistil. The petals on which the fertile stamina are inserted are much smaller and narrower than the others, as if exhausted by the greater development of the parts they nourish. These petals are called by Roxburgh outer laminæ of the filaments, which is contrary to all common analogy, while the other explanation might be supported by numerous examples of a similar structure. Thus in place of a diandrous flower with tripetalous appendiculate corolla and bifid stamina, we obtain 5 as the primary number of all the parts, only modified by the partial abortion of 3 of the stamina.

MILLINGTONIA SUMATRANA.—W. J.

Foliis impari-pinnatis, foliolis 3–6 jugis ovato-lanceolatis, petalis minoribus acutis, fructu ovato.

Found on the island of Pulo Nias.

It is a moderate-sized tree with grey bark. Leaves alternate, pinnate with an odd one which is rarely wanting; leaflets from 5 to 13, opposite, ovate, lanceolate, acuminate, entire, smooth, 6–9 inches long. Common petiole flat above and marginate, thickened at the base. Panicles terminal, many-flowered, rather coarctate, with stiff rigid divisions, slightly tomentose. Flowers white. Bracts minute. Calyx small, 5-leaved, the outer 2 smaller, resembling bracts. Corolla 5-petaled, the outer 3 large, subrotund, the inner 2 much smaller, lanceolate, acute. Stamina 5, inserted on the bases of the petals; 2 fertile, upon the smaller petals, with broad filaments expanding at top into a kind of cup, on which the anther rests, and to whose outer edge it is attached; the anther consists of 2 yellow lobes resembling masses of pollen which burst transversely. The 3 sterile stamina which are inserted on the larger petals have thick filaments without anthers, but marked with an oblong cup-like cavity on each side corresponding to the cups of the fertile ones. Before expansion, the 5 stamina connive over the pistil in such a manner that the cup-like cavities are mutually applied to each other; on expansion, the fertile stamina separate with a jerk, by which the pollen is in part dispersed, and the cup becomes erect with the anther resting upon it; the other 3 never separate but remain conniving over the pistil. Ovary embraced at the base by a nectarial cup with 5 toothlets; ovate, 2-celled, each cell containing 2 ovula attached to the centre of the partition. Style short. Stigma small. Berry ovate, oblique or recurved, somewhat less than an olive, containing a single 1-seeded nut. Nut obovate oblong, acute and curved at the base, carinate along one side, and having a large umbilical hollow above the base on the other, smooth, 1-seeded. Seed obovate oblong, acute at the base, covered with a dry loose brown skin; albumen none; embryo glutinous on the surface, erect, doubled on itself. Cotyledons thin, foliaceous, large, round ovate, reflected backwards upon the radicle, and half embracing it laterally. Radicle inferior, very large, thick, pointed, extending the whole length of the seed and partly doubled up or curved at the top.

Obs.—The cotyledons are wrapped round the embryo in such a manner as to give the whole somewhat of a chrysaloid appearance. This species has considerable resemblance to the M. pinnata of Roxburgh, but differs in having unequally pinnate leaves, with from 3 to 6 pair of leaflets, in having the smaller petals entire and acute, not tridentate, in the nectarial ring having 5 simple toothlets, not 3 bidentate angles, and in having a large ovate fruit with a smooth, not rugose nut. The abortive cell is generally observable near the umbilical foramen.

LAURUS INCRASSATUS.—W. J.

Foliis ovato-lanceolatis venosis, pedunculis fructûs incrassatis, rubris.

Machilus medius. Rumph. "Amb." iii. p. 70. t. 41.
Jaring-jaring tupai. *Malay.*
Found at Natal in the island of Sumatra.

A tree. Leaves alternate, petiolate, ovate lanceolate or lanceolate, acuminate, entire, very smooth, with lateral nerves proceeding from a middle rib; about 5 inches long. Petioles short. Peduncles axillary or lateral near the extremity of the branches, shorter than the leaves, supporting a small panicle of flowers. In the flower these peduncles and pedicels are slender and delicate, but as the fruit advances they become very much thickened, fleshy and red. Perianth 6-parted. Stamina 9, the 3 inner ones glandular at the base and somewhat villous; anthers opening by longitudinal valves. Style short. Stigma capitate, angled. Berry seated on the incrassated peduncle, and embraced at the base by the divisions of the perianth a little enlarged, about the size and shape of an olive, purple, 1-seeded. Seed oval, exalbuminous. Radicle superior, far within the edge of the cotyledons.

Obs.—I have met with another species at Bencoolen with larger leaves, from 9 to 12 inches in length, in which the pedicels alone are thickened, the peduncles remaining unaltered. In this particular it agrees perhaps still better with Rumphius's figure than the plant above described.

TETRANTHERA CORDATA.—W. J.

N. O. Laurinæ.

Racemis axillaribus, floribus umbellatis enneandris, filamentis pilosis, perianthii limbo sexpartito, foliis cordatis subrotundo-ovatis uninervibus costatis subtus ramulis pedunculis involucris-que ferrugineo villosis.

West Coast of Sumatra.

A moderate-sized tree. Leaves alternate, petiolate, cordate, sometimes sinuate-cordate, varying from subrotund-ovate to oblong oval, rather acute, smooth above, tomentose beneath, nerves proceeding from a middle rib, veins transverse, subreticulate. Peduncles axillary, shorter than the leaves, bearing a raceme of involucred umbels. Involucres 5-leaved, leaflets roundish, tomentose without, deciduous. Umbels sessile on the involucre, 4–7-flowered; flowers pedicelled. *Male.*—Perianth 6-parted. Stamina 9, hairy, the inner 3 filaments furnished with large glands; anthers 4-celled. *Female.*—Perianth 6-parted, segments narrow. Sterile stamina 9, the inner 3 with large double glands; filaments pilose with long hairs. Style 1, longer than the stamina. Stigma dilated, sublobate. Berry oblong, 1-seeded.

KNEMA GLAUCESCENS.—W. J.

N. O. Myristiceæ.—Br.

Glomerulis axillaribus 2–6 floris, floribus pedicellatis, baccis oblongo-ovalibus subpulverulentis, foliis oblongis sursum attenuatis subtus glaucis, antheris 12–15.

In the neighbourhood of Bencoolen.

A diœcious tree. The young parts covered with rusty down. Leaves alternate, short-petioled, oblong, generally rounded at the base, attenuated upwards, acute, very entire, deep green and shining above, glaucous beneath, the adult leaves nearly smooth, the young ones furnished with short stellate pubescence on the under surface; lateral nerves simple; about 7 inches long by 2 broad. Petioles somewhat rusty, a third of an inch in length. Stipules none. Flowers 2-6, glomerate on a short axillary knob, pedicellate; pedicels as long as the petioles, ferruginously tomentose. A minute bract about the middle of each pedicel. *Male.*—Perianth ferruginously tomentose without, deeply 3-parted, spreading, segments round ovate, thick; æstivation valvate. Stamineous column central, slender, expanding at top into a peltate disc, whose edge is divided into 12 or 15 rays, to the lower surfaces of which are attached an equal number of 2-celled anthers. *Female.*—Fruit axillary, generally solitary, hanging, oblong oval, considerably smaller than an olive, somewhat pulverulent and rusty, bursting into 2 valves. Nut invested by a thin aril, which is laciniate only at the top. Seed with ruminate albumen.

Obs.—The seed has a pungent taste and slightly aromatic smell. Mr. Brown has recognized the propriety of separating Knema from Myristica.

CONNARUS.—Linn.

This genus, with Cnestis, has been removed by Mr. R. Brown from the Terebintaceæ of Jussieu, and formed into a separate and very natural family under the name of Connaraceæ. They are rather a numerous tribe in the Malay islands, and besides the following species of Connarus and Cnestis, I have to add the new genus Eurycoma, which appears to be sufficiently distinct from both the former. I am doubtful whether the species which I have referred to Cnestis really belong to that genus, as they have all smooth capsules with arilled or carunculate seeds, or whether they ought not to be separated from those whose capsules are clothed with prurient hair. Some confusion appears also to have existed between the species of Cnestis and Connarus, the ripe capsules of the former being often solitary from the abortion of the remaining ovaries, and I am much inclined to think that Connarus santaloides, and mimosoides of Vahl in particular, are in reality species of Cnestis, a supposition which is supported by the analogy of the inflorescence, which is almost without exception terminal in Connarus and axillary in Cnestis. This distinction is of some importance between genera so nearly related.

CONNARUS FERRUGINEUS.—W. J.

Eerrugineo-tomentosa, foliis pinnatis, foliolis oblongis coriaceis subtus ferrugineo-villosis, paniculis terminalibus.

Bunga burutta. *Malay.*

Native of Pulo Pinang.

A small sized tree. Branches round, covered with ferruginous wool. Leaves alternate, pinnate, leaflets 9, sub-opposite, oblong lanceolate, acuminate, very entire, margins reflexed, coriaceous, green and tomentose above, ferruginously villous beneath. Petioles round, villous, thickened at the base. Stipules none. Panicles large, terminal, sometimes with a few axillary racemes. Flowers numerous, white. Bracts roundish, often curved, ferruginously villous, as well as the calyces and the whole panicle. Calyx 5-parted, laciniæ erect, oblong, acute. Corolla white, sprinkled with red dots, 5-petaled, longer than the calyx, petals erect, lanceolate. Stamina 10, erect, united at the base, the alternate ones much shorter. Anthers ovate. Style shorter than the long stamina. Stigma capitate, 3-furrowed. Capsule follicular, ferruginous, rather inflated, oblique, gibbous behind, opening on one side, 1-celled, 1-seeded. Seed bean-shaped, appendiculate at the umbilicus. Umbilical appendage or caruncle large, and glandular. Embryo dicotyledonous, conform to the seed, without albumen; radicle at a distance from the umbilicus.

Obs.—This fine species is well distinguished by its thick leathery leaves, and the ferruginous pubescence of their lower surface and of the branches and panicles.

CONNARUS VILLOSA.—W. J.

Villosissima, foliolis 5–7 lanceolatis longe acuminatis supra glabris, paniculis terminalibus dense stellato-villosis ferrugineis.

Native of Sumatra.

The whole plant densely and ferruginously woolly. Branches round. Leaves alternate, pinnate, leaflets 5 or 7, subopposite, oblong lanceolate, narrowing towards the base, terminating in a long acumen, entire, smooth above, villous beneath with stellate pubescence; about 6 inches long. In young leaves the upper surface is covered with deciduous pubescence. Panicles large, terminal, and from the upper axils densely villous, ferruginous. Bracts long, linear, thick, curved, villous. Calyx 5-parted, villous. Corolla 5-petaled, limb spreading. Stamina 10, united into a ring at the base, the alternate ones shorter. Ovary densely pilose with plumose hairs. Style longer than the stamina. Stigma capitate.

Obs.—This plant is covered with denser and rougher wool than the preceding, particularly on the panicles, and the leaves are much longer, acuminate, and not coriaceous.

CONNARUS SEMIDECANDRA.—W. J.

Foliis pinnatis, foliolis 3–5 lato-lanceolatis subtus villosiusculis, paniculis terminalibus axillaribusque villosis, filamentis alternis sterilibus.

Mangul, also Akar sedinka. *Malay.*

Abundant in thickets at various places on the West Coast of Sumatra.

It is a small tree, with wrinkled bark; the young shoots and leaves are softly and ferruginously villous. Leaves alternate, pinnate; leaflets from 3–5, ovate lanceolate, acuminate, entire, smooth above, slightly villous beneath, nerves lucid, 3–4 inches long. Panicles terminal or from the upper axils, villous and brownish. Flowers numerous. Bracts small. Calyx 5-leaved, erect, reddish, tomentose. Corolla of a light blush colour, 5-petaled; petals longer than the calyx, spreading at the limb. Stamina, filaments 5, fertile, exsert; 5 alternate ones, short, sterile, all united into a ring at the base. Style somewhat shorter than the stamina. Capsule tomentose, ferruginous, follicular, 2-valved, 1-seeded. Seed with an umbilical caruncle.

Obs.—This is one of the most common species in Sumatra, and, like all the rest of the genus, frequents thickets and copses, or what is called by the Malays "Belukar," rather than the great forests.

CONNARUS GRANDIS.—W. J.

Foliis pinnatis, foliolis quinis ovato-lanceolatis glabris, paniculis terminalibus, capsulis magnis glabris.

At Tappanuly, in Sumatra.

A moderate-sized tree. Leaves alternate, pinnate; leaflets generally 5, ovate lanceolate, acuminate, entire, smooth, 8 or 9 inches long. Panicles terminal, long, smooth. Capsules large, oblique, red, smooth, follicular, bursting on one side, 1-seeded. Seed with a large umbilical caruncle.

Obs.—I have not seen the flowers. It has larger leaves and fruit than any other species that I have met with, and is further distinguished by the smoothness of all its parts.

CONNARUS LUCIDUS.—W. J.

Foliis pinnatis, foliolis glaberrimis nitidis emarginato-acuminatis, paniculis terminalibus ferrugineis, calyce persistente.

Sumatra.

A small tree, with long divaricate subscandent branches. Bark brown and wrinkled. Leaves alternate; leaflets 5–9, ovate lanceolate or elliptic oblong, terminating in a long linear acumen, which is emarginate at the point, entire, very smooth, shining and lucid, 2–2½ inches long. Panicles terminal, small and delicate, ferruginously tomentose. Flowers pale red. Calyx 5-leaved, tomentose. Corolla 5-petaled, petals narrow. Stamina 10, monadelphous at the base, the alternate ones short. Style 1, longer than the stamina. Capsule obovate, less oblique than usual in the genus, embraced at the base by the enlarged persistent calyx, smooth, bursting on one side, 1-seeded. Seed attached nearly at the base, the umbilicus half embraced by the cup-shaped caruncula, which is rather smaller than usual.

Obs.—This is a small delicate species, having smooth, shining leaves with emarginate points; the panicles are small and seldom bring more than 1 or 2 fruit to perfection.

CNESTIS EMARGINATA.—W. J.

Foliolis 5–7, acuminatis apice emarginatis racemis axillaribus paucifloris, capsulis solitariis glabris, seminis umbilico caruncula semiamplexo.

Found in the neighbourhood of Bencoolen.

A small tree with weak diffuse branches. Leaves alternate, pinnate, leaflets 5–7, from ovate to oblong ovate, terminating in a long acumen which is emarginate at the point, entire, very smooth, the middle nerve pubescent underneath; the upper leaflet is the largest, and frequently 5 inches in length. Petiole thickened at top and bottom, almost articulate under the terminal leaflet. Racemis axillary, subsolitary, short, few-flowered. Pedicels alternate, 1-flowered; a bract at the end of each pedicel, small, tomentose as well as the peduncle. Calyx 5-parted, smooth, persistent. Corolla 5-petaled, petals oblong, acute. Stamina 10 distinct, the alternate ones shorter. Ovaries 5, smooth, with a line of hairs along the suture. Styles 5, shorter than the stamina. Stigmas emarginate. Capsule solitary, 4 ovaries aborting, embraced at the base by the thickened calyx, orange-coloured, smooth, bursting on one side, containing a single black seed. Seed furnished at the base with a cup-shaped orange-coloured fleshy caruncle which partially surrounds the umbilicus. Embryo inverse, without albumen.

Obs.—The umbilical caruncle in this species is similar in shape and situation to that observed in the *Connarus lucidus*, being smaller than usual in this tribe.

CNESTIS FLORIDA.—W. J.

Foliolis 3–5, rarius solitariis, oblongo-ovatis acuminatis glaberrimis, racemis fasciculatis axillaribus, seminibus arillo subinclusis.

Confer cum Connaro santaloide. Vahl, anne eadem?

Found in Sumatra and the island of Pulo Nias.

A small tree, with somewhat rigid divaricate branches. Leaves alternate, pinnate, leaflets 3–5, sometimes solitary, oblong ovate, attenuated into a longish blunt acumen, very entire, very smooth, rather rigid, shining above, veins reticulate, about 3 inches long. Racemes axillary, fasciculate, slender, shorter than the leaves, the lower pedicels 3–4 flowered. Calyx almost 5-leaved, erect, tinged with red towards the base. Corolla 5-petaled. Stamina 10, distinct, nearly equal, filaments flat and broader at the base. Ovaries 5, oblong, erect. Styles 1 to each ovary. Stigmas simple. Capsule solitary, the remainder aborting, ovate, pointed towards both ends, somewhat oblique, smooth, bursting on one side, 1-seeded. Seed almost enclosed in a bright red fleshy aril, originating from the umbilicus, and in its expansion enveloping the whole seed. Albumen none. Cotyledons plano-convex, solid. Radicle remote from the umbilicus, as in Gærtner's Omphalobium.

CNESTIS MIMOSOIDES.—W. J.

Foliis pinnatis subdecemjugis, foliolis ovato-oblongis emarginatis, seminibus arillo subinclusis.

Connarus mimosoides. Vahl and Willd.

Found at Tappanuly.

I can scarcely entertain a doubt of this being the very plant referred by Vahl to Connarus, and aptly named Mimosoides. Its analogy with the preceding is very close, having the seeds similarly enclosed in a large red aril, and the racemes axillary. I have not seen the flowers, but the four abortive ovaries are quite distinct at base of the perfect one. In all these three species only one capsule ripens, in which particular, as well as having smooth capsules and arilled seeds, they seem to differ from Cnestis.

EURYCOMA.—W. J.

Pentandria Monogynia. N. O. Connaraceæ.—BROWN.

Calyx 5-partitus. Corolla 5-petala. Stamina quinque. Glandulæ decem staminibus alternæ. Ovarium 5-lobum, lobis monosporis. Stylus 1. Stigmata quinque. Capsulæ 3-5, folliculares, glabræ, monospermæ. Semen nudum.

Polygama, foliis pinnatis fastigiatis, floribus paniculatis.

EURYCOMA LONGIFOLIA.

Kayu kabal. *Malay.*

Found at Tappanuly and Bencoolen, in Sumatra, and at Singapore.

This is a small tree, whose branches are thick, rough with the vestiges of fallen leaves and foliose at their summits. Leaves crowded at the extremity of the branches, 2 feet long, pinnated with numerous leaflets, which are oblong lanceolate, acute, very entire, very smooth, 2–3 inches in length. Panicles axillary, very long. Flowers male and hermaphrodite on different plants. Calyx small, 5-parted. Corolla longer than the calyx, purple, tomentose without, with glandular hairs, petals erect with inflexed margins. Stamina 5, erect, shorter than the petals, alternating with 5 pair of villous corpuscles, which are large and distinct in the male flower, very small in the hermaphrodite. Ovary 5-lobed, lobes monosporous, in the male very small and abortive. Style 1, short, curved. Stigmata 5, thick, recurved. Capsules from 3 to 5, nearly ovate, smooth, bursting on one side, 1-seeded. Seed naked (without aril or caruncle), exalbuminous.

Obs.—The corpuscles interposed between the stamina are remarkable in the male flower, being roundish, erect, yellow bodies, with somewhat the appearance of abortive anthers; in the hermaphrodite, however, they become simple scales. The genus differs from Cnestis in the number of the stamina, the single style, and the smoothness of the capsules, and from Connarus in the number of the ovaries and stigmas, and the want of the umbilical caruncula.

PERONEMA.—W. J.

Didynamia Angiospermia. N. O. Verberaceæ.—Br.

Calyx 5-partitus. Corolla tubo brevi, limbo irregulari 5-lobo, laciniis secundis. Stamino duo, exserta; rudimenta duorum sterilium. Stigma refractum. Fructus siccus, 4-partibilis, 4-spermus.

Arbor, foliis pinnatis petiolo alato, paniculâ terminali opposite corymbosâ.

PERONEMA CANESCENS.

Sungkei. *Malay.*

A large tree, native of Sumatra.

Trunk straight, but little branched. Leaves opposite, pinnate, nearly 2 feet long, with 7–9 pair of leaflets, which are alternate or subopposite, lanceolate, attenuated to both ends, acute, somewhat recurved, entire, smooth above, canescent beneath, veins reticulate on the under surface, 8–9 inches long. Petioles winged, finely and delicately tomentose, wings decurrent from the insertion of the leaflets. Stipules none. The branches are crowned by a vast terminal oppositely corymbose panicle, of which the ultimate divisions are dichotomous, with a flower in the bifurcations; the whole is finely tomentose and hoary. Bracts small, acute. Flowers inconspicuous, whitish. Calyx 5-parted, segments acute, erect.

Corolla not much longer than the calyx, limb expanding, irregular, 5-lobed, segments secund, the two upper ones diverging, the lowermost considerably longer than the rest. Stamina 2, reflexed backwards between the upper segments of the corolla, filaments subulate, thickened towards the base. Anthers long. Rudiments of 2 abortive stamina. Ovary 4-celled, ovula erect. Style rather longer than the stamina. Stigma simple, refracted. Fruit seated on the calyx, villous, dry, separating into 4 portions, each of which contains a single seed.

Obs.—This is a valuable timber tree, the wood being hard and tough, well suited for carriage shafts, which require to combine strength and elasticity with lightness. When long buried in the earth, it is said to become petrified. The genus is related to Vitex, but is abundantly distinct therefrom.

RHODAMNIA.—W. J.

Icosandria Monogynia. N. O. Myrtaceæ.

Calyx superus, quadrilobus. Corolla tetrapetala. Stamina numerosa. Ovarium uniloculare, pluri ovulatum, placentis duobus parietalibus. Bacca unilocularis oligosperma.

Arbuscula, foliis trinerviis, inflorescentia axillari.

RHODAMNIA CINEREA.

Frequent on the Western Coast of Sumatra and the islands which skirt it. Its Malay name is Marpuyan.

There are two varieties of this species, the one of which is larger than the other and has broader leaves, which are more decidedly tomentose below. These differences are scarcely sufficient for a specific distinction.

A small tree with greyish wrinkled bark and pilose branchlets. Leaves opposite and alternate, petiolate, roundish-ovate in the large variety, and broad lanceolate in the small one, acuminate, very entire, 3-nerved, often with a less distinct pair near the margin, smooth above, somewhat hoary beneath, pubescent, particularly on the nerves, but in the small variety nearly smooth, with little more than a glaucous tinge on the under surface. Petioles short, tomentose. Stipules small, linear. Peduncles short, axillary, 1-flowered. Flowers white. Calyx tomentose, persistent. Corolla twice as long as the calyx. Stamina inserted on the calyx, almost as long as the corolla. Ovary 1-celled, containing many ovula attached to 2 parietal placentæ. Style 1, erect. Berry reddish, subglobose, crowned with the calyx, 1-celled, containing a few seeds attached to the parietes, many of the ovula proving abortive.

DESCRIPTIONS OF MALAYAN PLANTS.

Obs.—This genus, which is nearly related to Myrtus, appears to be sufficiently distinguished by its ovary and placentation, from which, rather than from the fruit, the most important characters in this family are to be derived. It is peculiar in having 3-nerved leaves, in which particular it has a resemblance to Myrtus tomentosa, but differs widely from that species in its fruit and ovary.

ADINANDRA.—W. J.

Polyandria Monogynia.

Calyx 5-partitus, persistens, basi bibracteatus. Corolla pentapetala, petalis basi latis. Stamina 30, pluriseriata, subpolyadelpha, interioribus brevioribus; antheris bilocularibus apice mucronatis. Stylus unicus, subulatus. Bacca supera, stylo persistente acuminata, 5-locularis, polysperma, placentis ab angulo interiore loculos bipartientibus.

Arborescens foliis alternis exstipularibus, floribus axillaribus.

ADINANDRA DUMOSA.

Daun saribu. *Malay.*

Abundant in thickets throughout Sumatra and various parts of the Malay islands.

It grows to be a small tree; the bark is dark brown, and the branches are smooth. Leaves alternate, short petioled, elliptic oblong, acute at both ends, sometimes rounded, with an obtuse acumen at top, entire or obsoletely serrate, smooth, slightly glaucous beneath, almost veinless; 3–4 inches long. Stipules none. Peduncles axillary, subsolitary, 1-flowered, shorter than the leaves, recurved calyx bibracteate at the base, 5-parted, segments thick, subrotund, overlapping each other. Corolla white, twice as long as the calyx, erect or conniving, 5-petaled, petals ovate oblong, broad at the base, acute. Stamina about 30, closely arranged in several circles, the inner ones shorter; filaments divisible to their bases, but closely pressed against each other, sericeously pilose, particularly on their outer side; anthers of 2 parallel lobes, adnate to the sides of the filament, which is prolonged into a mucro at the summit. Ovary superior, smooth, 5-celled, polysporous; the cells are almost biparted by placentæ which project from the inner angle, and to whose edges the ovula are attached. Style single, subulate. Stigma simple. Berry globose, embraced at the base by the calyx, and acuminated by the persistent style; 5-celled, many seeded.

Obs.—In general habit and in the texture of the leaves this plant has some resemblance to Dyospyros, but differs widely in fructification.

IXONANTHES.—W. J.

Calyx 5-passim 6-partitus, foliolis subrotundis. Corolla 5 vel 6-petala, glutinosa. Stamina 10 vel 20. Nectarium germen cingens. Stylus 1. Capsula supera, calyce corollaque persistentibus cincta ovato-acuminata, 5-locularis, 5-valvis, valvularum marginibus introflexis. Semina singulo loculo duo, margini interiori dissepimentorum affixa, compressa, in alam membranaceam producta. Albumen semini conforme, embryone inverso foliaceo, plano.

Arbores, foliis alternis simplicibus, floribus, dichotome corymbosis axillaribus.

IXONANTHES RETICULATA.

Floribus decandris, foliis integerrimis.

Found at Tappanuly, on the West Coast of Sumatra.

A tree with smooth compressed branchlets. Leaves alternate, petiolate, elliptic oblong, emarginate, somewhat attenuated to the base, entire, smooth, firm and rigid, with thick revolute edges, shining above, rather glaucous beneath, veins reticulate, about 3 inches long. Petioles short, flattened above. Stipules minute, deciduous. Peduncles axillary on the younger shoots, much longer than the leaves, smooth, dichotomous at the summit, with a pedicel in the bifurcation, bearing generally about 7 flowers, which are small and green. Calyx 5-parted, segments rounded. Corolla glutinous as well as the calyx, 5-petaled, petals roundish. Stamina 10; filaments inserted below the petals; anthers yellow, 2-celled. Ovary surrounded at the base by a yellow fleshy nectarial ring, 5-celled, 10-seeded. Style erect. Stigma capitate. Capsule surrounded at the base by the persistent calyx and corolla, somewhat enlarged, oblong, pointed, smooth, 5-valved, 5-celled, septa formed by the introflexed margins of the valves, cells 2-seeded, but frequently only one comes to perfection; they are separated from each other by a ridge which projects from the middle of the valves. Seeds compressed, oblong, angular, winged at the lower end. Albumen conform to the seed. Embryo inverse, central. Cotyledons flat, oval. Radicle superior, cylindrical, not so long as the cotyledons.

IXONANTHES ICOSANDRA.

Floribus icosandris, foliis crenatis.

Found in the interior of Bencoolen.

A tree. Leaves alternate or scattered, short-petioled, lanceolate oblong, emarginate, dentato crenate, very smooth, shining above; about 6 inches long. Stipules small, deciduous. Peduncles axillary, nearly as long as the leaves, bearing a trichotomous umbel or corymb of greenish flowers. Bracts small. Calyx 5–6-parted. Corolla 5–6-petaled, glutinous as well as the calyx, petals spreading, subrotund, pale, and somewhat transparent. Stamina 20, much longer than the corolla. Nectarial ring crenate on the margin by the compression of the filaments which are inserted round it. Ovary 5–6-celled, each cell containing 2 ovula. Style a little longer than the stamina. Stigma capitate. Capsule ovate, pointed smooth, 5–6-celled, 5–6-valved, margins of the valves introflexed. Seeds 2 in each cell, attached by their middle to the inner edge of the valvular partitions, oblong, membranaceous to both ends, bifid at the lower.

CHIONOTRIA.—W. J.

Decandria Monogynia.

Calyx 5-partitus inferus. Corolla 5-petala. Stamina 10, erecta. Ovarium 2 loculare 2 sporum, ovulis pendulis. Stylus 1. Stigme capitatum. Bacca monosperma. Semen exalbuminosum apice umbilicatum. Cotyledonibus maximis convexo-planis, radiculâ superâ minimâ.

Frutex, foliis simplicibus oppositis pellucido punctatis, racemis axillaribus.

Genus Aurantiis affine.

CHIONOTRIA RIGIDA.

Native of Pulo Pinang.

A shrub with corrugated grey bark. Leaves opposite, very short-petioled, ovate lanceolate, acuminate, narrow at the base, very entire, very smooth, pellucidly punctate. Stipules subulate, acute. Racemes axillary, erect, rigid, branched, strict, shorter than the leaves, pedicels short, rigid, many-flowered. Flowers greenish, inconspicuous. Bracts very small. Calyx very small, 5-parted. Corolla a little longer than the calyx, 5-petaled. Stamina 10, exsert, erect. Anthers incumbent. Ovarium superior, 2-celled, 2-seeded, seeds pendulous. Style thick, as long as the stamina. Stigma capitate, obtuse. Berry of the size of a cherry, snow-white, globular, and somewhat flattened, umbilicate, consisting of a spongy farinaceous pulp, and containing a single large round seed. Seed globose, attached superiorly and there umbilicate. Integument coriaceous, marked with veins which diverge from the umbilicus. Albumen none. Embryo inverse, conform to the seed. Cotyledons plano-convex, of a deep green colour, somewhat rugose externally, and punctate on the inner surface. Radicle superior, obverse to the umbilicus, short, straight, cylindrical, obtuse, covered with ferruginous down; it is elongated into a short conical plumule.

SPHALANTHUS.—W. J.

Decandria Monogynia. N. O. Combretaceæ.—Br.

Calyx tubolosus, hinc gibbus, deciduus, limbo 5-partito. Corolla 5-petala, summo tubo calycis inserta et ejusdem laciniis alterna. Stamina 10, corolla breviora. Stylus tubo calycis hinc accretus. Ovarium uniloculare, ovulis paucis ab apice loculi pendulis. Capsula 5-alata, monasperma, semine 5-angulato. Semen exalbuminosum, cotyledonibus convexo-planis, radicula minimâ conicâ.

SPHALANTHUS CONFERTUS.

Kayu sumang.

A shrub with round nearly smooth branches. Leaves generally alternate, large and reflexly bifarious, short-petioled, ovate oblong, acuminate, subcordate at the base, entire, very smooth. Petioles short, somewhat recurved. Stipules none. Spikes 1–3, terminal, bending in an opposite direction from the leaves. Flowers crowded, sessile. Bracts lanceolate acute, much shorter than the flowers. Calyx superior, very long, tubular, gibbous on one side below, reddish and somewhat tomentose without, limb 5-parted, somewhat reflex, laciniæ acute, broader at the base. Corolla 5-petaled, white at first, becoming red after expansion, a little longer than the calyx, petals ovate oblong, acute. Stamina 10, inserted in a double series on the calyx, erect, shorter than the corolla; anthers oblong, yellow. Ovary small, oblong, 1-celled, containing 3 pendulous ovula, attached by filaments to the summit of the cell. Style green, filiform, rather longer than the stamina, adhering to or concrete with the tube of the calyx on one side along its whole length. Stigma simple. Capsule large, not crowned with the calyx, oblong, with 5 membranaceous wings, smooth, 1-celled, 1-seeded. Seed oblong, with 5 obtuse angles. Integument membranaceous, easily separated. Albumen none. Embryo conform to the seed. Cotyledons plano-convex, angled exteriorly. Radicle conical, very small.

Obs.—The structure of the seed is here different from what generally obtains in the Combretaceæ, the cotyledons being solid, not convolute.

PYRRHANTHUS.—W. J.

Decandria Monogynia. N.O. Combretaceæ.—Br.

Calyx 5-fidus, superus, persistens. Corolla 5-petala, calyce longior. Stamina 5–10, erecta, corollâ duplo longiora. Ovarium uniloculare, ovulis 3–5 pendulis. Drupa caryophylliformis, calyce coronata ; nuce oblonga monospermâ.

Arbor litorea inter Rhizophoras crescens ; foliis crassis ad apices ramorum confertis, floribus subcorymbosis.

PYRRHANTHUS LITTOREUS.

Malay, Miri batu, and in Sumatra Kayu api-api.

Native of Sumatra and the Malay Peninsula, growing among mangroves in salt swamps and near the mouths of rivers. It is one of the most ornamental trees that occur in these situations.

It grows to be a large tree, generally with an irregular crooked trunk. Leaves irregularly crowded at the extremities of the branches, which are rough with their persistent vestiges, subsessile, cuneiform, retuse, attenuated at the base into a very short petiole, obtusely crenate, often nearly entire, smooth, thick and fleshy, almost veinless. Stipules none. Racemes short, simple, terminal, subcorymbose. Flowers pedicellate, crowded. Bracts 2, small, acute, at the base of each flower. Calyx superior, 5-cleft, segments erect, thick, rather obtuse. Corolla crimson, 5-petaled, petals spreading, twice as long as the calyx, acute. Stamina varying in number from 5 to 10, erect, twice as long as the corolla, filaments red, subulate; anthers oblong, purple, attached by the middle. Ovary inferior, about the size and shape of a clove, 1-celled, containing from 3 to 5 ovula, which are pendulous from the top of the cell. Style 1. Berry or drupe somewhat compressed, obtusely angled, crowned by the thick persistent calyx; nut oblong, with 2 prominent angles, 1-seeded. Seed exalbuminous. Embryo inverse. Cotyledons convolute.

Obs.—The number of the stamina is very variable, 7 is perhaps the most frequent; 5 and 6 are common, but 10, the complete number, is rare. The number of ovula varies also. The genus is most nearly related to Laguncularia of Gærtner, but seems to differ in its corolla and stamina. It has some resemblance to Kada kandel (Rheed, "H. Mal." vi. p. 67, t. 37), a figure which has not, I believe, been quoted, and may possibly be another species of this genus. Kayu api-api is the name generally given to this tree in Sumatra, but is applied by Rumphius to his Mangium album ("H. A." iii. p. 115, t. 66), which is a species of Avicennia, probably the A. resinifera of Forster, known in Sumatra by the name of Pelandok kayu. It appears to be distinct from A. tomentosa, having lanceolate acute leaves, white beneath, but not tomentose, and the fruit being much smaller.

PHALERIA.—W. J.

Octandria Monogynia.

Perianthium coloratum, tubulosum, inferum, limbo 4-partito. Stamina 8, exserta. Ovarium biloculare, 2-sporum, ovulis pendulis. Stigma capitatum. Bacca bilocularis, disperma. Semina exalbuminosa, embryone inverso.

Frutex, foliis suboppositis, floribus axillaribus.

This genus is related to the Thymeleæ, but differs in having a bilocular ovary and fruit.

PHALERIA CAPITATA.—W. J.

Native of Sumatra.

A shrub with smooth branches. Leaves opposite, or subopposite, short petioled, ovate lanceolate, terminated by a long, sharp acumen, entire, very smooth, 8 inches long. Petioles thickened. Stipules none. Peduncles axillary, sometimes from the axils of fallen leaves, very short, bearing a head or umbel of sessile flowers which is embraced by an involucre composed of several oblong-ovate leaflets or bracts. Flowers large and white, resembling those of the jasmine. Perianth inferior, tube long, faux pervious, smooth, limb 4-parted, segments ovate. Stamina 8, inserted on the faux, exsert, rather long; anthers 2-lobed. Ovary embraced by a thin white nectarial cup, oblong, attenuated into a style, 2-celled, cells monosporous, ovula attached to the summit of the cell by a thread, which, passing along the back of the ovulum, is inserted into its base, so that the ovulum seems as if doubled upon its filament. Style a little shorter than the stamina. Stigma capitate, papilose. Berries crowded, somewhat pear-shaped, rounded above, acute at the base, cortical, 2-celled, 2-seeded. Seed exalbuminous, embryo inverse, cotyledons plano-convex; radicle small, superior.

PTERNANDRA.—W. J.

Octandria Monogynia.

Calyx ovatus, limbo quadridentato. Corolla 4-petala. Stamina octo, antheris introflexis, compressis, basi postice calcaratis, bilocularibus, loculis longitudinaliter dehiscentibus. Ovarium calyci infra adnatum, 4-loculare, polysporum, placentis parietalibus. Stylus declinatus. Bacca polysperma.

Habitus Melastomarum, foliis oppositis trinerviis, floribus paniculatis.

PTERNANDRA CŒRULESCENS.

Native of Pulo Pinang.

A large smooth shrub, with round branches. Leaves opposite, short petioled or subsessile, ovate, acuminate, tapering at the base into short petioles, very entire, very smooth; coriaceous, paler beneath, with 3 strong nerves, and 2 less conspicuous along the margins; the transverse veins are few and not prominent. Stipules none, but the petioles are connected by an interpetiolar line. Panicles oppositely corymbose, short, terminal, sometimes also from the upper axils. Peduncles 4-sided, smooth. Bracts small. Calyx united to the ovarium beneath, ovate, reticulately squamous, almost entire or obsoletely 4-toothed. Corolla blue, lighter at the margin, 4-petaled, petals ovate, acuminate, inserted into the calyx. Stamina 8, blue; filaments nearly erect, incurved at the apex. Anthers large, pointing inwards, compressed, elongated behind into an acumen or spur, cells anteriorly gibbous and bursting longitudinally. The anthers, before expansion, are turned downwards, as in the Melastomæ, but their points do not reach much below the top of the ovary. Style declinate, about as long as the stamina. Stigma conical and rather obtuse. Ovary adnate to the calyx, 4-celled, polysporous, ovula attached to convex parietal placentæ. Berry 4-celled, many-seeded.

Obs.—In general habit and appearance this plant has a close resemblance to my Melastoma glauca, and at first sight appears only to differ in having smaller flowers, and leaves with less distinct nerves and veins. In the structure of the anthers, however, it differs essentially from Melastoma, and has some affinity to Memecylon; the fruit and mode of placentation differs from both. The ovary might either be considered inferior, or superior and adnate to the calyx; the analogy of Melastoma has led me to assume the latter.

MEMECYLON PANICULATUM.—W. J.

Foliis petiolatis ovatis obtuso-acuminatis, paniculis axillaribus brachiatis.

Found at Tappanuly and on Pulo Bintangor, on the West Coast of Sumatra.

A large shrub, with grey bark and smooth branches. Leaves opposite, short-petioled, ovate or oblong ovate, terminating in a rather obtuse acumen, entire, very smooth, shining above, paler beneath, with pretty distinct nerves, which unite into a line near the margin; 7 or 8 inches long. Petioles short and thick. Stipules none. Panicles axillary, sometimes from the axils of fallen leaves, oppositely branched. Peduncles 4-sided, purplish; there is generally a single 1-flowered pedicel placed immediately below each of the principal divisions of the panicle, springing as it were from the same point. Flowers numerous, bluish. Bracts minute. Calyx nearly entire. Corolla light blue, 4-petaled, petals broad, acute. Stamina 8; filaments subulate; anthers blue, prolonged behind into a thick spur, the upper surface of which is marked with a nectariferous cavity; cells on the anterior surface perpendicular to the spur, which is nearly horizontal, bursting longitudinally. Ovary 1-celled, containing about 8 erect ovula attached to a small protuberance in the base of the cell, its disc marked with radii corresponding to the faces of the anthers, which are incurved before expansion. Style subulate. Stigma acute. Berry globular, 1-seeded. Seed erect, exalbuminous. Cotyledons peltate, hemispherical, their flat surfaces a little irregular or waved. Radicle erect, rising perpendicularly between the cotyledons to their centre, where it is inserted.

Obs.—This peculiar structure of the embryo is different from what obtains in all the other species of Memecylon that I have examined, where the cotyledons in place of being solid and hemispherical, are foliaceous and contortuplicate.

OCTAS.—W. J.

Octandria Monogynia.

Calyx 8-partitus. Corolla 8-loba. Stamina octo, laciniis corollæ alterna. Stigma sessile, 8-radiatum. Bacca 8-sperma, supera.

Frutex, foliis simplicibus alternis, spicis axillaribus.

OCTAS SPICATA.

Found at Tappanuly on the West Coast of Sumatra.

A shrub, with long branches, the young parts tomentose. Leaves alternate, petiolate, lanceolate oblong, acuminate, entire, smooth, 5 inches long. Stipules, small, acute. Spikes or racemes 2 from each axil, rather shorter than the leaves, many-flowered; pedicles in threes. Flowers small, white. Bracts minute. Calyx small, 8-parted. Corolla monopetalous, spreading, divided at the margin into 8 round lobes. Stamina 8, as long as the lobes of the corolla; anthers white, subsaggitate. Ovary superior, globular, 8-celled, 8-seeded. Stigma large, sessile, composed of 8 fleshy coadunate lobes. Berries about the size of peppercorns, purple, containing 8 seeds, which are angled interiorly.

CŒLOPYRUM.—W. J.
Octandria Monogynia.

Calyx 4-partitus. Corolla 4-petala. Stamina 8, alterna breviora. Stigma obtusum subsessile. Drupa supera, nuce biloculari, loculo exteriore lunato alterum fovente. Semen unicum, loculo altero vacuo.

Arbor, ramis apice foliosis, foliis simplicibus, floribus racemosis.

CŒLOPYRUM CORIACEUM,

Těrěntang. *Malay.*
In forests in the neighbourhood of Bencoolen.

A tree with thick branches, which are foliose at their summit. Leaves alternate, petiolate, elliptic, obtuse or emarginate, entire with reflexed margins, firm and leathery, smooth above, pale and tomentose beneath, costate with strong parallel ribs or nerves, 10 –12 inches long. Petioles about 3 inches long, marginate and flattened above. Racemes axillary, erect, shorter than the leaves, branched; flowers numerous, yellowish, small and inconspicuous, in small racemules or spikelets. Bracts small, acute. Calyx inferior, spreading. Corolla 4-petaled, petals longer than the calyx, ovate. Stamina 8, the alternate ones shorter. Ovary surrounded and nearly immersed in a large fleshy nectarial ring, whose sides are angled by the compression of the filaments. Style scarce any. Stigma obtuse. Drupe ovate, acute, smaller than an olive, containing a single nut. Nut 2-celled, cells unequal and dissimilar, the outer and lower crescent-shaped, and embracing the other, which is smaller, oblong and always empty; the larger cell contains a single conform seed.

Obs.—The structure of the fruit is very peculiar; the empty cell is placed obliquely in the upper part of the nut, the fertile one is, as it were, wrapped round the other. The extreme minuteness of the ovary prevented me from satisfactorily ascertaining its structure.

PETROCARYA EXCELSA.—W. J.
Heptandria Monogynia. N. O. Rosaceæ.—Juss.

Foliis oblongis acuminatis glabris, calycibus ore obliquis, staminibus undecim fertilibus.

Kayu balam pangkat. *Malay.*
A large timber tree. Leaves alternate, short, petioled oblong, acuminate, entire, smooth 4–5 inches long. Stipules longer than

the petioles, deciduous. Racemes axillary and terminal, forming a panicle towards the top, strict, erect, little branched; flowers very short, pedicelled and appressed to the principal peduncle; the whole ferruginous and tomentose. Bracts broad, deciduous. Cályx infundibular, ferruginous and tomentose, oblique at the mouth, furnished with a ring of stiff hairs which point downwards, lowest on the side to which the fertile stamina and ovary are attached, limb 5-parted, subreflex. Corolla 5-petaled, inserted on the mouth of the calyx and scarcely longer than its limb, petals subrotund. Stamina 11, fertile, twice as long as the petals, inserted in one phalanx along the lower edge of the mouth of the calyx, on the upper edge is a ring with 8 processes or abortive stamina. Ovary adnate to the side of the calyx below the fertile stamina, densely pilose, disporous. Style lateral, inserted near the base of the ovary, as long as the stamina. Stigma simple. Drupe enclosed in the enlarged calyx, which becomes adnate to it and crowned by its persistent limb; obliquely ovate, about the size of a filbert. Nut smooth, 1-seeded, with an abortive cell generally above the fertile one. Seed curved, corresponding to the cell, albuminous; embryo cylindrical inverse; radicle superior, clavato-cylindrical, longer than the ligulate cotyledons.

PETROCARYA SUMATRANA.—W. J.

Foliis elliptico-oblongis subtus canescentibus, calycis ore regulari, staminibus septem fertilibus.

A tree. Branchlets pilose. Leaves alternate, short petioled, elliptic-oblong, 6–8 inches long, terminating in a bluntish acumen, acute at the base, entire, the adult leaves smooth above, somewhat hoary, with close short wool beneath, the younger ones covered with deciduous pubescence above, nerves prominent beneath, veins reticulate. Petioles about a quarter of an inch in length, stipules longer than the petioles, oblong, acute. Racemes axillary and terminal, shorter than the leaves, tomentose; pedicels mostly 3-flowered, divaricate. Bracts rather large, concave, at the base of the peduncles, pedicels and flowers. Calyx tubular or campanulate, tomentose without, pilose at the faux, which is equal and regular, limb spreading, 5-parted, segments acute. Corolla 5-petaled, white, petals inserted on the mouth of the calyx, and as long as its segments. Stamina 14, of which 7 upper are fertile arranged in one phalanx, and the opposite 7 abortive; filaments short, flat, anthers roundish, 2-lobed. Ovary adnate to the upper side of the tube or calyx, pilose, 2-celled, containing 2 erect ovula. Style lateral, inserted at the base of the ovary, as long as the stamina. Stigma capitate.

Obs.—These two species, though nearly related, present abundant points of distinction. In the P. excelsa the leaves are smaller, smoother, and less strongly nerved, while the flowers are larger, the racemes longer, more erect and compact, and the stamina longer and more numerous than in the P. Sumatrana.

WORMIA EXCELSA.—W. J.

N. O. Dilleniaceæ.—DEC.

Foliis ellipticis acutis denticulatis, pedunculis multifloris oppositifoliis, pedicellis clavatis.

Kayu sipur. *Malay.*

In forests near Bencoolen.

A large tree. Leaves alternate, petiolate, from elliptic ovate to elliptic-oblong, acute, denticulate or obsoletely serrate, smooth, 8–12 inches long. Petioles deeply channelled above. Peduncles oppositifolious at the summit of the branches, many-flowered; pedicels alternate, clavate. Flowers large, yellow, 3 inches in diameter. Calyx 5-leaved, leaflets subrotund, concave, unequal. Corolla 5-petaled, spreading, petals ovate oblong. Stamina very numerous, the outer ones yellow, spreading, shorter than the inner, which are purple, erect and recurved above; anthers, lobes adnate to the filament. Ovaries 6–8, connate, polysporous. Stigmas as many, flat, recurved, diverging. Capsules 6–8, whitish, semi-transparent, bursting at the inner angle, and then spreading, containing no pulp. Seeds attached to the edges of the capsules, enveloped in a red aril.

Obs.—This is a large forest tree, which yields excellent timber, the wood having some resemblance to oak.

WORMIA PULCHELLA.—W. J.

Foliis obovatis integerrimis, pedunculis solitariis axillaribus unifloris, floribus pentagynis.

Found at Natal.

A small tree. Branches round, rather smooth. Leaves alternate, petiolate, oblong obovate, rounded at top, with a short round point, sometimes retuse, very entire, very smooth, thick and rather coriaceous, about 5 inches long. Petioles smooth, channelled and marginate above, less than an inch in length. Peduncles axillary and subterminal, solitary, 1-flowered, angled, about 2 inches long. Bracts none. Calyx 5-leaved, leaflets subrotund, smooth. Corolla 5-petaled. Stamina numerous. Ovaries 5, collected into a globe, terminating in as many flat, reflexed diverging styles. Stigmas thickened. Capsules 5, of a light semi-transparent rose-colour, bursting at their angles, and then spreading like a corolla. Seeds attached to the inner edges of the capsules, a few only coming to perfection, partly embraced by a red pulpy aril, which originates from the umbilicus.

Obs.—This species is very beautiful when in fruit, from the delicacy of the colours which the capsules exhibit.

FICUS OVOIDEA.—W. J.

Foliis cuneato-obovatis apice rotundatis, nervo medio dichotomo, fructibus axillaribus binis pedunculatis.

Found at Singapore, and on several parts of the West Coast of Sumatra and its islands.

A small tree, with smooth brownish bark. Leaves alternate, petiolate, cuneato-obovate, rounded above, attenuated to the base, very entire, very smooth, the middle nerve dichotomous; from $1\frac{1}{2}$ to 2 inches long. Petioles nearly half an inch long, round, with a slight furrow above, and covered with grey bark like the branchlets. Peduncles in pairs, sometimes solitary, axillary, shorter than the petioles, 1-flowered. Involucres embraced at the base by 3 short subrotund bracts, nearly globose, smooth, shut at the mouth by scales, and containing numerous pedicellate florets. Seeds naked, hard.

Obs.—The leaves are peculiar in having the middle nerve dichotomous, a character by which this species may be readily distinguished from its congeners.

FICUS DELTOIDEA.—W. J.

Foliis obcuneato-deltoideis apice latis v. retusis, nervo medio dichotomo, fructibus axillaribus binis pedunculatis.

A small tree, native of Sumatra, and very similar to the preceding, but having the leaves proportionally broader, more decidedly deltoid, and retuse or truncate, not rounded at top; the peduncles also are in pairs from the axils of the leaves and longer than the petioles. The breadth of the leaves is generally greater than their length in this species, which is not the case with their preceding; they are, however, precisely similar in their leathery texture, and in having the nerve dichotomous and not prominent.

FICUS RIGIDA.—W. J.

Foliis ovatis lineari-acuminatis rigidis, fructibus pedunculatis axillaribus globosis glabris.

Seribulan. *Malay.*

Sumatra, &c.

A tree, with grey cinereous bark and smooth branchlets.

Leaves alternate, petiolate, ovate or obovate, with long linear acumina which are obtuse or emarginate at the point, attenuated to the base, 3-4 inches long, entire, firm and rigid, smooth, shining above, rugose, with reticulate veins beneath; nerves prominent beneath, the lowermost pair springing from the base and running along the margins until they anastomose with the upper ones. Petioles brown with cracked skin. Berries 1-3, axillary, pedicelled, pedicels shorter than the petioles, smooth. Involucra globose, orange-coloured when ripe, smooth, with some whitish spots as large as a currant. Florets numerous, pedicellate. Female ones with a 4-5-parted perianth. Style inserted laterally. Seed naked.

Obs.—The bark of this species is fibrous, and I am informed that it is employed in Menangkabau in the fabrication of a coarse kind of paper.

JONESIA.—ROXB.

N. O. Leguminosæ.

Calyx tubolosus, basi bibracteatus, limbo 4-lobo. Petalla nulla. Stamina 3-7, summo tubo calycis inserta. Ovarium pedicellatum, pedicello calyci hinc accreto. Legumen oligospermum.

Frutices, foliis abrupte pinnatis, floribus fasciculatis.

The alteration I have here made in the terms of the generic description from that given by Roxburgh will remove all obscurity as to the true affinities of this genus, and establish its near relation to Macrolobium. The bracteal leaflets (the diphyllous calyx of Roxburgh) are found in both genera, though less conspicuous and not coloured in Macrolobium, the stamina are similarly inserted on the mouth of the tubular calyx, and are equally variable in number; the pedicel of the ovary is accrete to the calyx in both, and the only difference consists in the presence or absence of the single petal which is found in Macrolobium and is wanting in Jonesia.

JONESIA DECLINATA.—W. J.

Foliis 6-8 jugis, foliolis oblongis, floribus fasciculato-paniculatis tetrandris.

Kayu siturun. *Malay.*

A small straggling tree found generally in thickets; native of Sumatra.

Branches depending, whence the native name. Leaves alternate, composed of from 6 to 8 pair of leaflets, of which the lowest are situated on the base of the petiole; they are opposite, from 10 to 12 inches in length, oblong, rounded at the extremity, but terminating in a short thick recurved point, entire on the margin, smooth. Petiole roundish, thickened at the base. Stipule intrapetiolar, embracing the stem, broad at the base, ovate and pointed. Flowers in lateral fasciculate panicles, 2 subrotund bracts below each flower. Pedicels slender, the whole very smooth and delicate, and of a light semi-transparent red colour. Calyx reddish yellow, tubular; tube narrow; limb 4-parted, flat, segments subrotund, about the same size as the bracts. Corolla none. Stamina 4, more than twice the length of the calyx and inserted on its tube, their upper part deep red. Anthers deep purple, subrotund, 2-celled, each cell streaked with white. There are no rudiments of abortive stamina. Germen pedicellate, pedicel accrete to the tube of the calyx. Style long, red. Stigma round. Legume pedicellate, flat, compressed, containing several seeds.

The large branches of delicate flesh-coloured flowers render this a very beautiful shrub during the period of infloresence.

BAUHINIA EMARGINATA.—W. J.

Foliis cordatis subrotundo-ovalibus glaberrimis acumine brevi obtuso emarginato, floribus octandris, staminibus tribus superioribus fertilibus.

Dadâub. *Malay.*

Native of Sumatra.

A strong woody climber. Leaves alternate, petiolate, cordate, subrotund oval, terminating in a short blunt emarginate acumen, very entire, 4 inches long, 7-9 nerved with reticulate veins, very smooth. Petioles rather short. Cirrhi long, simple, revolute. Racemes terminal or sometimes lateral, corymbose, many flowered; pedicels long, tomentose. Calyx 5-parted, tomentose, bursting into 2 or 3 segments. Corolla large, 5-petaled, spreading, petals nearly equal, unguiculate. Stamina 8; 3 superior fertile, longer, with large 2-lobed anthers; 4 inferior short, with small abortive anthers; the fifth and lowest being a little longer, and entirely sterile. Ovary tomentose. Style about the length of the fertile stamina. Stigma peltate, round.

Obs.—The form of the leaf is very peculiar, and readily distinguishes this species from the others.

BAUHINIA BIDENTATA.—W. J.

Foliis cordatis acuminatis apice bidentatis glaberrimis, corymbis terminalibus, floribus octandris, staminibus tribus superioribus fertilibus.

Native of the Malayan forests, where it climbs over trees, and shows its flame-coloured blossoms on their very summits.

Shrubby, climbing far over the trees in its neighbourhood; bark brown; branches round, flexuose; branchlets covered with ferruginous tomentum. Leaves alternate, petiolate, cordate, acute, bifid at the point (not 2-lobed), divisions approximate, with a short thread interposed, very entire, 7-nerved, very smooth, the younger ones rather silky beneath with ferruginous deciduous hairs. Petioles thickened at the top and base. Tendrils simple, revolute. Corymbs terminal. Pedicels clavate, striated, tomentose. Calyx 5-parted, tomentose, for the most part bursting irregularly into three divisions. Corolla orange-coloured, becoming red after expansion, 5-petaled, petals nearly equal, subrotund, unguiculate, spreading. Stamina 8, ascending, of which the 3 upper are longer and fertile, and the 3 lowest short and sterile. Anthers subrotund. Ovary pedicellate, compressed, oblong, containing from 6–8 ovula. Style declinate, incurved at the point. Stigma large, capitate and glutinous.

Obs.—This species is at once distinguished by the peculiar form of the leaves, which are not 2-lobed as usual in the genus, but have the apex divided so as to make the leaf terminate in 2 acute points. The flowers are large and showy.

INGA BUBALINA.—W. J.

N. O. Mimoseæ.—BR.

Inermis, foliis conjugato-pinnatis, foliolis bijugis glaberrimis, capitulis paucifloris paniculatis, paniculis axillaribus et terminalibus, legumine recto cylindrico.

Bua karbau. *Malay.*

Sumatra, &c.

A tree, unarmed, with grey bark. Leaves alternate, conjugato pinnate, leaflets 2-paired, ovate, with rather an obtuse acumen, very entire, very smooth, nerves lucid, the upper pair of leaflets the largest. Primary petiole short, thickened at the base, bearing a gland at the point, secondary petioles without glands. Capitula few-flowered, panicled. Panicles axillary and terminal, peduncled, divaricate, shorter than the leaves. Bracts small. Calyx short, tubular, 5-dentate. Corolla white, much longer than the calyx, campanulate, 5-parted, segments spreading. Stamina many, monadelphous at the base, long and white. Style filiform, as long as the stamina. Ovary pedicellate. Legume dark green, straight, cylindrical, about 4 inches long, thick, obtuse, many-seeded, fetid. Seeds crowded, orbicular, piled one above the other and thus flattened above and below by their mutual compression.

Obs.—This species is nearly allied in habit and inflorescence to the Inga Jiringa ("Mal. Misc." vol. i.), but differs in the shape of the legume, which has a very offensive smell, but is eaten by the natives in the same manner as that of the Petek (Acacia graveolens, W. J.). Karbau in Malay signifies the Buffalo, whence the specific name.

INGA CLYPEARIA.—W. J.

Inermis, ramulis acutangulis, foliis bipinnattis, foliolis 10-jugis rhomboideis subtus tomentosis, paniculis terminalibus, leguminibus contortis rubris.

Clypearia rubra. Rumph. "Amb." iii. p. 176, t. 112.
Jering muñet. *Malay.*

A large tree. Branchlets smooth, acutely 5-angled, almost winged. Leaves alternate, bipinnate; pinnæ about 4 pair; leaflets about 10 pair, rhomboidal, inequilateral, rather acute, entire, smooth above, tomentose or silky and glaucous beneath, they are of unequal size, the uppermost often 2 inches long. Petiole or rachis acutely 4 or 5 angled, thickened at the base, eglandular. Panicles large, terminal; peduncles fascicled. Flowers white, pedicellate, in small capitula or heads. Calyx small, 5-parted. Corolla much longer than the calyx, quinquefid. Stamina numerous, monadelphous at the base. Style one. Legume red, flat, 2-valved, spirally contorted, containing many subrotund somewhat compressed black seeds.

Obs.—This species, which agrees with that described by Rumphius, is found in forests in the neighbourhood of Bencoolen, but I am not aware that it is there put to any particular use. These two species, together with the I. Jiringa, might perhaps with equal propriety be refered to Acacia, as the seeds are not arilled, though the legume (as in I. bubalina) is fleshy and esculent; the stamina are those of Inga and the paniculate inflorescence is more frequent in that genus than in Acacia. The distinction between these two sections of the Linnean genus Mimosa is an artificial one, and the characters of the present species are in some degree intermediate between the two.

TABERNÆMONTANA MACROCARPA.—W. J.

Foliis ovato-ellipticis basi attenuatis, corymbis terminalibus dichotomis, folliculis maximis subglobosis.

In the interior of Bencoolen.

A tree, branches smooth, somewhat compressed in contrary directions between each pair of leaves. Leaves opposite, petiolate, from elliptic-ovate to elliptic-lanceolate, tapering to the base, broader above with a short point, very entire, very smooth; nerves transverse, uniting into submarginal arches; 10–12 inches long. Petioles embracing the stem and uniting with the base of the opposite one. Peduncles 3–4, terminal, dividing at their summits into dichotomous corymbs. Flowers rather large, yellowish. Calyx 5-cleft, erect, thick. Corolla much longer than the calyx; tube gibbous, almost globose at the base, narrowing upwards; limb rotate, 5-parted; segments oblong, oblique. Stamina 5, within the tube. Ovary double. Styles 2, shorter than the stamina. Stigma small. Follicles 2, baccate, as large as citrons, red, diverging, subglobose, exuding a milky juice when cut, with a ridge along the middle and one at each side which unite in a short blunt point, 1-celled, many-seeded; the cell is recurved into the form of a crescent. Seeds contained in red fleshy arils or lobules which are angled by mutual compression, oblong, chrysaloid, hollowed on the one side with incurved rounded edges, convex on the other and longitudinally corrugated. Embryo contained in a conform albumen; cotyledons flat, round, cordate; radicle centripetal, cylindrical, longer than the cotyledons.

FAGRŒA CARNOSA.—W. J.

Foliis subrotundo-ovatis mucronatis carnosis, floribus terminalibus solitariis.

In the neighbourhood of Bencoolen.

A parasitic shrub growing on trees, with smooth greyish bark and somewhat dichotomous branches. Leaves opposite, petiolate, subrotund with a short reflexed point, entire with reflexed margins, very smooth, thick and fleshy. Petioles compressed, embracing the branch and furnished with an intrapetiolar ligula or stipule. Flowers terminal, solitary, nearly sessile, embraced at the base by a few sheathing bracts. Calyx 5-parted. Corolla of a dull yellowish white colour; tube about 4 inches long, expanding into a 5-parted limb. Stamina 5, rising a little above the tube; anthers large. Style little more than half the length of the tube. Stigma 4-lobed. Berry as large as a small egg, seated on the persistent calyx, ovate, rather pointed, 2-celled, many-seeded; seeds nidulant.

Obs.—This is the fifth species of Fagrœa that I have met with in the Malay Islands; the others have been already described in Roxburgh's "Flora Indica." The F. racemosa grows to be a small tree, and the F. volubilis, doubtfully proposed by Dr. Wallich as a distinct species, is the same plant. The F. auriculata is a large shrub, and from the size of its flowers is the most splendid of the genus. I originally met with it at Singapore, but have since found it also at Tappanuly. The following particulars may be added to the description given by Dr. Wallich.

F. Auriculata.—Flowers terminal, generally 3, rarely 5, on short thick pedicels, each embraced by 4 opposite calyculate bracts, of which the outer 2 are the smallest. Corolla very large, yellowish-white. Stamina inserted near the bottom of the tube. Stigma large and flattened. Ovary 2-celled, polysporous; the edges of the placentæ revolute. Fruit as large as a duck's egg, acuminated by part of the persistent style; seeds numerous, nidulant.

IXORA NERIIFOLIA.—W. J.

Foliis linearibus acuminatis glabris, corymbis terminalibus. Bunga Salûang. *Malay.*

Native of the West Coast of Sumatra.

A shrub, with round smooth branches. Leaves opposite, short petioled, linear, tapering to the point, acute, about 9 inches long, by little more than half an inch broad, entire, with revolute edges, very smooth. Stipules interpetiolar, subulate, longer than the petioles. Corymbs terminal, erect, trichotomous. Flowers red. Bracts small, acute. Calyx small, 4-toothed. Corolla tube long, slender; limb spreading, 4-parted, segments lanceolate, acute. Stamina 4, alternate with the laciniæ of the corolla. Style a little longer than the tube. Stigma clavate. Fruit a berry.

Obs.—The long narrow leaves readily distinguish this species; it is a handsome, delicate shrub.

LECANANTHUS.—W. J.

Pentandria Monogynia. N. O. Rubiaceæ.—Juss.

Calyx campanulatus, ampliatus, coloratus, irregulariter divisus. Corolla tubo brevi, limbo 5-partito. Ovarium biloculare, polysporum, placentis centralibus convexis. Stylus bifidus. Stigmata 2, linearia crassa. Fruticosa, floribus capitatis involucratis terminalibus, æstivatione valvatâ.

LECANANTHUS ERUBESCENS.

Found in the interior of Bencoolen.

A small erect shrub; stem 4-sided, 2 of the angles acute. Leaves opposite, short-petioled, ovate lanceolate, acute at both ends, rather attenuated to the point, entire, smooth; about 8 inches long. Stipules interpetiolar, large, ligulate, carinate towards the base. Flowers pale red, densely aggregated within the hypocrateriform cup of the involucre, forming a head which is terminal, nearly sessile, and turned backwards. Involucre monophyllous, entire. Pedicels none. Calyx superior, coloured, tomentose, thick and fleshy, much wider than the corol, expanding into from 2 to 4 irregular unequal obtuse lobes; the calyces of the outer flowers are often so much produced on one side as to seem bilabiate. Corolla, tube short, segments 5, acute, thick. Æstivation valvate. Stamina 5, inserted on the tube; anthers large. Ovary crowned with a prominent nectarial ring, 2-celled, polysporous; ovula arranged round central, semi-cylindrical placentæ. Style bifid. Stigmata 2, thick and linear.

PSILOBIUM.—W. J.

Pentandria Monogynia. **N. O.** *Rubiaceæ.*—Juss.

Calyx patens, 5-partitus. Corolla tubo brevi, limbo 5-partito. Stamina basi corollæ inserta. Stigma clavatum, 10-alatum, exsertum. Fructus cylindricus siliquæ formis, foliolis calycinis persistentibus coronatus, bilocularis, polyspermus. Semina duplici serie axi affixa.

Fruticosa, pedunculis axillaribus paucifloris, æstivatione valvatâ.

PSILOBIUM NUTANS.

Found in the interior of Bencoolen.

Stem erect, 4-sided, with rounded angles. Leaves opposite, petiolate, lanceolate, attenuated to both ends, acute, entire, smooth. Stipules interpetiolar, broad, acuminate, carinate. Peduncles axillary, drooping, bearing from 3 to 6 flowers. Bracts forming a kind of involucre at the base of the very short pedicels. Calyx superior, very large, composed of 5 leaflets or very deep segments, which are veined with red. Stamina 5. Filaments short; anthers long, erect. Style short. Stigma long, exsert, oblong-ovate, longitudinally 10-winged, the 5 alternate wings smaller. Fruit long, cylindrical, siliquose, crowned with the large persistent calyx, 2-celled, many-seeded; seeds arranged in a double series in each cell.

OPHIORRHIZA HETEROPHYLLA.—W. J.

Foliis oppositis subrotundo-ovatis, altero nano.

Found in the interior of Bencoolen.

This species is readily distinguished by the peculiarity of one of the opposite leaves being always dwarf or abortive; the other is subrotund-ovate, with a bluntish acumen, smooth, pale and whitish beneath. The stem is erect and tomentose. Flowers in a small terminal cyme. Capsule compressed, obcordate.

QUERCUS RACEMOSA.—W. J.

Foliis lato-lanceolatis integerrimis glaberrimis, spicis masculis paniculatis, fructibus spicatis nuce umbilicato-depressâ, calice fructûs tuberculato.

Punning-punning bungkus. *Malay.*

Native of Sumatra.

A large tree, with brownish bark. Branches smooth. Leaves alternate, short petioled, ovate-lanceolate, acuminate, attenuated to the petiole, very entire, very smooth, nerves well-marked and reddish beneath; 6–8 inches long. Stipules small, linear. Male spikes numerous, panicled, terminal, and from the axils of the upper leaves which are crowded round the thickened extremity of the branch, slender, hoary. Flowers sessile, aggregated. Female spikes at first terminal, becoming afterwards lateral by the shooting up of the branch. Flowers numerous, dense, sessile. *Male.*— Calyx 6-parted, segments acute. Stamina 15–20. The centre of the flower is occupied by a densely villous disc. *Female.*—Calyx rugose, turbinate, umbilicate. Ovary 3–5-celled, each cell containing 2 ovula attached by a thread to its summit. Acorns large, depressed, umbilicate, with a short mucro. Cup flat, embracing the nut for about half its height, nearly an inch in diameter, rough with angular imbricated tubercles, which are large towards the base, and become small towards the edge.

Obs.—This is a very splendid species, from the great size of the racemes and acorns. Punning-punning is the generic appellation of the oaks in Malay; in the Rejang dialect they are called Pasang.

QUERCUS URCEOLARIS.—W. J.

Foliis elliptico-oblongis acumine gracili integerrimis glaberrimis, fructibus spicatis, calyce fructûs subhemisphærico limbo patente.
Native of Sumatra.

A tree, with rough bark. Leaves alternate, petiolate, elliptic-oblong, terminated by a long slender acumen, very entire, smooth, coriaceous, pale beneath; 8–9 inches long. Fruit on lateral racemes. Acorns rounded and flattened at top, umbilicate in the centre and mucronate with the 3 short persistent styles, rather perpendicular at the sides, half embraced by the calyx, which is cup-shaped, marked on the outer surface with small acute scaly points concentrically arranged, and whose margin expands into a spreading, nearly entire, waved limb. The ovary is 3-celled, each cell containing 2 ovula, and is lodged in the bottom of the large funnel-shaped calyx. The acorn contains a single exalbuminous seed placed in a little obliquely.

Obs.—The spreading limb of the cups forms a good distinctive character, and renders this a very remarkable and curious species.

ARECA TIGILLARIA.—W. J.

Frondibus pinnatis, foliolis acutis, spadicibus ramosis, flore unico femineo inter duos masculos, fructibus globosis.
Nibong. *Malay.*

Abundant in Sumatra and the Malay Islands, where it is much used in the construction of houses, &c.

Trunk erect, generally thicker than that of the common Pinang (Areca catechu), armed, particularly on the lower part, with straight, slender, flattened spines. Fronds pinnate, leaflets linear, acuminate, reflexed at the edges so as to make the upper surface convex, smooth, with a few brownish scales on the middle nerve of the younger ones; they diminish in size to the top of the frond and the last 2 are partly united at their base. Stipes of the frond scaly while young, compressed, grooved above, the sheaths armed like the trunk. Spadix within the sheath of the frond, embracing the stem, flattened at the base, much branched; flower bearing branchlets about 2 feet long, drooping, the lower ones 3-4 together, the uppermost solitary or in pairs. Spathe single, completely enclosing the spadix before expansion, compressed, 2-edged, deciduous, partial spathes none. Flowers sessile, 1 female between 2 males, the latter considerably the largest and deciduous. *Male.*—Hermaphrodite. Perianth 6-parted, the outer leaflets small, the inner much longer, and acuminated with fine points. Stamina 6. Anthers sagitate. Ovary small, surmounted by 3 linear styles. *Female.*—Perianth 6-parted; leaflets nearly equal, rounder and shorter than those of the male. Stamina none. Ovary monosporous. Styles none. Stigmata 3. Fruit globose, about the size of a carbine bullet, of a deep purple colour when ripe, with a glaucous tint, containing under a reddish pulp a single smooth globular nut. Nut 1-seeded, having a thickened whitish scar on the side, and a small areola at the base opposite to the embryo. Seed solid; albumen ruminated. Embryo basilar, short, cylindrical, obtuse.

Obs.—This differs from the common Areca in the disposition of the flowers on the spadices, and in having the nut contained under a pulpy and not a fibrous covering. In A. catechu the ovary is likewise monosporous.

ENCHIDIUM.—W. J.

Monœcia Monadelphia. N. O. Euphorbiaceæ.—Juss.

Calyx 5-partitus. Corolla 5-partita. Nectarium glandulæ decem. *Mas.*—Filamentum columnare, 10-antheriferum; antheris radiatim patentibus. *Femina.*—Ovarium trilobum. Styli 3. Stigmata 6.

Flores masculi et feminei in eâdem spicâ.

ENCHIDIUM VERTICILLATUM.

Arbor spiculorum. Rumph. "Amb." iii. p. 167. t. 106.

Not unfrequent on hills in Sumatra and the Malay Islands.

A large shrub. I have not met with any that had attained to so great a size as mentioned by Rumphius. The leaves are arranged in a kind of irregular verticils at different distances along the branches, as exhibited in the figure quoted; on the young shoots they are sometimes irregularly disposed along the whole length; they are petiolate, lanceolate, acuminate, very entire, very smooth, firm and somewhat leathery, of various length, generally about 6 inches long by 2½ broad. Petioles from 1 to 2½ inches long, flattened above, striated. Spikes from among the upper verticils of leaves, bearing both male and female flowers, the former lowermost, all pedicellate. Calyx 5-parted. Corolla purple towards the centre, 5-parted, furnished with 10 callous nectaries or glands at the base. In the *male* the filament is columnar, bearing 10 anthers which diverge in a radiated circle round the summit. The *female* has a 3-lobed ovary surmounted by 3 styles with bifid stigmata.

Obs.—There can be little doubt of the identity of this plant with Rumphius's Arbor spicularum, of which he says he was never able to procure the flower. I have seen great numbers of these plants in the woods, but only once was successful in observing the flower, and have never met with the fruit. As the spike, however, fortunately contained both male and female flowers, its characters have been sufficiently determined to assign its proper place. It comes nearest to Cluytia, but differs in the corolla and in having 10 anthers with filaments united into a central column. Both its fructification and habit appear to distinguish it from all the present genera of the Euphorbiaceous family.

ANTIDESMA FRUTESCENS.—W. J.

Frutescens, foliis oblongo-ovalibus basi rotundatis supra glabris, racemis terminalibus et axillaribus subpaniculatis geminis solitariisque, nectarii glandulis quinis cum staminibus alternantibus.

Bencoolen.

A small diœcious shrub, not exceeding a few feet in height. Branchlets tomentose. Leaves alternate, petiolate, oblong oval, rounded and sometimes subcordate at the base, acute, sometimes terminated by a short mucro, or awn, entire, smooth above, subtomentose beneath, chiefly on the nerves; 3 inches long. Stipules long, subulate, acute. Racemes axillary and terminal, geminate and solitary, somewhat panicled, tomentose; when geminate, the outer raceme is simple, and the inner branched; male racemes generally longer than the leaves, female ones shorter. Pedicels solitary. Bracts shorter than the pedicels. *Male.*—Calyx 5-parted, tomentose. Nectary of 5 yellow pilose glands alternating with the stamina. Stamina 5; filaments much longer than the calyx; anthers bifid, cells bursting transversely on the summits of the lobes. Pistil abortive, pilose. *Female.*—Perianth 5-parted. Ovary superior, villous, oblong ovate, compressed, 1-celled, vesicular, containing 2 ovula, which are attached close together to one side near the top, and hang forward into the cell, which is in great part empty and inflated. Styles 2, 1 often bifid. Drupe subglobose, purplish, about the size of a peppercorn; nut 1–2 seeded.

Obs.—It has considerable resemblance to Roxburgh's A. pubescens; that, however, is a tree, while this is a small shrub. The most important difference appears to be in the nectary of the male flower.

SALACIA.—LINN.

This genus seems to require a little elucidation. It was originally referred to Gynandria, the fleshy nectary on which the stamina are inserted, having been mistaken for the germen, and the real ovary, on account of its smallness, having escaped the observation of Linnæus and Loureiro. This is now, I believe, generally admitted; there can therefore be no doubt of the identity of Roxburgh's Johnia with Salacia, and his I. salacioides agrees so well with S. chinensis, particularly in having entire leaves, that it is questionable whether they are not the same, for it is to be observed that in most of the species the leaves are only subopposite and may occasionally on the same tree be found both opposite and alternate. Tonsella prinoides (Willd. "Berl. Ges. Nat. Fr. Mag." iv.) is also without doubt a true species of Salacia, if it be not in fact the same plant as the Johnia Coromandeliana (Roxb. "Flor. Ind." i. p. 173). Calypso salacioides of Aubert du Petit Thouars agrees exactly with these in the structure of the flower but differs in having many-seeded berries. Some of the species of Tonsella appear likewise to have polyspermous fruit, but those which have definite seeds are probably true species of Salacia. It may be questioned whether the distinction founded on the number of seeds be really of generic value where the agreement is so exact in all other respects, especially if it should be found that a gradation exists from the one to the other in the fruit of the different species. This, however, can only be determined by an accurate examination of the ovaries and fruit of the various plants, at present ranged under Tonsella.

In the natural arrangement Salacia undoubtedly bears the greatest affinity to Hippocratea, it being scarcely possible to distinguish the two genera when only in flower. It also agrees in many particulars with the Celastrinæ, but differs in having exalbuminous seeds. The union of the Hippocraticeæ and Celastrinæ has, however, been suggested by Mr. Brown in his remarks on the Botany of Terra Australis. Under the above view the genus will be characterised as follows:—

Calyx inferus 5-fidus. Corolla 5-petala. Stamina, 3, disco

carnoso inserta. Ovarium 3-loculare, loculis 1–2 sporis, ovulis axi affixis. Bacca 1–3 sperma.

Frutices vel arbusculæ, foliis suboppositis simplicibus.

I have met with 2 species in Sumatra, 1 with anthers sessile on the nectary, which agrees very nearly both with S. chinensis and Roxburgh's I. salacioides; the other with anthers supported on filaments and nearly related to I. Coromandeliana Roxb.

VITIS RACEMIFERA.—W. J.

Tetrandra, foliis quinatis, foliolis spinescenti-serratis subtus incanis, cirrhis oppositifolis racemiferis, racemis compositis longissimis, baccis dispermis.

Akar charikan, or Bayur akar. *Malay.*

Native of Sumatra.

A large, strong, woody climber. Branches round, villous. Leaves alternate, quinate, leaflets pedicellate, oblong obovate, acute, subspinoso-serrate, the serratures being formed by the spinescent termination of the nerves, smooth above, hoary beneath, frequently with a ferruginous shade. Petioles villous. Cirrhi opposed to the leaves, very long, simple or bifid, when bifid 1 branch becomes the peduncle. Racemes very long, compound, consisting of numerous densely flowered racemuli inserted on a peduncle formed of the thickened tendril. The whole raceme is often a foot and a half in length. Peduncles ferruginously villous. Flowers sessile on the partial peduncles, small, green. Calyx minute, embracing the base of the corolla, quadridentate. Corolla deeply 4-parted. Stamina 4, anthers yellow. Ovary surrounded by a fleshy ring, tetrasporous. Style scarce any. Stigma thick, Berry of the shape of an olive and nearly as large, purple, juicy, 2-seeded.

Obs.—This would be a species of Cissus according to the Linnean division, but that genus has now been united to Vitis by Mr. Brown, as they differ in nothing but the number of parts.

RHOPALA OVATA.—W. J.

Foliis subsessilibus ovatis utrinque acutis integerrimis, pedicellis brevissimis cum calycibus ovariisque levissime tomentosis.

Found at Tappanuly.

A small tree. Leaves alternate and opposite, almost sessile, broad ovate, acute, sometimes acuminate, entire with revolute edges, very smooth, nerves distinct; 10 inches long by 6 broad. Petiole none, save the thickened base of the middle nerve. Racemes below the leaves from former axils. Pedicels 2-flowered; a bract at the base of each and at the subdivisions. Perianth, together with the pedicels, slightly tomentose or nearly smooth. Nectarial scales 4.

LINOCIERA ODORATA.—W. J.

Diandria Monogynia. N. O. Oleinæ.

Foliis lanceolatis utrinque acutis glaberrimis, paniculis axillaribus foliis brevioribus.

At Natal and on Pulo Mosella.

A large shrub, with subdichotomous branches. Leaves sub-opposite, short-petioled, oblong-lanceolate, acute at both ends, entire, smooth and coriaceous; 4–5 inches long. Panicles axillary, opposite, much shorter than the leaves; peduncles opposite, 3–5 flowered. Flowers subsessile, fragrant. Bracts small, oblong, Calyx 4-parted. Corolla white, almost 4-petaled, petals long, linear, united by pairs, by means of the filaments, slightly cohering at the other divisions. Stamina 2; anthers large, emarginate at the apex. Ovary 2-celled, each cell containing 2 linear pendulous parallel ovula. Style scarce any. Stigma bifid.

The following species have been discovered since the printing of this paper, and may be here briefly noticed:—

ADINANDRA SYLVESTRIS.—W. J.

Baccis trilocularibus.
Suka beranak. *Malay.*
A large forest tree, found at Moco Moco.

PTERNANDRA CAPITELLATA.—W. J.

Floribus axillaribus capitellatis.
Found at Moco Moco.

PTERNANDRA ECHINATA.—W. J.

Pedunculis axillaribus terminalibusque, calycibus ovariisque echinatis.
A large tree, found at Kataun. The leaves are 3-nerved in all the species.

PSILOBIUM TOMENTOSUM.—W. J.

Tomentosa, floribus axillaribus subsessilibus.
At Kataun. The fruit is baccate.

NOTE.

Since the foregoing article *On Malayan Plants* was printed, Sir J. D. Hooker has kindly supplied the Editor with the following references, while the Hon. D. F. A. Hervey has added some valuable corrections and suggestions concerning the Malay names. The former are here given in Italic, the latter in Roman type.

p. 211. Psychotria Malayana. (*Flora Brit. Ind.* iii. 165.)—Bâyam bâdak, *i.e.*, rhinoceros spinach, probably relished as food by that animal.
Rondeletia corymbosa. *Greenia Jackii, W. and A.* (*Ib.* iii. 41.)

p. 212. Phyteuma begonifolium, Roxb. *Pentaphragma begonifolium, Wall.* (*Ib.* iii. 437.)
Curculigo Sumatrana. (*Wight, Ic. Pl. Ind. or. t.* 2042.) Kalâpa, cocos nucifera, pûyû, a fish so named; but this is probably a mistake for pûyuh, the larger of the two quails found in the Archipelago, which frequents this plant.

p. 213. Loranthus coccineus. (*Flora Brit. Ind.* v. 206.)
Loranthus ferrugineus. (*Ib.* v. 210.)

p. 214. Nephelium lappaceum, Linn. (*Ib.* i. 687.)—There is a variety called rambutan pâchat (*i.e.*, leech rambutan) distinguished from the ordinary variety by the smaller size of the fruit, and the way in which the soft spines of the shell curl over, looking like the leech on his way to attach himself to some fresh point. It is used medicinally with other remedies in small-pox.
Sapindus rubiginosus. *Erioglossum edule, Blume.* (*Ib.* i. 672.) Kûlit lâyu, withered, faded bark.

p. 215. Melia excelsa. (*Ib.* i. 544.)
Microcos tomentosa. *Grewia paniculata, Roxb.* (*Ib.* i. 393.)

p. 216. Mimosa jiringa, W. J. *Pithecolobium lobatum, Benth.* (*Ib.* ii. 305.) *Mimosa Kaeringa, Roxb.*—Buah jĕring, a fruit eaten by Malays. Other varieties are jĕring tûpai (squirrel j.), Pith. oppositum, and j. hantu (spirit j.), Pith. bigeminum.

p. 217. Clerodendrum molle. *C. villosum, Blume.* (*Ib.* iv. 595.)

p. 218. Gmelina villosa. (*Ib.* iv. 582.)
Vitex arborea. *V. pubescens, Vahl.* (*Ib.* iv. 585.)—The wood is similarly used in the Peninsula.

p. 219. Sphenodesme pentandra. (*Ib.* iv. 602.)
Sterculia coccinea, Roxb. *S. laevis, Wall.* (*Ib.* i. 357.)—*This is an error of Jack's, it is not Roxburgh's coccinea, which is a N. Indian species.*

p. 220. Sterculia angustifolia. *S. rubiginosa, Vent.* (*Ib.* i. 358.)—Filet makes this a variety of the Sundanese hantap. *Roxburgh's S. angust. is a different species, referred to S. Balanghas, L.*

p. 220. Calla humilis. *Chamæcladon humile, Miq. (Engler, Monog. Arac.,* 345.)

p. 221. Clala angustifolia. *Chamæcladon angustifolium, Schott.* (*Ib.* 344.)

Calla nitida. *Aglaonema nitidum, Kunth.* (*Ib.* 438.)

Flacourtia inermis. (*Flora Brit. Ind.* i. 192.)—Variety of the fruit known as "rokam" or "rûkam," probably "rokam manis," or the sweet variety, also described as Flacourtia rukam. There are other varieties—viz., "r. asam" (Flacourtia sapida), and "r. sĕpat" (F. jangomas).

p. 222. Rottlera alba. *Mallotus albus, Muell. Arg. (De Cand. Prodr.* xv. 2, 965.)—Bâlik angin, turn wind, meaning that turns up its under side with the wind, and shows the whiteness of it.

p. 223. Didymocarpus crinita. (*Flora Brit. Ind.* iv. 351.)—Tĕmû. There are several other varieties—viz., tĕmû kunchi (Kæmpferia pandurata), "t. gîring" (Curcuma viridiflora), and "t. lawat" (Curcuma zerumbet).

p. 224. Didymocarpus reptans. (*Ib.* iv. 352.)—Tĕmû kunchi.
Didymocarpus corniculata. (*De Cand. Prodr.* ix. 265.)

p. 225. Didymocarpus frutescens. *Didissandra frutescens, Clarke.* (*Flora Brit. Ind.* iv. 355.)

Sonerila erecta. (*Ib.* ii. 530.)—Sambau, according to Johor aboriginal tradition, one of the first plants seen by the first parents of mankind. Used medicinally.

p. 226. Sonerila Moluccana. (*Ib.* ii. 537.)

p. 227. Rhopala attenuata. *Helicia attenuata, Bl.* (*Ib.* v. 190.)
Rhopala Moluccana. *Helicia petiolaris, Benn.* (*Ib.* v. 190.)

p. 228. Ixora pendula. (*Ib.* iii. 141.)
Epithinia Malayana. *Scyphiphora hydrophyllacea.* (*Ib.* iii. 125.)

p. 229. Morinda tetrandra. *M. umbellata, Linn.* (*Ib.* iii. 157.)
Morinda polysperma. *Lucinea morinda, De C.* (*Ib.* iii. 93.)

p. 230. Euthemis leucocarpa. (*Ib.* i. 526.)—There is a very hard timber tree, named pĕlâwan ("lâwan" to resist), of which there are several varieties in hill, plain, and swamp, according to Malays. This shrub, E. leucocarpa, which Jack gives as "pĕlâwan bĕruk," or the p. of the cocoa-nut monkey (Simius nemestrinus), is mentioned by Filet as mâta pĕlandok," eye of the Moschus javanicus, or an allied species, from the berry, which, when ripe, is of a lustrous black, but earlier of a bright scarlet, and perhaps white in the younger stages.

p. 231. Euthemis minor. (*Ib.* i. 526.)—Filet gives, as the Malay of this, "pûtat âyer," indicating a swampy habitat, but Jack has no hint on this point.

Celastrus bivalis. *Microtropis bivalvis, Wall.* (*Ib.* i. 614.)

p. 232. Leucopogon Malayanum. (*Ib.* iii. 477.)—Called "tĕrâtap" at Bangka according to Filet.

p. 233. Rauwolfia Sumatrana. (*De Cand. Prodr.* viii. 337.)—Used medicinally in conjunction with many other plants: "sĕmbu bâdak," horn of rhinoceros; "tampal," is a piece, to mend or to patch, but I am unaware of its application here.

p. 234. Tacca cristata. (*Miquel, Flora Ind. Bat.* iii. 578.)—"Pûar lîlipan," at Palembang, according to Filet, and would no doubt be a "pûar" of some kind in the Peninsula. These "pûar," mostly zingibers, are many of them used medicinally.

p. 234. Veratrum Malayanum. *Veratronia Malayana, Miquel.* (*Flora Ind. Bat.* iii. 553.)

p. 235. Memecylon cœruleum. (*Flora Brit. Ind.* ii. 559.)—"Kûlit nîpis," thin bark.

p. 236. Laurus parthenoxylon. *Cinnamomum parthenoxylon, Meissn.* (*Ib.* v. 135.)—"Kâyu gâdis," virgin wood. Filet gives this as Parthenoxylon porrectum, Bl., Nat. Fam. Laurineæ, a sort of pseudo-sassafras.

p. 237. Gomphia Sumatrana. (*Ib.* i. 525.)

p. 238. Murraya paniculata, W. J. *Murraya exotica, Linn., Van.* (*Ib.* i. 503.)—Filet gives it as "Kemûning Japan," or, as a Malay would say, "Jipún."
Aglaia odorata. (*Ib.* i. 554.)—Filet, "Kĕmûning Chîna."

p. 239. Rhizophora caryophylloides. *Bruguiera caryophylloides, Blume.* (*Ib.* ii. 438.)—Filet calls it "Kandaka (or gĕndâga) nasi," *i.e.*, boiled rice case.

p. 240. Acrotrema costatum. (*Ib.* i. 32.)

p. 241. Lagerstrœmia floribunda. (*Ib.* ii. 577.)
Ternstrœmia rubiginosa. *Sauraiya Jackiana, Kort.* (*Miquel, Flora Ind. Bat.* i. 2, 479.)

p. 242. Ternstrœmia pentapetala. *Sauraiya tristata, De C.* (*Flora Br. Ind.* i. 287.)
Elæocarpus nitida. (*Ib.* i. 401.)—"Bûah manik," jewel fruit.

p. 243. Monocera petiolata. *Elæocarpus integra, Wall.* (*Ib.* i. 408.)

p. 244. Monocera ferruginea. (*Ib.* i. 409.)
Tetracera arborescens. (*Miquel, Flora Ind. Bat.* i. 2, 9.)

p. 245. Uvaria hirsuta. (*Flora Brit. Ind.* i. 48.)
Careya macrostachya. *Barringtonia macrostachya, Kurz.* (*Ib.* ii. 509.)

p. 246. Clerodendrum divaricatum. (*Miquel, Flora Ind. Bat.* ii. 882.)
Hedychium Sumatranum. (*Ib.* iii. 608.)—"Gandasûli hûtan," the jungle or wild gandasûli, the ordinary being H. coronaium. "Ganda" seems to be Sanskrit for odour, which occurs in several Malay plant names, *e.g.*, "gandapûra" (Abelmoschus moschatus, Filet) and "gandarûsa" (Gandarussa vulgaris, Nees, or Justicia gandarussa.) "Suli" in this name comes, it is suggested, from the Sinhalese "sulinga," spiral (Rigg, quoted by Favre).

p. 247. Alpinia elatior. (*Ib.* iii. 606.)—"Bunga" flower; "Kinchong," the meaning of this is not easy to fix, as it is not certain how the word should be sounded; it might be "Kinchang," "Kĕnchang," or "Kinchong"—*i.e.*, strong, fine, or unfortunate.

p. 248. Alpinia capitellata. (*Ib.* iii. 607.)
Globba ciliata. (*Ib.* iii 592.)—"Pûar âmas," golden pûar. Filet calls it "pûar amut," speaking of the Sumatran variety also.

p. 249. Aristolochia hastata. *A. Jackiana, Steud.* (*Miquel, Flora Ind. Bat.* i. 1, 1067.)
p. 250. Begonia cæspitosa. (*De Cand. Prodr.* xv. 1, 397.)
Begonia orbiculata. (*Ib.* xv. 1, 398.)
p. 251. Begonia sublobata. (*Ib.* xv. 1, 353.)
p. 252. Begonia fasciculata. (*De Cand. Prodr.* xv. 1, 522.)
Begonia pilosa. (*Ib.* xv. 1, 398.)
p. 253. Begonia bracteata. (*Ib.* xv. 1, 316.)—" Bunko "=Bengkok or Bongkok. [See note above, p. 57.]
Begonia racemosa. (*Ib.* xv. 1, 322.)—" Lâyang-lâyang," means both the swallow, and a flying kite; " simpei " is a hoop, circle or loop, also the name of a monkey (Semnopithecus melalophos). Probably the name means "monkey's kite," referring to the round capsules of the female. It is common for Malays to give names of this kind to plants. Filet calls it Diploclinium racemosum.
Begonia geniculata, B. isoptera, Jack. (*Ib.* xv. i. 320.)—Filet (No. 6910) gives this as Diploclinium bombycinum, Bl. " Rumput ûdang-ûdang," shrimp or prawn grass. The Malays call many plants grass—*e.g.*, Ruellia repanda is called " rumput mâs," or golden grass, the Mimosa pudica is called " rumput kamâluan," the bashful grass, &c. &c.
p. 254. Sonerila heterophylla. (*Miquel, Flora. Ind. Bat.* i. 1, 582.)
Rhododendron Malayanum. (*Flora Brit. Ind.* iii. 462.)
p. 255. Vaccinium Sumatranum. (*Miquel, Flora Ind. Bat.* ii. 1063.)
p. 256. Haloragis disticha. *Anisophyllea disticha, Hook.* (*Flora Brit. Ind.* ii. 442.)—" Kâyu," wood, " Kanchil," small deer, (variety of Moschus javanicus), the cunning animal in Malay tales, like the fox in others.
p. 257. Elodea Sumatrana. *Cratoxylon Sumatranum.* (*Miquel, Flora Ind. Bat.* i. 2, 516.)—Tello Dalam, *i.e.*, " Tĕlok dâlam," deep bay.
p. 258. Elodea formosa. *Cratoxylon formosum, Benth. and Hook. f.* (*Flora Brit. Ind.* i. 258.)—" Kâyu gâgak," crow tree; " pĕdas," pungent, " bunga," flower. This would apparently indicate that there is another plant of the same name which is not supposed to flower.
p. 259. Ternstrœmia acuminata. *Not taken up in later works.*
Ternstrœmia serrata. (*Miquel, Flora Ind. Bat.* i. 2, 488.)
p. 260. Ternstrœmia cuspidata. *Not taken up in later works.*—Salumah is probably " Sri Lĕmak," one of the districts in the Mĕnangkâbau country in Sumatra.
p. 261. Millingtonia Sumatrana. *Meliosma Sumatrana, Hook. f.* (*Flora Brit. Ind.* ii. 6.)
p. 262. Laurus incrassatus. *Dehaasia microcarpa, Blume.* (*Ib.* v. 126.)—" Jĕring-jĕring tûpei," the squirrel jĕring. Filet gives it as Pithecolobium oppositum, the ordinary jĕring as P. lobatum, jĕring hantu as P. bigeminum, N.O. Mimoseæ.
p. 263. Tetranthera cordata. *Litsœa cordata, Hook. f.* (*Ib.* v. 177.)
Knema glaucescens. (?) *Myristica glaucescens.* (*Ib.* v. 111.)
p. 264. Connarus ferrugineus. (*Ib.* ii. 51.)

p. 265. Connarus villosus. (*Miquel, Flora Ind. Bat.* i. 2, 666.)
p. 266. Connarus semidecandrus. (*Flora Brit. Ind.* ii. 52.)—Filet calls it Karâbu. If it is called "akar," it should be a creeper. Connarus grandis. (*Ib.* ii. 53.)—Sundanese native name "Kilâja," Filet.
Connarus lucidus. (*Miquel, Flora Ind. Bat.* i. 2, 666.)
p. 267. Cnestis emarginata. *Not taken up in later works.*
Cnestis florida. (?) *Rourea simplicifolia.* (*Ib.* i. 2, 659.)
p. 268. Cnestis mimosoides. (?) *Rourea concolor, Blume.* (*Flora Brit. Ind.* ii. 49.
Eurycoma longifolia, W. J. (*Ib.* i. 521.) "Kâyu kĕbal" the invulnerable wood, whether used superstitiously or because the wood is hard. Jack gives no hint. Filet gives the Sumatran designation, 'bâbi kûrus,' thin pig, but without stating whether the porcine tribe value the fruit for anti-Banting properties.
p. 269. Peronema canescens, W. J. (*Flora Brit. Ind.* iv. 599.)—Javanese name "Kilangir" (Filet). It is also used for fences and for sheaths of common knives.
p. 270. Rhodamnia cinerea, W. J. *R. trineura, Blume.* (*Ib.* ii. 468.) —Filet gives it as "marampuyan," and also mentions R. concolor, and says "beide hooge boomen," so that the specimen Jack saw could not have been full grown. The "mĕrpôyan" of the Peninsula gives a hard wood, and is used in carpentering, and also, with other ingredients, medicinally in diarrhœa.
p. 271. Adinandra dumosa, W. J. (*Ib.* i. 282.)—In the Peninsula there is a shrub called "rîbu-rîbu," which seems to correspond with the description here given, but the berry is red, and Jack is silent as to the colour. It is used medicinally in a variety of ways, and is called "mĕrkâsih," by the aborigines of Johor. The Ligodium scandens is called "pâku" or "rumput sarîbu," the epithet "rîbu," thousand, having reference doubtless in this case, as in the text, to the countless number of leaves.
p. 272. Ixonanthes reticulata, W. J. (*Ib.* i. 417.)
Ixonanthes icosandra, W. J. (*Ib.* i. 416.)
p. 273. Chionotria rigida, W. J. (?) *Glycosmis pentaphylla, Corr.* (*Ib.* i. 500.)—Called "biârang" in Bangka.
p. 274. Sphalanthus confertus, W. J. *Quisqualis densiflora, Wall.* (*Ib.* ii. 460.)
p. 275. Pyrrhanthus littoreus. *Lumnitzera coccinea, Wd. and A.* (*Ib.* ii. 452.)—"Mîrî" for "kemîrî" (?), "bâtu," stone, meaning hard variety.
p. 276. Phaleria capitata, W. J. *Drymispermum phaleria, Meissn.* (*Miquel, Flora Ind. Bat.* i. 1, 884.)
p. 277. Pternandra cœrulescens. (*Flora Brit. Ind.* ii. 551.)
Memecylon paniculatum. (*Miquel, Flora Ind. Bat.* i. 1, 572.)
p. 278. Octas. *Genus not taken up by later authors.*
p. 279. Cœlopyrum. *Genus of unknown affinity.*
Cœlopyrum coriaceum. Filet gives "Tarantang" simply as

"Buchanania auriculata," Bl.,[N. O. Anacardiaceæ, and refers to B. macrophylla, which also appears under the native name of "mĕdang sangka." Then there are B. sessilifolia and B. splendens, native names "t. âyam" and "t. bûrong" respectively. Leaves and root of "t. pâya" (marsh-grower, Malacca), used medicinally.

p. 279. Petrocarpa excelsa. *Parinarium* (?) *Jackianum, Benth.* (*Flora Brit. Ind.* ii. 312.)—" Balam" is applied to one of the gutta-(gĕtah) producing trees, and generally to a red variety of any species. "Pangkat" means elevation, rank, and may refer to the situation or the good quality of this variety.

p. 280. Petrocarpa Sumatrana. *Parinarium costatum, Blume.* (?), (*Ib.* ii. 309.)—Filet gives the Sumatran name of this as "taijas" (tâyas), N.O. Chrysobalaneæ.

p. 281. Wormia excelsa. (*Miquel, Flora Ind. Bat.* i. 2, 10.)
Wormia pulchella. (*Flora Brit. Ind.* i. 36.)

p. 282. Ficus ovoidea. *Urostigma ovoideum.* (*Miquel, Flora Ind. Bat.* 1. 2, 345.)
Ficus deltoidea and Ficus rigida. *Not taken up in later works.*—"Sĕrî," the complexion, glorious, illustrious; "bûlan," the moon : this may refer to the appearance of the fruit, bark, or the leaves in the moonlight.

p. 283. Jonesia. *Saraca, Linn.*
Jonesia declinata. *Saraca declinata, Miquel.* (*Miquel, Flora Ind. Bat.* ii. 84.)—" Sitûrun," from "tûrun," to descend.

p. 284. Bauhinia emarginata. (*Flora Brit. Ind.* ii. 278.)
Bauhinia bidentata. (*Ib.* ii. 278.) Malay name "akar ka-kâtup;" used medicinally, the root being boiled with those of other plants, and the decoction drunk for diarrhœa.

p. 285. Inga bubalina. *Pithecolobium bubalinum, Benth.* (*Ib.* ii. 304.)

p. 286. Inga clypearia. *Pithecolobium clyperia, Benth.* (*Ib.* ii. 305.)—"Jĕring mûnyet"—*i.e.*, the monkey variety of jĕring, probably because that animal feeds on the fruit. Filet gives the Bangka name as "kâbu-kâbu" (which, in the Straits, is applied to the tree producing the cotton-pods), and says of it, "they make large canoes of the trunk, which are light, but not very durable, because the wood absorbs too much water and thus does not easily become dry again; they also make shields or "salowakkos" of it. The bark is used for the tanning of fishing-nets."
Tabernæmontana macrocarpa. (*Ib.* iii. 649.)

p. 287. Fagrœa carnosa. (*Ib.* iv. 82.)
Fagrœa auriculata. Filet only gives the Chinese name "Fan-nyin-won" as the native equivalent.

p. 288. Ixora neriifolia. *Not taken up in later works.*—Whether it be "bunga," flower, or "kâyu" or "poko," tree, makes no difference; the name "salûang," is taken from a fish which in form and dimensions resembles the leaves of this shrub.
Lecanthus erubescens, W. J. (*Ib.* iii. 110.)

p. 289. Psilobium nutans, W. J. (*Miquel, Flora Ind. Bat.* ii. 199.)
Ophiorrhiza heterophylla. (*Ib.* ii. 175.)
Quercus racemosa. *Quercus spicata, Smith.* (*De Cand. Prodr.*

xvi. 2, 85.)—"Pĕning-pĕning bungkus." The spelling in the text was a rough attempt to convey the sound which the word has in the Mĕnangkâbau dialect. "Ĕmpening" and "hĕmpĕning" are other forms.

p. 290. Quercus urceolarius. (*Ib.* xvi. 2, 89.)

p. 290. Areca tigillaria. *Oncosperma filamentosa, Blume.* (*Miquel, Flora Ind. Bat.* iii. 13.)—It is also used for floors and for boat decks, being split up into fine laths; poles of this also, with sharpened ends, are often used with fatal effect in riots.

p. 291. Enchidium. *Trigonostemon, Blume.*
Enchidium verticillatum. (*Ib.* i. 2. 363.)

p. 292. Antidesma frutescens. (*De Cand. Prodromus*, xv. 2, 250.)

p. 294. Vitis racemifera. *Not taken up by later authors.* — Filet identifies " bâyur ákar " with Canthium glomerulatum, Miq., N.O. Rubiaceæ.

Rhopala ovata. *Helicia ovata, Benn.* (*Miquel, Flora Ind. Bat.* i. 1, 984.)

p. 295. Linociera odorata. (*Ib.* ii. 554.)

Adinandra sylvestris. *Not taken up by later authors.*—" Sûka bĕrának "—*i.e.*, fond of having children.

Pternandra capitellata. (*Flora Brit. Ind.* ii. 551.)

Pternandra echinata. *Kibassia simplex, Korth.* (*Ib.* ii. 533.)

Psilobium tomentosum. *Not taken up by later authors.*

GENERAL AND GEOGRAPHICAL INDEX.

ACHEH, Achín, i. 214, 215
'Ádat sagala rája-rája Maláyu, ii. 46
Ambergris island, i. 222
Ant-eater, ii. 200 ff.
Arjuna vijaya, ii. 89
Aru, i. 216, 217
Attar of roses, i. 261
Ayer etam, i. 12
    kiti, ii. 58

BABAD, ii. 91
Bade, wadah, ii. 140 ff.
Bale, ii. 99, 141
Bali, i. 138, 139, 183, 184; ii. 69-200
    meaning, ii. 70; language, 71;
    its ingredients, 74 ff.; literature, 77 ff.; religion, 97 ff.;
    places of worship, 100 ff.;
    the gods worshipped, 102 ff.;
    Śiva's attributes, 104; the creation, 114 ff.; religious ceremonies and offerings, 121 ff.;
    dress of panditas, 124; dress of the gods, 126; feasts, 127;
    details of worship, 130 ff.;
    rishis, 136; trimûrti, 137; cremations, 137 ff.; castes, 151 ff.;
    Brahmans, 154 ff.; Kshatriyas, 158 ff.; Wesyas, 160 ff.;
    princely families, 162 ff.;
    further remarks on the castes, 183; feudal system, 184;
    Śûdras, 186; caste in Java, 189; calculation of time, 191;
    calendar, 193
Bali-sangraha, ii. 70
Banjermasin, i. 227
Banka, i. 202
Bantam, i. 179, 181
Bârata Yudda, ii. 86 ff.
Baruṇa, ii. 109

Batu Bayas, i. 11
    Birtam, i. 11
    Lanchong, i. 11
Beaju, i. 228
Bela, ii. 146
Bencoolen, ii. 57 ff.
Benko, Bengkok, ii. 57
Bidáyatu-lhidáyat, ii. 48
Billiton, i. 148, 151, 201
Bomakavya, ii. 89
Brahmâ, ii. 105
Brahmans, ii. 154 ff.
Brunei, i. 223
Búkit Chíná, i. 4
    Jalutong, i. 12, 16
    Kandís, ii. 60
    Mérah, i. 12, 16, 17
    Tangah, i. 13
Burning of widows, ii. 145 ff.
Bustánu-l'árifín, ii. 41
    ssalátín, ii. 15

CAMPHOR-BAROS, i. 260
Cassowary, i. 262
Chang-kwang, i. 133
Character of Balinese, ii. 189
Charitra nabí Allah Músá, ii. 39
Chinese geographical literature, i. 126

DAFTAR shajarah Charibon, ii. 22, 56
Duraka Juru, i. 13, 18, 19
Dvîpas, ii. 117

EXPIATORY feasts, ii. 128

FANTSÚR, i. 164; ii. 51
Farquhar Collection of Malay MSS., ii. 45-49
Funan, i. 239

304   GENERAL AND GEOGRAPHICAL INDEX.

GANA, Gaṇeśa, ii. 111
Giau-chi, i. 127, 128, 205
Grissé, i. 173, 179, 180
Grooved rocks, i. 25
Gunong Bau, i. 22
  Búbú, i. 10
  Belúmut, ii. 60
  Benko, Journey to, ii. 57 ff.
  Jerai, i. 12

HAKANG, i. 179, 181, 182
Hamzah, his works, ii. 51
Harivangsa, ii. 90
Hikáyat Ahmad Bisnu, ii. 35
  Bakhtiyár, ii. 39
  Bayan Budiman, ii. 6
  Bikermáditya, ii. 38
  Búdak miskín, ii. 53
  Barma Shahdán, ii. 12
  chábut tunggul, ii. 30
  Charang Kulina, ii. 13. 56
  Chikat Waning Pati, ii. 19
  Dalang Indra Kăsuma, ii. 19
    Panguda Asmara, ii. 17
  Damar Bulan, ii. 6
  Dewa Mandu, ii. 31
  endang Málat Rasmi, ii. 20
  Fátimah káwan, ii. 39, 54
  Ghulám, ii. 40
  Hang Tuah, ii. 1
  Indăra Kryángan, ii. 36
    Putra, ii. 10
  Isma Yatím, ii. 14
  Kalílah wa Damanah, ii. 28
  Khojah Meimún, ii. 6
  Mahárája 'Ali, ii. 42
    Boma, ii. 13, 52
  Mesa Indăra Dewa Kăsuma, ii. 32
    Lari Kăsumah, ii. 30
  Nága Barsăru, ii. 21
  Pălanduk Jináka, ii. 41
  Pandawa lima, ii. 18
    Jaya, ii. 3, 52
  Pangeran Kăsuma Agung, ii. 17
  Panji Wila Kăsuma, ii. 21
  partan islám, ii. 32
  Putri Bilkis, ii. 39
    Johor Mánikam, ii. 37
  rája Bábi, ii. 134
    Iskandar, ii. 46
  rája-rája Pásei, ii. 41
  Ranga Ariya Kuda, ii. 5
  Sări Rama, ii. 19
  Shah Kobád, ii. 22
  Shamsu-lbarri, ii. 38
  Si Miskín, ii. 35
  tamímu-ddári, ii. 34

Huiku, i. 232
Human sacrifices, ii. 129, 145

ICHNEUMON, ii. 205 ff.
Indra, ii. 108
Indragiri, i. 200

JAVA, Chinese accounts of, i. 131
Jilahati, i. 184
Jih-nan, i. 128
Johore, i. 254

KALA, i. 241, 243
Kalah, i. 243
Kalang, i. 149
Kaling, i. 138, 140, 183
Kandali, i. 185, 192, 193, 200
Kanyoh, i. 226
Karimata, i. 157, 236
Kataun, ii. 64, 65
Kaulan, Kolan, i. 201, 236
Kawi language, i. 282 ff.; ii. 73 ff.
Kelantan, i. 257
Kenhangrok, ii. 91
Kianchou, i. 239
Klaebang, i. 5, 7
Kora, i, 241, 243
Kubera, ii. 110
Kukang, i. 168, 169, 195, 197, 199, 200

LAMBRI, i. 169, 219, 220, 221
Land-shells of Pinang, i. 87 ff.
Langga, i. 135
Langpi, i. 140, 141
Law-books, ii. 93
Laye, Laïs. ii. 59, 62
Lignum-aloes, i. 260
Lingga, i. 203
Litai, i. 208, 219
Lubu Puar, ii. 58

MAHÁBHÁRATA, ii. 84 ff.
Majapahit, Mojopait, i. 149, 171; ii. 77, 79, 159
Makota sagala raja-raja, ii. 15
Malacca, i. 1-9, 243-254
Malagasy language, i. 263-286; its affinities, 263; grammatical structure, 266; idiosyncrasy, 267; Sanskrit and Arabic ingredients, 269; phonetic system, 271
Malat, ii. 97
Malay Archipelago, Notes on, from Chinese Sources, i. 126-262
Malay character, i. 17

GENERAL AND GEOGRAPHICAL INDEX. 305

Malay Manuscripts, Account of, ii. 1-56
Pantuns, ii. 65 ff.
Malayan Amphibia and Reptilia, i. 72 ff.
Plants Described, ii. 209-302
Mantras, Account of the, i. 286-307; other native tribes, 287; origin, 288; traditions, 289; habits and customs, 290; weapons, 292; character, 292; games, 293; ceremonies, 295; religion, 297; government, 301; language, 303; missions, 305
Marbukit, i. 22
Marigi, ii. 58
Mausu, i. 224, 257
Mayitung, i. 202
Ma'zijat rasúl allah, ii. 32, 39
Milikü, Moluccos, i. 183, 237

NAKUR, i. 208, 218
Núruddín, his works, ii. 49

PADANDAS, ii. 99 ff., 156
Pahang, i. 255, 257
Palembang, i. 163, 168, 184, 185, 188, 199
Pameṇḍanga, ii. 92
Paṇḍitas, ii. 157
Passier Ries, i. 21
Pekalongan, i. 166
Perak, i. 10
Permatang Pau, i. 12
Pinang, i. 9, 20, 87 ff.
Poli, i. 203, 205, 207, 242
Polo, i. 222
Porcupine, ii. 207 ff.
Prye, i. 12, 19, 20
Pulo Kindi, i. 10
  Riman, i. 10
  rondo, i. 222
  Sejahat, i. 23
  Tam (Ktam), i. 22, 39
  Tikang, i. 22, 26
  Ubin, i. 21 ff.; its rocks, plutonic and volcanic, 45
Puni, i. 225, 229, 257
Punjong, ii. 58
Purohita, ii. 157
Pyah Trubong, i. 12

RAFFLES' Collection of Malay MSS., ii. 1-45
Râmâyaṇa, ii. 80 ff.
Rangga Lawe, ii. 91
Rejak Bessi, ii. 58

Rejang, ii. 58, 62, 63
Rindowati, ii. 16

SALANGOR, i. 10
Salat Tambroh, i. 22
Salsalah rája-rája di tánah Jáwa, ii. 20
Samarkandí, ii. 53
San-bo-tsai, i. 187, 192, 193, 197
Sarbaza, i. 187, 200
Saríbu-masáil, ii. 38
Satya, ii. 146
Serawi, ii. 62, 63, 69
Sha'ir Angăreni, ii. 40, 56
  Bidasari, ii. 7
  buang, ii. 48
  íkan, ii. 35
    Tambara, ii. 10
  Jávan Tamâsa, ii. 53
  Johan anak rája Perak, ii. 48
  Ken Tambuhan, ii. 8, 40
  Kumpani Wolanda, ii. 46
  prang Angres di Batáwi, ii. 43
  Sări Buniyan, ii. 9
  Silindung dalíma, ii. 9, 54
Shajara Maláyu, ii. 16
Shamsuddin, his works, ii. 52
Shrew-mouse, ii. 203 f.
Sillebar, Selebar, ii. 62
Simpang ayer, ii. 58
Śivaites, ii. 98 ff.
S'kodo, i. 29
Smaradahana, ii. 88
Soli, i. 166
Sukitan, i. 179
Sulu, i. 225, 227
Sumâna Santaka, ii. 89
Sumatra, i. 162, 184, 208, 211
Sunda language, ii. 64, 69
Sungei Baru, i. 19
  Jara, i. 19
  Kalim, i. 19
  Labu Marijam, i. 19
  Lamau, Lemau, Limau, ii. 58
Surabaya, i. 171, 179
Sutasoma, ii. 90

TÁJU-SSALÁTÍN, ii. 16, 30
Tanjong Agung, ii. 58
  Jangy, i. 21
  Kling, i. 3
  Pamudang, i. 34
  Pongal, i. 21;
  Sanei, ii. 61
  Tajam, i. 32, 33
Tello Anou, ii. 61
Tiehli, i. 184
Timor, Timun, i. 236
Tiongkalo, i. 182, 237

Tuban, i. 171, 179
Tulloh Kumbar, i. 10
Tumapol, i. 149, 162, 165
Tunsun, i. 239, 240
Tuturs, ii. 93

UNDANG-UNDANG, ii. 26
   rája Maláka, ii. 46, 49
Usana Bali, ii. 70, 92
   Java, ii. 92

VIVÀHA, ii. 88
Vishṇu, ii. 106

WESYAS, ii. 160
Wriga Garga, ii. 191, 199

YAMA, ii. 109
Yortan, i. 179

INDEX OF LATIN TERMS.

ABLABES flaviceps, i. 84
Acrotrema cospatum, ii. 240
Adinandra dumosa, ii. 271
   sylvestris, ii. 295
Aglaia odorata, ii. 238
Aglaonema nitidum, ii. 297
Alpinia alatior, ii. 247
   capitellata, ii. 248
Alycæus gibbosulus, i. 95
Amomum biflorum, ii. 210
Anisophyllex disticha, ii. 299
Antidesma frutescens, ii. 292
Areca tigillaria, ii. 290
Aristolochia hastata, ii. 249
   jackiana, ii. 298
Aquilaria agallocha, ii. 260

BARRINGTONIA macrostachya, ii. 298
Bauhinia emarginata, ii. 284
   bidentata, ii. 284
Begonia bracteata, ii. 253
   cæspitosa, ii. 250
   fasciculata, ii. 252
   geniculata, ii. 253
   isoptera, ii. 299
   orbiculata, ii. 250
   pilosa, ii. 252
   racemosa, ii. 253
   sublobata, ii. 251
Bruguiera caryophylloides, ii. 298
Bulimus atricallosus, i. 114
   interruptus, i. 114

CALAMARIA stahlknechti, i. 80
Calla angustifolia, ii. 221
   humilis, ii. 220
   nitida, ii. 221
Cantoriana, i. 109
Careya macrostachya, ii. 245
Celastrus bivalvis, ii. 231
Chamæladon humile, ii. 297
   angustifolium, ii. 297
Chionotria rigida, ii. 273
Cinnamomum parthenoxylon, ii. 298

Clausilia filicostata, i. 116
   penangensis, i. 115
Clerodendrum divaricatum, ii. 246
   molle, ii. 217
   villosum, ii. 296
Cnestis emarginata, ii. 267
   florida, ii. 267
   mimosoides, ii. 268
Cœlopyrum coriaceum, ii. 279
Connarus ferrugineus, ii. 264
   grandis, ii. 266
   lucidus, ii. 266
   semidecandra, ii. 266
   villosus, ii. 265
Cratoxylon formosum, ii. 299
   sumatranum, ii. 299
Curculiga sumatrana, ii. 212
Cyclophis tricolor, i. 83
Cyclophorus borneensis, i. 89
   malayanus, i. 88
Cyclostomacea, i. 88

DEHAASIA microcarpa, ii. 299
Dendrophis caudolineatus, i. 84
Didissandra frutescens, ii. 297
Didymocarpus corniculata, ii. 224
   crinita, ii. 223
   frutescens, ii. 225
   reptans, ii. 224
Draco fimbriatus, i. 80
   quinquefasciatus, i. 79
Drymispermum phaleria, ii. 300

ELÆOCARPUS integra, ii. 298
   nitida, ii. 242
Elodea formosa, ii. 258
   sumatrana, ii. 257
Enchidium verticillatum, ii. 291
Ennea bicolor, i. 120
Epithinia malayana, ii. 228
Erioglossum edule, ii. 296
Euprepes olivaceus, i. 79
Eurycoma longifolia, ii. 268

INDEX OF LATIN TERMS.

Euthemis leucocarpa, ii. 230
    minor, ii. 231

FAGRŒA auriculata, ii. 287
    carnosa, ii. 287
Ficus deltoidea, ii. 282
    ovoidea, ii. 282
    rigida, ii. 282
Flacourtia inermis, ii. 221, 297

GLOBBA ciliata, ii. 248
Glycosmis pentaphylla, ii. 300
Gmelina villosa, ii. 218
Gomphia sumatrana, ii. 237
Gonyosoma oxycephalum, i. 84
Greenia jackii, ii. 296
Grewia paniculata, ii. 296
Gymnodactylus pulchellus, i. 79

HALORAGIS disticha, ii. 256
Hedychium sumatranum, ii. 246
Helicacea, i. 98
Helicarion permolle, i. 105
Helicia attenuata, ii. 297
    ovata, ii. 302
    petiolaris, ii. 297
Helix similaris, i. 113
Hipsirhina alternans, i. 86
Hystrix cristata, ii. 207
    torquatus, ii. 208

INGA bubalina, ii. 285
    clypearia, ii. 286
Ixonanthes icosandra, ii. 272
    reticulata, ii. 272
Ixora nerufolia, ii. 288
    pendula, ii. 228

JONESIA declinata, ii. 283

KIBASSIA simplex, ii. 302
Knema glaucescens, ii. 263

LAGERSTRŒMIA floribunda, ii. 241
Lagocheilus, i. 96
    striolatus, i. 97
    trochoides, i. 96
Laurus incrassatus, ii. 262
    parthenoxylon, ii. 266
Lecananthus erubescens, ii. 288
Leucopogon malayanum, ii. 232
Linociera odorata, ii. 295
Litsæa cordata, ii. 299
Loranthus coccineus, ii. 213
    ferrugineus, ii. 213
Lucinea murinda, ii. 297
Lumnitzera coccinea, ii. 300.

MACROCHLAMYS stephoides, i. 104
Mallotus albus, ii. 297

Manis brachyura, ii. 201
    macrura, ii. 201
Megalomastoma sectilabrum, i. 94
Melia excelsa, ii. 215
Meliosma sumatrana, ii. 299
Memecylon cœruleum, ii. 235
    paniculatum, ii. 277
Microcos glabra, ii. 216
    tomentosa, ii. 215
Microcystis palmicola, i. 105
Microtropis bivalvis, ii. 297
Millingtonia sumatrana, ii. 261
Mimosa jiringa, kaeringa, ii. 216, 296
Monocera ferruginea, ii. 244
    petiolata, ii. 243
Morinda polysperma, ii. 229
    tetrandra, ii. 229
    umbellata, ii. 297
Murraya exotica, ii. 298
    paniculata, ii. 238
Myristica glaucescens, ii. 299

NEPHELIUM lappaceum, ii. 214

OCTAS spicata, ii. 278
Olibanum, ii. 261
Oscosperma filamentosa, ii. 302
Ophiorrhiza heterophylla, ii. 289
    mungos, ii. 205
Ophites albofuscus, i. 85
    subcinctus, i. 85
Opisthoporus penangensis, i. 92
    solutus, i. 93
Oxycalamus longiceps, i. 81

PARINARIUM costatum, ii. 301
    jackianum, ii. 301
Pentaphragma begonifolium, ii. 296
Peronema canescens, ii. 269
Petrocarya excelsa, ii. 279
    sumatrana, ii. 280
Phaleria capitata, ii. 276
Philomycus, i. 116
    pictus, i. 118
Phyteuma begonifolium, ii. 212
Pithecolobium bubalinum, ii. 301
    clypearia, ii. 301
    lobatum, ii. 296, 299
Psilobium nutans, ii. 289
    tomentosum, ii. 295
Psychotria malayana, ii. 211
Pternandra capitellata, ii. 295
    cœrulescens, ii. 277
    echinata, ii. 295
Pupa, i. 119
    orcella, i. 120
    palmira, i. 120
Pupina aureola, i. 94
Pupisoma, i. 119

INDEX OF LATIN TERMS. 309

Pyrrhanthus litoreus, ii. 275
QUERCUS racemosa, ii. 289
  spicata, ii. 301
  urceolaris, ii. 290
Quisqualis densiflora, ii. 300

RANA fusca, i. 76
  lymnocharis, i. 77
  plicatella, i. 77
  porosissima, i. 78
Rauwolfia sumatrana, ii. 233
Rhizophora caryophylloides, ii. 239
Rhodamnia cinerea, ii. 270
  trineura, ii. 300
Rhododendron malayanum, ii. 254
Rhopala attenuata, ii. 227
  moluccana, ii. 227
  ovata, ii. 294
Rhysota cymatium, i. 98
Rondeletia corymbosa, ii. 211
Rottlera alba, ii. 222
Rotula bijuga, i. 101
Rourea simplicifolia, ii. 299
  concolor, ii. 300

SALACIA, ii. 293
Sauraiya jackiana, ii. 298
  tristata, ii. 298
Sapindus rubiginosus, ii. 214
Saraca declinata, ii. 301
Scyphiphora hydrophyllacea, ii. 297
Simotes bicatenatus, i. 82
  cruentatus, i. 82
  catenifer, i. 82
Sitala carinifera, i. 103
Sonerila erecta, ii. 225
  heterophylla, ii. 254
  moluccana, ii. 226
Sorex musaraneus, ii. 203
Sphalanthus confertus, ii. 274
Sphenodesme pentandra, ii. 219

Sterculia angustifolia, ii. 220
  coccinea, ii. 219
  lævis, ii. 296
  rubiginosa, ii. 296
Storax liquida, ii. 261
Styphelia, ii. 232

TABERNÆMONTANA macrocarpa, ii. 286
Tacca cristata, ii. 234
Tanarius major, i. 261
Ternstrœmia acuminata, ii. 259
  cuspidata, ii. 260
  pentapetala, ii. 242
  rubiginosa, ii. 241
  serrata, ii. 259
Tetracera arborescens, ii. 244
Tetranthera cordata, ii. 263
Trachia penangensis, i. 112
Trigonostemon, ii. 302
Trimeresurus wagleri, i. 87
Trocomorpha castra, i. 108
  timorensis, i. 109

UROSTIGMA ovoideum, ii. 301
Uvaria hirsuta, ii. 245

VACCINIUM sumatranum, ii. 255
Vaginulus birmanicus, i. 121
Veratronia malayana, ii. 298
Veratrum malayanum, ii. 234
Veronicella birmanica, i. 122
Vitex arborea, ii. 218
  pubescens, ii. 296
Vitrina nucleata, i. 110
Viverra mungos, ii. 204
Vitis racemifera, ii. 294

WORMIA excelsa, ii. 281
  pulchella, ii. 281

ZINGIBER gracile, ii. 209

INDEX OF MALAYAN AND CHINESE TERMS.

AJI, i. 158, 189
Akar charikan, ii. 294
   kakâtup, ii. 301
   sedingka, ii. 266
Aksara g'de, ii. 72, 76
   murda, ii. 72, 76
Anak-tumiang, i. 292
Anting-anting, ii. 134
Apus kupak, ii. 126
Aquilaria agallocha, i. 260
Aturan, ii. 132

BABAD, ii. 91
Babadong, ii. 126
Babandong, ii. 134
Babêdatti, ii. 126
Babing, i. 294
Bade, ii. 140
Badong, ii. 82
Baju, i. 290
Baju-panjang, i. 290
B'kel, ii. 161, 187
Balai, bale, i. 3 ; ii. 62, 99
Balam pangkat, ii. 301
Bale, ii. 139
Balian, ii. 136
Bâlik angin, ii. 222, 297
Bambu ribut, i. 294
Banten, ii. 132
   dagan, ii. 143, 148
Bapang, ii. 126
Batin, i. 288, 298, 301, 302
Batu-kapala, i. 130
Bâyam bâdak, byumbada, ii. 211, 296
Bâyur akar, ii. 294, 302
Begandai, ii. 63
Bela, ii. 110, 146
Bĕladan, i. 172
Bemban, ii. 66
Beo, i. 174, 206
Berdúwi, ii. 63
Biarang, ii. 300

Bindang, i. 4
Biola, i. 294
Buah jĕring, ii. 216, 296
   karbau, ii. 285
   manik, ii. 242, 298
Bunga salûang, ii. 288, 301
   burutta, ii. 264
   kĕnchong, ii. 247, 298
   yarum, ii. 228

CATI, i. 177
Chalêr, ii. 126
Chan-pi, i. 196
Charu, ii. 132
Chechandian, ii. 134
Chiang-chin-hsiang, i. 220
Ch'ien, i. 177
Chingkau, ii. 61
Chinkani, i. 301
Chintayn, ii. 67
Chitseh, i. 253
Chuundung, ii. 133
Çrîpâda, i. 135, 161

DADAUB, ii. 284
Daun saribu, ii. 271
Dinar, i. 210
Dukun, ii. 136
Durian, i. 209
Duung, ii. 101, 104

FAN-NYIN-WON, ii. 301
Fuyung, i. 187

GAMBANG, ii. 63
Gandasûli hutan, ii. 246, 298
G'de, ii. 168
G'dong chantêl, ii. 102
   tarik, ii. 102
Gê-kuei, i. 246
Gĕndâga nasi, ii. 298
Glang i. 290

INDEX OF MALAYAN AND CHINESE TERMS. 311

Glang batis, ii. 126
  kana, ii. 126
  kupak, ii. 134
Glung chandi, ii. 126
  kurung, ii. 126
Gomuti, i. 138
Guduha, ii. 104, 125, 134
  pawilangan, ii. 134
Guling buntut, ii. 129
Gusti, ii. 130, 151

HIPO-BATANG, i. 292
Hsiang-chên hsiang, i. 261
Hwo-siang, i. 240

IDA, ii. 151
Inga jĕring, ii. 285
Ingor-ingor karbau, ii. 259

JATA, ii. 124
Jawat, ii. 126
Jawi păkan, i. 7, 9
Jennang, i. 302
Jĕring-jĕring tûpei, ii. 262, 296
Jĕring munit, mûñet, ii. 286, 299, 301
Juru-krah, i. 295, 302

KABAHIA, i. 290
Kâbu-kâbu, ii. 301
Kadig jayan, ii. 87
Kahyangan, ii. 101
Kain kasoh, i. 299
Kajang, i. 166, 211, 244, 254
Kalâpa pûyuh, ii. 212, 296
Kalintang, ii. 63
Kalung, ii. 126
Kamben, ii. 126
Kampulan badan, ii. 137
Kampara, i. 204, 206
Kânda, ii. 81, 84
Kandis, ii. 59
Kan-man, i. 260
Kapas, kapeh, ki-pei, i. 142, 185, 206, 229, 259
Kara, i. 143
K'au-ni, i. 217
Kavi, ii. 73
Kavin, ii. 73
Kayu api-api, ii. 275, 300
  balam pangkat, ii. 279
  briang, ii. 218
  gâdis, ii. 236, 298
  gâgak, ii. 258, 299
  kabal, ii. 268, 300
  kanchil, ii. 256, 299
  sipur, ii. 281
  siturun, ii. 283, 301
  sumang, ii. 274
Kĕkavin, ii. 73

Kĕmûning, ii. 238, 239, 298
Kidung, ii. 77, 91, 137
Kilat bahu, ii. 134
Kilin, i. 249
Kladi ayer, ii. 220
Kobang, i. 177
Koorkup, ii. 221
Koyan, i. 15, 19
Krá, ii. 61
Kramat, ii. 57
Kranti, i. 294
Kris, i. 292
Kulak, i. 178
Kulang kaya, i. 246
Kûlit lâyu, ii. 214
Kûlit nîpis, ii. 235, 296, 298
Kunchah, i. 19
Kuniet, i. 295
Ku-pa, i. 206
Kun-tun-lu-lin, i. 143
Kwan, i. 249

LADANG, ii. 61
Lălakon, ii. 3
Landak, ii. 208
Langsap, i. 174
Larak, i. 176
Lâyang-lâyang simpei, ii. 253, 299
Lĕban, ii. 218
Lemu, i. 300
Li, i. 128
Liak, ii. 114
Liao-ko, i. 174
Lichi, i. 244
Linehêr, ii. 126
Lintangan, ii. 194
Lo-ki-lien, i. 143
Lûmut, ii. 60

MANGI-MANGI chengke, ii. 240
Mangul, ii. 266
Manis, ii. 201
Mangku, ii. 130
Marpûyan, ii. 270, 300
Mata pĕlandok, ii. 297
Mavinten, ii. 132
Máyin mandrah, i. 18
Máyong, i. 18
Mĕdang-sanka, ii. 300
Mengure glung, ii. 127
Mĕngkûdû kĕchil, ii. 229
Mĕnpuyan, ii. 300
Mĕntâda, ii. 232
Mĕrkâsih, ii. 300
Mîri bâtu, ii. 275, 300
Mutiara, i. 143

NAILI, i. 178
Nakhoda, i. 246

312 INDEX OF MALAYAN AND CHINESE TERMS.

Nálih, i. 19, 178
Nangka, i. 245
Natar, ii. 128
Nibong, ii. 290
Nipa, i. 211
Nyambri, ii. 63

ORANG kaya, i. 246, 288
 pútih, i. 4
Orlong, i. 18, 19

PABRISSIAN, ii. 140
Padaṇḍa, ii. 99
Palanduk, ii. 41
Panah, ii. 100, 104
Panataran, ii. 101, 104
Pangalasan, ii. 8
Pangâskaran, ii. 140
Pangastanan, ii. 101
Pangeran, i. 224
Panghulu, i. 15
Panluang, ii. 197
Pantun, ii. 13, 35, 49, 63
Panggoling, ii. 201
Papudukan, ii. 126
Pa-ra-man, i. 145
Parang, i. 292
Parâryangan, ii. 101
Parmata, ii. 134
Pasang, ii. 290
Patitis, ii. 126
P'au, i. 150
Pauh, ii. 226
Pavan, i. 300
Pedang, ii. 101, 104
Pĕlandok kayu, ii. 275
Pĕlâwan, ii. 297
Pĕning-pĕning bungkus, ii. 289, 290, 301
Permatang, i. 4, 12
Petek, ii. 285
Petinggi, i. 211
Pi, i. 193, 253
Pien, i. 204
Pinding, i. 290
Pînka, i. 140
Pi-pa, i. 174
Po-ho, i. 144
Po-ho, bahara, i. 210
Po-ho-pi-ni, i. 144
Po-lut, i. 261
Prakulit, ii. 122, 131
Pu, i. 188
Pûar amâs, ii. 248, 298
 lilîpan, ii. 234, 297
Pûtat âyĕr, ii. 297
Putu, ii. 169

RAGA, i. 293
Rambutan, ii. 214, 296

Rokam, rûkam, ii. 297
Ronron, ii. 126
Rumbing, ii. 127
Rumput udang-udang, ii. 253, 299

SADKAHYANGAN, ii. 100, 104, 107
Sagung, ii. 180
Sahala, i. 253
Sambau, ii. 297
Sambuk, ii. 101, 104
Samir, ii. 126
Sampat, ii. 126
Sanggar, ii. 101, 134
Sarbacane, i. 292
Sarong, i. 172, 260, 290
Sa-tien, i. 191, 259
Satya, ii. 110, 146
Sawah, i. 4; ii. 61
Sawit, ii. 126
Sĕmbu bâdak, ii. 233, 297
Senênan, i. 176
Sepĕdas bunga, ii. 258, 299
Seramba, ii. 63
Seribulan, ii. 282, 301
Shêng, i. 178
Shêw-chú, i. 2
Siamang, ii. 61
Sibûru, ii. 237
Silimpal, ii. 126
Simpai, ii. 61
S'ingo-ingo, ii. 241
Sin-tsai, i. 143
Siturun, ii. 301
S'kar taji, ii. 126
Slendang, i. 172; ii. 63
Śloka, ii. 76, 78
So-fu, i. 260
Subong, ii. 127
Sûka bĕrának, ii. 295, 302
Summow, sambau, ii. 226
Sumpitan, i. 292
Sungkei, ii. 269

TABU, i. 292
Tael, i. 177
Tambedana, ii. 126
Tampal bâdak, ii. 233, 297
Taṇḍak, ii. 122
Tanggal, ii. 197
Tangkal, i. 300
Tarantang, ii. 279, 300
Tâyas, ii. 301
Tazi, i. 139, 142, 145, 222
Tekan, ii. 104
Tĕmu, ii. 223, 297
 kechil, ii. 224
 kunchi, ii. 297
Tĕrâtap, ii. 297

INDEX OF MALAYAN AND CHINESE TERMS. 313

T'ieh, i. 206
Ti-mi, i. 143
Titiran, ii. 68, 149
Todak, ii. 25
Togog, ii. 132
To-lo, i. 193
To-lo-ni, i. 260
Tongkok,
Tou, i. 178
Toya tîrta, ii. 100
Trang-teja, ii. 127
Tuak, ii. 100, 104, 107
Tugu, ii. 132
Tu-man, i. 260
Tumbak, ii. 100, 104

Tumiang, i. 292
Tutur, ii. 74, 91

Ubas-ubas, ii. 104
Unka púteh, i. 287
Unting-unting, ii. 217, 296
Unting-unting bĕsar, ii. 220

Wadah, ii. 140
Wawalen, ii. 122, 130
Wáyang, i. 18

Yam-pa, i. 209

Zanggí, i. 140

END OF VOL. II.